The Poe Cinema

The Poe Cinema

A Critical Filmography
of Theatrical Releases
Based on the Works of
Edgar Allan Poe

by

DON G. SMITH

McFarland & Company, Inc., Publishers
Jefferson, North Carolina, and London

Front cover photo: A glimpse of the pendulum descending as Bela Lugosi tortures Samuel S. Hinds in *The Raven* (1935).

British Library Cataloguing-in-Publication data are available

Library of Congress Cataloguing-in-Publication Data

Smith, Don G., 1950–
    The Poe cinema : a critical filmography of theatrical releases based on the works of Edgar Allan Poe / by Don G. Smith.
       p.   cm.
    Includes bibliographical references (p.   ) and index.
    ISBN 0-7864-0453-1 (case binding : 50# alkaline paper) ∞
    1. Poe, Edgar Allan, 1809–1849—Film and video adaptations.
  2. Horror tales, American—Film and video adaptations.   3. Horror films—Plots, themes, etc. I. Title.
    PS2625.S58   1999
    791.43'6—dc21   98-3271
                                                                        CIP

Manufactured in the United States of America

McFarland & Company, Inc., Publishers
  Box 611, Jefferson, North Carolina 28640

For my parents, Eugene (Bud)
and Lola Smith,
and for Vincent Price

Table of Contents

Preface

Because this volume is intended primarily as a reference book, a source of ready information, the reader will find the Poe-based films arranged in chronological order. For each film the same information is provided, in a consistent order:

1. Title, date of release, production company, and country of origin.
2. Credits and cast.
3. Story synopsis.
4. Production and marketing history (the purpose here is fourfold: to comment on the degree to which the film is based on a work or works by Poe; to provide information on the careers of those working on or appearing in the film; to include thoughts, anecdotes, and observations from the principal participants; and to examine methods used to market the film).
5. Critique (this element involves summarizing representative and important reviews of a film in order to place it in a critical and historical context; commentary on previous criticism and the author's own analysis follow).

There are some Poe-inspired films which have been lost and some that are almost impossible to view; little if anything is known about these films. Since there is too little available information to support full entries, such films are discussed briefly in the context of other chapters. Readers seeking what little information is known about these films are invited to consult the index.

This book does not address nontheatrical productions based on Poe's works, such as short educational films made for school showings. Nor does it devote complete entries to made-for-television films, though the Afterword briefly addresses them.

Most of the entries are based on repeated viewings of the films. The few instances in which the author has not seen the film in question are identified in the text.

When an entry utilizes quotations from pressbooks or publicity material, the source is noted as such but no formal citation is given. Similarly, other than identifying the source, the text does not reference quotations from *The Overlook Encyclopedia of Film: Horror*. The films covered by the *Overlook Encyclopedia* are entered by year and title and are therefore easily accessible to readers who consult the annotated bibliography for details.

I want to thank my wife Diana and my daughter Cassandra for putting up with the many hours I spent watching films and sitting at the computer. I also extend sincerest thanks to my friend and proofreader, Gordon Speck, who retains his sense of humor even when I spell a character's name four different ways in the same chapter. Thanks also go to those who agreed to interviews—and to Vicki Moody of Craig's Video in Charleston, Illinois, who aided me in acquiring some films needed for this book.

Introduction

Looking back, it seems to have been inevitable that I would develop a lifelong interest in Edgar Allan Poe. A few years after my birth in 1950, my adoptive parents read me *Grimms' Fairy Tales,* and they introduced me at an early age to the world of the great authors. Since I was an only child who inherited a rather melancholy personality, Poe proved to be an ancient mariner who grabbed and mesmerized me on contact. My fourth and fifth grade teacher nurtured my interest in Poe by loaning me a book containing a handful of his poems, and a local library loaned me books of his collected stories. At the age of ten, I amazed Illinois historian John Allan by quoting "The Raven" to him during an impromptu chat we had at the library. But the big day came on August 28, 1960, when my aunt presented me with my own copy of Modern Library's *Selected Poetry and Prose of Poe.* Coincidentally, that same year American International released Roger Corman's version of *The Fall of the House of Usher,* starring Vincent Price. Since Price was my favorite actor as a result of my seeing *The Fly* (1958) and *The House on Haunted Hill* (1958), I could not resist the combination of Poe and Price. Although my parents were becoming concerned about my growing interest in horror, they somewhat reluctantly took me to see the film. Of course, *The Pit and the Pendulum* (1961) followed, and the Corman-Poe film cycle was well on its way to cinema immortality.

Today I look back upon those days with great nostalgia and appreciation. My parents really should not have worried so much about my attraction to Poe and Price. Poe, after all, today remains one of the greatest authors in America's literary canon, and at his death, Price was a highly respected Renaissance man of American cinema, art, and cooking. But more on Price later.

In 1992, I published my first contribution to Poe scholarship, "Shelley's *Frankenstein:* A Possible Source for Poe's 'MS. Found in a Bottle,'" in *Poe Studies* (vol. 25, nos. 1 and 2, 1992). Of all my professional writings, I am most proud of this. But let us turn now to Poe.

Born in 1809 in Boston to a pair of actors, Edgar Allan Poe had an unhappy childhood. His mother, Elizabeth Arnold Poe, was a truly talented actress, while his father, David Poe, barely adequate on stage, found his greatest talent in drinking. When David deserted the family and Elizabeth died, three-year-old Edgar was taken into the childless home of John Allan of Richmond, Virginia. The Allans did not get along well, and Edgar did not get along with John Allan. Poe received a classical education, but found himself an early loser at love. Engaged to marry Sarah Elmira Royster, he went off to the university at seventeen, only to have his letters intercepted by Sarah's parents. Shortly afterward, the girl married another man. Because the wealthy Allan refused to provide Edgar with adequate funds, the young man turned to gambling, which, combined with drinking, soon led to the end of his university career.

Although Poe was athletic, he was also nervous and unstable. His body could not tolerate alcohol, but he nevertheless imbibed whenever finances permitted and would go on sprees that left him ill for days.

Edgar ran away to Boston in 1827, worked at a variety of jobs, enlisted in the army, rose to the rank of regimental sergeant, and published his first book of poetry, *Tamerlane and Other Poems*. When Mrs. Allan died in 1829, Edgar left the service and returned to Virginia for a reconciliation with John Allan. When Poe's money ran out, however, he asked Allan to help him enter West Point. Although Poe was accepted after a one-year wait, absence from classes and roll calls terminated his career there after two years. When Allan remarried, he disinherited Poe, ending the young man's hope of financial security.

In 1833, Poe's "MS. Found in a Bottle" won the $50 first prize in a short story contest sponsored by the *Baltimore Saturday Visitor* and his poem "The Coliseum" took second place in the poetry contest. He was living with his father's sister, Mrs. Clemm, and her daughter Virginia in 1835 when he began to write for *The Southern Literary Messenger*. That year he published "Berenice," "Morella," and "Hans Pfaal." On May 16, 1836, he married his cousin Virginia, who was only fourteen years old.

Although Poe's stories, poems, and criticism were gaining attention, he continued to struggle in poverty while working for the *Messenger*. When drinking and disagreements led to Poe's dismissal from the magazine, he moved his wife and mother-in-law to New York, where he published "The Narrative of A. Gordon Pym" (1838). Unable to generate much income as a freelance writer, Poe moved Mrs. Clemm and Virginia to Philadelphia, where he undertook the coeditorship of *Burton's Gentleman's Magazine*. In this new environment, he published "Ligeia" (1838), "The Fall of the House of Usher" (1839), and "William Wilson" (1839). At the

same time, he contributed writings to *Alexander's Weekly Messenger*. He also published his *Tales of the Grotesque and Arabesque*, a collection of macabre short stories that failed to sell well, despite their quality.

Drinking, disagreements, and the desire to start his own literary magazine led to Poe's leaving *Burton's* in 1840, but when George Rex Graham bought out Burton, he reinstated Poe as editor. It was in *Graham's Magazine* that Poe published "Murders in the Rue Morgue" (1841), considered to be the first detective story. In 1842 he again lost his job and went through more years of poverty-level existence. During this period, however, he published "The Oval Portrait" (1842), "The Masque of the Red Death" (1842), "The Mystery of Marie Roget" (1842), "The Gold Bug" (1843), "The Pit and the Pendulum" (1843), "The Tell-Tale Heart" (1843), "The Black Cat" (1843), "The Premature Burial" (1844), and "The Oblong Box" (1844). At this time he was contributing to *The Broadway Journal*; he eventually became its editor and then its owner. In 1845, Poe became an overnight celebrity when his poem "the Raven" gained national acclaim. Unfortunately, as Poe was gaining fame, his young wife was suffering from the then-fatal disease of tuberculosis.

When *The Broadway Journal* ceased publication in 1846, Poe moved with Mrs. Clemm and his dying wife to a cottage at Fordham, New York, where he wrote "The Cask of Amontillado." Virginia died there the following year. As if the death of his beloved were not enough, Poe's critical writings soon led to a distasteful libel suit, which he won at great cost to his reputation.

Although a grieving and ill Poe published almost nothing in 1847, he rebounded the following year with "Ulalume," one of his most representative poems. Then in 1848 he published the book *Eureka*, a philosophical and pseudoscientific attempt to explain the nature of the universe.

In 1849, Poe pursued a platonic relationship with Annie Richmond, the inspiration for his poem "To Annie," and lectured in Richmond, where he renewed his romance with Sarah Shelton, formerly Sarah Royster, the now wealthy widow to whom he had been engaged at the age of seventeen. Although Poe earlier had been in a fairly serious relationship with Sarah Helen Whitman, he now seemed ready to settle down with his childhood sweetheart. As happiness and financial security appeared finally within reach, legend has it that on his way to New York he toasted a bride at a wedding, went on a drinking spree, and disappeared. He was found semiconscious on a Baltimore street on election day. He died four days later in a Baltimore hospital on October 8, 1849, his last words being, "Lord, help my poor soul."

The tragedy of Poe's life can account somewhat for the cult status he has enjoyed over the years, but only a glance at his work should convince anyone of its genuine literary importance. First consider Poe's versatility and range of approach. Vincent Buranelli explains:

> Poe is both a dreamy fantasist ("The Valley of Unrest") and a cerebral logician ("The Purloined Letter"). He lingers with science ("Eureka") and is chilled by its abstraction ("To Science"). He resolutely closes his eyes to factual reality ("Ligeia") and examines it

in detail ("Landor's Cottage"). He works with melancholy ("The Fall of the House of Usher"), and with humor ("Why the Little Frenchman Wears His Hand in a Sling"); with burlesque ("Bon Bon"), and with realism ("The Cask of Amontillado"). He probes fascinated, into horrible obsessions ("The Tell-Tale Heart"), and gazes, enchanted, at ethereal beauty ("To Helen").[1]

Poe invented the detective story, teased readers with science fiction so realistic that many confused it with fact, satirized his contemporary literary world, conjured ethereal fantasies, made a notorious but respected reputation as a critic, and spun poems of both beauty and terror. Beyond the world of literature and literary criticism, his work has also influenced the worlds of music (Debussy, Ravel, Prokofiev), art (Beardsley), and, of course, the cinema, where his horror tales and weird poems often serve as inspiration. And just as his literary creations have had a worldwide influence, especially in France, the cinema of Edgar Allan Poe reaches across the continents. This book will examine the films inspired by the works of the man Vincent Buranelli calls "America's greatest writer, and the American writer of greatest significance in world literature."[2]

The Films

Sherlock Holmes in the Great Murder Mystery (1908)
Crescent Films, U.S.A.

Credits: Based on "The Murders in the Rue Morgue" by Edgar Allan Poe and on characters created by A. Conan Doyle.

Cast: Unknown.

Story: Dr. Watson interests detective Sherlock Holmes in a series of murders being committed. The police are holding a young man as the prime suspect. Holmes, however, goes into a trance and discovers the real murderer to be a gorilla.

Production and marketing: *Sherlock Holmes and the Great Murder Mystery* was filmdom's third effort based on Conan Doyle's Sherlock Holmes, the first two being *Sherlock Holmes Baffled* (1903) and *The Adventures of Sherlock Holmes* (1905). Since *Sherlock Holmes in the Great Murder Mystery* was produced in the final months of 1908, one might guess that the producers had Poe's centennial celebration (January 19, 1909) in mind. The film discards Poe's master detective, C. Auguste Dupin, and has Conan Doyle's Sherlock Holmes solve a case based on Poe's "The Murders in the Rue Morgue." As in Poe's story, the detective investigates a baffling murder case and discovers that the killer is simian. Seventeen years before *Sherlock Holmes and the Great Murder Mystery*, Conan Doyle had Watson say to Holmes, "You remind me of Edgar Allan Poe's Dupin," to which Holmes replies, "No doubt you think that you are complimenting me in comparing me to Dupin. Now, in my opinion, Dupin was a very inferior fellow."

Personal jealousy on Holmes's part? No, of course not. Since Conan Doyle's Holmes is very egotistical, his words are quite in character. Yet Conan Doyle, who openly acknowledged his debt to Poe, knew better. Holmes was based on Poe's Dupin and therefore owes his very existence to his "inferior" predecessor. As Conan Doyle said before the Poe centennial celebration dinner of the Author's Society at the Hotel Metropole in March 1909, "Where was the detective story until Poe breathed the breath of life into it?"

Critique: Since I have not seen this lost film, I cannot offer critical comment.

Edgar Allan Poe (1909)
Mutoscope and Biograph Company, U.S.A.

Credits: Directed by D. W. Griffith; screenplay by D. W. Griffith and Frank Woods, based on the poem "The Raven" by Edgar Allan Poe; cinematography by Billy Bitzer.

Cast: Herbert Yost (Edgar Allan Poe), Linda Arvidson (Virginia Poe).

Story: Edgar Allan Poe is caring for his dying young wife, Virginia. When the author opens a window, a raven flies in and perches on "the pallid bust of Pallas just above his chamber door." Poe is inspired by the arrival of this bird of ill omen, immediately pens his famous poem "The Raven," and dashes out to sell it. When a first editor turns Poe away, he sells the poem to a second editor for ten dollars. Poe takes the money and buys medicine, food, and a wrap for Virginia. When the devoted husband arrives home, however, he finds his wife cold and still: "My God, she is dead!" The bird that is synonymous with death has taken his wife's soul to the Night's Plutonian shore.

Production and marketing: D. W. Griffith (1874–1948) an American film pioneer, was the industry's first major producer-director. He had made only a few one-reelers when, on the centenary of the author's birth, he undertook the Poe "biopic." Broadway actor Herbert Yost portrayed Poe, and Griffith's actress wife, Linda Arvidson (1884–1949), played Virginia. Griffith shot the picture on January 21 and 23, 1909. On February 3, Griffith registered his film with the Library of Congress in Washington, misspelling Poe's name and the film's title as *Edgar Allen Poe.* To interest prospective purchasers in the film, Lee Daugherty wrote the following in "Biograph Bulletin": "He was undoubtedly the most original poetical genius ever produced by America, and might be regarded as the literary lion of the universe, to which fact the public are becoming alive."[3]

The film appeared in America's nickelodeons on February 8. The choice of Poe as an early film subject demonstrates the legitimate reputation and cult following the author enjoyed at the turn of the century. Immediately after Poe's death, his literary executor, Rufus Griswold, wrote viciously of the deceased genius, after which others came to Poe's defense or attempted to inflict further damage. Partly as a result of the controversy, America became attracted to the growing legend of Edgar Allan Poe. Of course, the story of the struggling author and his dying wife and the national popularity of "The Raven" suggested a popular topic for filmmaker Griffith, who fused both attractions into a highly fictional and melodramatic account, somewhat as director Ken Russell might have done if Poe had been the topic of one of his 1960s BBC biographies.

The film must have been successful because Biograph rushed into a September production of *The Sealed Room,* which featured Henry Walthall as a minstrel in love with a duchess played by Marion Leonard. When Arthur Johnson, as the duke, unmasks the affair, he seals them behind a wall in the tradition of "The Cask of Amontillado."

Also in 1909, France's Henri Desfontaines directed *The Gold Bug,* based on Poe's short story. That film, unfortunately, appears to be lost.

Critique: In an article entitled "Pictures of Poe: A Survey of the Silent Film Era 1909–29," British film historian Denis Gifford writes that the only noteworthy element of the film is the cinematography of Billy Bitzer, who during the garret scenes shines lights through an angled window. Unfortunately, his stop-action stuffed raven comes off less well.[4]

The Raven (1912)
Eclair/American Standard, U.S.A.

Credits: From Edgar Allan Poe's "The Gold Bug," "The Black Cat," "The Murders in the Rue Morgue," "A Descent into the Maelstrom," "The Pit and the Pendulum," "The Raven," and "The Premature Burial."

Cast: Guy Oliver (Edgar Allan Poe).

Story: Edgar Allan Poe is looking after his invalid wife, Lenore, at their Fordham cottage. He falls asleep and dreams scenes from "The Gold Bug," "The Black Cat," "The Murders in the Rue Morgue," "The Pit and the Pendulum," "A Descent into the Maelstrom," and "The Premature Burial." Upon waking, he is sitting at his desk writing the poem "The Raven," when the bird itself taps at his window, perches above the bust of Pallas, and watches him write. Upon finishing, he rushes out to sell the poem in order to buy Lenore food and medicine. When he returns, he finds Lenore alive and waiting.

Production and marketing: While this two-reeler obviously derived much of its brief plot from D. W. Griffith's *Edgar Allan Poe* (1909), it changes Virginia's name to Lenore in order to correspond with the narrator's dead loved one in Poe's "The Raven." Also unlike Griffith's version, after selling his poem, Poe returns to find his wife alive, an ending more in line with fact. Virginia died two years after "The Raven" was published. Interestingly, the film uses actual location shots of Poe's Fordham cottage.

Advertising *The Raven* as "A Literary Film-Play Sensation," Eclair described its product in a full-page *Moving Picture World* ad as "The story of Poe's struggles and success, magnificently produced with a splendid corps of actors and scenes laid in the historic Poe cottage at Fordham, New York."[5]

France joined the United States in producing a film using Edgar Allan Poe as a character—*Une Vengeance d' Edgar Allan Poe* (1912). Though we know nothing about this lost film, its title indicates a highly fictional approach to the author.

Critique: According to all accounts, *The Raven* is a lost film.

The Pit and the Pendulum (1912)
Solax Film Company, U.S.A

Credits: From "The Pit and the Pendulum" by Edgar Allan Poe.

Cast: Darwin Karr (the prisoner), Blanche Cornwall, Fraunie Fraunholz.

Story: During the Spanish Inquisition, a prisoner is tossed into a dungeon, tied down, and subjected to the torture of a descending razor-sharp pendulum. At the last minute the prisoner smears food on the ropes binding him and entices some rats to gnaw through them, allowing him to escape his ordeal.

Production and marketing: On July 12, 1913, a two-page ad in *Moving Picture World* heralded *The Pit and the Pendulum*:

> Three reels of Thrill and Sensation Coming ... Adapted from the Great Edgar Allan Poe's Graphic, Lurid and Bloodcurdling Description of the Inquisition! ... Situations permeate with Genuine Thrills! A Bloodcurdling Classic! The screen story vibrates with all the virility and vitality of Poe's incomparable pen! The scenes mirror Poe's compellingly gruesome but not repellant verbal rhapsody![6]

If nothing else, these lines should serve to convince modern readers that the hyperbole of modern pressbooks has nothing over that of the silent era. If, however, the hyperbole is anywhere near the truth, this film is one of the first full-blown horror films ever made. The descriptions that remain indicate that it also probably stayed closer to the Poe story than later adaptations, though that is much easier to do when producing a three reel picture.

In 1910, Ambosio Films of Italy actually made the first cinematic version of *The Pit and the Pendulum*, along with a version of *Hop Frog the Jester*. Unfortunately, nothing more is known about the Italian films, both of which are considered lost.

Critique: On August 2, 1913, Stephen Bush reviewed the film, saying that he was indeed astonished at the effectiveness with which the fearful tortures of the story's hero have been illustrated by the Solax producer. The quiet occupants of many of the dungeons shown are skeletons, and all the mechanisms of torture, including the cell with the pit in its floor down which we see skulls and crawling serpents (the bottom of the pit is not so realistic as it might have been), have been extremely well conceived. The pendulum, massive and sharp, which swings back and forth and ever draws nearer to the bound victim, is also effective, as is the manner of his salvation from it. Rats gnaw the ropes that bind him.[7]

Since this is by all accounts a lost film, Bush must get the last word.

The Bells (1912)
Edison, U.S.A.

Credits: Directed by George Lessey; from the poem "The Bells" by Edgar Allan Poe.

Cast: Unknown.

Story: Lucy's stern father forces her to marry a miser. At the wedding ceremony, however, the church catches fire and the young woman is rescued by her true love. Lucy's bridegroom perishes in the blaze.

Production and marketing: *The Bells* is probably the first film to use the title of a Poe poem or story to produce a film having little or nothing to do with the original literature. Edison Studio, producers of the first cinematic version of *Frankenstein* (1910), uses snatches of Poe's onomatopoeic poem (e.g. "Hear the mellow wedding bells," "Hear the loud alarum bells," and "Hear the tolling of the bells—Iron bells!") to presumably add mood to the film's proceedings, which have nothing to do with Poe's poem. American International Pictures would use this technique (or subterfuge) in releasing Tigon Pictures' *Witchfinder General* (1968) to American audiences as Edgar Allan Poe's *The Conqueror Worm*.

Other films titled *The Bells* followed, one with Boris Karloff in 1926, but these were based upon an Erkmann-Chatrian play in which a man is haunted by the vision of his murder victim.

Critique: Reviews of the time were unfavorable to *The Bells*, one placing it among the weakest pictures produced by Edison and charging that the studio exploited Poe in order to give its poor product a poetic mood. According to all accounts, *The Bells* is today considered a lost film. If contemporary opinion was correct, perhaps it is no great loss. Then again, if the film served to introduce Poe's masterfully crafted poem to a wider audience, perhaps it served a useful purpose.

Le Système du Docteur Goudron et du Professeur Plume (1913); aka *The Lunatics*

Eclair, France

Credits: Directed by Maurice Tourneur; screenplay by André de Lorde, based on "The System of Dr. Tarr and Professor Fether" by Edgar Allan Poe and the play *Le Système du Docteur Goudron et du Professeur Plume*, also by André de Lorde, which was an adaptation of Poe's work.

Cast: Henri Gouget (madman), Henri Roussell (tourist), Renée Sylvaire (tourist's wife).

Running Time: 15 minutes.

Story: A tourist and his wife stop to visit an insane asylum, which has been taken over by the inmates. The head madman, now posing as the asylum's director, describes to the visitors his new insanity treatment, which consists of cutting out a patient's eye and slitting his or her throat. When offscreen noises interrupt his explanation, the "doctor" rushes into the next room and reappears with blood on his hands. Meanwhile a puddle of blood begins oozing slowly from under the door. As a thunderstorm roars outside, the inmates, excited by the gore, tar and feather the tourist.

Production and marketing: The First French film adaptation from a Poe source was *The Gold Bug* (1909). Nothing is known of it today. France's second Poe effort was *Le Système du Docteur Goudron et du Professeur Plume*. It should come as no surprise that two of the earliest cinematic adaptations of an Edgar Allan Poe short stories should come from France. After all, it was in the 1850s that French poet and literary critic Charles Baudelaire brought Poe to the attention of the French. Baudelaire, a decadent drug addict, was also a perceptive critic. A student of human nature's dark side and plagued as Poe was by impecuniousness, Baudelaire saw the American as a kindred soul. At the end of his study, the Frenchman described Poe in terms he probably would have used to describe himself:

> One could write on his tombstone: "All you who have ardently sought to discover the laws that govern your being, who have aspired to the infinite, and whose repressed emotions have had to seek a terrible relief in the wine of debauchery, pray for him. Now his bodily being, purified, floats amid the beings whose existence he glimpsed. Pray for him who sees and knows, he will intercede for you."[8]

Le Système du Docteur Goudron et du Professeur Plume (*The System of Dr. Tarr and Professor Fether*) was the third film of director Maurice Tourneur, who had been an interior decorator, an illustrator, a film and stage actor, and an assistant to Émile Chautard at Eclair. Screenwriter André de Lorde, a regular writer for France's Grand Guignol Theatre, transposed the story from his one-act play adapted from Poe's story "The System of Dr. Tarr and Professor Fether." Poe's short story is a comic tale in which the narrator is so dense that he does not realize that the inmates have taken over the asylum. De Lorde's screenplay retained the basic element of the Poe plot—the inmates of an insane asylum take over the place and confine their keepers. In order to increase audience concern for the tourists' safety, however, de Lorde turned the narrator's gentleman traveling companion in Poe's story into the narrator's wife. Little else of Poe appears to have been used, though the "treatment" of cutting out an eye may have been derived from Poe's "The Black Cat."

Tourneur filmed another play by de Lorde, *Figures de Cire* (1912), before departing for the United States. Although he never returned to the works of Poe, Tourneur did direct a few more films associated with the horror and science fiction genres: *Trilby* (1915), *The Mysterious Island* (1928), and *The Devil's Hand* (1942). Tourneur's son Jacques, following in his father's directorial footsteps, would go on to direct such horror genre classics as *The Cat People* (1942), *I Walked with a Zombie* (1943), *The Leopard Man* (1943), *Night of the Demon* (1958, aka *Curse of the Demon*), *A Comedy of Terrors* (1963) and the Poe-inspired *City Under the Sea* (1965, aka *War-Gods of the Deep*).

Critique: Although the film is now considered lost, we can assume that Tourneur and de Lorde attempted to inject none of Poe's humor into its short fifteen-minute running time, intending instead to reproduce the horror of the Grand Guignol. Reviewing for *Motion Picture World*, George Blaisdell called the film "A powerful story and a horrible one, yet fascinating in spite of its horror. However, don't show it to your patrons without looking at it for yourself, for it is no food for infants or weaklings."[9] According to Britain's *Bioscope*, "For sheer unadulterated horror and harrowing sensation this picture must stand practically unequalled."[10]

As many have noted, the technique of blood seeping under the door would later be copied by other horror film directors, the most notable and effective example appearing in Jacques Tourneur's *The Leopard Man* (1943). Like father, like son.

Der Student von Prag (1913);
aka *The Student of Prague;*
A Bargain from Satan;
From Life to Death;
Flight to the Sun
Apex/Bioscope, Germany

Credits: Directed by Stellan Rye; screenplay by Hans Heinz Ewers, from "William Wilson" by Edgar Allan Poe and "The Sand Merchant" by E. T. A. Hoffman; cinematography by Guido Seeber; art direction by Ronald A. Dietrich and K. Richer.

Running time: 60 minutes.

Cast: Paul Wegener (Baldwin), John Gottowt (Scapinelli), Greta Berger (Comtesse Magrit), Lyda Salmonova (Lyduschka), Lother Korner (Graf Swarzenberg).

Story: Baldwin, an impoverished, world-weary military student, rescues Comtesse Magrit when her horse runs away with her and deposits her in a lake. When he calls on her later with romantic intentions, he finds that he is financially no match for her official suitor, Swarzenberg. Baldwin then signs a contract with the sorcerer Scapinelli, an incarnation of Satan. Scapinelli promises Baldwin a woman and inexhaustible riches in exchange for Baldwin's mirror reflection. Baldwin signs Scapinelli's contract and watches as his mirror image steps out of the glass. Baldwin and the mirror image eye each other warily before the image leaves with Scapinelli. Baldwin then renews his attempt to win Magrit's heart. Angered at Baldwin's advances, Swarzenberg challenges Baldwin to a duel. When Magrit's father asks Baldwin, a fine fencer, to spare Swarzenberg, Baldwin agrees. Scapinelli, however, intervenes and detains Baldwin from the rendezvous, sending his mirror image instead.

The mirror image kills Swarzenberg, disgracing Baldwin. Although Baldwin tries to convince Magrit of his innocence, the mirror image turns up to frustrate his attempts. Baldwin lures the mirror image to an attic and shoots him, killing himself in the same act. Scapinelli enters and tears up the contract, the pieces of which fall and cover Baldwin's corpse.

Production and marketing: It is not surprising that in 1913 the German cinema would turn to the work of Edgar Allan Poe for inspiration. Poe's "Metzengerstein" is reputedly his tip of the hat to German gothicism. The German "shudder novel" was a popular product in a country steeped in Teutonic folk tales and ghost lore. Always of interest to Germans was the Doppelgänger theme, and they found in Poe's "William Wilson" a classic treatment. As in "William Wilson," Baldwin is a military student. As in "William Wilson," Baldwin is plagued by his double. As in "William Wilson," when Baldwin slays his double, he simultaneously slays himself (although in *Der Student von Prag* the slaying is literal, not figurative as it is in Poe). In a scene reminiscent of Poe's story, the mirror image confronts Baldwin at a playing card table after Baldwin has just won a game of cards.

Besides being inspired by Poe, *Der Student von Prag* is also inspired by Hoffman's idea of the malicious double and by the Faust legend. I would guess that *Der Student* itself proved inspirational in the sense that John Gottowt's Scapinelli seems the prototype for Werner Krauss's Dr. Caligari in Robert Wiene's later *Das Kabinett des Dr. Caligari* (1918).

Danish director Stellan Rye moved elements of the German Bioscope Company to Prague for location shooting, where they reconstructed Prague's Jewish cemetery in a forest when Hebrew officials would not allow filmmaking on hallowed ground. German actor-writer-director Paul Wegener (1874–1948) made his first meritorious starring appearance in *Der Student von Prag*. While in Prague for location shooting, he

learned of the legend of the Golem and would direct and star in versions of *Der Golem* in 1915 and 1920. He would also write, direct, and star in *Svengali* in 1927.

Screenwriter Hanns Heinz Ewers would later find Nazism compatible with his artistic talents. According to Siegfried Kracauer, "[Ewers] had the good fortune to be a bad author with an imagination reveling in gross sensation and sex—a natural ally for the Nazis, for whom he was to write, in 1933, the official screenplay on Horst Wessel. But precisely this kind of imagination forced him into spheres rich in tangible events and sensual experiences—always good screen material."[11]

Cinematographer Guido Seeber would introduce a tripod moving on wheels for Carl Mayer's groundbreaking German production *Sylvester,* aka *New Year's Eve.* In 1928 Seeber would suggest the foundation of a national film library.

Der Student von Prag would be remade by Henrik Galeen in 1926 and by the Nazis in 1936.

Critique: Although the Hanover newspaper *Volkswille* quotes a critic calling *Der Student von Prag* "incredibly naive and often ridiculous," the film has enjoyed a generally good reputation since it was found after decades of being considered lost. Carlos Clarens writes:

> It remains quite an achievement for a country as backward (in terms of cinema) as Germany was then.... The final showdown between Baldwin and his alter ego, in a studio set representing the garret, is beautifully lit in "the Rembrandt manner." The use of double exposure, albeit crude, confers on these scenes a quality exclusive to the film; no amount of stage trickery can make an actor appear as two people at the same time.... The film gains immeasurably from the restraint of Paul Wegener, who played Baldwin and, of course, his reflection.[12]

In my view, *Der Student von Prag* deserves a positive reputation for two reasons. First, the double exposure shots are symmetrically well mounted. The scenes in which poor, confused Countess Magrit sees both Baldwin and his mirror image are especially effective. Second, as Clarens points out, Wegener gives a fine performance, cutting a dashing figure as the military student and restraining himself in scenes in which some actors with extensive stage experience would fly over the edge. Particularly effective from the standpoint of foreshadowing is the scene in which Baldwin stands before the mirror, "shadow-fencing" with his reflection. Of course, he will later metaphorically fence with himself when the reflection takes on a life of its own. As the reflection, Wegener sometimes conjures an expression of disgust as though he has just swallowed

some food of revolting texture or taste. But this is believable, considering the disgust the soul would feel for the one having sold it to Satan. Indeed, Wegener's work in the horror genre places him in a silent triumvirate of terror with Lon Chaney, Sr., and Conrad Veidt, impressive company to say the least. Beyond Wegener's and Seeber's contributions, the sets, particularly that of the Jewish cemetery, are impressive. Judicious use of close-ups would have enhanced the final product (there are none in the film). Still, it stands as a fine example of the silent cinema in general and of the Poe cinema in particular. *Video Hound's Golden Movie Retriever 1996* correctly awards the film three bones.

The Avenging Conscience (1914)
Essanay, U.S.A.

Credits: Produced and directed by D. W. Griffith; cinematography by Billy Blitzer; based on "The Tell-Tale Heart" by Edgar Allan Poe.

Cast: Henry B. Walthall (the nephew, Edgar Allan Poe), Spottiswoode Aiken (the uncle), Blanche Sweet (Annabel Lee), Ralph Lewis (the stranger), George Seigmann (the Italian), Dorothy Gish, Donald Crisp, Mae Marsh.

Story: When a mother dies, her son is adopted by an indulgent uncle who wears a black patch over one eye. The boy grows into manhood and pursues a literary career. Still sharing his uncle's home, the nephew pores over Edgar Allan Poe's "The Tell-Tale Heart" while the old man attends to important paperwork, wishing that his nephew would get serious about a real career.

The nephew is invited to a garden party hosted by Annabel Lee, the young woman he loves.

> It was many and many a year ago,
>   In a kingdom by the sea,
> That a maiden there lived whom you may know

> By the name of Annabel Lee;—
> And this maiden she lived with no other
>   thought
> Than to love and be loved by me.
>   (from Poe's "Annabel Lee")

But when the young man tells his uncle of the invitation, the old man says, "You shall not go. You have important work to do!" Meanwhile, Annabel frees a puppy caught in a fence and walks toward the young man's house:

> Now all my hours are trances;
>   And all my nightly dreams
> Are where the dark eye glances,
>   And where thy footstep gleams.
>   (from Poe's "To One in Paradise")

The nephew defiantly leaves the house and meets Annabel beside a lake. When he returns, the uncle complains that he has sacrificed everything for his ungrateful nephew, and the two argue.

Later, Annabel visits the house and invites her lover to come out. He says he cannot come, so she enters and tries to speak in a friendly manner to the old man. He is unappeased, however, and charges, "You are after my boy like a common woman." The offended nephew threatens to punch his uncle but turns and leaves with Annabel instead. The uncle follows.

At the garden party, the couple sees a stranger, but they are too deeply trouble to pay him much attention. Shortly thereafter, because of the uncle's attitude, they agree to part forever:

> Thou was that all to me love,
>   For which my soul did pine—
> A green isle in the sea, love,
>   A fountain and a shrine
>   (from Poe's "To One in Paradise")

While the young lovers are preparing to say goodbye, Annabel's maid is laying plans to win the love of the grocery boy. As music and dancing commence, the nephew and Annabel give one another a last goodbye, and she goes into her house. Meanwhile, the uncle, who arrived at the party earlier, turns and heads for home. On the way, however, he notices the gaiety of the maid and the grocery boy, as well as the love shared by a young man and woman with a child. These experiences make him regret his actions, and he realizes that he has plunged his nephew into despair by denying him Annabel. Upon arriving home, the old man prays to God to guide him in the right path.

As the nephew is walking home, he speaks briefly with an Italian, who will be of significance later. Meanwhile, Annabel goes to take one last look at her love.

> But our love it was stronger by far than the
>   love
> Of those who were older than we—
> Of many far wiser than we—
>   (from Poe's "Annabel Lee")

Soon Annabel breaks down and cries. Unknown to her, however, she is watched by the stranger who attended her party.

At this same time, spurred on by the sight of a spider catching a fly and of ants swarming over their prey, the nephew begins to entertain thoughts of killing his uncle.

Later, at home, Annabel turns facedown a picture of her love:

> For the moon never beams, without bring-
>   ing me dreams
>   Of the beautiful ANNABEL LEE;
> And the stars never rise, but I feel the bright
>   eyes
>   Of the beautiful ANNABEL LEE.
>   (from Poe's "Annabel Lee")

When the nephew returns home, he hands his uncle a note which says, "If you will come to the house over the hill this afternoon, I will pay you the money I've owed you so long.—Jameson." Of course, the old man immediately sets off for the house over the hill. The nephew, who composed the note, follows his uncle and asks several townspeople where the old man is going. They say they don't know, at which point the nephew invites them into a nearby building, probably a tavern, thereby leaving no witnesses to see the old man return home. His plan working, the nephew soon returns home to find his uncle asleep in a chair. He plays with the idea of shooting the old man with a pistol but cannot bring himself to pull the trigger. At that moment, the Italian and a woman, both drinking heavily, stagger past. The Italian orders the woman away and continues his trek.

Inside the house, the uncle awakens and the nephew says he will go away if the old man will give him money. The two struggle, and the nephew strangles his uncle. Outside the house, the Italian apparently hears the struggle. He observes the murder through the window, and then blackmails the nephew. Later the young man conceals the corpse within the aperture of the fireplace and seals the opening with bricks.

When the uncle has been missing for a sufficient amount of time, the nephew comes into his inheritance and pays off the Italian. There are those, however, who are suspicious. One day one of the uncle's friends brings the stranger to visit the nephew. The

Henry Walthall is haunted by Christ himself in D. W. Griffith's *The Avenging Conscience* (1914).

nephew gives the stranger a rose. As the friend and stranger are leaving, the stranger remarks about the oddly shaped fireplace.

Feeling he has gotten away with his crime, the nephew renews his courtship of Annabel. But as they talk, he hallucinates about his uncle's ghost and acts strangely. Annabel, fearing something more than mental derangement, suspects guilt. Later the nephew tries to sleep but is once again visited by his uncle's ghost. This precipitates a mental breakdown, and the young man is consigned to a mental sanatorium. When he returns, apparently cured, he fears that the stranger is actually a detective on his trail. For insurance, he hires the Italian to blow a whistle if unfriendly intruders approach, and he shows the Italian a trap door in his barn that will lead to escape.

Convinced that the nephew's strange actions were not caused by guilt, Annabel renews interest in her former love. The nephew, however, is still stung by remorse, as is illustrated through a quotation from Poe's "The Tell-Tale Heart," with the word *heard* replaced by *saw*: "I saw all things in Heaven and Earth. I saw many many things in Hell." The nephew hallucinates about Christ and a stone reading "Thou shalt not kill." He falls to his knees, praying to a vision of Christ on the cross. The stranger, actually a detective hoping to force a confession from the nephew, places his posse in waiting and goes into the house to question the young man. As the detective questions the nephew, the posse discovers the trap door in the barn and nails it shut. At the same time, the detective taps his pencil upon the table and taps his foot on the floor, all reminding the nephew of the beating of the dead man's heart. A swinging pendulum and the monotonous hooting of an owl add to the effect. Soon, guilt overcomes the nephew, and he hallucinates about ghouls and demons in hell. When he also envisions himself haunted by a skeleton, he breaks down and explains to the detective how he strangled his uncle to death. Then he flees.

The detective's posse, seemingly led by the Italian, who has switched allegiance, corners the nephew in the barn. The nephew tries to hold off his pursuers with rifle fire, but he soon realizes that his standoff is in vain. As Annabel runs to be with him, he hangs himself. Upon gaining knowledge of her lover's death, she commits suicide by throwing herself off a cliff.

The nephew then awakens and realizes that all that has transpired has been a dream. He hugs his uncle, joyous to find the old man still alive, and goes outdoors with his wife Annabel to read to her from his latest writings. The young man is actually Edgar Allan Poe.

Production and marketing: *The Avenging Conscience*, or *Thou Shalt Not Kill*, is D. W. Griffith's second excursion into Poe, his first being *Edgar Allan Poe* (1909). This time, rather than attempting to film a slice of Poe's life, he turns to Poe's "The Tell-Tale Heart" for inspiration. He also liberally quotes from Poe's poetry.

Critique: *The Avenging Conscience*, although it draws upon Poe's actual life, is largely based upon the author's "The Tell-Tale Heart." The "Tell-Tale Heart" element is that of a mentally deranged man murdering his one-eyed elder and concealing the body from view, only to confess later when hallucinating about the beating of his victim's heart. Griffith clearly draws from Poe's life in patterning the uncle after John Allan, who, as Poe's guardian, broke up his youthful courtship with Sarah Elmira Royster.

In the film, Griffith demonstrates how far the cinema had come since his first 1909 foray into Poe. Much of the cinema's progress clearly can be credited to Griffith him-

self. Here the director makes good use of the close-up, casting off the idea of film as a moving stage play. Particularly effective are Griffith's shots of a spider devouring a fly, superimposed shots of the murdered uncle as a ghost, and the hallucinatory shots of Christ and the demons in hell.

Unfortunately, Griffith does not capture the true horror of "The Tell-Tale Heart." In Poe's story, the old man has only one seeing eye, the other being described as a "vulture eye." In the film, the old man wears a patch over one eye. In Poe's story, the killer has no rational motive for killing the old man, but in the film Griffith supplies the motives of lost love and financial gain. In Poe's tale, the narrator claims that the vulture eye itself drives him to murder. No such deranged defense exists in the film. Consequently, Poe's focus is upon the mind of an insane killer, while Griffith's version supplies a rational motive, thereby dissipating the horrors of the mind conjured by Poe. Griffith's nephew cannot claim as can Poe's deranged narrator: "Object there was none. Passion there was none. I loved the old man. He had never wronged me." Poe's tale is an exercise in psychological horror, while Griffith's film is a morality play, weakened by the dream ending, which, in all fairness, was not yet cliché when Griffith employed it.

As for the cast, Henry Walthall delivers a top-notch performance as nephew Poe. As any effective silent performer must do, he acts with his gestures and eyes. His eyes are particularly effective when he contemplates shooting his uncle and when he experiences those hellish hallucinations. The rest of the cast is at least adequate. Although *Video Hound's Golden Retriever* awards the film only two bones, I find *The Avenging Conscience* both an above-average silent horror picture and a worthy entry in the cinema of Edgar Allan Poe.

The Raven (1915)

Essanay, U.S.A.

Credits: Directed by Charles J. Brabin; from the play by George C. Hazelton and the poem "The Raven" by Edgar Allan Poe.

Running time: 80 minutes.

Cast: Henry Walthall (Edgar Allan Poe), Ernest Maupain (John Allan), Warda Howard (Virginia Clemm and Helen Whitman), Marion Skinner (Mrs. Clemm), Harry Dunkinson (Tony, Poe's chum), Charles J. Harris (Mr. Pehlham).

Story: In 1811, David Poe dies, leaving his wife Elizabeth and their two children, Edgar and Rosalie, without provision. The woman becomes ill. When Mrs. Allan brings the receipts of a benefit to Elizabeth's bedside, she realizes that the money has arrived too late. When Mrs. Allan entreats her husband John to become Edgar's guardian, he at first refuses, but soon agrees at his wife's romantic insistence. The Allans adopt Edgar, who takes the name Edgar Allan Poe.

After 15 years, Edgar is at the University of Virginia, deeply in debt and under the sway of wine. As he sits drinking, a pendulum swings on the shelf in the background. At the table, he dreams of a pistol duel he wins. He awakens from the dream shaken, but regains his composure, smiles rather madly, and quaffs more wine. Meanwhile, Mr. Allan is angry upon receiving word of Edgar's debts at the university.

At this point, Poe and his buddy Tony begin to court Virginia Clemm, a playful and rather voluptuous young woman who lives with her mother. Poe takes Virginia on a horseback ride, and while pausing for an interlude beside a "glassy pool of romance" (presumably a pond or lake), he tells her a story of a hunter stopped by a young woman from shooting a deer. Pan plays his flutes and the hunter and girl fall in love as nymphs joyfully dance. After Poe concludes his story, he and Virginia kiss. As they are returning to Virginia's house, they encounter a slave owner beating a helpless slave. Moved to pity, Poe walks up and buys the slave with an IOU for $600. Later, when the slave owner presents Allan with Edgar's IOU, Allan grumbles: "Bills, bills, bills, nothing but bills. Where is that scoundrel Edgar?"

It so happens that Edgar is draining a tankard of beer with his friend Tony in a tavern. When Edgar excuses himself to keep an appointment, Tony takes advantage of the opportunity to visit Virginia, only to find that Poe has arrived there before him. As Edgar and Virginia are getting cozy on the couch, Tony knocks on the door. Poe soon leaves and hides in the cellar. When Tony sweet-talks Virginia, she gently rebuffs him, after which he leaves. Poe then comes out from his hiding place and resumes his position with Virginia on the couch. They are interrupted again, however, when Tony returns to the window, laughing at the situation.

The next day Edgar and Tony visit the Allan home and begin drinking. Virginia arrives and discreetly takes the glass from Edgar's hand, initiating a little guessing game between her two suitors. After she arranges for Edgar to win, John Allan appears and begins shouting about Edgar's debts. "Let us not discuss my shortcomings here," Edgar protests. Allan, at the end of his patience, banishes Edgar from his presence forever. As Edgar leaves, Virginia rushes to him, saying, "Not alone Edgar, if you will take me." Edgar gladly takes her along, as well as his recently purchased slave.

Later, Edgar struggles to support himself, Virginia, and Mrs. Clemm with his writings. One evening he is awakened by the sound of something tapping at the door. "'Tis some visitor," he thinks to himself. But when he opens the door, he finds only "Darkness there and nothing more."

...long I stood there wondering, fearing,
Doubting, dreaming dreams no mortal ever dared to dream before;

Poe then envisions himself struggling up a steep hill, his path blocked by a huge rock which represents his addiction to wine. An angel appears and he struggles on.

> ...and the stillness gave no token,
> And the only word there spoken was the
> whispered word, "Lenore!"

Poe, amazed and addled, reaches for wine. As he lifts the glass, it takes on the appearance of a skull. Poe shrinks from the sight and buries his head in his arms, fearing madness.

> Surely...that is something at my window
> lattice;
> Let me see, then what thereat is, and this
> mystery explore—
> Let my heart be still a moment and this
> mystery explore;—

When Poe throws open the window, a raven enters and perches upon the bust of Pallas above his chamber door.

Henry Walthall as Edgar Allan Poe in Charles J. Brabin's *The Raven* (1915).

> "Tell me what thy lordly name is on the
> Night's Plutonian shore!"
>   Quoth the Raven, "Nevermore."

Poe considers the bird.

> "On the morrow *he* will leave me, as my
> hopes have flown before."
>   Then the bird said, "Nevermore."

The bird remains, and Poe's mind searches for the meaning of what is happening.

> ...I betook myself to linking
> Fancy unto fancy, thinking what this ominous bird of yore—
> What this grim, ungainly, ghastly, gaunt,
> and ominous bird of yore
>   Meant in croaking "Nevermore."
> ...With my head at ease reclining
> On the cushion's velvet lining that the
> lamp-light gloated o'er,
> But whose velvet lining with the lam-light
> gloating o'er,
> *She* shall press, ah, nevermore!

Poe is then again visited by the angel.

> "Wretch," I cried, "thy God hath lent
> thee—by these angels he
> hath sent thee

> Respite—and nepenthe from thy memories
> of Lenore!
> Quaff, oh quaff this kind nepenthe and forget this lost Lenore!"
>   Quoth the Raven, "Nevermore."

At that point Poe orders the raven out.

> "...tell me truly, I implore—
> Is there—*is* there balm in Gilead?—tell
> me—tell me, I implore?"
>   Quoth the Raven, "Nevermore."

Poe drops to his knees before a vision of the angel holding a sword as the gates of heaven close to him.

> "Prophet!" said I, "thing of evil!—prophet
> still, if bird or devil!—
> By that Heaven that bends above us—by
> that God which we both adore—
> Tell this soul with sorrow laden if, within
> the distant Aidenn,
> It shall clasp a sainted maiden whom the
> angels name Lenore—
> Clasp a rare and radiant maiden whom the
> angels name Lenore."
>   Quoth the Raven, "Nevermore."

Poe then harangues the bird further.

"Be that word our sign of parting, bird or
  fiend!" I shrieked, upstarting ...

Poe orders the bird to leave through the
window that it entered.

"Leave my loneliness unbroken!—quit the
   bust above my door!
Take thy beak from out my heart, and take
   thy form from off my door!"
                Quoth the Raven "Nevermore."
And the Raven, never flitting, still is sitting, *still* is sitting
On the pallid bust of Pallas just above my
   chamber door;
And his eyes have all the seeming of a
   demon's that is dreaming,
And the lamp-light o'er him streaming
   throws his shadow on
the floor.
And my soul from out that shadow that lies
   floating on the floor
                Shall be lifted—nevermore!

Some years later at the cottage in Fordham, New York, Poe, after vainly endeavoring to sell his manuscripts, is in dire poverty
and broken in spirit. He is sitting at his desk,
exasperated and desperate, when Virginia
comes to him. They talk for a moment, but
then she is suddenly seized by a terrible fit
of coughing. For Poe, this symptom of tuberculosis signals only more misery ahead.

The next day Poe tramps about the city,
vainly trying to sell his manuscripts:

Ah, dream too bright to last!
   Ah, starry Hope: that didst arise
But to be overcast!
(from Poe's "To One in Paradise")

Virginia is nursed by Mrs. Clemm as
the slave goes out to gather wood. Meanwhile, Poe, with lantern in hand, wanders
"By a route obscure and lonely" on his way
back to the cottage. When he arrives, Mrs.
Clemm despairs to see that his manuscripts
are unsold. He then embraces his dying wife
and leads her back to bed, where he places
his "West Point Gray" coat over her to keep
her warm and sits beside her through the
night. The next morning he slowly realizes
that Virginia has died. In a fit of grief, he
throws himself over the bed and weeps:

And the fever called "Living"
   Is conquered at last.
                (from Poe's "For Annie")

Later Poe grieves at Virginia's tomb, his
mental health wavering, and while seated
outside, he hallucinates a vision of her at a
spinning wheel. When she appears, he realizes that he is losing his mind.

Helen Whitman is sitting outdoors
reading when she receives a letter from John
Hammond asking her to come and help tend
to their ill friend, Joseph Reed. She goes immediately, and her appearance lifts the ill
man's spirits.

Poe meanwhile goes down to the sea
and again envisions the angel. He runs to
Virginia's tomb:

I dwelt alone
In a world of moan
And my soul was a stagnant tide ...
                (from Poe's "Eulalie")

He hears only the lonely word "Lenore."

...an echo murmured back the word
   "Lenore!"
Merely this and nothing more....
                Quoth the Raven, "Nevermore."

Production and marketing: *The Raven*
is a six-reel reworking of D. W. Griffith's
Edgar Allan Poe (1909) and the 1912 *The
Raven*. It is presumably also based on a play
by George C. Hazelton and, of course, on
Poe's famous poem.

Because Henry Walthall had scored
such a success as Edgar Allan Poe in D. W.
Griffith's *The Avenging Conscience* (1914), he
was awarded the role of Poe in *The Raven*.
Essanay was correct in advertising Walthall
as "the image of Poe." Whether he was also
"a man of the same mold and temperament,"
we can only speculate. Walthall, a major
leading man of the silent era, survived the
transition into sound and continued to work
until his death in 1936 at the age of 58. Aside
from his performances as Poe, his most important credits include *The Birth of a Nation*
(1914), *The Scarlet Letter* (1925), *Abraham
Lincoln* (1931), *Dante's Inferno* (1934), *A Tale*

Poster art for *The Raven* (1915). Note the misspelling of Poe's name. Courtesy of Ron Borst/Hollywood Movie Posters.

of Two Cities (1935), and *The Devil Doll* (1936). Warda Howard, who plays both Virginia and Helen Whitman, failed to carve out a career as successful as Walthall's.

Director Charles Brabin, an Englishman who went on to success in Hollywood, would direct two other noteworthy films. The first, *So Big* (1925), is the popular soap opera of a teacher who brings up her son to be self-sufficient. The second, *The Mask of Fu Manchu* (1932), is a thriller based upon one of Sax Rohmer's Fu Manchu novels. The performances of Boris Karloff and Myrna Loy make it one of the best non-Universal horror pictures of horror's golden age (1931–1936).

As a biography of Poe, *The Raven*'s historical accuracy is spotty. David Poe actually deserted his family several years before he died. When Elizabeth became ill with tuberculosis, her theatrical compatriots did hold a fun-raising concert on her behalf. Edgar did lose at cards, drink excessively, and run up debts while at the University of Virginia, all of which disgusted his guardian, John Allan. One interesting falsehood, however, is the sequence in which Poe is moved by pity to buy a slave for $600. The source of this seems to be an event that occurred in 1915 when Poe was only six years old. On June 22, while preparing to take his wife, his sister-in-law, and Edgar to England, Allan wrote a letter asking Charles Ellis to sell Scipio, a slave, for $600 and to hire out others at $50 a year. Edgar Allan Poe shared the prejudices of his time and region, opposed abolition, believing blacks inferior.

Contrary to sequences in the film, I can find no evidence that Poe had to compete against other suitors for the love of his cousin Virginia. Repeating the obvious error of its predecessors, the film incorrectly portrays Poe's encounter with the raven as an actual historical event.

Critique: *The Video Hound's Golden Movie Retriever* awards *The Raven* only two bones, calling it "An early, eccentric pseudo-biography of author Edgar Allan Poe." *The Raven* is a flawed product, owing most of its success to the performance of Henry Walthall. The film opens with a portrait of Poe and cuts to a medium close-up of Walthall in order to show the remarkable resemblance between the two men. Walthall displays a wide range of emotions as Poe. Most memorable are the wicked gleam in his eye as he contemplates a glass of wine, the touches of humor that he exhibits as the young Poe, the facial expressions of complete despair at his circumstances and those reflecting Poe's fear of insanity. A critic for *The Dramatic Mirror* observed with only slight hyperbole that Walthall's performance "ceased to be acting and becomes at times almost uncanny."[13]

The rest of the cast also remarkably resemble those they portray. Still, though Warda Howard effectively captures Virginia's reported playfulness and devotion to her "Eddie," she comes across as somewhat more voluptuous than Poe's actual young cousin.

The film's generally successful pace is marred only occasionally. Particularly out of place is the pictorial rendering of Poe's Pan and hunter story that he tells Virginia during their courtship. Besides being merely silly, it fails to add any depth to the obvious fact that Edgar and Virginia are in love. If Brabin was attempting an allusion to Poe's occasional playing of the flute, the attempt fails. Also confusing and annoying is the film's ending, at which point it appears that Brabin simply ran out of film and prematurely wrapped. We are introduced to Helen Whitman, with whom Poe began a romance after Virginia's death, but the romance is never depicted. Helen, whose significance is never explained, simply responds to a letter asking her to aid an ill friend and is seen no more as the film cuts to Poe at Virginia's tomb and quickly ends.

Though nothing is known of their contents, two early Russian films were apparently based on Poe sources: *Isle of Oblivion* (1917) and *A Spectre Haunts Europe* (1923). Poe's appeal in Russia must have been limited since no more of his works were adapted to the Russian screen.

Unheimliche Geschichten (1919); aka *Tales of the Uncanny; Five Sinister Stories; Tales of Horror; Weird Tales*

A Richard Oswald Film, Germany

Credits: Produced and directed by Richard Oswald; screenplay by Richard Oswald and Robert Liebmann, based on "The Black Cat" by Edgar Allan Poe, "The Suicide Club" by Robert Louis Stevenson, "Die Erscheinung" by Anselma Heine, and "Der Spuk" by Richard Oswald; cinematography by Carl Hoffmann.

Running time: 112 minutes.

Cast: Conrad Veidt, Anita Berber, Reinhold Schuenzel, Georg John, Hugo Doeblin, Paul Morgan.

Story: In an antiquarian bookstore, the portraits of a young woman and three strange men come to life. One of the apparitions opens a book and begins to read "Die Erscheinung," or "The Phenomenon," the story of a man who rescues a young woman from the mad husband she has recently divorced. She disappears into a hotel room and is later carted out, the victim of pestilence.

In the second story, "Die Hand," or "The Hand," two men are in love with the same woman. One murders the other and three years later reestablishes his relationship with the woman, who is now a professional dancer. During one of her performances, the murderer sees the hands of his victim pull back the stage curtain. Later the hands reappear during a seance attended by the murderer and the dancer, and the ghostly victim gains his revenge.

The third story is Edgar Allan Poe's "The Black Cat." Two men are drinking at an outdoor cafe. One draws the attention of the other to an inebriate at a nearby table, saying, "The drunk over there has a pretty wife." With obvious interest in meeting the wife, the other man walks over as a stranger

and befriends the drunkard. Later the drunkard returns home to his pretty wife, who is cuddling her black cat. First he taunts his wife and threatens to strike her, but he settles for batting at the woman's cat, which runs away.

The next day the wife comes to the tavern to get her besotted husband, who introduces her to the stranger. Taking an obvious liking to the wife, the stranger accompanies them home. The wife immediately picks up her black cat while her husband fetches drinks. Soon the drunkard passes out, and the stranger leaves. When the drunkard awakens, he threatens to beat his wife but again settles for physically abusing the cat. When his wife tries to stop him, he kills her in a fit of temper and hides her corpse behind a wall in the cellar. But where is the cat?

The next day the killer feels remorse for his act but decides to keep the corpse hidden in order to avoid punishment. When the stranger returns, the drunkard says that his wife has gone to the countryside. The stranger leaves but quickly returns after hearing neighbors suggest that the drunkard has murdered his wife. The stranger disputes the drunkard's story, and the two nearly come to blows. Without proof, however, the stranger leaves. He summons the police and returns with them to the drunkard's house. When the police ask to search his home, the drunkard invites them to do so.

When a search of the house does not prove fruitful, the stranger suggests that they search the cellar. As the search commences, the drunkard is jovial. Suddenly, however, a noise comes from behind the newly erected wall. The stranger grabs an ax and opens a hole in the wall, out of which runs the black cat. "He has walled up the cat with his wife."

In the fourth story, Robert Louis Stevenson's "The Suicide Club," a man goes to a supposedly deserted house to find it occupied by the members of a strange club. It is a suicide club, and whoever draws the ace of spades agrees to die that night. The stranger joins the club, draws the deadly card, and is restrained in his chair by the club president, who tells him that he will die at midnight. The man becomes hysterical as the moments tick away and finally pretends to die of a heart attack shortly before midnight. The club president is pleased with the outcome, but soon finds himself trapped in the chair when the intended victim, presumed dead, jumps up to reveal the hoax.

In the fifth story, "Der Spuk," or "The Horrific Episode," a woman is upset because her husband takes care of many important things but does not take care of her. One night a stranger who was injured during an attack on his coach is brought into their home. The husband tells the stranger to make himself at home for the evening, which he does by romancing the restless wife. The husband says he must leave because of an emergency and leaves the wife in the "capable hands of their guest." The husband later returns to confront the guest, frightening him so badly that the trembling man runs off, leaving the husband to win the day.

Production and marketing: Richard Oswald (1880–1963), an unimaginative director who nevertheless managed a few interesting films, became best known for making sex education pictures and costume dramas. His first omnibus film was *Hoffmanns Erzaehlungen* (1916), based upon the stories of T. A. Hoffmann. For *Unheimliche Geschichten* he turned, among other sources, to a story by Edgar Allan Poe. Oswald's other work in the horror/science fiction genre includes two attempts at *Der Hund von Baskerville* (1914 and 1929), both based on Sir Arthur Conan Doyle's *The Hound of the Baskervilles*. He also filmed *Ein seltsamer Fall* (1914), a version of Robert Louis Stevenson's *Dr. Jekyll and Mr. Hyde;* Oscar Wilde's *Das Bildnis des Dorian Gray* (The Picture of Dorian Gray, 1917); and *Alraune* (1930), an inferior remake of director Henrik Galeen's masterful film of a prostitute artificially inseminated by a scientist with the semen of a hanged man. In 1932, Oswald would remake his *Unheimliche Geschichten* as a comedy. His son, Gerd Oswald, would be a successful German-American film director. Unlike his father, Gerd would not turn his attention to the horror genre.

The cast of *Unheimliche Geschichten* is effectively headed by Conrad Veidt (1893–1943), who in the framing narration looks as eerie as he did as Cesare in Robert Wiene's groundbreaking *Das Kabinett des Dr. Caligari* (*The Cabinet of Dr. Caligari*, 1919). Veidt, whom many consider the screen's first "horror actor," would distinguish himself in such genre films as *Das Wachsfigurenkabinett* (*Waxworks* 1924), *Orlacs Haende* (*The Hands of Orlac*, 1924), *Der Student von Prag* (*The Student of Prague*, 1926), *The Man Who Laughs* (1927), *The Last Performance* (1928), and *The Thief of Baghdad* (1940). While he would give many excellent starring performances in critically acclaimed mainstream films in both the United States and Great Britain, he is probably best known to casual American audiences for his supporting role in the Bogart/Bergman classic, *Casablanca* (1942). Although he successfully escaped typecasting in the horror genre, his "almost liquid villainy" led to his frequent casting as "heavies." "No matter what roles I play," he later said, "I can't get Caligari out of my system."

Although many sources claim that the film's third story is based on both Poe's "The System of Dr. Tarr and Professor Fether" and "The Black Cat," I see no evidence that the former was consulted. The story is a straight adaptation of "The Black Cat" and nothing else. Since the film was considered lost until a copy surfaced in 1992, perhaps some early incorrect accounts of the film led all subsequent writers astray, or perhaps indications that Oswald used "The System of

Dr. Tarr and Professor Fether" in his 1932 remake may have incorrectly suggested that it was part of his 1919 original.

Oswald and Liebmann's adaptation of "The Black Cat" stays relatively true to Poe's narrative, truer than most future screenwriters would stay. The Germans provide the drunkard's wife with an admirer not present in Poe's story, a device that Richard Matheson would later employ in his adaptation of "The Black Cat" for director Roger Corman's *Tales of Terror* (1962). Conrad Veidt is the suave admirer in Oswald's film, a role Vincent Price would assume in Corman's remake.

In both the 1919 screenplay and the original story, alcohol ("the Fiend Intemperance," as Poe calls it) is a key factor in accounting for the murderer's behavior, and both narratives hint that the killer projects hatred for his wife onto the black cat. By showing the killer's remorse after the murder, Oswald and Liebmann also incorporate Poe's theme of perversity.

Critique: Except for fine performances by Conrad Veidt and the actor who portrays the drunkard in Poe's "The Black Cat," Oswald's omnibus film is rather stodgy. The framing device manages to create a weird aura, but the final impression is less than impressive. As for Veidt, in several of the stories his skeletal appearance and fluid manner add a sense of the macabre that few other actors could have delivered, but as the hero of "The Black Cat," he dispenses with some of the more obvious horror-inspiring qualities to stand as a contrast to the completely reprehensible drunkard.

While the film does incorporate key narrative elements of the Poe story, it focuses primarily on the pitiful situation of the drunkard's wife and the interest in her shown by the stranger, rarely allowing us to study the personality of the killer, as Poe does so effectively. Indeed, the drunkard largely remains a loathsome sot with little to recommend him to our attention. Although the film's third tale falls short in capturing Poe's psychological subtlety, it is still probably the most interesting of the five. The fifth story, *Der Spuk*, is a lighthearted finale that spoofs the straight horror of the other tales.

Die Pest in Florenz (1919); aka *The Plague in Florence*

Decla Film, Germany

Credits: Directed by Otto Rippert; produced by Erich Pommer; screenplay by Fritz Lang, based on "The Masque of the Red Death" by Edgar Allan Poe; cinematography by Willy Hameister and Emil Schuenemann.

Running time: 96 minutes.

Cast: Otto Mannstaedt (Cesare), Anders Wikman (Cesare's son), Theodore Becker (Franciscan monk), Marga Kierska (beautiful stranger), Julietta Brandt (Death), Karl Bernhard, Franz Knaak, Erner Huebsch, Hans Walter.

Story: Cesare, the ruler of Florence, and his son are sexually attracted to a sensuous female stranger who has entered their city. In a fit of jealousy, Cesare orders that his son be tortured, driving the young man to patricide. As the new ruler, the son turns the churches into places of uninhibited sexual frenzy. When a Franciscan monk tries to restore decency and order, he too falls under the spell of the female stranger and kills his rival. Eventually, the woman, who is actually Death, stalks through Florence, claiming rich and poor alike as plague victims.

Production and marketing: Screenwriter Fritz Lang (1890–1976) incorporated several elements from Poe's "The Masque of the Red Death" into *Die Pest in Florenz*. Anders Wickman, who plays the leader of the city at the time of the plague, stands in for Poe's Prince Propero, and Julietta Brandt plays Death, the surrogate for Poe's Red Death. The themes of hedonism and debauchery as symbolic of mankind's materialism in the face of death and eternity and the theme of our illusions being wiped out by the plague are also lifted from Poe's tale. In Lang's *Lilith und Ly* (1919), the story of a vampiric black widow of a woman, Lang combines Death and the woman into one figure, whereas in *Die Pest in Florenz* he keeps them as two separate figures. *Femme fatales* continued to populate Lang's films when he became both a screenwriter and director. Now considered one the great directors of film history, Lang made a number of pictures with ties to the horror/science fiction genre. Perhaps his most famous work is the science fiction masterpiece *Metropolis* (1926), based upon the novel by Thea von Harbou. Lang's other genre-related films include *Der müde Tod* (1921, aka *Destiny*), *Dr.*

Mabuse der Spieler (1922), *Siegfried* (1923), *Frau im Mond* (1928, aka *Girl in the Moon*), *M* (1931, starring Peter Lorre), *The Testament of Dr. Mabuse* (1932), and *Die tausend Augen des Dr. Mabuse* (1960, aka *The Thousand Eyes of Dr. Mabuse*). Among Lang's mainstream successes in Hollywood are *Fury* (1936), *You Only Live Once* (1937), *The Woman in the Window* (1944), and *The Big Heat* (1935). As Andrew Sarris said of Lang in 1968, "His cinema is that of the nightmare, the fable, and the philosophical dissertation."

Decla spared little expense in bringing this story to the screen. Not only did it hire thousands of extras, but it also employed four separate artists to create the lavish sets. Architect Franz Jaffe designed the set of Florence, Hermann Warm constructed the interiors, and Walter Reimann and Walter Roehrig produced the murals and backgrounds. All of the above save Jaffe designed the unforgettable sets of the classic *Das Kabinett des Dr. Caligari*, also a Decla film.

Critique: As I have not seen this film, I will reserve comment.

Der Student von Prag (1926);
aka *The Student of Prague;*
The Man Who Cheated Life
Sokal-Film, Germany and Austria

Credits: Directed by Henrik Galeen; screenplay by Henrik Galeen, based on a novel by H. H. Ewers and "William Wilson" by Edgar Allan Poe; cinematography by Gwenther Krampf and Erich Nitzschmann; sets by Hermann Warm.

Running time: 85 minutes.

Cast: Conrad Veidt (Baldwin), Werner Krause (Scapinelli), Agnes Estherhazy (Comptesse Magrit), Fritz Alberti (Waldis), Erick Kober, Ferdinand Von Alten, Elizza La Porta, Sylvia Torf, Max Maximilian, Marian Alma.

Story: Baldwin, an impoverished, world-weary student, comes under the scrutiny of Scapinelli (the Devil). Scapinelli magically arranges for Comptesse Magrit to lose control of her horse in Baldwin's presence during a fox hunt. Baldwin catches Magrit as she falls from her horse and later visits her at her palace with an eye toward courtship. During his visit, Magrit's wealthy suitor, Waldis, arrives and presents Magrit with a much larger bouquet of flowers than Baldwin could ever afford. Despondent, Baldwin returns to his garret. Scapinelli arrives and promises Baldwin riches in exchange for Baldwin's mirror image. When the deal is complete, the mirror image walks out of Baldwin's mirror and leaves with Scapinelli. Baldwin then renews his attempt to win Magrit's heart. During a ball, Baldwin passes a love note to Magrit, asking her to join him on the terrace. As they talk, Scapinelli causes the note to fall to the ground, where it is discovered by Lyduschka, a peas-

The French pressbook cover for Germany's *Der Student von Prag* (1926). Courtesy of Ron Borst/Hollywood Movie Posters.

ant girl in love with Baldwin. Lyduschka later takes the note to Waldis, who soon commits to a duel with Baldwin, the best swordsman in the country. To please Magrit's family, Baldwin agrees not to meet Waldis at the appointed time for the duel. Unfortunately, Baldwin's mirror image keeps the appointment and kills Waldis, turning Magrit's family against Baldwin. Baldwin then engages in an evening of self-destructive revelry at the tavern with Lyduschka.

Baldwin is soon dismissed from the university. Meanwhile, Magrit prays for him. Baldwin goes to Magrit and tells her that his mirror image killed Waldis. To prove his point, he stands before a mirror which remains empty. At that point, the mirror image enters the room and Magrit faints. Baldwin runs home, pursued by the mirror image at every turn. In the garret, the mirror image steps back into the mirror and bears his breast to Baldwin's pistol. Baldwin fires and the mirror shatters. Before dying, Baldwin holds up a shard of glass and is relieved to see his reflection. Baldwin's tombstone reads:

> Here Lies Baldwin ...
> He fought with the Devil and lost.

Production and marketing: Henrik Galeen's *Der Student von Prag* was the screen's second film of that title based in part on Poe's "William Wilson," the first having been directed by Stellan Rye thirteen years earlier. In 1926, Dutch writer-director Henrik Galeen (1881–1949) was already one of the silent cinema's most important horror-film makers. He had written and directed *Der Golem* (1915) and written *Der Golem* (1920), *Nosferatu* (1922), and *Das Wachsfigurenkabenett* (1924, aka *Waxworks*). In 1927 he would direct *Alraune*.

The sets of *Der Student von Prag* were constructed by Hermann Warm, who had cobuilt the magnificent expressionistic sets of *Das Kabinett des Dr. Caligari* (1919). Heading the cast were Conrad Veidt (1893–

1943) and Werner Krauss (1884–1969). For details on Veidt's career, see *Unheimliche Geschichten* (1919). Werner Krauss, who costarred with Veidt in *Das Kabinett des Dr. Caligari* (1919) and *Wachsfigurenkabinett* (1924), is otherwise known for his work in films inspired by great authors such as Dostoevsky and Shakespeare. These films include *The Brothers Karamazov* (1920), *Othello* (1922), and *A Midsummer Night's Dream* (1925).

Although the plot of *Der Student von Prag* (1926) is essentially the same as that of its 1913 predecessor, the emphasis has shifted from Scapinelli as the puller of strings to Baldwin as split personality. In the earlier version, for instance, Scapinelli's magic stalls Baldwin while the mirror image kills Magrit's wealthy suitor in a duel. In Galeen's version, Baldwin stands as though in a trance as the mirror image walks past him to the duel. In fact, after Scapinelli arranges for Baldwin to meet Magrit, he plays little if any part in the rest of the film. The implication is that Baldwin is his own devil and that the mirror image is an illusory projection of the dark side of Baldwin's own soul—much as is the case in Poe's "William Wilson." One scene in Galeen's version seems particularly lifted from Poe. When Baldwin is expelled from the university, he plays a game of cards with his friends and wins big, after which one of the vanquished players observes that "The devil has fingers in this game."

At the climax, Baldwin kills the mirror image (his evil self) much as Poe's William Wilson kills his double (his better self). The result is the same in both cases—the killer's own death by suicide.

Critique: The greater psychological implications of Galeen's version help lift it in quality over its predecessor. Other elements also help make Galeen's *Student* superior to Rye's. Both employ excellent trick photography, but three scenes stand out in Galeen's version that overpower anything shot by Rye. First is the scene in which an umbrella-carrying Scapinelli, wearing a long coat and stovepipe hat, stands upon a hillside beside a twisted tree stump. Against a white sky, he stands in the wind and, with the use of malevolent arm and body gestures, manipulates Magrit's horse in Baldwin's direction. Second is the expressionistic scene in which Scapinelli's shadow slowly rises up along the wall to the top of the terrace, where it knocks Baldwin's love note to the ground. Third are the truly eerie scenes in which the camera tracks the fleeing Baldwin through the dark, wind-swept streets of Prague. The state of Baldwin's soul is reflected in the night's turbulent weather,

and the student's haunted face and eyes are the picture of madness.

While Paul Wegener's Baldwin is a rather dashing figure, Veidt's is a tense, gaunt portrait in terror. Of all the films inspired by Poe's "William Wilson," this one is the best. A third version of *Der Student von Prag* would be made in Vienna by the Nazis in 1936. The film, which starred Adolph Wohlbruck (later Anton Walbrook) and Dorothea Wieck, contained musical scenes that reputedly provided an operatic flavor injurious to any mood of horror.

La Chute de la Maison Usher (1928); aka *The Fall of the House of Usher*
Jean Epstein Films, France

Credits: Directed and produced by Jean Epstein; screenplay by Jean Epstein, based on Edgar Allan Poe's "The Oval Portrait" and "The Fall of the House of Usher"; cinematography by George Lucas and Jean Lucas.

Running time: 55 minutes.

Cast: Margaret Gance (Madeline Usher), Jean Debucourt (Roderick Usher), Charles Lamy (Usher's friend), Abel Gance (doctor).

Story: A man enters an inn and says to those assembled, "Do you have a carriage that can bring me to the house of Usher this evening?" "Usher!" those in the inn exclaim, refusing the traveler any assistance. Finally, someone agrees to transport the stranger by horse-drawn wagon to the house of Usher.

At the house, Usher is painting a portrait of his wife Madeleine, who appears to suffer with each brush stroke. The traveler arrives and notes that "There was a sad, oppressive feeling about the place, as if it were inhabited by spirits." Usher is happy to see his friend, who has traveled far out of concern for Roderick's health. Usher then shows his friend around a bit, pointing out a paint-

ing of Ligeia Usher, 1717. Usher then introduces his friend to Madeleine's doctor; she suffers from a strange illness that the doctor is unable to diagnose. Both the doctor and friend comment upon Madeleine's portrait in progress which seems to be alive. Usher explains that "Everyone of the Usher family has painted a portrait of his own wife." Usher appears to be obsessed with the portrait. With an ethereal glare, he stares at the painting.

At the dinner table with his friend, Usher is strumming quietly upon a stringed instrument when the butler brings word that "Her grace is tired and requests to be excused from diner." Shortly afterward, Usher's attention is again drawn to the painting which again seems to be alive. His attention then focuses on his paint palette. The narrator announces: "Already Roderick regretted the intrusion into his isolation. His visitor was becoming annoying. He *wished* to return to his painting."

"My dear friend," Usher says, "your concern for my health is touching, but think also of yourself. A short stroll will help you to rest better after your long trip." The friend agrees to Usher's suggestion and leaves the house.

An obviously ill Madeleine enters the room. Usher continues his work on the portrait as the candles burn low. Finally, unable to stand, Madeleine sinks into a chair as though utterly exhausted. Usher kneels at her side and comforts her as the candles burn still lower.

After a while, the friend returns. Madeleine has reluctantly returned to her feet, and Usher continues to paint. Slowly, however, Madeleine collapses onto the floor. As the friend enters the room, he and Usher examine the finished portrait. "Truly it is like life itself!"

Suddenly, after the friend spots Madeleine on the floor, Usher shrieks and carries her along a wind-swept corridor and up to her room. She is, however, pronounced dead, after which a coffin is prepared for her burial. As the time for burial approaches, Usher shows his friend and the doctor a book he has been reading and exclaims: "Listen to me! Perhaps she is not really dead!" But no one will offer Usher any hope. "She will not leave me!" Usher persists. "We will bring her back again."

When Madeleine is placed in the coffin, Usher objects to having the lid nailed shut. His friend tries to comfort him, but Usher is inconsolable. Finally, Usher, his friend, the doctor, and the servant carry Madeleine's coffin along a path on its way to burial. Aboard a boat, they row the coffin toward its resting place as the wind creates waves upon the water. On the other side, Usher grieves as the coffin is placed inside a vault and the lid nailed down. Finally, Usher and his friend walk away.

Back at the house, a black cat watches and a pendulum swings to and fro. That evening Roderick is tense as though expecting some kind of sign, the least sound seeming to irritate him. "Roderick no longer dared to repeat his insane conviction that Madeleine had been smothered in her coffin." As a thunderstorm breaks upon the land and the air becomes charged with elec-

tricity, Usher's friend passes the time reading from a book: "There are two kinds of sleep," he reads. "One is the body's sleep, not to be feared. But if your brother falls into Fate's dark shadow, in this other, nameless sleep that is at once life and death, commend his soul to God!" The friend obviously takes the words to heart in regard to Usher. Then, as the curtains billow and the lightning crashes without, Usher enters the room carrying a candelabra. "Now do you hear it?" he asks. He and his friend throw open the window and look out into the storm. "Roderick, you must not keep searching," the friend warns. "Let me read to you. It will distract you." Usher agrees, and the friend opens a book and begins to read: "Ethelred rose, and with a few quick blows of his club broke through the planks of the door. And with his iron hands, he pulled himself inside."

At that moment, Madeleine's coffin slides from its resting place and crashes to the ground. The friend continues to read: "Ethelred struck a blow to the dragon's head, and it fell before him, and surrendered its breath with a terrible roar." At that moment Madeleine emerges from her tomb and walks into the stormy night.

The reading continues: "The brave champion went toward the place on the wall where hung the shield. As soon as he approached, it fell to the ground at his feet as if by its own volition." At that moment a row of books collapses to the floor as Usher rocks smiling to and fro in his chair. Meanwhile, Madeleine walks across the desolate countryside toward the house of Usher, her white burial vestments trailing in the wind.

"Yes, I understand," Usher says. "I have understood for a long time…since the very first day…We have buried her alive." At that moment, Madeleine enters and lightning strikes the house of Usher, spreading flames all about. Usher's friend flees the burning building, and Madeleine helps her husband to safety moments before the portrait burns and the house falls amid lightning and conflagration.

Madeline Usher (Margaret Gance) lies in her coffin still alive in Jean Epstein's classic *La Chute de la Maison Usher* (1928, aka *The Fall of the House of Usher*).

Production and Marketing: Polish-born Jean Epstein (1897–1953) moved to France and became a leading director in the French avant-garde cinema. His early experimental films, often mystical in theme and filled with trick camerawork, include *Mauprat, Le Coeur Fidèle, L'Affiche, La Glace a Trois Faces*, and *Six et Demi × Onze*. His first seriously acclaimed film was *La Chute de la Maison Usher*. Already popular in France largely due to Baudelaire's translations, Poe's work provided Epstein with two short stories that the director could adapt to his own cinematic and thematic purposes: "The Oval Portrait" and "The Fall of the House of Usher."

The opening of Epstein's film borrows from Friedrich Murnau's *Nosferatu* (1928), which is based on Bram Stoker's novel *Dracula*. In Murnau's film, a traveler to the castle of Count Orlock (Dracula) raises eyebrows and fear in the village inn when he mentions his destination. In Epstein's film, a traveler to the house of Usher evokes a similar reaction. Such foreshadowing, which appears in Stoker's novel but not in Poe's short story, would be used often in horror films to come. Epstein further alters Poe's "The Fall of the House of Usher" by making Madeline (spelled "Madeleine" in the film) Usher's wife rather than his twin sister. However, in Poe's "The Oval Portrait," upon which the film is also based, the painter and his subject are husband and wife. Faced with which relationship to adopt for the film, Epstein chose that of "The Oval Portrait."

Another difference between Poe's "House of Usher" and Epstein's is Madeline's burial. In Poe's story, Roderick's sister is buried in a vault located in the lower portion of the Usher house. In Epstein's film, on the other hand, the coffin of Roderick's wife is transported some distance from the house itself. The change of scene clearly allows Epstein more outdoor cinematography, an opportunity he uses effectively.

A final and most striking difference is that of the respective endings. In Poe's tale, Roderick and Madeline perish along with the house itself. In Epstein's version, Madeleine returns from the grave, not to bear Usher's body to the floor as a corpse, but rather to save him.

Epstein's faithfulness to Poe's "The Oval Portrait" is a little more exact. In Poe's tale, a traveler's attention is arrested by the oval portrait of a young woman in the bedroom of a house where he has stopped for the night. When he reads a history of the painting, he discovers that it was done by a painter, a wild and moody man, who labored obsessively to produce a portrait of his reluctant new bride. When the portrait was completed, the painter cried in a loud voice, "This is indeed *Life* itself" and turned to find his beloved wife dead. In Epstein's film, Usher and the painter are one, and while the vampiric effects of Usher's art drain the vitality from Madeleine, she does not die as she does at the finale of Poe's story, but rather is buried alive to satisfy the requirements of the Usher tale.

Epstein's decision to merge Poe's "The Oval Portrait" and "The Fall of the House of Usher" was probably suggested by Poe's description of Roderick Usher's proclivity for painting:

> From the paintings over which his elaborate fancy brooded, and which grew, touch by touch, into vagueness at which I shuddered the more thrillingly, because I shuddered knowing not why;—from these paintings (vivid as their images now are before me) I would in vain endeavor to educe more than a small portion which should lie within the compass of merely written words. By the utter simplicity, by the nakedness of his designs, he arrested and overawed attention. If ever mortal painted an idea, that mortal was Roderick Usher. For me at least—in the circumstances then surrounding me—there arose out of the pure abstractions which the hypochondriac contrived to throw upon his canvas, an intensity of intolerable awe, no shadow of which felt I ever yet in the contemplation of the certainly glowing yet too concrete reveries of Fuseli.

Interestingly, Epstein initially had an assistant director on the Poe project. His name was Luis Buñuel. Dissatisfied with Epstein's conception, Buñuel became disgusted and quit. That same year he directed his own avant-garde masterpiece, *Un Chien Andalou* (aka *A Mad Dog*), which presents as its opening scene a man walking up behind a woman and very realistically slicing her eyeball in half with a razor blade. That scene is one of only a handful in the history of the cinema that once seen can never be forgotten. Buñuel, of course, went on to eclipse Epstein as a world-renowned director of international importance, no mean feat since the latter would direct such important classics of the French cinema as *Finis Terrae* (1928, aka *World's End*), *Morvan* (1930), and *Le Tempestaire* (1947, aka *The Tempest Calmer*)

La Chute de la Maison found itself sandwiched between two other French films based on the work of Edgar Allan Poe: *The Chess Player* (1926) and *The Chess Player* (1938). Although little is known of these films, they were apparently inspired by Poe's "Maelzel's Chess-Player," in which the author exposed the hoax of a chess machine built in 1769. The "Automaton Chess Player," which astonished audiences on both sides of the Atlantic, was actually operated by a concealed man. What Poe did not acknowledge was that he drew his explanation largely from an earlier published article which he failed to credit.

Critique: Epstein's *The Fall of the House of Usher* is a visual feast: the long hallway of the Usher house lined with curtains billowed by the wind; low-lying fog rushing across the land; waves rippling upon the tarn (as opposed to Poe's stagnant tarn); shots of the bleak beauty of barren trees, sometimes silhouetted against a gray sky. In the hands of cinematographers George and Jean Lucas, the camera is almost a living participant in the film as it tracks wild-eyed Jean Debucourt (Usher) carrying Madeleine along the long corridor after she has "died," or as it tracks along the floor of a wind-blown corridor, placing the audience in the position of the wind itself as it buffets the dead leaves before it. Epstein evokes a sense of autumn melancholy in line with Poe's brilliant first paragraph of "The Fall of the House of Usher." Visually, the only disappointment is the poorly executed exterior set of the house of Usher, which serves only to hamper the poetic mood of the rest of the film.

Although Epstein's film is a visual feast, it unfortunately suffers from the liberties the director took with Poe's original "House of Usher." In making Madeline the wife rather than the twin sister of Usher and in having her serve as Usher's savior rather than as an agent in his death, Epstein obliterates Poe's intent of spiritually linking Roderick, Madeline, and the Usher family to the house itself, an intent suggesting that spirit is present in inanimate nature. Epstein's aim, on the other hand, is to deliver a Christian message. Although the director presents no overtly Christian symbolism, he does interpolate symbolically regenerative scenes of copulating frogs into Madeleine's funeral sequences. Madeleine's resurrection to save the man who self-centeredly hastened her "death," is obviously Christ-like. All of this, unfortunately, deviates too far from Poe. A contemporary parallel is Stanley Kubrick's film of Stephen King's novel *The Shining*.

The film is good Kubrick but disappointing King. Perhaps that is why *The Overlook Film Encyclopedia* calls Epstein's film "basically an empty exercise in style. Roger Corman's *House of Usher* (1960) captured the troubled undertones of Poe much more honestly."

While the film is thematically problematic, the cast is exemplary. Jean Debucourt, a perfect Roderick Usher, embodies Poe's description:

> A cadaverousness of complexion; an eye large, liquid, and luminous beyond comparison; lips somewhat thin and very pallid, but of a surpassingly beautiful curve; a nose of a delicate Hebrew model, but with a breadth of nostril unusual in similar formations... The now ghastly pallor of the skin, and the now miraculous lustre of the eye, above all things startled and even awed me. The silken hair, too, had been suffered to grow unheeded, and as, in its wild gossamer texture, it floated rather than fell about the face, I could not, even with effort, connect its Arabesque expression with any idea of simple humanity.

Margaret Gance gives a fine, sympathetic performance as Madeleine Usher, her vitality seeping away as Roderick's portrait nears completion. The rest of the cast, too, leaves nothing to be desired.

The Fall of the House of Usher (1928)
Webber, U.S.A.

Credits: Directed by James Sibley Watson; screenplay and scenic design by Melville Webber, based on "The Fall of the House of Usher" by Edgar Allan Poe; cinematography by James Sibley Watson.
Running time: 20 minutes.
Cast: Herbert Stern (Roderick Usher), Hildergarde Watson (Madeline Usher), Melville Webber (a traveler).
Story: The film opens with a prismatic effect of Poe's title page of "The Fall of the House of Usher." A traveler arrives at the

house of Usher. Madeline carries flowers into the dining room and places them in a vase on the table. Roderick pulls out Madeline's chair for her, and they sit down for dinner. They are affectionate toward one another. He gives her a drink.

When Madeline discovers a miniature coffin under her dinner dish she is startled and passes out. Usher comes to her side; she rises as though in a trance and walks away through superimposed images of coffins.

Raindrops fall into a body of water. The

bell of the house of Usher rings, and the traveler enters. Madeline walks about, still trancelike. The traveler enters and sees Madeline collapse on the stairs. Usher approaches Madeline, who rises to her knees.

Madeline is in a coffin. Usher's gloved hands close her eyes, but her lips move. The coffin is hammered shut. The hammer and gloves drop to the floor.

Madeline rests in her coffin. Usher climbs the stairs. Madeline rises from her coffin, her arms raised heavenward. Hands turn the pages of a book, and alphabet letters float across the screen suggesting words such as "b-e-a-t," "c-r-a-c-k," and "s-c-r-e-a-m." Madeline walks upstairs. She opens the door, enters the room, and falls upon Roderick. The traveler flees and the house collapses.

Production and marketing: The same year that Jean Epstein made his visually arresting *The Fall of the House of Usher*, Americans Webber and Watson made a highly experimental version of the story. Produced by the Film Guild, it took an even more *avant-garde* approach than Epstein did. The first Edgar Allan Poe film regarded as "experimental" was Charles F. Klein's *Caligari*-inspired *The Tell-Tale Heart* (1928), now lost. Weber and Watson follow suit in the source of their inspiration. Although their *The Fall of the House of Usher* languished largely unseen, it received high praise from the American *avant-garde* community. No one involved went on to achieve any cinematic renown, however, and the film today remains largely ignored.

Critique: The story synopsis above is much more concrete than the film itself. In fact, story, character, and the themes of Poe finish a distant second to the visuals, which attempt not so much to tell a story as to create a mood through cinematic poetry. The sets look as though they were borrowed from *The Cabinet of Dr. Caligari* and painted over by Pablo Picasso. Madeline Usher looks like a twenties vamp, but that too is secondary. The visuals dominate: *Caligari*-like use of light and shadow, optical distortions created by filming through prisms, and multiple exposures and dissolves. There is no dialogue, but who needs dialogue if there is really no story? The following is a fairly accurate review written by Padraic Colum in *The Dial*:

> *The Fall of the House of Usher* produced by the Film Guild develops from *The Cabinet of Dr. Caligari*. In that memorable photoplay the settings were made accessories to the story; they expressed the fantastic mood of the play. In *The Fall of the House of Usher* an experiment is made that goes further in this direction; the cast is of the smallest and the settings quite dominate the people in the film. What goes to establish the mood is the interior of the strange house, with its corridors and vaults, its dimly lighted rooms, its toppling walls and arches. Motion is given to things which should be inanimate and the strange shapes that fill the interior are made more sinister by this device...It is as if it was the expression, not of Poe's story, but of some music that accompanied that story.[14]

The overall effect is one of having been abused by pretension, of having witnessed an experiment gone sour.

Unheimliche Geschichten (1932); aka *Tales of the Uncanny; The Living Dead; Extraordinary Tales; Asylum of Horror*

Roto Film, Germany

Credits: Directed by Richard Oswald; produced by Gabriel Pascal; screenplay by Heinz Goldberg and Eugen Szatmari, based on "The System of Dr. Tarr and Professor Fether" and "The Black Cat" by Edgar Allan Poe and "The Suicide Club" by Robert Louis Stevenson; cinematography by Heinrich Gaertner.

Running Time: 89 minutes.

Cast: Paul Wegener, Harald Paulsen, Bert Reisfeld, Roma Bahn, Mary Parker, John Gottowt, Paul Henckels, Ilse Feurstenberg, Viktor de Kowa.

Story: A mad scientist kills his wife and is locked away in a mental institution. He takes over the institution and turns it into a suicide club.

Production and marketing: *Unheimliche Geschichten*, finished in late 1931, sees director Oswald remake his 1915 film of the same title as a comedy. According to *The Overlook Film Encyclopedia: Horror*, the film "pokes fun at all the classic motifs of the genre but seems to single out Paul Leni's *Das Wachsfigurenkabinett* (1924) as a special target for parody." The film's star, Paul Wegener, who earlier directed and starred in *Der Golem* (1914) and later became a Nazi collaborator in the realms of theater and cinema, apparently enjoyed sending up the genre he had helped make famous.

Critique: As I have not seen this film, I cannot comment.

The Murders in the Rue Morgue (1932)

Universal, U.S.A.

Credits: Directed by Robert Florey; screenplay by Tom Reed and Dale van Avery, based on "The Murders in the Rue Morgue" by Edgar Allan Poe; adaptation by Robert Florey; cinematography by Karl Freund; art direction by Charles D. Hall; special effects by John P. Fulton; art direction by Charles D. Hall; edited by Milton Carruth; makeup by Jack Pierce.

Running time: 62 minutes.

Cast: Bela Lugosi (Dr. Mirakle), Sidney Fox (Camille L'Espanaye), Leon Waycoff ([later Leon Ames], Pierre Dupin), Bert Roach (Paul), Betsy Ross Clark (Mme. L'Espanaye), Brandon Hurst (prefect of police), D'Arcy Corrigan (morgue keeper), Noble Johnson (Janos, the Black One), Arlene Francis (woman of the streets).

Story: The scene is a carnival in Paris. Pierre Dupin, his fiancée Camille L'Espanaye, Pierre's roommate Paul, and Paul's girlfriend are drawn to a sideshow exhibit for "Erik the Ape—the beast with a human soul." When they enter the tent, they are directed by Dr. Mirakle to sit near the front. Quickly, Mirakle walks to the stage and addresses the twittering audience: "Silence! I am Dr. Mirakle, Messieurs and Mesdames, and I am not a sideshow charlatan. So if you expect to witness the usual carnival hocus-pocus, just go to the box office and get your money back. I am not exhibiting a freak, a monstrosity of nature, but a milestone in the development of life! The shadow of Erik the Ape hangs over us all—the darkness before the dawn of man." Mirakle then signals his servant, Janos, to unveil Erik's cage. "Behold!" Mirakle cries. "The first man." This reference to Darwinism causes the audience to shout, boo, and leave their seats.

Someone charges Mirakle with heresy, to which he replies, "Heresy! Heresy? Do they still burn men for heresy? Then burn me, Monsieur. Light the fire. Do you think your little candle will outshine the flame of truth? Do you think these walls and curtains are my whole life? They are only a trap to catch the pennies of fools! My life is consecrated to great experiment! I tell you I will prove your kinship with the ape. Erik's blood shall be mixed with the blood of man!"

By this time, Pierre and Camille are among the few remaining customers. Pierre, who is quite intrigued by Mirakle's diatribe, accompanies Camille to Erik's cage. The ape takes an immediate liking to Camille, grabs her bonnet, and destroys it. When Mirakle insists on sending her another bonnet as part of a ruse to acquire her address, Pierre, distrusting Mirakle, forbids Camille to divulge her address and hustles her quickly out of the exhibit. When they are gone, Mirakle sends Janos to follow them and learn Camille's address.

Later Mirakle's carriage stops along a stone street where two men are fighting over a prostitute. When the men fatally injure each other, Mirakle leaves his carriage and offers assistance to the frightened prostitute. Shortly afterward, as the carriage pulls away with Mirakle and the girl inside, her laughter dissolves into screams.

In Mirakle's laboratory, as the girl moans in the background, tied to a cross, the doctor tests her blood to see if it mixes with Erik's. "Are you in pain, mademoiselle?" he rants. "It will only last a little longer. Just a few more minutes and we shall see. We will know whether you are to be the bride of sci-

ence!" As the girl's screams intensify, Mirakle learns that the experiment is a failure. "Rotten blood!" he cries, shaking his fist in her face. "Your blood is rotten! Your beauty was a lie!" At that moment, she falls limp. "Dead. You're…you're dead," he sadly mutters, sinking to his knees as if in prayer before the girl. Janos then approaches and cuts the girl's ropes, allowing her to fall through a trap door into the Seine below. "Will my search never end?" Mirakle wonders.

Sometime later Pierre goes to the morgue in order to acquire blood from two recently deceased girls pulled from the Seine. He is obviously intrigued to learn that a third female corpse has been found, all three having a similar mark on their arms. Pierre makes arrangements to have the morgue attendant bring a blood sample from the latest corpse to his home that evening.

When evening arrives, Pierre is at home working obsessively on the case of the three female corpses, attempting to discover what links their deaths. All the while, Pierre's effeminate roommate Paul fusses over a macaroni dinner and berates Pierre for turning their home into a morgue. After the morgue attendant brings the medical student the blood sample, Paul again admonishes Pierre to lead a more balanced life: "Oh, Pierre, pull yourself together! You're becoming fanatical. Look at yourself in the mirror—your eyes are getting glassy just like that old charlatan." Suddenly reminded of Mirakle's tirade at the sideshow, Pierre wonders if the strange doctor could be behind the three recent deaths.

Meanwhile, Camille receives a new bonnet accompanied by a note which reads: "Great things are written for you in the stars. Erik and I will read them for you tonight." Pierre and a group of medical students then arrive, singing a song consisting in part of "Her father wanted her to wed a funny, funny little man." Camille joins in the singing, after which everyone retires to a park, where Pierre pushes Camille in a swing. When she tells him of Mirakle's invitation, Pierre stops the swing suddenly and

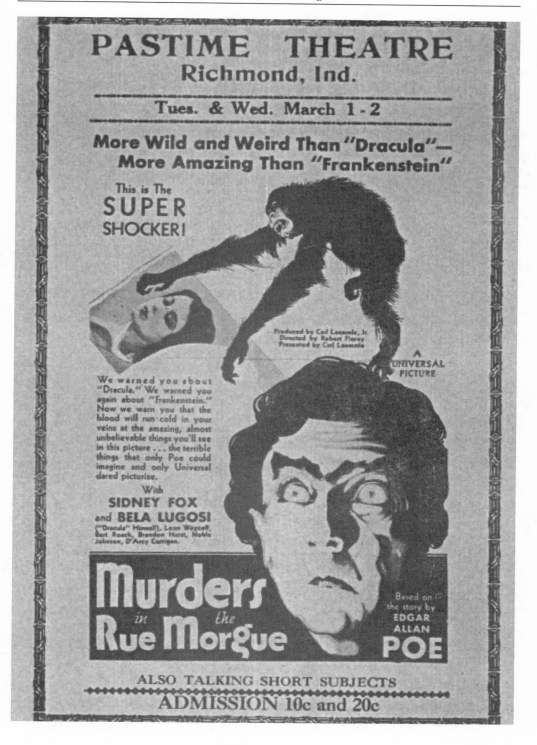

An original herald for *Murders in the Rue Morgue* (1932).

tells his fiancée to remain at home while he goes to meet Mirakle instead.

That night Pierre goes to the carnival and finds that the show is packing up to leave. He enters Mirakle's exhibit and finds the doctor writing at a table. Mirakle is obviously disappointed at seeing Pierre instead of Camille, and when the student presses him about his theories, Mirakle says that he is busy preparing to leave the city and dismisses the young man. Upon leaving, however, Pierre learns that Mirakle is not leaving Paris at all. Later Pierre follows Mirakle through the streets of Paris, much as Mirakle earlier followed Pierre and Camille.

When Pierre returns to Camille, he tells her of his evening and reveals that Mirakle is actually staying at a house in Paris. He obviously believes Camille is in danger. After Pierre leaves, Mirakle arrives and tries to persuade Camille to leave with him. Camille, frightened but polite, finally has to force the door shut in Mirakle's face to make him leave. She then prays before a crucifix as Mirakle sends Erik the ape up the side of the building on a kidnapping mission.

As Erik murders Madame L'Espanaye, stuffing her body up the chimney, and abducts Camille, several onlookers listen to the screams and noises issuing from behind the women's locked door. Meanwhile, Pierre is at home discovering that the blood of the three dead women is contaminated with ape's blood. Rushing off to warn Camille again about Mirakle, he arrives as the police are investigating the disappearance of Madame L'Espanaye. Unfortunately, Pierre quickly becomes their major suspect. When the onlookers disagree about what language the intruder was speaking, Pierre struggles without success to convince the police that the intruder was indeed an ape and that Dr. Mirakle is behind the killings and the abduction of Camille.

Suddenly, when the head and shoulders of Madame L'Espanaye fall into view from the fireplace chimney where the body has been hidden, Pierre is able to convince the police that the hair clutched in the dead woman's hand is that of an ape. He then leads the police to Mirakle's house, where the doctor has just discovered that Camille's and Erik's blood are compatible. For no apparent reason, the ape then kills Mirakle, grabs Camille, and ascends to the rooftops of Paris. With pistol in hand, Pierre follows the ape and is able to shoot it to death when it puts Camille down and attacks him.

Production and marketing: When Universal was preparing to make *Frankenstein* (1931), the first choice to play the monster was Bela Lugosi (1882–1956), who had just completed *Dracula* (1931) and whom Universal considered its next Lon Chaney. However, after considering the script and submitting to a makeup test, Lugosi declined the role. Likewise, Robert Florey (1900–1956) was set to direct *Frankenstein*. Formerly from France, Florey was heavily under the influence of the German expressionistic cinema. Although Florey went so far in preparing *Frankenstein* as to co-author a detailed screenplay and direct a two-reel test, Universal took him off the project and brought in director James Whale. Boris Karloff landed the role of the Frankenstein monster, and the rest is history. Part of that history, of course, is that Lugosi and Florey were given Edgar Allan Poe's *The Murders in the Rue Morgue* as a consolation prize. But it wasn't even as easy as all that.

Universal, still in financial difficulty in 1932, wanted to replace the period settings with modern sets in order to save money. When told this, Florey, still smarting from his experience with *Frankenstein*, threatened to walk out. In order to appease the flustered director, the studio restored the nineteenth-century setting and kept Florey on board. Shooting began on October 19, 1931, on a budget of only $164,220, considerably less than the budgets provided for *Dracula* and *Frankenstein*. Within eight days, Florey was finding it necessary to film retakes of the scenes in Mirakle's tent, a decision that pushed the shooting five days past its projected eighteen-day schedule. After the film wrapped on November 13, 1931, Carl Laemmle, Jr., thought it so inferior to *Dracula* and *Frankenstein* that he ordered it back into production for $21,870 of new scenes, including the climactic rooftop scenes. Florey finally wrapped on December 22, 1931, after spending his final day shooting scenes of a real monkey in the Selig zoo. This footage was then clumsily inserted into the film at various places to add "realism." Most of the ape scenes, of course, featured Charles Gemora in a gorilla suit. When the film finally opened in February of 1932, Universal had gone $4000 over its revised budget.

Posters and ads for *Rue Morgue* featured a large head of Lugosi and a drawing of an ape reaching for a sleeping young woman. "More wild and weird than 'Dracula'—More amazing than 'Frankenstein,'" barked the ads. "This is the super shocker!…We warned you about 'Dracula.' We warned you about 'Frankenstein.' Now we warn you that blood will run cold in your veins at the amazing, almost unbelievable things you'll see in this picture…the terrible things that only Poe could imagine and only Universal dared picturize."

Realart Pictures rereleased *Rue Morgue* in 1948. This time the image of the ape is featured more prominently in the poster and ad art and Lugosi is somewhat de-emphasized. Still, when the ballyhoo dubs the film "the horror monster show," everyone knows who the horror monster is.

Interestingly, the more films Universal would base on the works of Edgar Allan Poe, the less Poe's writings would actually figure in the scenarios. In *The Murders in the Rue Morgue*, the key element from Poe is the sequence in which the ape enters the home of the Espanayes as onlookers confuse the ape's growls for different spoken languages that, ironically, they have never heard. Also from Poe is the discovery of the body in the fireplace chimney where it has been jammed by the murderous ape. The rest of the tale is pure Hollywood, influenced by German expressionism.

The nightmarish sets of Robert Weine's *Das Kabinett des Dr. Caligari* (1919, aka *The Cabinet of Dr. Caligari*) obviously influenced Florey's sets. But as Ken Hanke explains in his definitive article on *Rue Morgue*, Florey also lifts the plot from *Caligari*:

> The carnival side-show setting is there. Lugosi's Dr. Mirakle stands in nicely for Caligari, as does Erik the Ape for Cesare. Erik even carries off the heroine after the fashion of Cesare in *Caligari*. The most notable difference is the removal of the madhouse framing device, which in *Caligari* turns the film around by explaining the distorted settings as the warped perspective of an inmate.[15]

This should not be held against the film, however. Karl Freund's *The Mummy* (1932) is basically a remake of *Dracula* with Karloff standing in for Lugosi and Edward van Sloan standing in for himself, but no one disparages the Karloff film because of it, nor should anyone.

Hanke also notes that Florey emphasizes the relationship between Dr. Mirakle and Pierre Dupin: "Mirakle is Dupin—as reflected in a funhouse mirror. This complex linking of hero and villain, which Florey develops throughout the film, indicates that the division between good and evil almost disappears when both are obsessive"[16] In pointing out this unmistakable linking of Dupin and Mirakle, Hanke fails to note that in this instance perhaps Florey owed something to Poe. It is Poe in the "The Murders in the Rue Morgue" who subtly links amateur detective C. Auguste Dupin with the opposing forces of darkness. As John G. Cawelti observes in his book *Adventure, Mystery, and Romance*, "When one thinks about it, the close resemblance between Dupin and the gothic villain is immediately clear. Both are demonically brilliant, night-loving figures, and both are involved in plotting out elaborate and complex stratagems. One might interpret Poe's invention of the detective as a means of bringing the terrifying potency of the gothic villain under the control of rationality and thereby directing it to beneficial ends."[17] Of course, Florey's Dupin is not demonically brilliant. He is, however, fascinated by evil. Note his obsessive interest in Mirakle and his work, as well as his single-minded pursuits, which make him a frequenter of the morgue. If Universal had been interested in producing Poe's story faithfully, Dupin should more have resembled their Sherlock Holmes of the forties rather than their typical thirties and forties heroes who were always in love, sometimes persistent, but never brilliant.

Critique: *The Murders in the Rue Morgue* (1932) is probably the most controversial film of cinematic horror's golden age (1931–1936). Reviews at the time of the film's release were mixed. The *New York Times* noted that Poe contributed the title, but little else, saying, "This synthetic blood curdler, with its crazy scientist and its shadowy ape, is not in any important respect to be confused with Poe's ratiocinative detective story."[18] The reviewer concluded, "The entire production suffers from an overzealous effort at terrorization, and the cast, inspired by the general hysteria, succumbs to the temptation to overact."[19]

On the other hand, The New York *Daily News* found things to like about the film:

> It's an artificial story...nevertheless Bela Lugosi's Dr. Mirakle does make you shrink back a little in your seat and the ape, Eric (*sic*), sends your thumping heart up into your throat when he...carries his lovely victim over the rooftops of Paris. Lugosi's suggestion of the insanely criminal doctor is effective. Sidney Fox gives the necessary touch of beauty to the macabre tale.[20]

In his book *The Count: The Life and Films of Bela "Dracula" Lugosi,* Arthur Lennig writes:

> Certainly Dr. Mirakle is on the verge of being one of Lugosi's best performances, but the actor is so hampered by a stodgy script and by the uninspired direction of Robert Florey, as well as by an excess of bad comedy relief, that the film as a whole is only mildly interesting and by no means up to what one

would expect, considering the creatively rich period during which it was made.[21]

In recent years the film has come under great scrutiny, largely initiated by Brian Taves's book *Robert Florey, the French Expressionist* (Scarecrow Press, 1987). Taves's most controversial claim is that Florey would have directed a better *Frankenstein* than James Whale did. His assertion has resulted in a renewed interest, both positive and negative, in *Rue Morgue*. Taves, of course, praises Florey and blames the film's shortcomings on Lugosi's overacting.

The best and most balanced positive examination of the film is the 1989 Ken Hanke article mentioned above. The most negative response to the film is found in *Universal Horrors* by Michael Brunas, John Brunas, and Tom Weaver.

Hanke summarizes the film's positive aspects as follows:

> That the film is primarily famous as one of the better Bela Lugosi vehicles isn't surprising, but it is ironic. A mere handful of Lugosi films—*White Zombie, The Black Cat, The Raven, Dark Eyes of London*—do as well by the actor as Florey's strange pastiche. A brilliant Lugosi performance in a well conceived, intelligently written role to one side, *Murders in the Rue Morgue* is an unusually good—almost great film in its own right. It certainly has its own atmosphere with its cold-blooded—even slightly sick—sense of humor and its no-nonsense grimness, at the core of which is a heavily offbeat, often warped sexuality. Sexual fantasy, of course, is central to the horror film, but Florey's use of it here is unique by virtue of its sheer convolutions, encompassing bestiality, sexual transference and homosexuality—not to mention sadism.[22]

Hanke makes his case, which is too detailed to repeat here, by closely and accurately examining the film scene by scene. Suffice it to say that Florey's masterful touches include the *Caligari*-like sets, expert use of atmospheric lighting and cross-cutting, the effective direction of the actors' physical movements, the linking of Dupin and Mirakle as warped reflections of one another, and the sheer bravado of attempting to integrate so much nastiness into one picture. Florey's failure to achieve a clear focus, however, is one of Hanke's strongest and most accurate criticisms.

> *Murders in the Rue Morgue* comes across as one of those maddening films that dot cinema history—films that are better in part than as a whole. This is particularly regrettable here where those separate components achieve a brilliance suggestive of a truly major talent needing just a little more control…Florey's inherent bitterness and irony are almost certainly factors in the film's inability to achieve a clear focus—but this bitterness and irony are also its strengths and its beauty.[23]

Brunas, Brunas, and Weaver call *Rue Morgue* "easily the worst acted Universal horror film,"[24] which, if we leave Lugosi aside, might be true. They cite reediting as being responsible for the film's obvious unevenness, but unlike Hanke, they criticize Florey's conception and direction for its debt to *Caligari*. Interestingly, when evaluating Karl Freund's approach to *The Mummy*, they uncritically note that film's debt to *Dracula* but leave Freund unscathed—as they should. However, when noting *Rue Morgue*'s debt to *Caligari*, they brand Florey a thief. Do not Florey and Freund deserve to be judged by comparable standards? Brunas, Brunas, Weaver, and Hanke are all correct however, in ridiculing the insipid love talk between Waycoff and Fox. In fact, in examining the dialogue as a whole, one could almost conclude that an amateurish bumbler concocted the Waycoff-Fox exchanges, while a much firmer hand produced Lugosi's speech. Brunas, Brunas, Weaver, and Hanke also all correctly agree that the clumsily added scenes of the live ape detract greatly. In fairness, Brunas, Brunas, and Weaver admit that the sets are striking and that the film contains some impressive scenes. They remain, however, far less pleased with the final product than is Hanke.

Brunas, Brunas, and Weaver had not read Hanke's fine article before going to press with *Universal Horrors*. Weaver, the primary author of the book's *Rue Morgue* chapter, has since read Hanke's article and finds it generally accurate and provocative. Nevertheless, he says, while Hanke's excellent criticism makes the film more interesting, it does little to enhance its entertainment value.

Finally, it would seem that *Rue Morgue* is an admirable film with a number of regrettable flaws. Florey cannot be dismissed as a minor talent, nor can he be heralded as superior to James Whale. Lugosi is the greatest horror-film personality of all time, even if (or possibly even because) he paints his performances with large brush strokes. Largely due Lugosi's ripping performance, I find the film enjoyable after repeated viewings, but also of enduring interest are Florey's expressionistic moods and his none-too-subtle religious symbolism suggesting traditional Christianity's struggle against the threat of Darwinism. Unfortunately, Edgar Allan Poe contributes little, though what little he does add goes to the positive side of the film's ledger.

The Black Cat (1934)
Universal, U.S.A.

Credits: Directed by Edgar G. Ulmer; production supervisor—E. M. Asher; screenplay by Peter Ruric, based on a story by Edgar G. Ulmer and Peter Ruric suggested by *The Black Cat* by Edgar Allan Poe; assistant directors—W. J. Reiter and Sam Weisenthal; director of photography—John J. Mescall; edited by Ray Curtiss; musical director—Heinz Roemheld; art direction by Charles D. Hall; makeup by Jack Pierce.

Running time: 66 minutes

Cast: Boris Korloff (Hjalmar Poelzig), Bela Lugosi (Dr. Vitus Werdegast), David Manners (Peter Alison), Jacqueline Wells ([later Julie Bishop], Joan Alison), Lucille Lund (Karen Werdegast Poelzig), Egon Brecher (the majordomo), Henry Cording (Thamal), Albert Conti (the lieutenant), John Peter Richmond ([later John Carradine], cultist).

Story: Newlyweds Peter and Joan Alison are traveling by train on their honeymoon to a European resort. When a seating mistake is made, a somber and sinister-looking stranger enters their car, excuses himself, and prepares to leave. The couple, however, insist that he stay since there is not far to go. The stranger, who introduces himself as Dr. Vitus Werdegast, says that he is going to visit an old friend. Later, when Peter awakens to find Werdegast lovingly stroking Joan's hair, the doctor explains:

> I beg your indulgence, my friend. Eighteen years ago I left a girl—so like your lovely wife—to go to war. For Kaiser and country, you know. She was my wife. Have you ever heard of—Kurgaal? It is a prison below Omsk on Lake Bakail. Many men have gone there. Few have returned. I have returned. After fifteen years—I have returned!

Since they are all going in the same direction they board a bus together and set out into the stormy night. Amidst thunder and lightning, the bus driver provides "tourist" information:

> All of this country was one of the greatest battlefields of the war. Tens of thousands of men died here. The ravine down there was piled twelve deep with dead and wounded men. The little river below was swollen—red—a raging torrent of blood. That high hill, yonder, where engineer Poelzig now lives, was the site of Fort Marmaros. He built his home on its very foundation. Marmaros! The greatest graveyard in the world!

Because of weather conditions, the bus crashes, killing the driver and leaving Joan injured and unconscious. Peter and Werdegast, aided by Thamal, Poelzig's servant, carry the girl to Poelzig's house, which is nearby.

Upon entering Poelzig's house, Werdegast sends someone for Poelzig and begins to attend to Joan's injuries. When Poelzig rises from his bed and goes downstairs, it is obvious that he and Werdegast know each other, and they exhibit an obvious animosity toward one another.

When Werdegast and Poelzig are alone, the psychiatrist accuses Poelzig of war crimes: "You sold Marmaros to the Russians. Scuttled away in the night and left us to die. Is it to be wondered that you should choose this place to build your house? The masterpiece of construction—built upon the ruins of the masterpiece of destruction—the masterpiece of murder. The murderer of 10,000 men returns to the place of his crime!" Werdegast recounts the tortures he endured as a prisoner and tells Poelzig that he has returned for his wife Karen. Poelzig attempts to evade the subject as Werdegast becomes increasingly hostile.

At that point, Peter walks innocently into the room, and Poelzig suggests that they all have a drink. As Werdegast proposes a toast, a black cat runs across the room. The sight of the animal makes the psychiatrist hurl a knife into the cat as he succumbs to a fit of anger and hysteria. Joan enters in a trancelike state, and Poelzig explains Werdegast's problem: "You must be indulgent of Dr. Werdegast's weakness. He is the unfortunate victim of one of the commoner phobias, but in the extreme form. He has an intense and all-consuming horror—of cats." Peter is worried and persuades Joan to return to her room. Werdegast composes himself and explains that he does indeed fear cats and tells Peter that, according to superstition, the black cat is a symbol of evil, and at death that evil enters into the nearest living thing. With a smile, Poelzig adds that the black cat never dies. Then the high priest of

Satanism shows his guests to their bedrooms.

Later, in the dead of night, Poelzig strokes a black cat and prowls his Marmaros cellars, where he has preserved his many female sacrifices to Satan. His prize, displayed upright behind glass, is Karen, Werdegast's former wife. Suddenly Werdegast enters and discovers the perverse exhibit. Poelzig tells the grieving psychiatrist that his wife died two years after the war and that his daughter later died also. Werdegast calls Poelzig a liar, vows that he will help Joan leave the house alive, and pulls a pistol. Before he can fire, however, the black cat approaches, completely immobilizing Werdegast with fear. When Werdegast recovers, Poelzig suggests that they play a game of chess to decide whether Joan leaves or stays.

The next day Joan appears recovered, and Peter tries to make plans to leave. Poelzig conveniently arranges a series of excuses to keep the newlyweds in the house, one ruse being that of a dead phone. As Poelzig and Werdegast play chess, Poelzig smiles and says: "You hear that, Vitus? The phone is dead. Even the phone is dead."

When Poelzig wins the game of chess and the Alisons try to leave, the servant Thamal knocks out Peter and takes Joan back to her room. Shortly afterward, Joan meets a young woman who identifies herself as Karen, the daughter of Vitus Werdegast, whom she believes dead. She reveals that she is Poelzig's wife and warns Joan to get out of the house before it is too late. When Werdegast comes to rescue Joan, she tells him of having met his daughter Karen. Werdegast is enraged and disrupts Poelzig's Black Mass. He then forces Poelzig down into the cellar and skins his nemesis alive. When Werdegast later tries to help Joan escape, Peter misunderstands his actions and shoots him. Joan and Peter flee the house, and the dying Werdegast sets off dynamite in the cellar, destroying the house and everything in it.

Production and marketing: After the success of Boris Karloff (1887–1969) in *Frankenstein* (1931), *The Old Dark House* (1932), and *The Mummy* (1932), Universal was eager to get his name back up in lights in projects with proposed titles *The Return of Frankenstein, A Trip to Mars,* and *The Golem.* When for various reasons these proposals were scotched, Edgar G. Ulmer (1900–1972) approached Carl Laemmle, Jr., (1908–1979), with an idea to film Poe's "The Black Cat." Universal already had a 1932 Richard Schayer script titled *The Black Cat* in which Karloff was to the play the drunkard of Poe's tale in a scenario at least roughly following the original story. They also had a 1932 script titled *The Brain Never Dies,* based on Poe's "The Fall of the House of Usher" and "The Black Cat," as well as yet a third script, penned in 1933, titled *The Black Cat,* which was to feature the wicked, torture-laden plans of a mad count in a Carpathian castle.

Upon receiving permission to make *The Black Cat,* Ulmer left the other scripts in the vault and ignored the original Poe tale as well, although he was under orders to feature Poe prominently in the advertising. While the resulting screenplay is a masterpiece, one of the most intriguing of horror's golden age, it owes little to Edgar Allan Poe.

The only plot connection between Poe's "The Black Cat" and Ulmer's film is just that—a black cat. In Poe's story the narrator's wife refers to the superstitious belief that black cats are "witches in disguise." In the film, Werdegast refers to the black cat as "the living embodiment of evil," and Poelzig adds that the black cat is deathless. This last concept may have been gleaned from Poe because in his story the narrator is convinced that the black cat he killed has returned to life, and in the film, after Werdegast has killed a black cat, another (or the same one) soon appears.

If *The Black Cat* borrows little from Poe's plot, most contemporary reviewers acknowledge that Ulmer does expertly convey the Poe atmosphere. In his book *Classics of the Horror Film,* William K. Everson grants

Bela Lugosi cringes at the sight of his nemesis in *The Black Cat* **(1934).**

that "in its mood and in its oppressive, claustrophobic, and generally unhealthy atmosphere, [the film] does evoke a very definite feeling of Poe."[25] In *Cinema of Mystery*, Rose London agrees that "Ulmer's direction of the film and his inventive and brooding atmospherics and contrasted black-and-white effects are possibly more faithful to the world of Poe than those of any other film maker; he is, indeed, the Aubrey Beardsley of the cinema as an illustrator of Poe."[26] In his book *Karloff and Lugosi*, Gregory William Mank also notes the film's Poesque spirit:

> True, Poe's tale of revenge is suggested only by the black cat pet of Poelzig. Nevertheless, Poe probably would have found much to admire in this moody, sinister movie; indeed few films have ever evoked the twisted nightmarish Evil that haunted Poe's stories as did *The Black Cat*. The motifs of revenge, souls that have been "killed," and the demonic flamboyance would have fascinated Edgar Allan—as would have the marriage of Poelzig and stepdaughter Karen. Poe, after all, had married his beloved Virginia

(who was truly the "core and meaning" of his life, and whose death destroyed him) when she was only 13 years old; and as Philip Van Doren Stern noted in his introduction to *The Portable Poe*, Poe's personality indicated "he was sexually abnormal, but there is no way of proving it"[27]

Beyond the connections cited above, Ulmer left Poe unconsulted. Instead, the main source of inspiration seems to have been the reputation of Aleister Crowley, an infamous self-proclaimed Satanist who also inspired Somerset Maugham's 1908 story "The Magician."

Initially, Universal estimated a meager $91,125 production cost, much lower than that of *Dracula* and *Frankenstein*. Apparently, the studio believed that the dual billing of Karloff and Lugosi could nearly carry the film to financial success regardless of other circumstances. Universal also planned for a mere 15-day shooting schedule. Ulmer began shooting on February 28, 1934, and wrapped on March 17, 1934, after which

Laemmle, Jr., ordered alterations to tone down the film's sadism and suggested necrophilia. In addition, Lugosi, who wanted to play a sympathetic role this time around, was particularly unhappy when he found his character attempting to rape poor Joan in the original print. That, among other unsavory footage, was cut and reshot.

Of course, the ads for *The Black Cat* heralded the first-time teaming of Karloff and Lugosi, and for once when the ads promised "Stranger things than you have ever seen or even dreamed of," they were probably right. Most of the pressbook ballyhoo recommended that theaters exploit the black cat angle. Typical of the feline-infested showmanship were recommendations that two men in a giant black cat outfit roam the streets, that a sidewalk projector beam the image of a black cat, that the theater sponsor a black cat contest and an art contest for the best black cat drawing, and that an illuminated cat's head be used. There was, however, one appeal based upon Edgar Allan Poe:

> Because of the tremendous reputation which Edgar Allan Poe enjoys, his words are used in many literature classes throughout American schools. Under the circumstances, tie-ups with the showing of your picture should be easily arranged.
>
> Contact principals or teachers in your locality and arrange for visits of pupils to see the picture in groups, or to stimulate extra interest, sponsor an essay contest on the subject of Edgar Allan Poe's life or why "BLACK CAT" can be considered one of his most outstanding masterpieces. Be sure that bulletins or cards announcing your showing appear in every school and at spots patronized by school children.

One can only imagine the real horrors that would have been created had well-meaning teachers carted off busloads of impressionable pupils to see this dark tale of necrophilia, sadism, and torture, only to discover that the goings-on had little to do with the story in their literature books. In 1960, when Roger Corman approached American International with an idea of filming Poe's "The Fall of the House of User," the executives reportedly balked partly because they believed that youngsters subjected to Poe in school textbooks would hardly rush out to repeat the unwelcome experience at a movie theater, all of which reminds us of W. H. Auden's sad observation that Poe was "Doomed to be used in school textbooks as a bait to interest the young in literature, to be a respectable rival to the pulps."

When the screen season ended, *The Black Cat* turned an impressive $140,000 profit for Universal. Realart Pictures rereleased it in 1953 as *The Vanishing Body*.

One original pressbook merchandising angle recommended that theaters pass out black cat good-luck charms. Perhaps many individuals associated with the film acquired such charms, for the future was bright for most of them. Boris Karloff, of course, was soon to give two of his finest performances in *The Black Room* (1935) and *The Bride of Frankenstein* (1935). David Manners (1901–) would play in several more good films before retiring as Universal's most recognizable horror-film leading man, and Edgar G. Ulmer would go on to leave a greater mark on the horror genre by directing such films as *Bluebeard* (1944), *The Man from Planet X* (1951), *The Daughter of Dr. Jekyll* (1957), *The Amazing Transparent Man* (1960), and *Beyond the Time Barrier* (1961). As for Bela Lugosi, though a sad career decline was about to commence, he was soon to star in *The Raven* (1935) and *The Son of Frankenstein* (1939), the only two films in which he undeniably outshines his career rival, Boris Karloff.

For those interested in knowing virtually *all* there is to know about the production of *The Black Cat*, I heartily recommend Gregory William Mank's *Karloff and Lugosi*, which is the last word on the subject.

Critique: When *The Black Cat* opened at New York's Roxy Theater on May 18, 1934, the *New York Times,* almost always deprecatory toward horror films, first informed readers that the film "is not remotely to be identified with Poe's short story." While the review goes on to grudgingly commend the camera work and the screams of Jacqueline Wells, the final verdict is that "*The Black Cat* is more foolish than horrible. The story and dialogue pile the agony on too thick to give the audience a reasonable scare."[28]

Variety was also unkind:

> Because of the presence in one film of Boris Karloff, that jovial madman, and Bela Lugosi, that suave fiend, this picture probably has box office attraction. But otherwise and on the counts of story, novelty, thrills and distinction, it is subnormal. Skinning alive is not new. It was done in a Gouverneur Morris story, *The Man Behind the Door*, filmed during the war. A truly horrible and nauseating bit of extreme sadism, its inclusion in a motion picture is dubious showmanship. That devil-worshipping cult is also close to the border.[29]

In his book *Horror in the Cinema*, Ivan Butler pronounced the film a failure:

> There is not much of Poe in this, and in spite of a splendidly sinister performance by Karloff and a surprisingly moving one from Lugosi the final result is a rather scrappy and ineffectual film. Karloff's Latin incantations are impressively delivered, but otherwise the Satanic rites, admittedly interrupted before they can get under way, look like being even less diabolical than English Druid junketings, and the guests are clearly not going to allow any orgiastic carryings-on to disarrange their elegant evening dresses and coiffeurs. The black cat of the title (and Lugosi's abhorrence of it) is completely expendable. Even the final revenge fizzles out in shadows and switch-triggered castle-dynamiting.[30]

More recent perspectives on *The Black Cat*, however, have been more positive, many lauding it as a classic horror film:

> *The Black Cat*, with its weird and terrifying clashes between good and evil, is one of the most genuinely horrific films of the genre....Few films have managed to gener-

ate such dread, and in such a stylish and shadowy way. That *The Black Cat* succeeds so singularly well makes it a memorable addition to the cinema of fantastic horror."[31]
> —Chris Steinbrunner and Burt Goldblatt, *Cinema of the Fantastic*

> The striking pictorial quality of the film creates a decidedly non-Hollywood and non-stereotyped horror film....The cold modernistic sets, the rich quality of eroticism (often involving the change of focus within a shot to give added sexual emphasis), and the slow gliding camerawork of John Mescall are all helped in their creation of mood by a brilliant musical score which draws heavily on the classics.[32]
> —William K. Everson, *Classics of the Horror Film*

> *The Black Cat* is quintessential Poe in that it weaves an almost abstract web of anguish out of its all-pervasive sense of evil.... Strange, hypnotic, tormented and eliciting the best performances of their careers from Karloff and Lugosi, *The Black Cat* is one of the masterpieces of the genre.
> —*The Overlook Film Encyclopedia: Horror*

> A work of great artistry and sinister beauty, *The Black Cat* occupies a very special niche in the history of macabre cinema....The picture is rife with excellent lines and Karloff, getting the lion's share, serves them up with chilling understatement.[33]
> —Michael Brunas, John Brunas, and Tom Weaver, *Universal Horrors*

> All the morbid quirks of *The Black Cat* serve as the ideal backdrop for the first teaming of Karloff and Lugosi, a wonderful showcase for the macabre chemistry which would make the unions of these men vital movie history....Karloff's Lascivious Lucifer versus Lugosi's Avenging Angel makes *The Black Cat* transcend the horror movie genre, and become a grand lunatic fairy tale, sparked by a wickedly imaginative director, a bewitched camera and a properly romantic score.[34]
> —Gregory William Mank, *Karloff and Lugosi*

The superior assessments of the modern critics again prove that the passage of time is necessary for maximum critical insight. The greatness of the film lies in five areas. First, Edgar G. Ulmer's direction is creative, eliciting the best from the actors involved. Second, the expressionistic sets create a mood of pervasive, sick evil. Third, John Mescall's camera is sometimes itself catlike as it creeps about the chilling sets. Fourth, Boris Karloff and Bela Lugosi each give one of the best performances of their careers. And fifth, the musical score perfectly evokes Ulmer's intended moods.

Still, there is a flaw. As Arthur Lennig points out in *The Count*, the film plot contains holes. For example, Poelzig refers to

Werdegast as "one of the world's greatest psychiatrists," even though the latter has just spent fifteen years in prison and three years in the army. When did he have time to establish this marvelous reputation? There are other small slips, but they are all small indeed, detracting little from the overall horror and artistic cohesion of the film. Finally, *The Black Cat* must take its place as one of the great horror films of all time, though not one of the greatest Poe adaptations.

Maniac (1934)
Roadshow Attractions, U.S.A.

Credits: Directed and produced by Dwain Esper; associate producer—Louis Sonney; assistant director—J. Stuart Blackton, Jr.; screenplay by Hildergard Stadie (Esper), from "The Black Cat" by Edgar Allan Poe; cinematography by William Thompson; edited by William Austin.

Running time: 67 minutes.

Cast: Bill Woods (Maxwell), Horace Carpenter (Dr. Meirshultz), Ted Edwards (Mr. Buckley), Phyllis Diller (Mrs. Buckley), Theo Ramsey (Alice Maxwell); Jenny Dark (Maizie); Marvel Andre (Marvel); Cilia McCann (Jo); J. P. Wade (embalmer); Marion Blackton (neighbor).

Story: The film opens with these words on the screen:

> The brain, in and of its physical self, does not think, any more than a musical instrument can give out melody without the touch of the musician's hand. The brain is indeed the instrument of thinking, but the mind is the skillful player that makes it give forth the beautiful harmony of thought....
>
> It is because of the disastrous results of fear brought not only on the individual but on the nation that it becomes the duty of every sane man and woman to establish quarantine against fear. Fear is a psychic disease which is highly contagious and extraordinarily infectious. Fear thought is most dan-

gerous when it parades as forethought. Combat fear by replacing it with faith. Resist worry with confidence.

> Unhealthy thought creates warped attitudes which create criminals and turn criminals into maniacs.
>
> The Chicago Crime Commission made a survey of 40,000 convicted criminals and found them all suffering from some mental disease.
>
> William S. Sadler, M.D., F.A.C.S., Director of the Chicago Institute of Research and Diagnosis

Dr. Meirschultz and his assistant Maxwell plan to bring a human being back to life. Meirschultz commands Maxwell to procure a corpse from the morgue and suggests that the assistant's ability to impersonate others will come in handy. "Once a ham, always a ham," the doctor intones. When Maxwell expresses reservations, Meirschultz reminds him that the police would be interested in his whereabouts, a threat that elicits Maxwell's reluctant agreement.

That night Meirschultz and Maxwell (disguised as the coroner) enter the morgue. The doctor injects a young suicide named Maria Altura with his experimental drug, after which he and his assistant massage her limbs. Soon after, they remove the girl from the morgue to their laboratory.

Back at the lab, after Dr. Meirschultz rants and raves about needing another corpse into which to transplant a beating heart, he orders poor Maxwell out into the night to steal a body from the undertaker's establishment. Maxwell breaks in, but as he is about to remove a body, he sees several cats in the room. Suffering from a horror of cats, Maxwell flees empty-handed. Upon hearing of Maxwell's aborted mission, Meirschultz insanely harangues the young man about his weaknesses, finally deciding that Maxwell must shoot himself in order to provide a body for the experiment. Maxwell takes the gun but shoots the doctor instead.

Again words appear on the screen.

> Dementia Praecox: This is the most important of the psychoses, both because it constitutes the highest percentage of mental disorders and because recovery is so extremely rare.
> Dementia praecox patients show blunting of the emotions, serious defects of judgment, development of fantastic ideas, belief that they are being forced to do things or are being interfered with.

As we return to the story, Maxwell is racked by guilt at having killed his benefactor. He quickly decides to continue the doctor's work and eventually resurrect him. At that moment, the door buzzer interrupts Maxwell's mad reveries. He answers the door and admits a Mrs. Buckley who wants Dr. Meirschultz to see her husband immediately. It seems that Mr. Buckley is having hallucinations in which he imagines himself to be the murdering orangutan from Poe's "The Murders in the Rue Morgue." When Mrs. Buckley goes out to get her husband, Maxwell makes himself up as the doctor. Then, in a exhibit of mad grandiosity, he proclaims, "Not only do I look like Meirschultz, I am Meirschultz! I will be a great man!"

When Mrs. Buckley returns with her husband, Maxwell (as Meirschultz) gives him an injection of the wrong drug, which immediately sends him into paroxysms of madness, ending with his mental "transformation" into the murdering orangutan. When the resurrected suicide walks into the room, Mr. Buckley, all the while emitting simian growls and cries, carries her out of the house and rapes her in the bushes.

Another quotation appears on the screen: "Paresis: General paralysis of the insane, paresis is the most serious disorder for the criminologist. There are marked failure of memory, poor attention, impaired judgment, and failure on the part of the patient to curb criminal tendencies" (*Crimes and the Criminal*, Phillip a. Parsons, Ph. D.).

As we return to the story, Mrs. Buckley discovers Meirschultz's body on the floor, but assumes that it is actually the assistant's body. Maxwell tells her that he hopes to bring the man back to life. Mrs. Buckley says: "Doctor, I have often heard of your uncanny experiments, but this tops them all. But I think we speak the same language. Am I right?" She goes on to suggest that when the doctor brings the assistant back to life, the mind of the revived corpse will be under the doctor's command. Mrs. Buckley wants the doctor to put her husband's mind under *her* command.

When Mrs. Buckley leaves, a neighbor comes over looking for several cats he says have escaped from his yard. Maxwell says he doesn't use cats in his experiments because he is so attached to Satan, the black cat owned by Dr. Meirschultz. Of course, Maxwell really loathes the cat. When the neighbor leaves. Maxwell becomes fearful that Mr. Buckley, who might have seen Meirschultz's body, will go to the police. He therefore decides to seal up Meirschultz behind a brick wall in the basement. As he is engaged in the task, he is distracted by Satan, the black cat of the lab. Temporarily unhinged by the cat, he loses control, catches the animal, and gouges out its eye. Observing that the eyeball is "not unlike an oyster or a grape, but the gleam is gone," he pops it into his mouth and eats it. Upon finishing his "snack," he returns to the basement to finish the task of concealment, unaware that the cat has climbed behind the wall with the corpse.

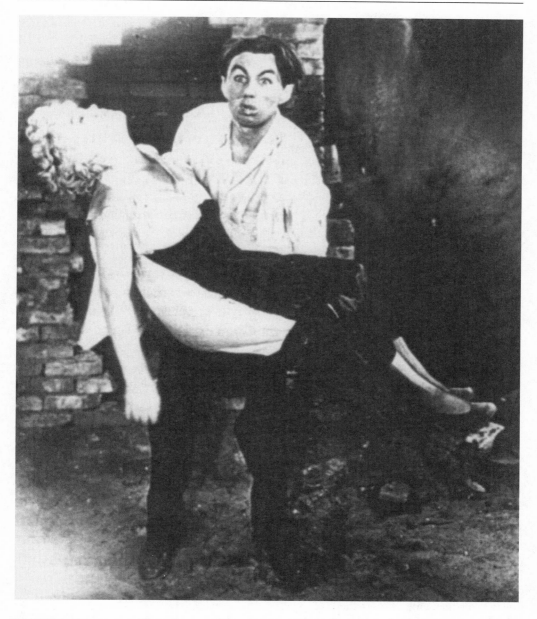

Ted Edwards menaces Theo Ramsey in a publicity still from *Maniac* (1934). Courtesy of Ron Borst/Hollywood Movie Posters.

Words again appear on the screen. "Paranoia: This is an extremely rare but very curious disease. Characteristics of it are fixed suspicions, persecutory delusions. The paranoiac is often particularly dangerous because of the difficulty of detecting his disease."

A police officer investigating the ab-

duction of the suicide's corpse from the morgue questions Dr. Meirschultz's neighbors. When he questions the man who had earlier asked Maxwell about his lost cats, we discover that the man raises cats for their fur. He lets rats run about the place to feed the cats. Cats eat the rats, rats eat the skinned cats, and the neighbor gets the furs. The police officer seems unsuitably impressed.

Meanwhile, Maxwell's wife, who hasn't seen her husband for years, learns that he has come into an inheritance, but the authorities cannot find him. Wondering if Maxwell could still be with that "goofy professor," she goes to the lab as part of a plan to get her hands on the money. She first talks to Maxwell—disguised, of course, as Meirschultz—and tells him that her husband has inherited a fortune. He tells her to return that evening when her husband will be there.

This description then appears on the screen.

> Manic-depressive psychoses: There are three phases of the manic-depressive psychoses; the manic phase, the depressed phase, and the mixed phase.
>
> In the manic phase, ideas come so rapidly that there is no time to select the proper reaction, and judgment accordingly appears impaired. Such patients are often able to commit sex offenses.

As Maxwell "treats" female patients in various stages of undress, he hallucinates kissing and fondling them. Later, upon deciding that his wife Alice wants to kill him to get the inheritance, he hatches a plan to have Mrs. Buckley and Alice kill each other. He sends both women downstairs, convincing each that the other is a dangerous mental patient. When he closes the basement door, the two women begin fighting each other for their lives. The noise quickly brings the police, who decide that Maxwell is mad. After going into the basement, they break up the fight between the women and hear a cat meowing behind the brick wall. When an officer breaks a hole in the wall, the corpse of Meirschultz falls forward and Satan, the black cat, leaps out.

Words again appear on the screen.

> Maniacs are created by inability to adjust to the world as it is. Insanity is our defense against a world which is not of our making or to our liking. The normal person can make such an adjustment. It is not always easy, but it is being done constantly. The person of inferior mental capacity cannot do this. He

therefore creates a world in his mind which is his own idea of the world of his choice. He retreats to this world whenever the other world becomes unbearable. This explains the periods of rationalism all mental cases have. The periods of rationalism depends *(sic)* upon the unbearableness of the real world.

> There are many people of sound mind who find one particular thing unbearable. When this is the case, he is said to be the victim of such a complex.

Maxwell is behind bars. He cries out that he only wanted to amuse, to entertain, but no one appreciated him. But he showed them! A brilliant impersonation!

Production and marketing: *Maniac* was made by the husband and wife team of Dwain Esper and Hildergard Stadie, the creators of such disreputable junk as *Marihuana, Weed with Roots in Hell* (1936), *Narcotic* (1937), and *How to Undress in Front of Your Husband* (1937). Like *Maniac, Marihuana* and *Narcotic* paraded as films with socially redeeming values, when in reality they were all low-budget exploitation films aimed at burlesque houses and roadhouses.

The connection with Poe is flimsy indeed, though not as flimsy as the connection in many better, higher budget pictures. In Poe's "The Black Cat," the narrator is clearly mentally disturbed, though not to the degree that Maxwell is in *Maniac*. As Poe's narrator relates:

> One night, returning home, much intoxicated, from one of my haunts about town, I fancied that the cat avoided my presence. I seized him; when, in his fright at my violence, he inflicted a slight wound upon my hand with his teeth. The fury of a demon instantly seized me. I knew myself no longer. My original soul seemed, at once, to take its flight from my body; and a more than fiendish malevolence, gin-nurtured, thrilled every fibre of my frame. I took from my waist-pocket a pen-knife, opened it, grasped the poor beast by the throat, and deliberately cut one of its eyes from the socket! I blush, I burn, I shudder, while I pen the damnable atrocity.

In *Maniac*, Maxwell has a phobia of

cats, much as Bela Lugosi does in *The Black Cat* (1934), which may have served as an inspiration. In his madness, Woods overcomes that fear and attacks the animal, gouging out the beast's eye with his finger. If Poe could sometimes test the limits of good taste, Esper and Stadie plunge headlong into tastelessness by having Woods gobble up the eye with "ghoulish relish."

Maniac also borrows its entombment scene and dénouement from Poe's story, though the contexts are totally different, Poe's being infinitely superior in every way. There is, of course, the reference to Poe's "The Murders in the Rue Morgue," a fact that gives one solace to know that the author did not live long enough to see the release of this film.

In scenes featuring the mad rantings and ravings of Bill Woods, Esper superimposes scenes from Benjamin Christensen's *Haxan* (1922, aka *Witchcraft Through the Ages*) in order to signal to the audience that the character is indeed experiencing a "mad episode." (Critic Bret Wood says these scenes are *not* from Christensen, but I still believe they are.) Unfortunately, Christensen did not escape the fate of Poe, that of being an innocent party to this abysmal film.

In 1938, examiners from the New York Censor Board failed to accept the film as an educational picture about mental illness and instead banned it from the state, citing it as "inhuman, immoral, would tend to corrupt morals, and would tend to incite to crime."

Interestingly, Dwain Esper would go on to rerelease Tod Browning's *Freaks* (1932), a film that in its day was regarded as tasteless and exploitational, but which today is heralded as a genre classic. While the passage of time does allow for greater perspective, it is safe to say that Esper's own *Maniac* will never rise above its current reputation, that of a grossly poor exploitation film.

Critique: Some films are so bad that they nearly defy description. *Maniac* is such a film. While outrageous enough in its ineptitude to avoid being boring, it otherwise manages to commit every conceivable cine-matic sin. Let us begin with its pretentiousness. One can imagine members of the audience of this burlesque house atrocity being told that they are watching a film designed to make them more cognizant of America's mental health problems and being informed that they are seeing accurate and serious examples of mental illnesses of concern to eminent criminologists and physicians. Of course, *Maniac* has no more to do with the real world of mental illness than most MTV rock videos (themselves the contemporary embodiment of pretentiousness) have to do with serious artistic expression. And, as noted above, the New York Censor Board knew it.

The screenplay is laughable throughout, and all that might rise above the laughable in the hands of competent actors draws unintended derision because of the dreadfully poor performances that abound. Horace Carpenter outrageously overacts as Dr. Meirschultz. It is as though he wants to outdo Bela Lugosi at his most extravagant but is unable to conjure up any of that actor's charisma and polish. Bill Woods is likewise unrestrained by director Esper, and the performance of Ted Edwards as Mr. Buckley has to be seen to be believed (or disbelieved). Still, worst-acting dishonors must go to Phyllis Diller as Mrs. Buckley. No performer in any Ed Wood, Jr., film ever sank to such dismal depths of thespian ineptitude as does the *completely* incompetent Diller, whose performance would be cut from any self-respecting grade-school play.

Despite all the flaws, *Maniac* has at least one credible defender. In *Guilty Pleasures of the Horror Film*, critic Bret Wood writes: "Detailing *Maniac*'s technical flaws would be a tiresome endeavor and would diminish the raw beauty of the film."[35] Despite Wood's valiant defense, I fail to see the raw beauty. Wood asserts: "Consciously or not, Dwain Esper's *Maniac* is a mockery of Hollywood, refusing to mimic its veneer of sophistication and its idea of artistry, delivering the same sex, violence, and intrigue in slop buckets rather than pearly teacups."[36]

Armed with a good knowledge of Esper and the times in which he worked, Wood makes as good a defense of *Maniac* as is humanly possible, asserting that what appears as (and may be) incompetence aids the film in its depression era attempt to portray madness. Here is an example of Wood's logic. When Esper uses one actress twice in the film by changing her hair color from blond to brunette, Wood argues:

> One could write this substitution off as ineptness but again, it functions as an example of Esper's flagrant disregard for Hollywood rules of continuity. If an audience is going to suspend its disbelief enough to accept an in-

dependently funded scientist who discovers a way to reanimate the dead, the saps shouldn't complain about a brunette subbing for a blonde or a tabby sitting in for a black cat when it comes time to flash the breasts and gaping eye sockets.[37]

While this film (that makes *Plan Nine from Outer Space* look altogether competent by comparison), might someday achieve the status of "camp classic," it is ultimately so tasteless and amateurish that I sincerely regret seeing Poe's name attached to it at all. *Video Hound's Golden Retriever* 1996 appropriately gives the film a "Woof!" (its lowest score).

The Tell-Tale Heart (1934); aka *A Bucket of Blood*

DuWorld, Great Britain

Credits: Directed by Brian Desmond Hurst; screenplay by David Greene, based on "The Tell-Tale Heart" by Edgar Allan Poe.

Running time: 51 minutes.

Cast: Norman Dryden (young man), John Kelt (old man), Yolande Terrell, Thomas Shenton.

Story: A young man befriends an elderly man who has a film over one of his eyes. The young man becomes obsessed by the "vulture eye" and decides to kill the old man in order to rid himself of the eye forever. Each night the disturbed man enters the chamber of his proposed victim, shines a light upon the old man's face, but finding the eye closed, retreats. After each attempt, he heartily greets the old man as though nothing were wrong. Finally, the young man enters the old man's chamber and hears his victim awaken in terror. The room is silent except for the beating of the old man's heart. The young man turns the light upon his victim's face, fully illuminating the "vulture eye." Seized by fury, the young man pounces upon his victim and kills him, after which he buries the body beneath the floor boards of the chamber.

Later, during an investigation of the old man's disappearance, the killer fancies he hears the beating of the old man's heart beneath the floor boards and assumes the investigators can hear it too. Are they mocking him? Are they playing a game with him? Suddenly he breaks down and confesses the crime, demanding that the investigators acknowledge the beating of the old man's heart.

Production and marketing: Little if anything is known about the production and marketing of this film. The first known version of Poe's "The Tell-Tale Heart" was a 1928 silent picture, of which even less is known, directed and written by Charles Klein. In his 1934 version for DuWorld, Brian Desmond Hurst stuck very close to the original source, interpolating a few love scenes to flesh out the production. The film opened in New York to favorable reviews at the Fifty-fifth Street Playhouse in mid-June of 1934.

Critique: In an uncharacteristically positive review for a horror film, the *New York Times* reported: "The British producers have clung almost literally to the original tale, and in so doing have supplied further evidence that it is not absolutely necessary to distort a great author's work in order to create a fascinating motion picture."[38] This observation is an obvious reference to Universal's *The Murders in the Rue Morgue* (1932) and *The Black Cat* (1934), both of which the *New York Times* considered crimes against Poe. Addressing the film's pace, the review found: "At no time is there any slackening of interest. Even persons familiar with the gripping pen portrait...are bound to be entertained by the remarkable manner in which the camera produces the early nineteenth-century atmosphere. The light effects are particularly impressive. The very sparseness of the dialogue adds to the illusion."[39] The review lavished high praise upon the cast, noting that "While all the actors are excellent, the honors naturally go to Norman Dryden as the insane young man and to John Kelt as the aged victim of the youth's delusions. It is hard to imagine anybody making their parts more real."[40]

As I have been unable to review the film, the *New York Times* will have the last word.

The Raven (1935)
Universal, U.S.A.

Credits: Directed by Louis Friedlander (later Lew Landers); associate producer—David Diamond. Screenplay by David Boehm, suggested by "The Raven" by Edgar Allan Poe; cinematography by Charles Stumar; art direction by Albert S. D'Agostino; makeup by Jack Pierce; musical score by Clifford Vaughan, Heinz Roemheld, and Y. Franke Harling; dance staged by Theodore Kosloff.

Running time: 61 minutes.

Cast: Boris Karloff (Edmond Bateman), Bela Lugosi (Dr. Richard Vollin), Lester Matthews (Dr. Jerry Halden), Irene Ware (Jean Thatcher), Samuel S. Hinds (Judge Thatcher), Spencer Charters (Colonel Bertram Grant), Inez Courtney (Mary Burns), Ian Wolfe (Geoffrey "Pinky" Burns), Maidel Turner (Harriet Grant), Arthur Hoyt (Chapman).

Story: When a car crash critically injures Jean Thatcher, her father, Judge Thatcher, stands by as her fiancé, Dr. Jerry Halden, and a team of doctors announce that only Dr. Vollin can save her. Meanwhile at his home on Hillview Heights, Vollin sits at his desk, which supports a stuffed raven, and declaims lines from Poe's poem:

...suddenly there came a tapping,
As of someone gently rapping, rapping at my chamber door.
Open then (*sic*) I flung the shutter, when, with many a flirt and flutter
In there stepped a stately raven.

Nearby is Mr. Chapman, a diminutive man who has come to see Vollin's Poe collection. When Vollin identifies the raven as his talisman, Chapman remarks that it is a curious talisman, "the bird of ill omen, a symbol of death," to which Vollin replies: "Death is my talisman, Mr. Chapman. The one indestructible force, the one certain thing in an uncertain universe. Death!" As their conversation continues, Vollin expresses pride in the fact that he has actually constructed Poe's torture devices in his cellar. When the astonished Chapman calls this "a very curious hobby," Vollin intones that "it's *more* than a hobby."

When Chapman leaves, Judge Thatcher arrives and begs Vollin to come to the hospital and save his daughter's life. Vollin refuses, even turning down Thatcher's offer to pay him anything he wants. "But someone is dying," Thatcher begs. "Your obligation as member of the medical profession." "I respect no obligation," Vollin interrupts. "I am a law unto myself. Death hasn't the same significance for me as it has for you."

Only when Thatcher explains that all the other doctors say that he, Vollin, is the only man capable of saving Jean, does the doctor beam with pride and agree to help. During the operation, it is obvious that Vollin is taken with the young girl's beauty.

When Jean recovers, she visits Vollin, who plays Bach's "Toccata" for her on the organ. Fascinated by the doctor's talent as both a physician and a musician, she tells Vollin that he is almost greater than a human being, almost...

"A god?" he asks, in obvious agreement. "A god—with the taint of human emotions."

When Jean asks if there is anything she can do to show her gratitude, Vollin, betraying his growing desire to possess the girl, replies: "There is. The restraint that we impose upon ourselves can drive us mad!" Jean withdraws slightly from Vollin's passionate advance, reminding him that she is engaged to Dr. Jerry Halden and thanking Vollin for taking him as an assistant. The doctor stares into the distance and explains, "I did it to give him something to take the place of what he's losing."

Jean, who is a professional dancer, does do something to show her gratitude for Vollin. She performs an original ballet for him called "The Spirit of Poe," which the doctor attends with obvious relish. After the performance, Vollin goes to Jean's dressing room, takes her hand, and exults, "Whom the angels call Lenore!"

When Judge Thatcher notices the growing attraction between Vollin and his impressionable daughter, he goes to Vollin's home and politely suggests that Jean is in danger of becoming infatuated. Vollin erupts with anger and orders Thatcher to send Jean to him. The judge refuses, calls Vollin mad, and leaves, after which the doctor plots revenge.

Meanwhile, across town, escaped killer and bank robber Edmond Bateman finds Vollin's address, pays the doctor a visit, and asks him to change his face through plastic surgery. Vollin, recognizing Bateman, refuses money but agrees to perform the surgery anyway if the criminal will return the favor by performing acts of torture and murder. When Bateman balks, Vollin reminds him of his criminal deeds, to which Bateman responds: "I'll tell you somethin', Doc. Ever since I was born, everybody looks at me and says, 'You're ugly.' Makes me feel mean. Maybe because I look ugly, maybe if a man looks ugly, he does ugly things." Vollin, who begins to grin as this idea settles in, muses aloud: "You are saying something profound. A man with a face so hideously ugly!"

Thus the plan is hatched. During the operation, Vollin gives the poor man a hideous face and blackmails him into remaining as his servant with the promise that he will later change Bateman's face. Of course, Vollin plans to use Bateman as part of his revenge plot against Judge Thatcher, Jean, and Dr. Halden, all three of whom he invites to his house for a weekend party along with two other older and somewhat comical couples. Although Judge Thatcher is suspicious, he agrees to attend upon learning that Jean and Jerry are going.

That evening while the other guests are playing a spinning horse game, Jean is fixing her hair upstairs when Bateman enters the room and frightens her. When her screams interrupt the game, Vollin goes up and orders Bateman out, after which he explains to everyone that his servant was mutilated by Arab bandits while serving in Vollin's army regiment. When the guests return to Vollin's study, they ask him how he interprets Poe's "The Raven."

VOLLIN: I will tell you. Poe was a great genius. Like all great geniuses, there was in him the insistent will to do something big, great, constructive in the world. He had the brain to do it. But—he fell in love. Her name was Lenore.

JEAN: [with a sigh] Longing for the lost Lenore.

VOLLIN: (also with a sigh) Longing for the

Upstaged by a stuffed omen of death, Bela Lugosi peers with ill intent at Samuel S. Hinds in *The Raven* (1935).

lost Lenore. (Then with growing resentment) Something happened. Someone took her away from him. When a man of genius is denied his great love, he goes mad. His brain, instead of being clear to do his work, is tortured—so *he* begins to think of torture. Torture for those who have tortured him.!

Realizing that he is about to incur the suspicion of his guests, Vollin smiles and adds, "My interest in Poe, the way I speak about torture and death, you people being laymen perhaps do not understand. As a doctor, a surgeon, I look upon these things differently (his obsessive tone returns). A doctor is fascinated by death—and pain. And how much pain a man can endure."

As the guests retire for the evening, Jean apologizes to Bateman for having been frightened. Her kindness softens the crimi-

nal's heart, and it is obvious that he looks upon her with affection.

A bit later Vollin gives Bateman a tour of his cellar and points out the torture devices from Poe's stories. When Vollin lies on the slab beneath a gigantic pendulum, Bateman pulls a lever and traps the doctor in his own creation. When the pendulum begins to descend, Bateman gloats that the evil doctor is about to get what he deserves. Although in mortal danger, Vollin, while fighting to retain his composure, points out to Bateman that if the pendulum does its work, Bateman will forever own the hideous face that he presently wears. Convinced by Vollin's logic, Bateman releases his nemesis and agrees to help carry out the rest of Vollin's mad plan.

First, Bateman pulls a struggling Judge Thatcher from his room and locks him in

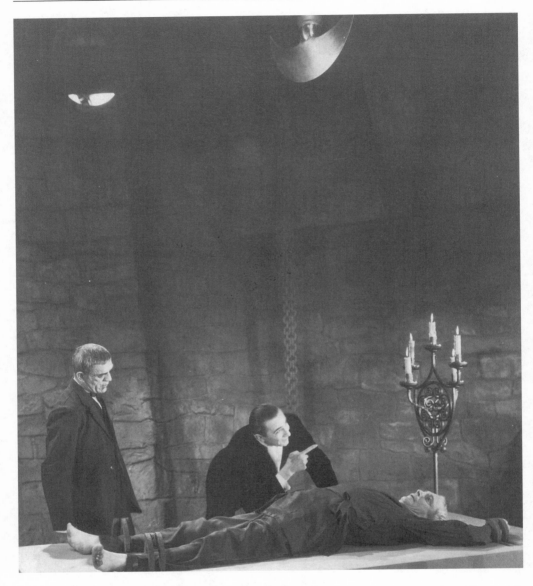

No pit is evident, but the pendulum descends as Boris Karloff and Bela Lugosi torture Samuel S. Hinds in *The Raven* (1935).

the manacles on the slab where Vollin has recently been trapped. Vollin then cruelly teases the judge about the descending pendulum that will soon cut him in half. "What are you trying to do to me?" Thatcher asks. "Torture you," Vollin calmly answers. "Oh, try to be sane, Vollin!" Thatcher pleads, to which the doctor ecstatically replies: "I am the sanest man who ever lived! But I will not be tortured! I tear torture out of myself by torturing *you* !"

Then, at a large control panel, Vollin pulls a lever that lowers Jean's bedroom into the cellar. When Jerry and several of the other guests run to aid Jean, Vollin stops them at gunpoint. Then he orders Jean and Jerry into a room and commands Bateman to pull the lever that closes the door. Acting upon Vollin's orders, Bateman pulls another switch that causes the walls of the lovers' room to come together, another torture inspired by Poe's "The Pit and the Pendulum."

His mind at a breaking point, Vollin exults, "What torture! What a delicious torture, Bateman! Greater than Poe! Poe only conceived it! I have done it, Bateman! Poe, you are avenged!" He then waves his arms and laughs insanely. He quickly recovers his composure, however, when Bateman objects to the girl being crushed. Acting upon impulse, the hideous servant pulls the lever that stops the moving walls. This, of course, causes the insane Vollin to fire a bullet into Bateman, who rushes at the doctor, knocking him unconscious. He then frees Jean and Jerry from the torture room. As the guests rush to free Judge Thatcher, Bateman drags Vollin into the torture room and, before dying, pulls the levers that close the door and send the walls together. When Vollin regains consciousness, he is quickly sent into a state of terror upon realizing his situation. After vainly trying to stop the walls from closing in, he falls to the floor and is crushed by his own device.

Production and marketing: Encouraged by the financial returns of *The Black Cat* (1934), Universal decided to reunite Karloff and Lugosi in another picture ostensibly based on a work by Edgar Allan Poe. The victim this time was Poe's most famous poem, "The Raven." Universal paid a total of $16,162.56 to seven script writers, finally crediting only David Boehm, who took home $5,375 for his contribution. The original budget for *The Raven* was $109,750. The film began shooting on March 20, 1935, and wrapped on April 5, 1935. Although Lugosi's part was much bigger than Karloff's, Lugosi earned $1000 per week for five weeks while Karloff made $2500 per week for four weeks. The film opened in New York City on July 4, 1935.

As was the case with Universal's *The Murders in the Rue Morgue* and *The Black Cat*, *The Raven* owes little to its Poe sources. Of course, Lugosi is a mad scientist inspired

to the point of madness by Poe's "The Raven" and "The Pit and the Pendulum," but that is the extent of Poe's contribution. Unfortunately, the seven screen writers were not equally inspired. Lugosi refers to Poe throughout the film, offers an idiosyncratic and completely unsustainable interpretation of "The Raven," and uses the pendulum as a torture device, and we see Irene Ware (or a stand-in) ineptly perform a dance to "The Spirit of Poe."

Universal's *Raven* pressbook, larger than the one it produced for *The Black Cat*, heralded "The uncanny master of make-up in a new amazing shocker. Carl Laemmle presents Karloff in an adaptation of Edgar Allan Poe's *The Raven* with Bela (Dracula) Lugosi." Since Lugosi carries the film, he could not have been pleased with his trivial billing compared to that of Karloff.

In one of the pressbook's suggested advance stories, we are asked to ponder the question "Was Poe mad?"

Was Edgar Allan Poe a mental derelict?
The great American poet has supplied the topic of discussion for many debates in the last century, due to his super-imaginative writing. There are those who claim Poe was perfectly normal in his own way, but that he lived in a world apart. There are others who do not share this belief in his normality, maintaining that his fictitious characters were but a reflection of himself.
Poe's characters, it is pointed out, are complex and difficult: self-willed; self-indulgent and easily swayed by moods. Poe himself was like that; a dreamer whose imagination dwelt constantly in the mystic and horrible. But his mind was brilliant and acute.
The themes of his poems were few. Man's loneliness, the hopelessness of struggle and remorse for a wrecked life constituted the basis for his writings. His stories were invariably weird and filled with horrors. He emphasized the power of fear on a sensitive soul and his analysis of morbid and tortured souls was unsurpassed. His speculation hovered around the improbable and the horrible, but his originality and literary craftsmanship never have been questioned.
"The Raven," his greatest imaginative effort, has been made into a motion picture by Universal....Poe wrote "The Raven" at a

time when his dearly beloved wife was suffering untold pain and torture from a illness of which she ultimately died. It is this suffering and torture that supplied the theme for the picture.

Besides the usual ballyhoo suggestions, the pressbook continues to stress the Poe link:

> Exploit the greatest writer of shocker stories that ever lived. Edgar Allan Poe is famous for his thrilling fiction, and his stories are considered classics in American schools.
> This enables you to make tie-ups with local educational institutions and it should be possible to make contacts with teachers, offering passes to the pupils as prizes for the best essays submitted on the following topic: "Why I Consider 'THE RAVEN' One of Poe's Greatest Works." Or you can have a poetry contest, offering similar inducements for the best poem about the picture submitted in "The Raven" style.

The pressbook also suggests that theater owners send the following letter to high schools and colleges:

> Dear Sir (or Madam): We feel that your students will be interested in seeing on the screen a remarkable entertainment, inspired by Edgar Allan Poe's literary classic, *The Raven*. Karloff and "Dracula" Lugosi are the featured players.
> The atmospheric mood of this poetic masterpiece has been captured and re-created in a story based on its famous lines. Introducing a character, Dr. Vollin, whose admiration of the poem causes him to become a victim of a peculiar mania, the screen play reproduces that atmosphere of horror and terror that is so typical of Edgar Allan Poe's tales.
> In the Universal picture, "The Raven," the pit yawns, the pendulum swings, as Dr. Vollin actually creates those devices which Poe conceived. The great writer's lines are frequently quoted throughout the picture, and you and your students will feel a new interest and appreciate more keenly the dramatic power of this famous verse, if you see "The Raven" on the screen. Please pass on the word to your students, or post this conspicuously on a bulletin board.

The pressbook also refers to "Franken-stein" Karloff, "Dracula" Lugosi, and "Goose-Pimple" Edgar Allan Poe as the "big three," encouraging theater owners to sponsor art contests in which students submit drawings of Edgar Allan Poe. It also pushes the Grosset and Dunlap hardcover tie-in of Poe's tales. Altogether, the campaign for *The Raven* placed much greater stress on Edgar Allan Poe than did the one for *The Black Cat*. Still, one has to wonder what the reaction of teachers and students would have been to this film, which shocked audiences and critics with its overt brutality and sadism while delivering nothing of an edifying nature from the pen of Edgar Allan Poe.

Reaction to the film was harsh and swift as states demanded a variety of cuts, the main offending scene apparently being Hinds on the slab below the swinging pendulum. In apparent agreement, critics castigated the film for its gross horrors. *The Raven* was banned outright in Ontario, Canada, and Holland, and it caused a major furor in England, where the X rating for horror films was soon established, bringing an end to Universal's golden age of horror.

Lugosi and Karloff would appear together in five more films. Lugosi would outshine Karloff in *Son of Frankenstein* (1939), the inaugural film of Universal's silver age of horror (1939–1946), but thereafter Karloff would reign supreme. Anyone interested in the Karloff-Lugosi collaboration is referred to Gregory William Mank's *Karloff and Lugosi*, which is the last word on the subject.

Louis Frielander would go on to direct two more horror genre films of little note: *The Boogie Man Will Get You* (1942, a comedy spoof of Karloff's *Arsenic and Old Lace* starring Karloff and Peter Lorre), and *The Return of the Vampire* (1943, starring Bela Lugosi).

Critique: The immediate critical reaction to *The Raven* was even more negative than that which greeted *The Murders in the Rue Morgue* and *The Black Cat*. The *New York Times* quickly pointed out the film's shameless exploitation of Poe's name:

Suddenly there came a tapping
As of some one gently rapping—
But there will be no gentle rapping from this corner of the curious photoplay, "The Raven," which Universal, with amazing effrontery, describes as having been inspired by two Edgar Allan Poe classics, "The Raven" and "The Pit and the Pendulum." ... If "The Raven" is the best that Universal can do with one of the greatest horror story writers of all time, then it had better toss away the other two books in its library and stick to the pulpies for plot material.[41]

Agreeing with the *Times,* the *Los Angeles Herald-Examiner* called the Karloff and Lugosi vehicle "their most dreadful effort to date."[42] Although *Variety* called the film "a good horror flicker"[43] and the film made money, the charge of bad taste and over-the-top horrors combined with the British ban of American horror films ended Universal's golden age of horror.

While *The Raven*'s reputation still lags well behind that of *The Black Cat,* time has smiled on it as well. Although in *An Illustrated History of the Horror Film,* Carlos Clarens writes that *The Raven* is "at heart an old fashioned serial, memorable mainly for Lugosi's unwitting self-burlesque,"[44] Arthur Lennig calls the film one of Lugosi's greatest outings. In his book *The Count: The Life*

and Films of Bela "Dracula" Lugosi, Lennig correctly praises the film's good pace and argues that its story is superior to that of *The Black Cat.* It is Friedlander's "workmanlike" direction, Lennig concludes, that robs the film of the gloom and foreboding it would have enjoyed in more inventive hands.

In his book *Karloff and Lugosi,* Gregory William Mank writes: "*The Raven* is a movie one regards with much affection if little admiration. It is almost a celebration of Bela and Boris."[45] In *Universal Horrors,* Michael Brunas, John Brunas, and Tom Weaver agree with Mank that "in spite of its many faults... true *aficionados* (particularly Bela fans) find great pleasure in the movie's uninhibited madness."[46] In the 1992 edition of his *Movie and Video Guide,* Leonard Maltin awards the film three stars, calling it "great fun throughout." In a similar vein, *Video Hound's Golden Retriever 1996* grants the film three bones.

I cannot fault *The Raven*'s current reputation. It is indeed great fun, largely as a result of fast pacing and Bela Lugosi's splendid performance as Dr. Vollin. While Karloff does not appear to take the proceedings very seriously, Lugosi throws himself into the role as if it were his last, delivering one of his most memorable, charismatic portrayals.

The Crime of Doctor Crespi (1935)
Republic, U.S.A.

Credits: Directed and produced by John H. Auer; story by John H. Auer; screenplay by Lewis Graham and Edwin Olmstead, based on "The Premature Burial" by Edgar Allan Poe; cinematography by Larry Williams; art direction by William Saulter.

Running time: 63 minutes.

Cast: Erich von Stroheim (Dr. Andre Crespi), Harriet Russell (Estelle Ross), Dwight Frey (Dr. Thomas), Paul Guilfoyle (Dr. John Arnold), John Bohn (Dr. Stephen

Ross), Geraldine Kay (Nurse Rexford), Jeanne Kelly (Miss Gordon), Patsy Berlin (Jeanne), Joe Verdi (Di Angelo), Dean Raymond (the minister).

Story: Dr. Thomas enters the office of Dr. Andre Crespi, chief of surgery at the Taft Clinic, and tells the doctor that a certain patient of interest to Crespi has died. Crespi expresses regret at the loss and begins to fill out the death certificate. When Dr. Thomas says that he thinks the patient died at 3:45, Crespi barks: "You think! I wonder!

Dr. Thomas, please. Let's understand each other once and for all. I don't pay you to think! I pay you to know!"

When Estelle Ross comes to the clinic to see Crespi, he tells his nurse that he does not want to see her. Estelle enters Crespi's office anyway and pleads with him to operate on her husband, Dr. Stephen Ross, who is in critical condition following an automobile accident. Crespi reminds her that Stephen took her away from him, but Estelle argues that Stephen never knew that Crespi loved her. When Crespi suggests that there are many competent physicians in the city to whom Estelle could turn, she explains that all the other physicians agree that Dr. Crespi is the only one who can save Stephen. At this point, Crespi relents and arranges for Stephen to be transferred to the Taft Clinic. Afterward, Crespi sits at his desk plotting revenge.

Dr. Thomas, knowing of Crespi's bitterness at having lost Estelle to Stephen Ross, is skeptical of his boss's motives in agreeing to save a former rival. When Crespi operates, however, the procedure is heralded a success. Soon afterward, though, after being given a mysterious injection by Crespi, Ross appears to die. Actually, he is in a twelve-hour, drug-induced cataleptic state. When Dr. Thomas discovers that Crespi has filled out the time of death on the death certificate before the fact, his suspicions regarding Crespi are heightened. After comforting Estelle, Crespi goes to the morgue and administers another injection to Ross, after which he explains to his paralyzed victim what is about to happen. Ross is to be buried the next day. He will not regain the use of his muscles until he is safely six feet under the earth, at which point he will regain full control of himself, only to die horribly as a result of premature burial. Crespi also promises Ross that he will order his favorite flowers—carnations—for the funeral.

Crespi later prevents an autopsy from being performed on Ross and returns to his office, only to be confronted by the suspicious Dr. Thomas. Crespi slaps Thomas,

strangles him into unconsciousness, ties him up, and conceals him behind a locked door. Crespi then attends the funeral of Dr. Ross.

After Ross is buried, Crespi returns to the clinic and frees Dr. Thomas, saying to the very ruffled Thomas that he did what he did for the sake of everyone concerned. He also warns Thomas to keep his wild ideas to himself. Undeterred, Dr. Thomas talks Dr. Arnold into helping him dig up Ross for the purpose of performing an autopsy that would incriminate Crespi. After the two surgeons transport Ross from the grave to the hospital, the "corpse" regains the use of its limbs and staggers down the hospital corridor and into Crespi's office. The doctor, who has been drinking, at first mistakes Ross for a ghost but soon realizes that his intended victim has somehow escaped from the grave. When Crespi pulls a pistol from his desk, Dr. Thomas, Dr. Arnold, Estelle, and the nurse all rush into the room and confront Crespi, who then turns the gun upon himself.

Production and marketing: *The Crime of Dr. Crespi* was shot in New York by Liberty Pictures, a struggling film studio on the brink of failure. When Herbert J. Yates (1880–1966) formed Republic Pictures, he acquired Liberty and released *Crespi* under the Republic banner.

Far from being a mad-scientist tale, Poe's "The Premature Burial" is the account of a narrator who fears being buried alive. This narrator relates several tales of actual premature burial in an effort to demonstrate the horror of the experience and then goes on to reveal his own obsessive fear of being buried alive. When the film's Dr. Crespi visits the cataleptic Dr. Ross in the morgue, he explains in detail how Ross is about to die by premature burial:

> Your eyes are open; you can see. You can hear everything. Yes, and you can feel, but you can't make the slightest sound, and you can't move an eyelash. And here you lie, helpless, paralyzed, unable to shield yourself, and you wonder why. I'll tell you. You have made me suffer for five long years by marrying

Erich von Stroheim, "the man you love to hate," journeys into Poe territory in *The Crime of Dr. Crespi* (1935).

Estelle. …How would you like to see your own funeral, huh? How would you like to see me on your grave's edge? Hearing the earth fall on your casket. How would you like to feel the cold of your own grave? Tomorrow around midnight your muscles will be alive again, but it will be too late. And in your frenzy you will pound and scratch, and you will gasp and suffocate.

Although the above monologue is more eerie when delivered by the villainous Stroheim, it pales next to Poe's vivid, unforgettable description:

It may be asserted, without hesitation, that no event is so terribly well adapted to inspire the supremeness of bodily and of mental distress, as is burial before death. The unendurable oppression of the lungs—the stifling fumes of the damp earth—the clinging to the death garments—the rigid embrace of the narrow house—the blackness of the absolute Night—the silence like a sea that overwhelms—the unseen but palpable presence of the Conqueror Worm—these things, with the thoughts of the air and grass above, with memory of dear friends who would fly to save us if but informed of our fate…

In addition to that general passage from Poe's story, two tales told by Poe's narrator also seem to have suggested *The Crime of Doctor Crespi*. In the first instance, a beautiful young girl from an illustrious family is courted by a poor journalist and a powerful banker. Although she loves the journalist, she marries the banker out of family pride. After several years of ill-treatment, she "dies" and is buried. When the journalist quickly digs her up in order to acquire some locks of her hair, to his shock and relief he finds that she was buried alive. Fate having smiled upon them, they leave the graveyard to begin a life together in another land. In the second instance, a body snatcher delivers a recently buried corpse to a group of doctors intent upon performing a *postmortem* examination. Before they commence the dissection, one of the doctors performs a galvanic battery experiment upon the "corpse," with the effect of rousing it from

the cataleptic state responsible for its having been buried alive.

A greater influence than Poe, however, seems to be Universal's *The Raven* (1935). In both films a mad doctor is flattered into performing a life-saving operation by being told that he is the only one with skill enough to succeed. Because they feel tortured, both doctors plot revenge against those whom they believe are responsible. Erich von Stroheim's Dr. Crespi is obviously patterned after Lugosi's Dr. Vollin.

Erich von Stroheim (1885–1957), who had established himself as one of film's most inventive directors in the twenties, made his first horror film appearance in *The Great Gabbo* (1930), wherein he plays a schizophrenic ventriloquist. He would return to the horror genre as an actor in *The Lady and the Monster* (1944).

Third-billed Dwight Frye (1899–1943), who was once chosen as one of the ten best legitimate actors on Broadway, came to *Crespi* after performing memorable supporting roles in *Dracula* (1931, as Renfield), *Frankenstein* (1931, as Fritz), *The Vampire Bat* (1933), *The Invisible Man* (1933), and *The Bride of Frankenstein* (1935). Frye would also darken the door of horror in *The Son of Frankenstein* (1939), *The Drums of Fu Manchu* (1940), *The Ghost of Frankenstein* (1942), *Frankenstein Meets the Wolf Man* (1943), and *Dead Men Walk* (1943).

The Crime of Doctor Crespi was the second American credit for Hungarian director John H. Auer (1901–1975). He would remain a "B" film director throughout his career, though his *Gangway for Tomorrow* (1943) and *The City Never Sleeps* are highly regarded by many critics. He ended his career as a television director, dying in 1975 at the age of 66.

Posters for the film featured the large head of Stroheim next to a rather hideous skull (probably an allusion to the skull Crespi keeps in his office), below which appear a man and woman in fearful embrace beside a cemetery. "The Man You Love To Hate!" the poster boasts. "Erich [*sic*] von

Stroheim in Edgar Allan Poe's Super Shocker—*The Crime of Dr. Crespi.*"

Critique: When *The Crime of Doctor Crespi* opened in New York in mid-January of 1936, the *New York Times* reported that "Even as 'horror pictures' go, which is pretty far South as a rule, 'The Crime of Dr. Crespi' ...is an almost humorously over-strained attempt at grimness. There were spots when the Rialto audience was unable to restrain a kind of uncalled-for mirth."[47] The reviewer wrote that Stroheim "is unconvincing and looks somehow a rather seedy stranger, photographed through the test-tubes, phials and steaming retorts of the conventional sinister-scientific shots to which the horror school remains incurably addicted."[48] "The only redeeming presence in the picture," the *Times* concludes, "is that of Dwight Frye."[49]

The Hollywood Reporter was more generous, saying that Stroheim "out-Karloff's Karloff without a make-up," giving "such a cruel, cold, malignant and malevolent portrayal of a fiend in human flesh, that one gets an insane urge to up and let him have it."[50]

According to *The Overlook Film Encyclopedia: Horror.* "Cheap, lurid and hesitantly directed, [*Crespi*] nevertheless can boast some moody camerawork and excellent supporting performances to counterbalance Stroheim's over- the-top portrayal of lecherous sadism."

Both *Leonard Maltin's 1996 Movie and Video Guide* and *Video Hound's Golden Movie Retriever 1996* award the film a mediocre two stars, the *Hound* calling Stroheim's performance "very campy."

The film's first half is definitely very slow. The camera often lingers on von Stroheim for what seems an eternity, capturing his every expression, sniff, and twitch. Unfortunately, though villainous enough, Stroheim does not exude the grand charisma of a Bela Lugosi, upon whose Dr. Vollin the Crespi character is based. Whereas the camera loves Lugosi, its intimacy with von Stroheim leaves the audience impatient rather than enthralled.

Although it falls far shot of capturing Poe's mood of stifling terror, Stroheim's monologue in the morgue is one of the film's most chilling sequences, another being the burial of Dr. Ross. In the latter scenes, Auer employs rapid camera cuts from Stroheim to Russell to Raymond as Dr. Ross is "laid to rest." The camera then assumes a prone position at the bottom of the grave as the dirt comes tumbling down upon it from above. Dwight Frye gives a good performance, and Harriet Russell is adequate. Otherwise, *The Crime of Doctor Crespi* is creepingly mediocre. Perhaps the last word should go to Erich von Stroheim himself, who suggested the film be known as "The Crime of Republic."

The Black Cat (1941)
Universal, U.S.A.

Credits: Directed by Albert S. Rogell; associate producer—Burt Kelly; screenplay by Robert Lees, Frederic I. Rinaldo, Eric Taylor, and Robert Neville, suggested by "The Black Cat" by Edgar Allan Poe; cinematography by Stanley Cortez; special photographic effects by John P. Fulton; art direction by Jack Otterson; musical direction by Hans J. Salter; edited by Ted Kent.
Running time: 70 minutes.

Cast: Basil Rathbone (Montague Hartley), Broderick Crawford (Gilbert Smith), Bela Lugosi (Eduardo Vitos), Gale Sondergaard (Abigail Doone), Hugh Herbert (Mr. Penny), Anne Gwynne (Elaine Winslow), Gladys Cooper (Myra Hartley), Cecilia Loftus (Henrietta Winslow), Claire Dodd (Margaret Gordon), John Eldredge (Stanley Grable), Alan Ladd (Richard Hartley).
Story: When the relatives of Henrietta

Winslow, an eccentric old woman who keeps her house full of cats, are informed of her impending death, they flock to the Winslow mansion like vultures. When, to the disappointment of most of her relatives, the old woman recovers, she reveals the contents of her will, which heavily favors her granddaughter Elaine, the only one present who really seems to care about the old woman's well-being. Meanwhile Gil Smith and Mr. Penny arrive to appraise the furniture at the request of Henrietta's son-in-law Montague Hartley.

When Abigail, the housekeeper, brings Henrietta a glass of milk, a hand reaches from the shadows and puts poison into it. Gil feeds some of the milk to a pesky cat, which quickly falls dead, suggesting to Gil that something is amiss. Later Henrietta is found dead in the cat crematorium, stabbed by a knitting needle. Although most of those present conclude that the death was accidental, Gil suspects that the old woman was murdered.

After Mrs. Winslow's death, the group discovers that she had not revealed to them the entire contents of the will. In reality, none of the previously read provisions are to go into effect until after the death of the cats and of Abigail, whom Henrietta charged with the care of the felines. Montague immediately decides to contest the will and leaves for town.

As those assembled begin to bicker among themselves, a powerful electrical storm rises. Meanwhile, Mr. Penny is going about the house appraising the furniture and turning newer pieces into "antiques" with the help of a drill that creates "worm holes" when he discovers Abigail unconscious in a box. Upon recovering, Abigail hypothesizes that she was looking for something in the box when the lid fell upon her head. Gil, again suspecting foul play, goes to phone the police, only to find that the phone cord has been cut. Following Elaine's advice, Gil orders Eduardo, the groundskeeper, to go for the police. Montague returns, however, and informs everyone that the bridge has been

washed out, that he has brought Eduardo back to the mansion, and that they all must stay the night.

Conversations soon reveal that the marriage of Montague and Myrna Hartley is in trouble. Also, a series of escapades reveals that the house is honeycombed with secret passages.

When Gil cannot find Elaine, he rushes out into the rain as Eduardo is loading a suspicious sack into a wagon bed. Fearing that the groundskeeper is spiriting Elaine away, Gil opens the bag, only to release a passel of cats. Eduardo sadly protests that he was only trying to get the cats in out of the rain, after which he crawls off crying, "Here, kitty, kitty."

Soon afterward, an attempt is made on Gil's life in the crematorium. A comedy of errors then follows in which Gil wakes up the house looking for Elaine when she has only gone downstairs for a book, and Gil disturbs the peace a second time when he mistakes Abigail's whistling tea kettle for a scream. Later, as Gil keeps watch outside Elaine's door, a mysterious cloaked figure enters the room through a secret passage and leaves a pile of ashes and a black cat on Elaine's bed. Elaine awakens and fearfully tells Gil what happened. A short time later, however, another scream leads to the discovery of Abigail's body near the sack of ashes. Although her hanging appears to be a guilty suicide, Gil's examination of the rope allows him to prove that Abigail was murdered.

After a dizzying encounter with a revolving panel, Gil finds Mrs. Winslow's will in Myrna's room. When the unconscious Myrna is revived, she identifies Eduardo as her attacker. As the household hunts for Eduardo, he returns to Myrna's room and protests his innocence. Myrna, however, takes the opportunity to kill the groundskeeper with a pistol.

Soon afterward, when Myrna is rescued from hanging, Elaine examines the rope and discovers that Myrna has actually staged the act herself. Furthermore, she accuses Myrna

Bela Lugosi mugs for the camera beside a Poe-inspired feline statue in *The Black Cat* **(1941).**

of having killed Mrs. Winslow and Abigail. It seems that Myrna wanted the inheritance in order to hold onto Montague. Exposed as the killer, Myrna knocks Elaine unconscious and carries her through a secret passage to the crematorium. There, she places Elaine and the black cat into the oven. When Gil cannot find Elaine, he goes to the crematorium just in time to interrupt Myrna's plan. When the cat meows from inside the oven, Gil pushes Myrna aside and rescues the girl and the cat. Myrna meanwhile has caught her gown afire and goes screaming off into the night, a human torch. The mystery solved, Gil and Elaine presumably live happily ever after.

Production and marketing: When Paramount resurrected the "old dark house" horror subgenre with *The Ghost Breakers* (1939), a remake of *The Cat and the Canary*, they did it as a Bob Hope comedy. The combination of shadowy chills and aggressive American humor proved popular with audiences unable to respond any longer to the straight haunted house formula. Sensing a way to make a buck, Universal jumped on the bandwagon in 1941 with its second version of Poe's *The Black Cat*. Why the studio felt it necessary to pillage Poe for such a vehicle is the biggest mystery suggested by the film.

At least the cat of the title is more prominent in the 1941 version than it was in 1934. Still, its presence is merely a forced attempt to justify the title. Again Universal serves up the old mumbo jumbo of the black cat as a symbol of death without any convincing attempt to integrate the legend into the film itself. The only borrowing from Poe is the scene in which Myrna Cooper places Elaine and the black cat into the crematorium oven (rather than behind a wall), only to have the cat's meowing unmask her as the killer.

Interestingly, though there is very little horror in the film, the studio hyped it as a horror picture, a strategy guaranteed to disappoint and anger the target audience. Posters showed the looming image of a fearsome black cat above the sinister or frightened faces of the cast.

Basil Rathbone (1892–1967), Hugh Herbert (1887–1952), and Brod Crawford (1911–1986) received top billing. The British Rathbone had starred in such genre classics as *Son of Frankenstein* (1939), *The Hound of the Baskervilles* (1939, as Sherlock Holmes), and *Tower of London* (1939, with Boris Karloff and Vincent Price). He had also starred or made important appearances in such general classics as *David Copperfield* (1935, as Murdstone), *Anna Karenina* (1935), *Captain Blood* (1935), and *The Adventures of Robin Hood* (1938). Spurred by his stature in the industry at the time and irked by having to appear in a lowly horror film, Rathbone reportedly demanded that his first scene in the film appear before those of any other performers so that his importance would immediately register with the audience.

Hugh Herbert was an American comedian remembered for his nervous "woo woo" exclamation. Among his more important films preceding *The Black Cat* were *A Midsummer Night's Dream* (1935), *Helzapoppin* (1941), and *Mrs. Wiggs and the Cabbage Patch* (1942, with W. C. Fields).

Brod Crawford, the son of actress Helen Broderick, began his film career playing comic stooges and gangsters. At the time of *The Black Cat,* he was still largely seen as a comic character or supporting ruffian. He would, however, go on to win an Academy Award for his starring role as a politician modeled after Hewey Long in *All the King's Men* (1950) and would become a household name as a result of starring in the popular television series "Highway Patrol" (1955–1958).

Interestingly, it was primarily the second-billed players whom filmgoers most remember today. First and foremost, of course, is Bela Lugosi. Although he appears in a minor role, Bela manages to be both menacing and comic as the *The Black Cat*'s most obvious red herring. It is sad that Universal had so little confidence in Lugosi as to cast him in such a minor role.

Gale Sondergaard (1899–1985) came to *The Black Cat* having won an Academy Award in *Anthony Adverse* (1936) and having turned in fine performances in such acclaimed films as *Maid of Salem* (1937), *The Life of Emile Zola* (1937), *The Cat and the Canary* (1939), and *The Bluebird* (1940). She would later play Sherlock Holmes's nemesis in *The Spider Woman* (1944), fall prey to *The Invisible Man's Revenge* (1944), join Boris Karloff in *The Climax* (1944), and revisit the arachnids in *The Spider Woman Strikes Back* (1946). Because she was suspected of Communist tendencies, her film career was damaged by the hunt for Communists in the early 1950s. She made final horror film appearances in the made-for-television *The Cat Creature* (1974) and in *Echoes* (1983). Although Sondergaard did not respect the horror films she made, it is largely for those films that she is most remembered today.

Then we have a minor player named Alan Ladd (1913–1964), who had kicked around in minor roles in minor films since 1932. He did have a small role in a big picture called *Citizen Kane* (1941), but that appearance also failed to gain him recognition. After *The Black Cat,* however, he earned great critical acclaim as a psychotic hired killer in *This Gun for Hire* (1942, with Veronica Lake). He followed up with acclaimed starring roles in such films as *The Glass Key* (1942), *The Blue Dahlia* (1946), *The Great Gatsby* (1949), and *Shane* (1953). Ladd received eleventh billing in the 1941 release of *The Black Cat.* When Realart Pictures later rereleased the film, Ladd miraculously soared to second billing behind Basil Rathbone. Brod Crawford, billed third in 1941, was relegated to seventh billing.

Critique: *Film Daily* reported: "The cast is fine, the horror element in the story is sufficient, with a full complement of secret passages, yowling cats and sinister characters. Picture should serve well as a supporting feature ... where audiences go for this type of film. Rathbone is properly sinister and heartless, Herbert is amusing as an antique buyer, Bela Lugosi adds a note of horror to the cast. Direction and screenplay are both good."[51]

Rathbone's sinister presence does add a touch of class to the film. His starring role in Universal's Sherlock Holmes series also allows Crawford to get a laugh by muttering "Who does he think he is, Sherlock Holmes?" as Rathbone fumbles about trying to solve the mystery.

Although the *Film Daily* found Hugh Herbert amusing, it appears to be one of the few critical sources that has. As Michael Brunas, John Brunas, and Tom Weaver write in *Universal Horrors,* "Playing the archetypical scatter-brained friend of the hero, Herbert looks as if he were thrown in the film at the last minute to bolster the feeble comedy. His hijinks as an antique dealer whose *idée fixe* is to batter every furnishing in sight to make them look more like antiques is repetitious and relentlessly unfunny. His character is so dense, obnoxious and outlandishly stupid that it's painful to watch him in action."[52]

If Bela Lugosi adds a "note of horror to the cast," it is a weak note indeed. Of little interest to Universal by this time, Lugosi is almost unrecognizable as he creeps about as the seedy groundskeeper, his "horror" usually limited to peering through windows. Universal would use him in a small but effective role in *The Wolf Man* (1941), as Igor in *The Ghost of Frankenstein* (1942), as a red-herring butler in *Night Monster* (1942), and as the Frankenstein Monster in *Frankenstein Meets the Wolf Man* (1943) before releasing him entirely, leaving him at the mercy of low-budget studios such as Monogram for most of the rest of his film career. In *The Black Cat,* he makes the "sack of cats" scene the funniest in the film with his unlikely "Here kitty, kitty." Also of note, in an early scene, a close-up of Lugosi's staring eyes (a cliché since *Dracula* and *White Zombie*) effectively fades to a shot of the headlights of Crawford's car.

Broderick Crawford carries the comic leading man role well, and with Gladlys Cooper, shares the film's best acting honor. Ironically, Alan Ladd, the actor with the smallest part, would soon become one of Hollywood's biggest stars of the forties. In *The Black Cat,* however, he has little to do.

Albert S. Rogell directs competently, but only competently, his greatest contribution being the film's fast pace. More on the positive side is the fine camera work of Stanley Cortez, particularly in the film's eerie introduction and early scenes and in the shots of the cloaked killer as she creeps through the mansion's secret passageways.

In *The Psychotronic Encyclopedia of Film,* Michael Weldon calls *The Black Cat* "an unfunny old-dark-house murder-mystery comedy with a good cast."[53] Leonard Maltin awards the film 2½ stars.

Fans of Edgar Allan Poe and the horror genre have always found *The Black Cat* disappointing. While 1941 high school literature students would not have been shocked and horrified by this film as they would have been by the 1934 version, they would not have been edified either.

The Tell-Tale Heart (1941)
MGM, U.S.A.

Credits: Directed by Jules Dassin; screenplay by Doane Hoag (or Lewis Jacobs), based on "The Tell-Tale Heart" by Edgar Allan Poe; music by Sol Krandel.

Running time: 20 minutes.

Cast: Joseph Schildkraut (murderer), Roman Bohnen (old man), Oscar O'Shea and Will Wright (investigators).

Story: A feebleminded young man, obsessed by the filmy eye of an old man acting as his guardian and spinning master, decides to murder the old man to rid himself of the "vulture eye." Apparently the old man has mistreated the young man for years and has dared him to try to find other employment, knowing that he cannot. At night, during a thunderstorm, with a lantern that controls the width of the light beam, the young man opens the door of the old man's bedroom. The predator opens the lantern's shutter and shines the light upon the old man's eye. "You are not strong enough to have blood on your soul," the old man warns. Nevertheless, the young man leaps upon his victim and kills him. Just as the old man dies, the young man listens to the last beats of his victim's heart. Afterward, the young man buries the body under the floorboards and falls asleep in a chair. Waking in the morning, he believes he again hears the beating of the old man's heart. It is, however, the ticking of a pendulum and the dripping of a faucet, both of which the young man terminates.

Shortly afterward, a knock comes to the door. It is two men wondering about the whereabouts of the old man. The young man says that his master has left and will probably return the next day. The men, who are leaving, suddenly stop. The young man's explanation is curious, they say, since the old man promised to attend the auction today. Agitated at being questioned, the young man quickly blurts out that the old man probably forgot. As the young man continues to address the suspicions of his visitors, however he begins to hear the repetitious beating of the old man's heart. Becoming frightened, the young man glances about the room. The pendulum is still, and the faucet is not dripping. Still the beating continues. When one of the visitors begins tapping his fingers on the table, the young man grabs his arm and angrily orders him to quit. By now the visitors are quite suspicious. "Where *is* the old man?" one asks pointedly. The young man retreats to a chair, which he begins to scrape across the very floorboards concealing the victim. "Why are you looking at me?" he asks nervously. "Are you deaf! Can't you hear it!" The visitors stare at him accusingly. "You do hear it!" the young man cries. "Stop it! Stop it! Tear up the planks!"

The visitors kneel down and peek under the floorboards. Then they walk over to the young man, who stands looking out the window. "It is quiet now," the young man says, and with a peaceful countenance, he is led away.

Production and marketing: Jules Dassin (1911–), a former radio writer and actor, joined MGM in 1941 to direct short features, one of which was *The Tell-Tale Heart*. He would go on to direct feature films, among the best being *Brute Force* (1947), *The Naked City* (1948), *Thieves' Highway* (1949), and *Rififi* (1954).

Unlike the Poe tale, the screenplay seems to account for the killer's act via the explanation of slight mental retardation. Otherwise, the film is a faithful adaptation.

Joseph Schildkraut (1895–1964), an Austrian leading man and character actor, had many films behind him when he was chosen for the lead in *The Tell-Tale Heart*. Films featuring his most well-known performances include *King of Kings* (1927), *Showboat* (1929), *The Garden of Allah* (1936), *The Life of Emile Zola* (1937), and my personal favorite, *The Diary of Anne Frank* (1959). In his 1959 autobiography, *My Fa-*

ther and I, he wrote that *The Tell-Tale Heart* "was to a great extent in pantomine, accompanied by movie and sound effects. In fact I did not speak more than four sentences in the whole picture." (He actually has substantial dialogue).

Roman Bohnen (1894–1949), an American character actor known for playing hardworking immigrants, appeared in such memorable pictures as *Of Mice and Men* (1939), *The Hitler Gang* (1944), *The Best Years of Our Lives* (1946), and *Brute Force* (1947, also directed by Dassin).

Will Wright (1894–1962), another well-known character actor whose face is immediately recognized by most filmgoers, had his biggest role in *The Blue Dahlia* (1946) as the killer. He also appeared in the riotous Tracy/Hepburn comedy *Adam's Rib* (1949).

The Tell-Tale Heart won the Oscar in 1941 for best short feature, one of the few times in the history of the cinema that a horror film has won one of the prestigious statues.

Critique: The firm directorial hand of Jules Dassin, the faithful screenplay, and the film's excellent cast make this two-reeler a solid Poe entry. Of course, the shorter length gives it a natural edge over most feature films, which require padding, usually to their detriment. The stark, small house of the old man and his apprentice provides a simple setting, but it is not that which provides the horror. As D. W. Griffith before him, Dassin relies on the eerie sound effects of the beating heart and on the growing madness of the guilty party to produce the terror. Indeed the nervousness and paranoia of Schildkraut are palpable as the film moves to its satisfying conclusion. In terms of faithfulness to Poe and the terror invoked, this version of *The Tell-Tale Heart* is undoubtedly the best of its kind.

The Mystery of Marie Roget (1942); aka *Phantom of Paris*;
Universal, U.S.A.

Credits: Directed by Philip Rosen; associate producer—Paul Malvern; screenplay by Michel Jacoby, based on "The Mystery of Marie Roget" by Edgar Allan Poe; cinematography by Elwood Bredell; art direction by Jack Otterson and Richard H. Riedel; edited by Milton Carruth; musical direction by Hans Salter

Running time: 60 minutes.

Cast: Patric Knowles (Dr. Paul Dupin), Maria Monte (Marie Roget), Maria Ouspenskaya (Mme. Cecile Roget), John Litel (Henri Beauvais), Edward Norris (Marcel Vigneaux), Lloyd Corrigan (Prefect of Police Gobelin), Nell O'Day (Camille Roget), Frank Reicher (Magistrate), Clyde Fillmore (M. De Luc).

Story: Paris, 1889. The entire city is excited and intrigued when musical comedy star Marie Roget disappears. Although M. Beauvais, minister of naval affairs and a family friend, scolds inspector Gobelin, the perfect of police, for failing to find her, Dr. Paul Dupin, chief medical officer for the police, remains confident that the mystery will be solved. It was, after all, Dupin who solved the recent case of the murders in the Rue Morgue.

When the body of a young woman is fished from the Seine, Dupin notes that "her face has been torn to a pulp by the claws of an animal." Gobelin is so sure that the corpse is that of Marie Roget that he, Beauvais, and Dupin go to notify Mme. Roget (Marie's elderly and wealthy grandmother) and Marie's sister Camille of the discovery. As Beauvais relates Gobelin's conclusions to the family, Marie herself walks cheerfully into the house and feigns surprise that her disappearance has caused such a fuss. When Mme. Roget demands to know where her granddaughter has been, the young woman simply brushes her off, proclaiming that her private comings and goings are her own business. When Gobelin notices that Mme. Roget keeps a leopard as a house pet, he suspects that the old woman might have been responsible for the death of the victim recently pulled from the Seine.

Later, Marcel Vigneaux, the handsome aide to Beauvais, becomes engaged to Camille. When Camille leaves the room, however, Vigneaux and Marie plot to divert a large inheritance from Camille to Marie. When Marie demands to know why he has proposed marriage to Camille, Vigneaux answers he did so to divert suspicion from himself since Camille is going to disappear the following night at a party given for Marie by the De Lucs. Mme. Roget overhears their plotting, however, and calls for Dupin. Without telling Dupin what she knows, the old lady offers him 50,000 francs to act as Camille's bodyguard at the party. Dupin balks at the offer until he is struck by Camille's beauty.

Meanwhile, Dupin has discovered that the corpse pulled earlier from the Seine was that of an English girl murdered shortly after her arrival in France. At the Le Duc party, Beauvais makes advances toward Marie, but she rebuffs him politely. Dupin tries to become friendly with Marie, but she is aloof. After Marie sings a song for the assemblage, Vigneaux, who has arrived at the party late, tells her in the garden that he is afraid to carry out their plan as long as Dupin is keeping a watchful eye on Camille. Marie, however, plays Lady Macbeth, urging Vigneaux on with the argument that they will be suspected less if Camille is killed under the very nose of the police.

Shortly afterward, however, Marie screams. When the partygoers rush to a garden wall overlooking the river, she is nowhere to be found. Beauvais offers his assistance, claiming that he was walking in the garden alone when he heard the scream. Dupin discovers a handkerchief covered with Camille's perfume near the spot where Marie disappeared, but there are no arrests.

As Parisian newspapers report the second disappearance of Marie Roget, Dupin suggests that a diver search the river below the De Lucs' garden wall. The diver brings up the body of Marie Roget, her face mutilated in the same manner as the corpse discovered earlier.

Beauvais takes charge of the body and denies Dupin autopsy rights. Later, however, a figure garbed in a black coat and hat steals into the morgue and removes Marie's brain. When Gobelin is understandably upset at this news, Dupin confesses that he stole the organ in order to perform experiments which could lead to the capture of the killer. Meanwhile, Mme. Roget has given her leopard to the zoo, claiming that it bit her arm and was too dangerous to maintain any longer as a house pet. Gobelin, however, jumps to the conclusion that she has simply disposed of the murder weapon.

Certain that Mme. Roget is innocent, Dupin recovers a hand cultivator in a tool shed at the De Lucs. Tests, he claims, will demonstrate that the cultivator was the instrument used to disfigure the two dead women. Gobelin's suspicions turn next to Beauvais when the latter seems to fall for a trap hatched by Dupin involving Marie Roget's diary. Beauvais, however, denies any guilt and is freed when Mme. Roget proclaims that she told Beauvais to get the diary for her. Mme. Roget then reveals to Camille that Marie was a wicked woman who plotted kill her in order to inherit money. Vigneaux responds by confessing that it was he who must have dropped Camille's handkerchief at the scene of the crime after killing Marie. Dupin, however, claiming to know the identity of the killer, convinces a reluctant and angry Gobelin to drop charges. Still, Dupin refuses to tell the frustrated Gobelin whom he suspects. Meanwhile, Vigneaux threatens to kill Dupin for his role in getting the charges dropped.

Dupin then sets another trap involving the diary to capture the murderer. When an unforeseen twist occurs, however, he rushes to the Roget home, fearful that the killer will soon strike against Camille. Indeed, as Camille sleeps, a figure dressed in a black cloak and hat creeps across the rooftops and into her room. Dupin, who arrives just in time to save Camille's life, pursues the killer across the rooftops. A shot finally drops the fleeing killer, who is revealed to be Vigneaux. Dupin later explains that Vigneaux killed his actual wife as soon as she arrived in France from England. Intending to marry Camille for her money, he then killed Marie. Dupin, fearing that the killer would receive a verdict of justifiable homicide, interfered with Vigneaux's trial in order to later prove premeditation. Dupin also explains that he first suspected the killer's identity when Beauvais saved Camille and himself from being poisoned by Vigneaux at the Le Duc party. With the mystery solved, the budding romance between Dupin and Camille is free to blossom.

Production and marketing: Few of Edgar Allan Poe's stories are less suited for a straight screen adaptation than "The Mystery of Marie Roget." In fact, in Poe's tale, which is a sequel to "The Murders in the Rue Morgue," Dupin solves the murder of Marie Roget simply by sitting in his room and poring over newspaper accounts of the case.

Poe based his story on an actual murder case that was mystifying and intriguing New York City at the time. In October 1838, two and a half years before her death, Mary Rogers disappeared from her home after leaving a note threatening to kill herself. When she returned home unharmed, the *Times and Commercial Intelligencer* reported that she had simply gone to visit a friend in Brooklyn. Several years later, however, the *Herald* reported that she had disappeared after being seduced by an officer of the U.S. Navy and had been kept at Hoboken for two weeks.

On July 25, 1841, Mary Rogers told her fiancé, Daniel Payne, that she was going to visit her aunt, after which she disappeared for a second time. Never having reached the home of her aunt, Mary was found three days later floating in the Hudson River. The corpse was bound, the face butchered and battered. A piece of lace knotted tightly around her neck was cited at the autopsy as the cause of death and the knots were reputed to be sailor's knots.

In August, Mrs. Frederick Loss, a roadhouse proprietor, informed the Hoboken police that her sons had discovered some articles of a woman's clothing in a thicket about 300 yards from her establishment. The items, which included a handkerchief, were identified as having belonged to Mary Rogers.

Rumors that a rowdy gang committed the murder persisted, as did whispers of a botched abortion attempt. Although he was not a suspect, Daniel Payne committed suicide in October 1941 near the spot where his fiancée was murdered. Despite hefty rewards, the mystery was never officially solved.

Although Poe resets the mystery in Paris, he closely reproduces the key elements of the Rogers case, making only minor changes in some sequences of events and often quoting nearly verbatim from contemporary newspaper accounts. Poe's Dupin uses evidence from the clothing found at the supposed murder site to disprove the gang theory. Seizing on the rumor that the murdered girl's first disappearance involved a naval officer and also upon evidence that the knots used to bind the corpse were sailor's knots, Poe has Dupin point the finger of guilt at M. Beauvais. According to Dupin, Marie was eloping with the officer when they were detained in the thicket by the rainstorm. Beauvais then violated Marie in a fit of passion and murdered her in a frenzy of guilt. Finally, Dupin traces the boat used by the naval officer to dispose of Marie's body with the aid of a newspaper account fabricated by Poe. As the story appeared in installments in the *Companion* magazine, Poe boasted to have solved the actual Mary Rogers case. Readers interested in a full account of the circum-

Maria Montez, Maria Ouspenskaya, Edward Norris, John Litel, Patric Knowles, and Lloyd Corrigan in the dénouement of *The Mystery of Marie Roget* **(1942).**

stances surrounding Poe's "The Mystery of Marie Roget" are directed to John Walsh's definitive study *Poe the Detective* (Rutgers University Press, 1968).

When Universal decided to turn "The Mystery of Marie Roget" into a "B" horror picture, it handed the story, which is nearly devoid of both characterization and action, to Michel Jacoby. Struggling to mold the tale into a marketable film, Jacoby retained from Poe's story, the Parisian setting, the two disappearances of Marie Roget, and the discovery of a scarf at the murder scene. (In the film it becomes a handkerchief belonging to the victim's sister rather than to Marie herself.)

Interestingly, an account of the actual case indicates the victim's face was "battered and butchered to a mummy." Although Poe's story does not cite this report, Jacoby has Marie's face disfigured beyond recognition

by a garden weeder in order to throw suspicion upon Mme. Roget's leopard, which obviously does not appear in Poe's story.

In creating the film's characters, Jacoby turns Dupin into someone quite different from Poe's reclusive detective or the morbid but love-struck medical student of Universal's *The Murders in the Rue Morgue*. Jacoby's Dupin, as portrayed by Patric Knowles, is the typical charming leading man of the forties, intelligent but not intellectual, a "regular guy" with a pleasant sense of humor. As in Poe's story, Jacoby's Dupin enjoys a measure of fame as a result of having solved the Rue Morgue murders.

Poe's prefect of police is long-winded and ineffectual, while Jacoby's Gobelin, as portrayed by Lloyd Corrigan, though equally unimaginative, is infused with a jovial personality missing from Poe's model.

Poe's Mme. Duluc, the roadhouse proprietor of the original case, becomes Jacoby's Mme. De Luc, the woman at whose home Marie Roget makes her second and final disappearance. The rest of Jacoby's characters either do not exist in Poe's story or are rendered in the film in such ways as to be unrecognizable.

Jacoby probably created the film's two black-garbed phantoms to add a greater aura of mystery to the picture and to allow Universal to engage in horror film hype. One poster asks "What is the secret of this baffling beauty? Maddening—with her soft caress! Murdering—with steel-clawed terror! Fiction's spine-clutching classic of the Phantom Mangler of Paris!" The pressbook disingenuously announces the film as "Edgar Allan Poe's CLASSIC OF TERROR!" On the showmanship page, the pressbook recommends that theater owners "tap the sources where mystery fans are certain to be reached" and pushes the Edgar Allan Poe connection.

> Edgar Allan Poe's books are standard sellers in all book stores, popular stand-bys at all public and circulating libraries. Make up book-marks listing his classics with emphasis on the volume of short stories in which "The Mystery of Marie Roget" is published…. Your public library might go for a display of their best horror novels… among which Poe's would naturally top the list. This would permit a still display from your picture to command the attention of the many readers who are attracted to mystery and horror stories.

Director Phil Rosen (1888–1951) began his career at the helm of some major silent-film productions. Later, when he became associated with poverty-row studios such as Mascot and Monogram, he would direct such low-budget horror films as *Spooks Run Wild* (1941, with Bela Lugosi) and *Return of the Ape Man* (1944, with Bela Lugosi and John Carradine).

Marie Montez (1919–1951), who debuted in Universal's *The Invisible Woman* (1941), would become known as an exotic leading lady in adventure films such as *Arabian Nights* (1942), *Cobra Woman* (1944), and

Ali Baba and the Forty Thieves (1944). Commenting upon her physical assets, she once remarked, "When I see myself on the screen, I am so beautiful I jump for joy."

Patric Knowles (1911–) had appeared in such critically acclaimed films as Michael Curtiz's *The Charge of the Light Brigade* (1936) and *The Adventures of Robin Hood* (1938), John Ford's *How Green Was My Valley* (1941), and *The Wolf Man* (1941). He would go on to distinguish himself as the leading man in Universal's excellent *Frankenstein Meets the Wolf Man* (1943).

Russian character actress Maria Ouspenskaya (1876–1949) enlivened many Hollywood films after the mid-thirties. Among her best-known films are *Love Affair* (1939), *The Rains Came* (1939), *Dr. Ehrlich's Magic Bullet* (1940), *Waterloo Bridge* (1940), and of course, *The Wolf Man* (1940) and *Frankenstein Meets the Wolf Man* (1943), in which she gives her horror genre classic performances as Maleva the Gypsy.

Critique: When *The Mystery of Marie Roget* opened in May 1942, the *New York Times* wasted no time in savaging Universal's latest horror release:

> Usually, when murder is done in fiction, it is best to show some motive for the crime. But that very obvious essential is just one of the conventions which has been overlooked… in Universal's butchered retelling of Edgar Allan Poe's "The Mystery of Marie Roget." …Why a certain party kills the beautiful Parisian musical star is never explained. Why Dr. Paul Dupin, an amateur detective, should suspect the killer is never made clear. Indeed, why every one in the picture acts with such strange evasiveness is by far a more irritating mystery than who killed Marie and why.
> For the conclusive fact of the matter is that this is a dreary, aimless film, devoid of logic or excitement or even a shadow of suspense. Vaguely it leaves an impression of wretched futility. Several fairly good actors have been buried beneath a molehill of dust.[54]

In truth, this review is unfairly harsh, but not by much. It is correct in charging that Vigneaux's motive for murdering Marie Roget is vague at best. On the other hand, Dupin clearly explains at the end of the picture why he initially suspected Vigneaux. The film's pace is slow, but it does pick up in the last fifteen minutes, albeit not soon enough to save the picture. Michael Brunas, John Brunas, and Tom Weaver fairly accurately assess the film in their book *Universal Horrors*:

> It's never explained why Vigneaux murders Marie, nor why he disfigures her face before dumping her body in the river. Although it's understandable that he should mutilate the face of the first victim (his wife), the fact that he indulges in this sadistic excess a second time with Marie seems particularly ill-advised, and would serve only to eventually link him with the earlier murder....Vigneaux's curious plan to win over a jury (he figures if he claims to have murdered Marie in order to protect Camille, he will be acquitted) seems similarly wrongheaded; here again, his senseless mutilation of Marie's face would obviously work very strongly against him and surely lose for him the sympathy of any jury. The fact that Dupin is able to ascertain Marie's criminal nature through an examination of her brain is a quaint but preposterous notion which probably fooled no one even in the less sophisticated 1940s .

(Marie's criminal nature is actually revealed by Mme. Roget.)[55]

Brunas, Brunas, and Weaver also accurately observe that there is too little horror for this offering to be a horror film and too few viable suspects for it to be a successful mystery. Everyone, I think, would agree that Edgar Allan Poe is ill-served by this particular adaptation, which wastes a fine cast.

A somewhat dissenting voice is *Leonard Maltin's 1996 Movie and Video Guide,* wherein the film receives 2½ stars and is judged a "Fairly good murder mystery."

By the way, what ever happened to Mme. Camille L'Espanaye, Paul Dupin's great love from the 1932 film *The Murders in the Rue Morgue*? Could he have finally dumped her because of the insipid sentences that so frequently issued from her lips? Anyway, he has another Camille now. May they rest in peace.

Realart Pictures rereleased *The Mystery of Marie Roget* as *Phantom of Paris* in 1951, at which time it died a quick and well-deserved death at the box office.

The Loves of Edgar Allan Poe (1942)
Fox, U.S.A.

Credits: Directed by Harry Lachman; produced by Bryan Foy; screenplay by Samuel Hoffenstein, Tom Reed, and Arthur Caesar; cinematography by Lucien Andriot; edited by Fred Allen; music by Emil Newman; art direction by Richard Day and Nathan Juran.

Running time: 67 minutes.

Cast: Linda Darnell (Virginia Clemm), John Shepperd [later Shepperd Strudwick] (Edgar Allan Poe), Virginia Gilmore (Elmira Royster), Jane Darwell (Mrs. Clemm), Mary Howard (Frances Allen), Frank Conroy (John Allan), Henry Morgan (Ebenezer Burling), Walter Kingsford (T. W. White), Morris Ankrum (Mr. Graham), Skippy

Wanders (Poe, age 3), Freddie Mercer (Poe, age 12), Erville Alderson (schoolmaster), Peggy McIntyre (Elmira, age 10), William Bakewell, Jr. (Hugh Pleasant), Frank Melton (Turner Dixon), Morton Lowry (Charles Dickens), Gilbert Emery (Thomas Jefferson), Ed Stanley (Dr.. Moran), Francis Ford (tavern keeper), Harry Denny (Kennedy), Hardie Albright (Shelton), Jan Clayton (Poe's young mother), Mae Marsh (Mrs. Phillips), Alec Craig (printer), Leon Tyler (boy), Arthur Shields (Somes, the proctor).

Story: In 1911, actress Elizabeth Arnold Poe dies, and her son Edgar is taken into the childless home of John and Frances Allan. The foster father mistreats the boy, and the two do not get along. At the age of seventeen, Edgar falls in love with Elmira Royster and becomes engaged to her. When Edgar enters the University of Virginia, the romance is cut short when Elmira's parents intercept Edgar's letters and fail to pass them on to Elmira. Elmira soon marries Shelton, leaving Edgar brokenhearted. Edgar leaves the university after a time of heavy drinking and after accumulating gambling debts. John Allan refuses to pay the debts, and Edgar runs away to Boston. After a stint in the military, Edgar is accepted at West Point and begins to publish poetry. Later he takes up residence with his father's sister, Mrs. Clemm, and her daughter, Virginia. Edgar develops a deep affection for Virginia and marries her. When Edgar is dismissed from the *Southern Literary Messenger,* he, Virginia, and Mrs. Clemm move to New York and then to Philadelphia, and he eventually becomes editor of *Graham's Magazine.* Soon Poe is famous for his short stories and poetry, particularly for the overnight success "The Raven." He then moves Virginia and Mrs. Clemm to a cottage in Fordham.

Virginia, however, develops tuberculosis and drifts slowly and painfully toward death as Edgar attempts by writing to overcome their poverty. Still apparently unhinged by his earlier mistreatment at the hands of John Allan, Edgar drinks excessively in the face of Virginia's imminent death. After her sad passing, Edgar renews his engagement to Mrs. Shelton (formerly Elmira Royster), who is now a widow. Before the wedding can take place, however, Edgar drinks himself to death.

Production and marketing: *The Loves of Edgar Allan Poe* primarily addresses Poe's love for his cousin Virginia Clemm and for Elmira (Royster) Shelton. Also addressed is his deep affection for Mrs. Clemm. Unaccountably absent, however, is his important relationship with and engagement to Sarah Helen Whitman which occurred after Virginia's death and before his engagement to Elmira Shelton. Also untouched is the problematic relationship between Poe and Frances

Sargent Osgood. The film portrays John Allan as the decisive negative influence of Poe's life, largely responsible for both his heavy drinking and his subsequent mental difficulties.

By 1942, Anglo-American director Harry Lachman (1886–1975) had already done his best work, including the films *Dante's Inferno* (1935), a carnival-based Spencer Tracy vehicle, and *Our Relations* (1936), a critically successful Laurel and Hardy comedy. Lachman also directed Warner Oland, Keye Luke, and J. Carrol Naish in the pleasing mystery *Charlie Chan at the Circus* (1936). In 1941, Lachman returned to the Charlie Chan series to direct Sidney Toler and George Reeves in the moody *Dead Men Tell.*

Top-billed Linda Darnell (1921–1965) was a major screen star throughout the forties, appearing in such acclaimed films as *Brigham Young* (1940), *The Mark of Zorro* (1940), *The Song of Bernadette* (1943, as Virgin Mary), *It Happened Tomorrow* (1944), *Hangover Square* (1945), *Anna and the King of Siam* (1946), *My Darling Clementine* (1946), and *Forever Amber* (1947). The hard-drinking Darnell would lose her life in a fire shortly after appearing in an A. C. Lyles Western called *Black Spurs* (1965).

American actor John Shepperd, aka Shepperd Strudwick (1907–1983), landed the potentially juicy role of Edgar A. Poe after turning in a notable performance as a presidential nominee in *Remember the Day* (1941). Among his other notable films would be *All the King's Men* (1949, with Academy-Award winner Broderick Crawford), *A Place in the Sun* (1951), with Montgomery Clift and Elizabeth Taylor), and *Autumn Leaves* (1965, with Joan Crawford).

American leading lady Virginia Gilmore (1919–1986) appeared in routine films throughout the forties but ultimately failed to carve out a memorable career. The same cannot be said, however, for Jane Darwell (1880–1967). Having appeared in *Gone with the Wind* in 1939, she won an Academy Award for her moving performance as the indomitable Ma Joad in *The Grapes of Wrath*

(1940) and followed up with a fine performance in *All That Money Can Buy* (1941). She would go on to give many excellent performances as strong women in such notable films as *The Ox-Bow Incident* (1943), *Captain Tugboat Annie* (1946, in the title role), *My Darling Clementine* (1946), and *The Last Hurrah* (1958). In 1964 she would play the tender "bird lady" in Disney's popular *Mary Poppins*.

British stage actor Frank Conroy (1890–1964), who plays the villainous John Allan, made a career of playing domestic tyrants. Among his most memorable films are *Grand Hotel* (1932), *The Call of the Wild* (1935), and *The Ox-Bow Incident* (1943).

Another performer worthy of note is American character actor Morris Ankrum (1896–1964). Ankrum appeared in films of all types, usually as lawyers, judges, and Western villains, but it is for his roles as authority figures in horror/science fiction films of the fifties that he is now best remembered. Among those many credits are *Rocketship X-M* (1950), *Flight to Mars* (1951), *Invaders from Mars* (1953), *Earth versus the Flying Saucers* (1956), and *Kronos* (1957).

Critique: When *The Loves of Edgar Allan Poe* opened, *The New York Times* found it "dull, prosaic, and uninspired ... no more than a postured and lifeless tableau."[56] Both Leonard Maltin and *Video Hound's Golden Movie Retriever* award the film a mediocre two stars, Maltin calling it "plodding" and the *Hound* calling it "bland." Although I saw the film many years ago, I can remember little about the experience other than my great disappointment. While I found the cast enjoyable, the film itself was dull. Perhaps if I saw it as an adult, my perspective would change. Unfortunately, *The Loves of Edgar Allan Poe* is unavailable on video (one source incorrectly lists it for sale from Fox Video), and it rarely, if ever, shows on television.

The Fall of the House of Usher (1949)
G.L.B./Vigilant, Great Britain

Credits: Directed and produced by Ivan Barnett; screenplay by Kenneth Thompson and Dorothy Catt, adapted from the story "The Fall of the House of Usher" by Edgar Allan Poe; cinematography by Ivan Barnett; music by De Wolfe; sound by Leeves Rich; art direction by Hugh Gladwich.

Running time: 70 minutes.

Cast: Kaye Tendeter (Lord Roderick Usher), Gwendoline Watford (Lady Madeline Usher), Irving Steen (Jonathan), Lucy Pavy (the hag), Vernon Charles (Dr. Cordwell), Gavin Lee (the butler), Tony Powell-Bristow (Richard), Connie Goodwin (Louise).

Story: Members of the Gresham Club meet and begin discussing horror stories. One member says that he knows a story that will chill everyone to the bone. Pulling a book from the shelf, he announces that he will read to his friends "The Fall of the House of Usher" by Edgar Allan Poe. Thus begins the story of the Usher family.

While Roderick Usher's house guest, Jonathan, sleeps upstairs, Dr. Cordwell explains to Usher that the true cause of his and his sister Madeline's illness is a curse put upon the family years ago. The doctor reminds Roderick of his father's warning never to venture into the forest and marshland sough of the estate because no one who has entered there has ever come back alive. Although the land is indeed dangerous, Roderick's father actually wanted the young man to stay clear of a temple which stood just beyond the forest and marsh. The doctor produces a map made by Roderick's father and tells Roderick that they must follow the map to the temple. When the two journey into the night, Madeline, who was listening at the door, follows.

After a long trek through the marshland woods, the party arrives at the temple, at which point the doctor continues his explanation of the Usher curse. It seems that years ago Roderick's beautiful mother took a lover, whom she frequently met clandestinely in the temple. One day Roderick's father followed the lovers, rushed into the temple, tortured the lover on the rack, and beat his unfaithful wife. While on the rack, the lover cursed the Usher family, willing Roderick and Madeline to die before the age of thirty, at which time the house of Usher would fall. Roderick's father then chopped off the lover's head.

Now, Roderick's mother sits inside the temple an insane, silent hag, watching over her lover's head, which is mounted on a chamber wall at the end of a short passage. The doctor explains that the hag, who will let no one near the head, still has enough strength to tear a man apart.

Upon returning to the house, Cordwell explains to Roderick that the curse is too strong for modern medicine and that the only way to remove the curse is to destroy the head. The doctor suggests that three men return to the temple, two to restrain the hag and one to destroy the head. Reluctant to bring his friend Jonathan into the difficulties, Roderick proposes that Richard, the gardener, join them. Then Roderick asks, "What if we fail?" "The alternative," Cordwell intones, "is to take the life of Lady Madeline."

Later that night, the three men go to the temple and attempt to put Cordwell's plan into effect. Unfortunately, the hag stabs Roderick, and Richard is caught in a leg trap that lies near the preserved head. Cordwell forces Roderick out of the mission and back to the house, abandoning Richard to die at the hands of the hag.

The next day Roderick explains to a worried Madeline that Richard has been let go as gardener and will not be returning. Suspicious of foul play, Madeline learns from Louise, a servant, that Richard left the previous evening with Cordwell and Roderick

and that only the latter two returned. That night, with the aid of Louise, Madeline leaves the house and goes to the temple to help Richard. When she enters the temple, however, she sees Richard's corpse and barely escapes a knife attack by the hag. Running back toward the house, she has a vision of the severed head and faints. Upon awakening, she finds herself back at the house. While reclining, she receives what appears to be a glass of milk, as is her nightly custom.

Unknown to the occupants of the house of Usher, the hag leaves the temple, walks through the woody marshland, and enters the house through a secret passage. She then enters Madeline's bedroom, but flees through a secret passage when the young woman wakes up and screams. As Madeline cries hysterically, Cordwell admits that he was afraid the hag would some day venture to the house. Still, no one knows how she got in.

A short time later Madeline is found "dead." Roderick announces the news to Jonathan, who helps in the funeral preparations. A hammer repeatedly slams down on the final coffin nail, after which Roderick and Cordwell place Madeline in the family vault downstairs.

As time passes, Roderick becomes increasingly disturbed. His mind dwells upon the head in the temple, the ticking of the clock's pendulum, and the repetitious hammer blows upon the nails of Madeline's coffin.

Eight nights later, a rising storm wakes Jonathan. Meanwhile, Roderick also awakens in an uneasy state. As the minutes pass, Roderick thinks he hears Madeline moaning in her coffin. Moments after he has fearfully removed a pistol from a drawer, Cordwell enters. When Roderick expresses his fears, the doctor gets a pistol and announces his intentions to kill the hag. When Cordwell fails to heed Roderick's warning to desist, Roderick shoots him. At that point Jonathan enters the room and, apparently unaware of Cordwells' death, suggests that the reading of one of Roderick's favorite books might help them pass the stormy, disturbing night together.

Jonathan reads the story of Ethelred: "And Ethelred, on account of the powerfulness of the wine he had drunk, waited no longer to speak to the hermit, who, in truth, was of an obstinate and maliceful turn, but, feeling the rain upon his shoulders, and fearing the rising of the tempest, uplifted his mace, and with blows, quickly made room for his gauntleted hand. And pulling sturdily, he cracked, and ripped, and tore asunder [*sic*], that the noise of the dry and hollow-sounding wood reverberated throughout the forest." At that moment Roderick thinks he hears Madeline escaping from her coffin below. Jonathan continues. "But the good champion Ethelred, now entering within the door, was enraged and amazed to perceive no signal of the hermit; but instead, was a dragon of a scaly and prodigious demeanor, and with a fiery tongue, which sat on guard before a palace of gold, with a floor of silver. And Ethelred uplifted his club, and struck the dragon on the head with a shriek so horrible and fearsome... "Suddenly, Madeline forces open the coffin and climbs out with a shriek. Meanwhile, Roderick waits, his head in his hands, as the pendulum swings, followed by the sound of the hammer on the coffin nail—all resembling a haunting heartbeat.

Suddenly Roderick jumps to his feet, breaks the face of the clock with a large candlestick, and confesses to Jonathan his fear that they have buried Madeline alive:

> Didn't you hear it? I heard it for a long time. Yet I dared not ... I dared not speak. She's alive, I tell you. We have put her living in the tomb. I tell you I heard her first feeble movements in the hollow coffin many hours ago. Yet I dared not speak. And now tonight—Ethelred and the breaking of the hermit's door—the cry of the dragon and the clanging of the shield. Say, rather, the rending of her coffin and the breaking of the iron hinges of her prison, and the struggles within the coppered archway of the vault! Haven't I heard her footsteps on the stairs? Haven't I

heard the horrible heavy beating of her heart? Madman! I tell you she is now standing outside the door!

Fearfully, Usher opens the door and comes face to face with his sister, at whom he fires his pistol with little effect. As Roderick continues to fire shots at her, Madeline stalks him up the stairs and to the roof. As the hag watches, Roderick continues to retreat from his sister through the pouring rain until he finally falls to his death from the roof. The hag then looks down at where Roderick has fallen.

Madeline's coffin, however, is still closed and sealed. Has Roderick merely imagined his sister's return?

Suddenly, a bolt of lightning ignites the house. Jonathan flees the holocaust and stands alone in the rain, the lone witness to the fall of the house of Usher.

As we return to the Gresham Club, those who have listened to the reading of Poe's "The Fall of the House of Usher" are perplexed. Was Madeline slowly poisoned? Was she really buried alive? "I don't know," the reader says slowly. "Your guess is as good as mine."

Production and marketing: Britain's *The Fall of the House of Usher* was the third film version of Poe's famous story. The screenwriters, too loose with Poe and too untalented to produce a worthwhile alternative, adapt the main characters from Poe's tale but place them into the universe of a typical low-budget British forties horror-mystery. The illness of the Ushers is fantastically attributed to a curse, which allows the writers to drag in a torture chamber, a mad, knife-wielding hag, and a preserved severed head. Poe's identification of the Ushers and the house is missing from the film. The writers adapt Poe more faithfully during the last fifteen minutes when Madeline's escape from her coffin fairly accurately parallels Jonathan's reading of Ethelred as Poe conceived it. Otherwise, this nominal adaptation owes little to Poe's short story.

Critique: This version of Poe's "The

Fall of the House of Usher" begins as a typical entry in the late forties/early fifties low-budget horror sweepstakes. The first three-quarters of the film owes little to Poe. The last quarter, however, interpolates many of Poe's lines and plot elements from the original story, ending, of course, with the promised fall of the house itself.

Probably the most outspoken critic of the film is Rose London. In her book *Cinema of Mystery*, she writes:

> The first full feature made of the subject ... has to be seen to be discredited. It opens to a prologue, which naively declares: "Talking of horror stories, those of Edgar Allan Poe take quite a lot of beating." It commences with a wooden showing of the tale that would be laughable, if it were not so dull. Its makers are best left fallen with the fragments of the House of User into the waters of the tarn and merciful oblivion.[57]

There is clearly no explanation for why a medical doctor so easily attributes a family illness to a curse. Nor is there any character motivation explaining why the doctor did not long ago place the hag under institutional care or why he waited so long to tell Roderick of his mother's grisly situation. And why, if the destruction of the head failed, would Madeline have to be killed to break the curse? The camera's lingering on Madeline's empty glass of milk suggests she was poisoned. But if so, by whom? And why Roderick's fearful and guilty response if he is not the culprit? While I am sure the writers intended these questions to be intriguing, they are ultimately annoying. Based upon the camera's apparent role as objective recorder, the best that a careful viewer can conclude from the proceedings is that Roderick Usher is mad and that he imagines much that occurs at the end of the film. Still, the uneven nature of the exposition leaves the suspicion that the writers were simply unskillfully "playing" with the audience. Critics have, of course, suggested that Poe's tale is itself inconsistent, providing the reader with no final answers. While this is so, there is a world of difference between the

carefully constructed inconsistencies of a masterful short story writer and the clumsy inconsistencies of hack screenwriters. Possibly no other film makes that point so well as this version of "The Fall of the House of Usher."

Of course, if one wishes to see here a fairly accurate Poe adaptation, the results can only disappoint. Missing are the personality of the house itself and the identification of the house with the Ushers. Missing is Poe's theme of rationality versus irrationality (except as a hack device). Missing is the all-important point of view of the narrator, so central to any interpretation of Poe's story. In fact, as a character, Jonathan is as much a nonentity as one is likely to see. He is there apparently only because Poe's story calls for a narrator. Neither his relationship with Roderick nor the reason for his visit is ever clarified. Perhaps these are among the reasons that *Video Hound's Golden Movie Retriever 1996* calls the film a "poor adaptation of the Poe classic" and awards it only one bone.

Technically, the film has little to recommend it. While the actors are relatively competent and do not ruin the film, they also do not create characters of any particular interest. The sets of the house of Usher are so cheap that in some scenes they burn far too quickly to be believable, and the severed head, which is supposed to shock each time it appears, conveys all the realism of a Halloween mask.

While *The Fall of the House of Usher* must get a "thumbs down," some positive aspects should be acknowledged. First, the hag, who detracts from the film's success as a Poe adaptation, nicely fills the role of bogey-woman, especially if we consider the picture simply as a low-budget shocker. For example, the scene in which she, with knife raised, approaches the helpless gardener in the temple should send a slight chill down the spine of even seasoned horror-film patrons. Again, if we consider the film simply as a low-budget shocker, we must applaud its fast pace, a virtue that can often hide otherwise serious flaws from a Saturday matinee audience eager for an hour's mindless entertainment. From that perspective, I would rather watch this film again than be subjected to certain ponderous, pretentious horror films which, while technically superior in every way, fail to raise a hackle.

The Man With a Cloak (1951)
Metro-Goldwyn Mayer, U.S.A.

Credits: Directed by Fletcher Markle; cinematography by George J. Folsey; music by David Raskin; edited by Newell P. Kimlin; art direction by Cedric Gibbons and Arthur Lonergan; makeup by William Tuttle; produced by Stephen Ames; screenplay by Frank Fenton, based on a story by John Dickson Carr; music by David Raskin.

Running time: 81 minutes.

Cast: Joseph Cotten (Dupin), Barbara Stanwyck (Lorna Bounty), Louis Calhern (Charles Thevenet), Leslie Caron (Madeline Minot), Margaret Wycherly (Mrs. Flynn), Joe De Santis (Martin), Jim Backus (Flaherty), Roy Roberts (policeman), Nicholas Joy (Dr. Roland), Richard Hale (Durand), Mitchell Lewis (Walter).

Story: "In the lives of all men there are moments of mystery—for man often yearns, and sometimes chooses to wander alone and nameless. This is the tale of such a wanderer, once less known and less respected, whose real name later became immortal."

In 1848, Madeline Minot travels from France to New York City in order to visit her lover's rich grandfather, Charles Thevenet, who was formerly a marshal of France under Napoleon. Minot wants the irascible, partially paralyzed old man, who disapproves of his grandson's political activities in France, to provide financial help to her struggling fiancé. Upon arriving in the city, she befriends a mysterious man in a black cloak who calls himself Dupin. Although sporting a French name, the man is an impoverished American who drinks heavily on credit at his favorite haunt, Flaherty's Tavern.

Minot, who is invited to stay the night, soon discovers that Thevenet is drinking himself to death. She also suspects that Lorna Bounty, a former actress who now serves as housekeeper and "kept woman," and Martin the butler are attempting to hasten the old man's death. Late that night Thevenet wakens Minot and warns her to be careful because "They [Lorna and Martin] want my money." The old man also grudgingly admits that blood is thicker than water and gives the young woman a key with which to lock her door against intruders.

When the doctor leaves some medicine for Thevenet, Minot, suspecting that it is poison, takes it to Dupin and asks for help. Dupin takes Minot to a local pharmacist, who determines the contents to be sugar water. When Minot is relieved, Dupin points out there are two ways to kill a man being kept alive by medicine—by poisoning his medicine or by denying him the medicine he needs. He advises Minot to take further action on behalf of her fiancé's grandfather.

Later Dupin visits the Thevenet residence and accepts a glass of wine. When Lorna Bounty subtly romances the stranger, Martin is jealous and suspicious. At one point when he is left with the maid, he reads to her some lines from "The Raven." Minot then tells Dupin of a Halloween party, charging that Bounty and the butler are encouraging Thevenet to continue his self-destructive drinking.

At the Halloween party, Dupin observes the interactions of those in the household. When Lorna is asked to sing for Thevenet, she tells Dupin, "He wants me to sing for him, but I'm going to sing for you." Shortly after Lorna's song, the old man orders everyone out of the room so he and Dupin can talk. Dupin warns Thevenet that he is in danger of being murdered by those around him. That evening, much to the dismay of the plotters, Thevenet summons Durand, his lawyer, to appear at the house in the morning. Realizing that Dupin is having an influence on Thevenet's actions, Bounty tells him, "I believe I have underestimated you," to which Dupin replies, "So has my generation." Bounty then tries to buy off Dupin while simultaneously sweet-talking him.

When Dupin leaves the house, Martin follows him with nefarious intentions. Dupin, however, realizes he is being followed and takes up with a policeman on the beat.

The next morning Thevenet dictates a will leaving all of his money to his grandson and prepares to commit suicide. The lawyer, however, reenters the room, sees the poisoned glass of liquor, and unwittingly drinks it before Thevenet, stricken by a stroke, is able to stop him. Durand immediately dies, and Dupin goes to the paralyzed Thevenet's bedside. The old man makes some eye movements regarding the whereabouts of the new will, but Dupin is unable immediately to make sense of the directions.

Soon after, Thevenet dies. Dupin, suspecting foul play, takes the death glass to the pharmacist to have the residue analyzed. "This is the first time," Dupin quips, "that I've ever been interested in an empty glass." Upon learning that the contents of the glass contained arsenic, Dupin reasons out the actual order of events that occurred.

Bounty finds Dupin at Flaherty's and asks him to find the new will, after which the two of them will leave with the money. After implying to Flaherty, the owner of his favorite tavern, that he is going to the Thevenet residence and may never return alive, Dupin sets off to locate the hidden will. Once inside the dead man's house, he pours himself a drink and announces to Bounty and Martin that he can indeed discover the location

of the new will. Going to the bedroom, he recalls Thevenet's eye movements and discovers the will in the fireplace. As he tries to run from the house with the will, Martin attacks him. Before the big butler can inflict damage, the policeman, tipped off by Flaherty, arrives on the scene and restores order. Dupin then reads the will aloud, verifying that Thevenet's grandson is to inherit the money, while Martin and Bounty are to inherit the house—as long as they both agree to live together in it.

When Minot goes to Flaherty's to thank Dupin, the owner explains that the mysterious stranger has left. All that remains is a piece of paper containing scribbled lines from the poem "Annabel Lee." On the reverse side is an IOU for $7.80, signed by Edgar Allan Poe.

Production and marketing: *The Man with a Cloak* was a major MGM production. Fletcher Markle (1921–1991), a Canadian director, was working in America when he got the call to direct this slow but satisfying mystery. He would later direct Walt Disney's *The Incredible Journey* (1963).

The film's star, Joseph Cotten (1905–1994), began his film career in Orson Welles's *Citizen Kane* (1941), *The Magnificent Ambersons* (1942), and *Journey into Fear* (1942). Before assuming the role of Edgar Allan Poe, he also worked in such critically acclaimed pictures as *I'll Be Seeing You* (1945), *Portrait of Jennie* (1948), and *The Third Man* (1949). Later, his vita would include such science fiction/horror films as *From the Earth to the Moon* (1958), *Hush, Hush, Sweet Charlotte* (1964), *Latitude Zero* (1969), *The Abominable Dr. Phibes* (1971), *Lady Frankenstein* (1971), and *Baron Blood* (1971). In *The Man with a Cloak*, Cotten gives an engaging performance as Edgar Allan Poe, a hard drinker with dignity and a strong sense of justice. He has the lion's hare of the film's best lines, all of which he effectively delivers with bittersweet humor and irony.

Barbara Stanwyck (1907–1990) was a major Hollywood star at the time she acquired the role of Lorna Bounty in *The Man with a Cloak.* Among her most memorable pictures were *Miracle Woman* (1931), *Night Nurse* (1931), *The Bitter Tea of General Yen* (1933), *Baby Face* (1933), *Annie Oakley* (1935), *Stella Dallas* (1937), *The Lady Eve* (1941), *Meet John Doe* (1941), *Ball of Fire* (1941), *Double Indemnity* (1944), *The Strange Love of Martha Ivers* (1946), *Sorry, Wrong Number* (1948), and *The Furies* (1950). Later, besides starring in such horror films as *The Night Walker* (1965), she would distinguish herself as the matriarch of the successful television series *The Big Valley* (1965–1968).

Louis Calhern (1895–1956) was a distinguished character actor at the time he was awarded the meaty role of Charles Thevenet. He had recently won acclaim for three of his best performances in *Annie Get Your Gun* (1950, as Buffalo Bill), *The Asphalt Jungle* (1950), and *The Magnificent Yankee* (1950).

Leslie Caron (1931–) had just turned in a bravura performance dancing to the rousing music of George Gershwin in her first American film, *An American in Paris* (1951). Fresh in an appreciative audience's mind, she landed the role of the French Miss Minot in *The Man with a Cloak.* Caron would later turn in fine performances in such memorable pictures as *Gigi* (1958), *Fanny* (1961), and *The L-Shaped Room* (1962).

Screenwriter John Dickson Carr (1905–1977) was one of America's most well-known writers of detective fiction, but how good was his own detective work in producing this Edgar Allan Poe scenario? Living in Fordham, New York, Poe began in 1848 to work on his cosmological treatise *Eureka* and issued a prospectus for *The Stylus,* his proposed literary magazine. Letters place Poe for a brief period in New York City (the setting of the film) in January. On February 3, he delivered a lecture titled "The Universe" in New York City. The lecture, a three-hour condensation of *Eureka,* drew a small but appreciative audience. Poe clearly returned to Fordham in February. Probably Poe returned to New York in late April, when George P. Putnam was considering publication of *Eureka.* Poe was in New York in late May to

sign the contract, and he returned there several times later in the year. Carr, therefore, probably used the evidence of Poe's stay in New York during the contract negotiations over *Eureka* as the basis for his fictional tale. Carr also cleverly has Minot refer to Baudelaire, the man who would later play a major role in establishing Poe's literary reputation in France.

Critique: When the film opened in New York, the *Times* reported: "It is obvious from the opening shot ... that the producers were endeavoring to fashion a brooding, suspenseful story about a mysterious stranger who was destined for fame. But the [film] ... is merely leisurely fare no more intriguing than the routine melodrama despite a stellar cast and some stately dialogue."[58]

It is true that Dupin's true identity is strongly suggested in several scenes. First of all, a raven flits about Thevenet's rooms. Second, Dupin quotes lines from "The Raven" to Thevenet's maid. Third, during a conversation between Thevenet and Dupin, the phrase "death in life" is uttered. Poe's short story "The Oval Portrait" was originally titled "Life in Death."

While the film's pace is slow, it is not so slow as to render affairs boring. Indeed, the performers all rise to the occasion and engage audience interest throughout. Cotten, Caron, and Calhern deserve special commendation. Blessed with most of the good lines, Cotten is a mysterious and believable world-weary character, though not necessarily a faithful embodiment of the actual Poe. From all accounts, had Poe drunk as much and as often as Cotten does in the film, his low tolerance for alcohol would have rendered him incapable of being much help to Caron at all. Speaking of Caron, the *New York Times* was correct in calling her "pert and fetching in the billowing skirts of the period as she was in the ballet costumes of 'An American in Paris.'"[59] Calhern has a number of flamboyant scenes as the recalcitrant old Thevenet, and Stanwyck, a fine actress of whom the screenplay requires only a stereotypical scheming-woman performance, is all that one could wish. Unfortunately, the film requires Stanwyck to sing. While she can carry a tune, she is not a singer.

Leonard Maltin awards the film 2½ stars, calling it an "intriguing little mystery … Not bad, with spooky David Raskin score, but having Barbara sing was a mistake."

The Man with a Cloak is a well-written, well-acted mystery drama. Although doing little to bring a realistic Poe to the screen, as a fifties period-mystery, it delivers 81 minutes of better-than-average intrigue.

Some sources suggest that one year after the release of *The Man with a Cloak*, Joseph Losey directed a Poe-inspired film called *The Assignation*. While I include the film in the appendix of this book, I am unconvinced that it is a Poe adaptation.

The Tell-Tale Heart (1953)
Columbia, U.S.A.

Credits: Directed by Ted Parmelee; production manager—Herbert Klynn; story adaptation by Bill Scott and Fred Grable, based upon "The Tell-Tale Heart" by Edgar Allan Poe; color by Technicolor; cinematography by Jack Eckes; animation by Pat Matthews; music by Boris Kremenliev.

Running time: 7 minutes.

Cast: James Mason (narrator).

Story: "True, I'm nervous. Very, very dreadfully nervous, but why will you say that I am mad? See how calmly and precisely I can tell the story to you."

The narrator prepares to kill an old man who lives in the same boardinghouse as he. He does not want to kill the old man for his gold, if there even is any gold. No, he wants to kill the old man because of his eye: "staring, milky-white film, the eye everywhere—in everything."

The narrator is never so kind to the old man as immediately after planning to kill him. He looks after the old man every minute of every day. But night after night, the narrator opens the old man's door. The eye is always closed. For seven days, he waits. "What madman could wait so patiently, so long?" On the eighth night, the narrator again opens the door to the old man's room. With a start, the old man awakens. In the darkness and stillness, both the predator and his victim wait. Then the narrator hears, dull and muffled, the beating of the old man's heart. The old man knows. Louder and still louder grows the beating of the heart. The

narrator quickly dispatches the old man, but not before the victim emits a scream. Soon, however, the heart is still, the eye dead. The narrator is free.

The murderer places the corpse below the floorboards of the old man's bedroom. Later there is a knock at the door. The police are investigating the report of a scream. The narrator claims that the scream was his own, the result of a nightmare. After looking about the premises, the police are satisfied and are about to leave. The narrator, however, as though compelled by perversity, invites the police to stay and warm themselves with a cup of tea. Then what appears to be the dripping of water from a faucet becomes for the murderer the repetitious beating of the old man's heart. As the "heartbeat" becomes louder, the murderer suspects that the seemingly indifferent police are cruelly playing with him. Finally he screams in anger for them to tear up the planks in the floor. "Yes, yes, you devils, I did it. It is there, under the floor. Stop it. It is the beating of *his* hideous heart."

From a locked cell, the narrator states: "True, I am nervous—very, very dreadfully nervous. But why will you say that I am mad?"

Production and marketing: *The Tell-Tale Heart*, a seven-minute animated short released by Columbia, was the work of United Productions of America (UPA), the Academy Award–winning creators of *Gerald McBoing-Boing*. Other well-known UPA animated productions included *Nearsighted*

Poster art for the animated version of Poe's *The Tell-Tale Heart* (1953).

Mr. Magoo, *Madeline*, and *The Unicorn in the Garden*, Although most of UPA's previous animated ventures were of the light-hearted variety, *The Tell-Tale Heart* most definitely was not. On the contrary, it was the first animated short feature to tell a short story of tense dramatic impact. Although the screenwriters trim Poe's tale, Poe's words overwhelmingly compose the narration.

Reportedly, James Mason (1909–1984) was on a sight-seeing tour of UPA's cartoon studios in Hollywood when he saw the preliminary sketches for *The Tell-Tale Heart* and made an on-the-spot pitch for the job of narration. Mason, of course, had already established himself as a screen villain and as a top-flight actor in such films as *I Met a Murderer* (1939), *The Night Has Eyes* (1942), *The Man in Grey* (1943), *The Desert Fox* (1951), and *Julius Caesar* (1953). He would go on to play Captain Nemo in Walt Disney's *20,000 Leagues Under the Sea* (1954), to distinguish himself opposite Judy Garland in *A Star is Born* (1954), and to compile a most impressive lifetime film vita that would include, almost last but clearly not least, one of the screen's best portrayals of Conan Doyle's Dr. Watson in *Murder by Decree* (1979).

Columbia produced a four-page pressbook for their new animated horror short. Receiving the most hype, of course, were James Mason and Edgar Allan Poe. "Put James Mason Name to Work!" the pressbook urged. "There's a big star in 'The Tell-Tale Heart!' James Mason, who delivers the narration in one of the best jobs of his career, is a marquee name. Put him in your brightest lights!" The pressbook reminded exhibitors that "Poe's works are perennially best-selling classics. Approach both your book stores and libraries for tie-up displays and promotions." One angle was the tired pitch exhorting exhibitors to interest schools in the Poe connection: "Invite the school children of your town by the classful to see 'The Tell-Tale Heart.' This Edgar Allan Poe classic is right down the alley for every English class from the first grade to the top! It's prime meat for all the art classes from clas-

sic to Picassic! It's in the groove for music students from bop to Bach! Invite school officials to private screenings." One must agree that this particular Poe adaptation recommended itself to such promotion better than any of its predecessors.

While Columbia obviously took its short subject seriously, its publicists could not avoid the usual poor-taste hijinks commonly associated with pressbook hoopla, of which the following is a typical example:

> Dramatize the blood drive in your town by putting big glass hearts in all public buildings, terminals, stores etc., including your lobby, representing the current blood collection quota. Pour in red liquid daily representing each day's blood collection. Make the slogan 'Give a Heartful!' and call the receptacles 'Tell Tale Hearts' because they keep record of the collection. See that the blood agency sends daily pictures to the papers and also try to get the papers to run a front-page "Tell Tale Heart" drawing, marking the daily gains in the blood drive.

Critique: While short subjects usually receive little critical attention, *The Tell-Tale Heart* was unique and received four-page spreads in both *Life* and *Time*. The former pronounced the film "Good entertainment and a leading contender for the Oscar as best movie short of the year," and the latter opined that The *Tell-Tale Heart* proves "the animated film can be used for drama and melodrama as well as humor."

The film is indeed engrossing. The expressionistic art aptly represents the world as seen through the eyes of a madman. The musical score is appropriately eerie, and Mason's narration is on the mark, especially his anguished cries at the film's finale. In conclusion, there is probably no seven minutes in film history so Poe-esque as this version of "The Tell-Tale Heart."

In 1955, Dynamic Films produced *The Cask of Amontillado*, a black and white fifteen-minute version of Poe's tale of the same name. Starring Monty Woolley, the short subject tells the story of how Montressor lures Fortunado to his death in a walled-in wine cellar.

Phantom of the Rue Morgue (1954)
Warner Brothers, U.S.A.

Credits: Directed by Roy Del Ruth; produced by Henry Blanke; screenplay by Harold Medford and James R. Webb, based upon "The Murders in the Rue Morgue" by Edgar Allan Poe; cinematography by J. Peverell Marley; art direction by Bertram Tuttle; sound by Stanley Jones; music by David Buttolph; makeup by Gordon Bau.

Running time: 84 minutes.

Cast: Karl Malden (Dr. Marais), Claude Dauphin (Inspector Bonnard), Patricia Medina (Jeannette Rovere), Steve Forrest (Prof. Paul Dupin), Allyn McLerie (Yvonne), Veola Vonn (Arlette), Dolores Dorn (Camille), Anthony Caruso (Jacques), Merv Griffin (Georges Brevert), Paul Richards (René), Rolphe Sedan (LeBon), Erin O'Brien-Moore (wardrobe woman), the Flying Zacchinis (specialty).

Story: Paris at the turn of the century. As an ominous shadow hulks above a Paris rooftop, a woman runs into the street screaming "Help! Police! Murder! Murder! Murder in the Rue Morgue!"

Later at the prefecture of police, Inspector Bonnard judges that the recent murder of a young woman was a crime of passion. Unfortunately, he is able to learn little from a scarf with a Maltese sailor's insignia, the only clue discovered in the apartment of death.

The scene shifts to a dance hall, where René and Yvonne, his beautiful dancing partner and assistant, are arguing even as they perform. René is jealous of Yvonne's new unknown suitor, and she taunts him with the news that her new beau is not just another poor student, but rather a man of some stature. René is further infuriated by the new bell bracelet, obviously a gift from this new admirer, that jingles on Yvonne's wrist. After completing a dance number, René and Yvonne launch into a knife-throwing act. At one point, René, with anger in his eyes, throws a knife so close as to nick

Yvonne's arm. In the audience are the handsome young Professor Paul Dupin, his fiancée Jeannette Rovere, and several students and their dates.

After the performance, Yvonne argues further with René and leaves the dance hall. Upon arriving at her upper-floor apartment, she closes the window and opens her closet door. As her eyes focus upon what is within, she begins to scream hysterically. A crowd quickly gathers below, and a resident named Albert, still in his night-clothes, races upstairs and into the room. Within moments, Albert is tossed through the window like a ragdoll to the street below. By the time the police arrive, the terrible sounds from the apartment have ceased. Entering the room, the officer discovers Yvonne's broken corpse amid the shambles. The phantom killer has disappeared, and Yvonne has become the latest victim in a series of murders. Outside, onlookers spot a hulking shadow as it ambles along the rooftop. Shortly afterward, it disappears down a manhole on a deserted street. One witness later claims that he heard the killer speaking German.

Inspector Bonnard's suspicions immediately fall upon René, whom he reluctantly releases when the entertainer produces an alibi. After René's release, Bonnard ponders the bell bracelet taken from Yvonne's body. Once locked, the gift, which obviously symbolized undying love, can only be opened with a file.

At the university, after Bonnard has grilled several students without success, Dupin suggests that the killer is "a schizophrenic, a split personality governed by pronounced sadistic tendencies." As a result of his studies in psychology, he further explains to Bonnard that while a blind urge to kill seems to run throughout the animal kingdom, most people learn through the civilizing influence of society to control the urge. The conversation is interrupted when

Poster art for *Phantom of the Rue Morgue* (1954) questions whether a human could have committed such grisly crimes.

a rude, one-eyed sailor with a Maltese insignia tattooed on his arm delivers an animal in a cage to the laboratory. When the sailor leaves, Dr. Marais, the middle-aged psychologist and director of the Paris zoo, enters the lab. Picking up on Dupin's theories, Marais explains to Bonnard that the killer instinct lies dormant in most human beings. But for some, acting under the influence of sudden hatred, passion, or frustration, the urge to kill reasserts itself with deadly results.

Paris is soon shocked again when artist Arlette's model is brutally murdered in the same fashion as the other young women. Again, a bell bracelet is found upon the corpse's wrist. Contradicting a report made after the first murder, one onlooker insists that the killer spoke Italian. When a brooch once purchased by Dupin is found at the scene of the crime, the young psychologist becomes Bonnard's prime suspect. In his defense, Dupin explains that the brooch, intended for Jeannette, was earlier stolen from his apartment. Jeannette suggests that the real killer must have left the brooch at the scene to falsely implicate Dupin.

Time passes without any arrests. Then one night a young woman in Dupin's boardinghouse begins to scream. Dupin, who is shaving, sees the shadow on the rooftop and gives chase, dropping his razor in the process. As the killer escapes, the police arrest Dupin, arguing that the razor he dropped was probably the murder weapon used to mutilate his victims.

Going to the apartment from which came the screams, Bonnard is unable to find a body. He is puzzled when he discovers that the door and the windows are all locked. How did the attacker leave the scene, and where was the victim? The inspector soon discovers the body of the murdered girl jammed feet first up the chimney, but there is still no indication of how the killer escaped. Dupin then discovers a small catch on one of the windows and demonstrates that the killer could have opened the window by pushing it. Unfortunately, Bonnard

takes Dupin's discovery as further proof of the hapless psychologist's guilt. When an onlooker identifies Spanish, rather than German or Italian, as the language spoken by the killer, the inspector is quite confused. He soon triumphantly produces Dupin's university transcript, however, which reveals Dupin as a student of all three languages.

Because of the great arm reach and exceptional strength required of the killer, Dupin suggests to Bonnard that the killer must have been an ape, to which the inspector sarcastically replies that before killing women, apes do not buy them bracelets. While Paul remains in police custody, Dr. Marais keeps his promise to look after Jeannette.

Meanwhile, Jacques, the Maltese sailor, is drinking in a bar when another sailor enters and begins talking about how they once shipped out of Malta together and how strange it was that Jacques had a pet ape that clawed his eye out. Realizing that the sailor's tales will soon implicate him in the Rue Morgue murders, Jacques lures his jovial pal outside, kills him, and dumps the body into the river.

At his house on the zoo grounds, Dr. Marais advises Jeannette to stop thinking about Paul. He then confides to her that his young wife committed suicide five years ago and that her death was what inspired him to study psychology. He also explains that the bars on the windows of his former wife's room were a result of her fear of the zoo animals. He then takes Jeannette into the basement and shows her his caged ape, Sultan, who is being tended by Jacques. The ape immediately takes a liking to the girl.

After Jeannette goes upstairs, a conversation between Jacques and Marais reveals that the ape earlier escaped from the sailor and committed the first Rue Morgue murder. Marais convinced Jacques not to go to the police and trained the creature to kill several of his intended wives when they proved unfaithful.

Returning upstairs to Jeannette, Marais grabs the startled woman, forces a kiss upon her, and confesses that he has fallen in love with her. Repulsed, Jeannette screams and suddenly realizes that the bars on the window were to keep Marais's wife inside, not to keep the animals out. Marais is angry, but he quickly softens and tells Jeannette that Paul had asked him to buy a particular bell bracelet for her. Because she believes it comes from Paul, Jeannette accepts the gift, only to discover that once it is locked on her wrist, she cannot get it off. Marais then locks her in the room, saying: "I have never killed anyone. My foolish man-made conscience is as clean as my hands."

Going downstairs, Marais finds that the ape has killed Jacques and escaped. In the now-darkened city streets, he hunts for the creature, finally tracking it to a clothing store, where it has murdered a seamstress who was working late. This time, however, witnesses see the ape, and a lamplighter reports observing a well-dressed man escape with the monster into a manhole.

At police headquarters, Dupin suggests that only a man knowledgeable of conditioned reflexes could use bracelets with bells to control an ape. Handing the confession he has been asked to sign back to Bonnard, he demands that the inspector give it to Dr. Marais instead, explaining that Marais has employed classical conditioning to create a killer ape. Because of the witnesses, Bonnard believes Dupin and orders the police to Marais's house on the zoo grounds.

Having already returned, Marais sends Sultan up the side of he house and into the room wherein Jeannette is held prisoner. The ape grabs the terrified woman and, instead of killing her as Marais commands, carries her out into the night.

When Dupin, Bonnard, and the police arrive, Marais frees a lion to create confusion. The police gun down the lion, however, and take Marais into custody. Sultan leaps into a tree with Jeannette and is fired upon by officers. When the ape drops Jeannette, the police break her fall. The simian then leaps from the tree onto Marais, quickly killing the surprised psychologist. At that

point, police open fire on Sultan, killing the creature with a hail of gunfire.

At Bonnard's office, Paul and Jeannette are reunited, and the inspector closes the file on the murders in the Rue Morgue.

Production and marketing: In 1953, Warner Brothers released *House of Wax*, starring Vincent Price, history's first 3-D horror film. It was a great success, as was Universal's 3-D horror/science fiction outing of the same year, *It Came from Outer Space*. Hoping to repeat the success of *House of Wax*, the studio quickly produced a second 3-D horror picture, *Phantom of the Rue Morgue*. Choosing Poe's tale for their subject, screenwriters Medford and Webb incorporated a bit more of Poe's original story than did Universal's 1932 version. As in Poe, the ape escapes from its owner, a Maltese sailor, and commits a horrendous crime. In the Medford and Webb version, however, the ape and its owner come under the influence of a nefarious psychologist who uses the murderous ape for his own purposes.

Having been a struggling medical student in the 1932 *Murders in the Rue Morgue* and a police pathologist in the 1942 *The Mystery of Marie Roget*, Dupin is this time a psychologist. In none of the films was he recognizably close to Poe's brilliant, eccentric Dupin.

Medford and Webb follow the 1932 version of "Murders" in supplying a love interest and in making the real villain a psychopathic scientist of sorts. Of course, the writers include the famous corpse in the chimney scene without which no version of Poe's original story would be complete. Concerning the experience of hanging upside down in the chimney, actress Dolores Dorn quipped, "I've heard girls say they'd stand on their heads for a chance in the movies, but I'm the first girl I've known who's done it."

The film's star, Karl Malden (1913–), had won an Academy Award for his performance in Elia Kazan's hard-hitting *A Streetcar Named Desire* (1952). In the same year as *Phantom*'s release, he would distinguish himself in *On the Waterfront*, and a year later he would appear in the then shocking *Baby Doll*, both directed by Elia Kazan, and, like *A Streetcar Named Desire*, based upon work by Tennessee Williams. Malden would later become familiar to television audiences as the costar of the popular series "The Streets of San Francisco" (1972–1976).

Frenchman Claude Dauphin had been in pictures since 1930. Two seasons before undertaking the role of Inspector Bonnard, he starred on the New York stage in *The Happy Time*, in a role whose film version went to his compatriot Charles Boyer.

The British-born leading lady, Patricia Medina (1921–), was in her second decade as a film actress when she landed the role of Jeannette in *Phantom*. Although her career would consist only of routine films, her face would become a familiar sight to patrons of international cinema.

Steve Forrest (1924–), the brother of actor Dana Andrews, would appear with Ronald Reagan in *Prisoner of War* (1954) and in *The Living Idol* (1957), another excursion into psychotronic cinema. Forrest would also show up frequently on television.

Roy Del Ruth (1895–1961) had distinguished himself as the director of the first film version of *The Maltese Falcon* (1931), *Blessed Event* (1932), *Lady Killer* (1933), *Thanks a Million* (1935), *Topper Returns* (1941), and many others. Toward the end of his career he returned to the horror genre to direct Lon Chaney, Jr., in *The Alligator People*. Unfortunately, his direction of *Phantom* would garner little praise.

Interestingly, post-1960 reviews of the film almost always call attention to two facts. First, Charles Gemora, the man in the ape suit in *Murders in the Rue Morgue* (1932), dons the ape costume again in *Phantom*. Second, Merv Griffin, who would become a popular late-night talk show host in the sixties, shows up briefly as a student host in this fifties horror film. One review actually says that spotting Griffin in a small role is one of the few positive experiences the film offers.

For their follow-up 3-D extravaganza,

Warner Brothers issued a large pressbook emphasizing the lurid aspects of their tale. "IT MAULS ... IT RIPS ... IT VANISHES!" cried the ads. "A MAMMOTH MONSTROUS MAN-OR-CREATURE RISING OUT OF THE DEPTHS BENEATH THE CITY!" Rather than give away the fact that the killer is an ape, the ads show a half-human, half-ape creature wearing human clothing. As for Poe, one pressbook ad exploits the film's origin:

> It was in 1843 that Edgar Allan Poe's story, "Murders in the Rue Morgue," was first published in Philadelphia. In 1954, 111 years later, the Poe classic was made into a movie. [They apparently forgot about the 1932 version.] ... Known as the father of the modern mystery-murder story, Edgar Allan Poe and his works have provided much of the inspiration for today's mystery story writers. School children throughout the nation are familiar with the spine-tingling tales of terror which include "The Tell-Tale Heart," "The Gold Bug," "The Pit and the Pendulum," "The Red Death," and many others. Scholars, on the other hand, agree that Poe's technique of constructing a suspenseful and terrifying tale still stands as the master guide for all such stories.

When *Phantom* failed to distinguish itself critically or financially, Warner Brothers scrapped any plans for future 3-D horror films, though Universal would give the gimmick a successful whirl with *Creature from the Black Lagoon*, also in 1954.

Critique: When *Phantom of the Rue Morgue* opened in New York in late March of 1954, the *New York Times* was predictably unimpressed. Reminding readers of the 1932 version which featured Bela Lugosi, the *Times* judged *Phantom* to be "proof that time has not worked wonders." After pronouncing Malden "properly neurotic as the deranged scientist, despite the technical dialogue that is his lot," and after judging that "Mr. Dauphin, Miss Medina, and Steve Forrest behave as well as they can under the circumstances," the review concludes that "Their Phantom is less a menace than a bore."[60]

Unlike its 1932 predecessor, *Phantom* has not seen an improvement in its reputation over the years. In *A Pictorial History of Horror Movies*, Denis Gifford regrets that "This reworking of the Poe piece cast Karl Malden, a method man, as Dr. Marais the Darwinian, but although he rolled his stereoscopic eyeballs he was no Lugosi."[61] In *Cinema of Mystery*, Rose London calls the film "messy and simplistic," concluding that "The threat of bestial rape was exaggerated at the expense of Poe's prose and the result was predictably dull."[62] In *The Psychotronic Encyclopedia of Film*, Michael Weldon pronounces the film "pretty pathetic." Leonard Maltin assigns *Phantom* a two-star rating, judging that it "suffers from Malden's hamminess in the Lugosi role, plus little real atmosphere." Most recently, *The Overlook Film Encyclopedia: Horror* finds Malden "overacting like mad in the Lugosi role." The *Encyclopedia* concludes that "The abysmal dialogue is full of psychoanalytical bilge, the murders are repetitive in the extreme (the best scene, paradoxically, is one in which the ape attacks a window-display dummy), and the 3-D effects are tamely restricted to the usual hail of hurled knives and clutching paws."

In my view, *Phantom*'s primary fault is its lack of atmosphere. From scenes of bright Parisian gaiety, we cut to darkened scenes of shadows and brutal murder. Then come long talky stretches, which, while sometimes engaging, do little to sustain an atmosphere. It is largely the atmosphere of Robert Florey's sets and the presence of Bela Lugosi that give the 1932 version whatever interest it has. Those strengths, though, are enough to elevate it slightly above *Phantom* in quality.

The murders themselves are most effective. Although the killer is off-camera throughout most of the film, the terror it elicits from its victims, the wild, animalistic fury with which it kills, and the complete destruction it leaves in its wake should raise the hackles of all but the most jaded audience. Gemora is effective in the ape suit, but the horror he creates is not as great as that merely suggested by the off-camera killer of earlier scenes.

The cast is clearly adequate to the task; Malden does what he can with the role, but he is no Bela Lugosi. Lugosi's overacting could save an otherwise tedious picture, but Malden's cannot. Still, the latter does a credible job. Particularly effective, however, is Claude Dauphin, whose sometimes thoughtful, sometimes humorous, and often sarcastic delivery makes Inspector Bonnard the most likable character in the picture. Also of note is unheralded Allyn McLerie, who gives a brief but saucy performance as the ape's second victim.

The aging director, Roy Del Ruth, then nearing the end of his career, proved himself still sturdy at the helm. Unfortunately, he seems to have been more concerned with directing a film with good 3-D effects than with making a film that works equally well on all levels.

Finally, though the writers of *Phantom* borrow a few more elements of Poe's tale than did their 1932 counterparts, they fail to lay the foundation for a superior adaptation in the process.

Manfish (1956)
United Artist, U.S.A.

Credits: Directed and produced by W. Lee Wilder; story by Myles Wilder, based upon "The Gold Bug" and "The Tell-Tale Heart" by Edgar Allan Poe; screenplay by Joel Murcott; music by Albert Elms; cinematography by S. Wellborn.

Tessa Prendergast, Victor Jory, John Bromfield, and Lon Chaney, Jr., struggle in *Manfish* (1956).

Running time: 75 minutes.

Cast: John Bromfield (Brannigan), Lon Chaney, Jr. ("Swede"), Victor Jory ("Professor"), Barbara Nichols (Mimi), Tessa Prendegast (Alita), Eric Coverly (Chavez), Vincent Chang (Domingo), Theodore Purcell ("Big Boy"), Vera Johns (Bianco), Arnold Shanks (Aleppo), Clyde Hoyte (Calypso).

Story: A Scotland Yard official arrives in Jamaica to seek extradition of a criminal known as "the Professor." The Jamaican police chief says that extradition is impossible and explains the latest events.

When Bianco threatens to confiscate the *Manfish*, Captain Brannigan's turtle boat, Brannigan's big, good-hearted but slightly retarded "first mate," Swede, hunts for the captain. He finds Brannigan in a poker game and explains that he will lose the *Manfish* unless he pays the 300 pounds he owes Bianco. Brannigan, who is winning at cards, brushes off Swede and goes on playing.

That night Brannigan confesses to Swede that he ended up losing at cards and doesn't even have enough money to buy a drink. He then begins a flirtation with a native girl named Alita, whom everyone considers the girl of the Professor, an older, bearded mystery man from another island. A native warns Brannigan to leave Alita alone because the Professor is "a little crazy." The Professor soon returns and starts trouble with Brannigan, but before a fight can erupt, the Professor is told to return to his own island. Before going, however, he vows that someday he will kill Brannigan.

The next day Brannigan, Swede, and two swimmers are turtle fishing when Swede spots a shark. Brannigan dives in and saves the swimmers from the killer fish, but Swede makes the mistake of allowing the swimmers back on board before getting the captain's permission. When Brannigan rather unfairly upbraids Swede, the big dimwit apologizes but then explodes when Brannigan spits on the deck of the *Manfish*. Even though Brannigan did win the *Manfish* in a poker game, Swede considers the boat the only woman he has.

Suddenly the swimmers report finding a skeleton clutching a bottle. Brannigan dives in and brings up the bottle, which contains half of a coded map and a skull-and-crossbones ring similar to the one he saw on the Professor's hand the previous night.

Later Brannigan taunts Swede for being unable to read and subsequently tries to get his girl Mimi to translate the French code. Although she can translate the words, they make no sense because they represent only half the message. Brannigan returns to the boat, wakes Swede, and sets sail for the Professor's island.

After arriving at the island, Brannigan resumes his flirtation with the willing Alita but is interrupted by the arrival of the Professor. It seems that the Professor has been staying in the Caribbean for five years for no apparent reason. Brannigan suggests that the Professor has been staying there in order to find the half of the coded map now owned by Brannigan.

Equipped with an aqua lung, Brannigan dives underwater to search the coral cove. Another swimmer appears and fires a deadly compressed air spear at him, barely missing. A fight ensues underwater. When the two men surface, Brannigan finds his adversary to be the Professor. On shore, Alita hands Brannigan the other half of the map belonging to the Professor. As he is the only one who can decode the map, the Professor and Brannigan are forced to be partners, and both of them set out in the *Manfish* to dig up the treasure of the pirate Lafitte.

Soon the Professor has translated the French: "The dead man stares from the rocky peak. He guards the treasure that live men seek. Who finds the two rings will hold the key. One death head points, but the other can see. And a wise man walks backwards until he has learned the beginning and the end of the trail that has been joined." The

Professor calls Brannigan stupid for being unable to understand the meaning. The Professor then explains that one must turn the map upside-down to find the treasure, which is on the island of Hispaniola. Realizing that Brannigan will kill him if he reveals enough for the captain to find the treasure alone, the Professor burns both halves of the map, telling the enraged Brannigan that, as the location of the treasure is now only in his mind, that will be his "life insurance."

The *Manfish* anchors off Hispaniola, and Brannigan, the Professor, and Swede row ashore, trek through the wilderness to the designated spot, and unearth an ancient treasure chest full of gold and jewels. Brannigan now conspires to kill the Professor but is thwarted when the Professor produces another treasure map from the chest which will lead them to Lafitte's second treasure. As the Professor is the only one who can decode the map, he and Brannigan are again forced to remain partners.

While Swede is in town to sell some of the gold to finance their second trip, the Professor kills Brannigan with a compressed air spear, gleeful that he has finally delivered on his threat. The Professor then experiences great anxiety as events conspire to delay his disposal of the corpse. Finally, he is able to weight the body with compressed air tanks and throw it overboard.

Soon, however, bubbles begin to rise to the surface from an opened valve. When Swede returns, the Professor tries to get him to move the boat away from the maddening bubbles, but Swede refuses to leave without Brannigan. The police arrive with Bianco to claim the ship on which £300 is due him. Suddenly Swede sees Brannigan's cap floating on the water amidst the tell-tale bubbles. He dives into the water and finds Brannigan's body.

The police arrest the Professor for the crime. As Swede, who now owns the *Manfish*, sails out to sea, the propeller cuts the rope to which the Professor had attached the treasure chest under water and it sinks to the bottom.

Production and marketing: Although set in Jamaica rather than South Carolina, the film retains a number of basic elements from Poe's story "The Gold Bug," in which two white men, one eccentric, and a Negro servant decode a Captain Kidd map in order to find hidden treasure. Based loosely on the character of Jupider, the Negro servant, Swede has a below-average IQ, allowing Lon Chaney, Jr., to give a performance similar to the acclaimed one he gave as Lennie in *Of Mice and Men* (1939). While referred to in the film as dumb, illiterate, and brainless, he nevertheless possesses "a stubborn streak of decency." In fact, though playing a character slow of mind, Chaney relies heavily on facial expression to create the only sympathetic role in the whole scenario. Jory's horrified reaction to the rising bubbles from the submerged oxygen cylinder is suggested by a similar reaction from the narrator of Poe's "The Tell-Tale Heart," when he hears the beating heart of his murder victim, whom he has buried beneath the floor. Although not entirely successful, Jory's almost immediate plunge into madness is given some credibility by the natives' suggestion that he is "a little crazy." Another element of Poe's "The Gold Bug" woven into the film is the discovery of a skull from whose eye treasure hunters must drop a line in order to get a bead on the booty.

United Artists hyped the film with a medium-sized ad campaign relying heavily on the adventure angle. "Battling Aqua-Lung Adventure!" the posters screamed. "Man against man ... Man against beast ... in the deep of the mysterious Caribbean." In order to mislead potential patrons, one poster suggested a horror element: "Manfish —Floating Monster of the Sea!" Of course, one of the ads hyped the Poe connection:

A modern adaptation of two of the immortal Edgar Allan Poe's greatest works, "The Gold Bug" and "The Tell-Tale Heart," this double barreled action shocker is charged with all the suspense, eeriness and fascinating horror which are the legendary trademarks of that master story teller. While the terrifying deeds of derring-do have been heightened and intensified by such modern day devices as compressed air spear guns and aqua lungs, basically the characters and situations are the same as those penned by the great master.

Obviously, while there are some similarities between Poe's tales and the film, the characters and situations of the latter are not basically the same as those penned by Poe.

While Poe is a respectable foundation upon which to base the selling of a film, the hype-meisters for *Manfish* also engaged in typical lowbrow hoopla. For example, the pressbook encourages theaters to "Find Champ Manfish of your community!" The idea was to stage a contest at a local swimming pool or beach "to find the local swimmer or deep sea diver whose prowess most closely comes up to that of the intrepid skin divers of the film." The pressbook also recommends that theaters "Cash in on the built-in kid appeal of the film" by plastering playgrounds and swimming pools with announcements, holding a contest for a "junior Manfish," and by organizing a parade of young sea scouts carrying banners stating they're on their way to see *Manfish*.

The film was made in Jamaica, affording the producer no shortage of native labor in the poverty-stricken location. John Bromfield (1922–), considered at the time to be a rising young star, never really made the big time, finally settling for lead roles in the short-lived television Westerns *Sheriff of Cochise* (1956–1957) and *U.S. Marshall* (1958–1959). Until 1947, he reportedly owned and operated his own commercial tuna fishing boat in the waters of Southern California, an experience that possibly made him feel at home while making *Manfish*.

Victor Jory (1902–1982) had scored as Injun Joe in *The Adventures of Tom Sawyer* (1938) and had garnered a few minutes of screen time as the carpetbagger in *Gone With the Wind* (1939) before going to the Caribbean to make his only Poe film. He made a career of playing villains, not the least of whom is the Professor.

Lon Chaney, Jr. (1906–1973), was fifty years old when he made *Manfish*. He was also suffering a career decline which began in the late forties. Behind him at that time was *Of Mice and Men*, which had challenged for an Academy Award as best picture in 1939, a year marked by the release of many great films. Also in his past were the six years he spent as Universal's top horror star in such films as *Man-Made Monster* (1941), *The Wolf Man* (1941), *The Ghost of Frankenstein* (1942), *The Mummy's Tomb* (1942), *Frankenstein Meets the Wolf Man* (1942), and *Son of Dracula* (1943). Although Chaney would carve out an impressive career as a character actor in both films and television, his later years would be marred by the results of a lifetime of heavy drinking, immoderate eating, and excessive smoking. Interestingly, he insisted on doing his own underwater stunt work in *Manfish*, just as he had done in such earlier sea outings as *Bird of Paradise* (1932) and *Sixteen Fathoms Deep* (1934).

Manfish marked the first film appearance of Barbara Nichols (1929–1976), who would go on to score in comedies and straight dramas as a not-so-dumb blonde. On her vita at the time of her suicide were such films as *The Scarface Mob* (1960), *The George Raft Story* (1961), *The Disorderly Orderly* (1964), and *The Loved One* (1965).

Tessa Prendergast, billed by Allied Artists as "The Lollobrigida of Jamaica," was one of the most famous actresses of the island (which, however, is not necessarily saying much). She apparently flew from Rome to make *Manfish*.

The film's producer and director, W. Lee Wilder (1904–), was the Austro-Hungarian brother of highly acclaimed writer and director Billy Wilder. Unfortunately, W. Lee, lacking the talent of his brother, was relegated to making such low-budget curiosities as *Phantom from Space* (1953), *The Snow Creature* (1954), and *Bluebeard's Ten Honeymoons* (1960).

Critique: Not suprisingly, *Manfish* garnered little positive critical attention. While it maintains a mild suspense throughout, it is simply an average adventure film. One of the major drawbacks is that Swede, played well by Lon Chaney, Jr., is the only sympathetic character in the picture. Bromfield's Brannigan, whom one would expect to be the handsome, brave adventurer, amuses himself by taunting poor Swede, uses his "girlfriend" Mimi simply as a sex object to be ignored whenever more pressing matters claim his attention, and is not above killing for financial gain. Jory's slightly unhinged Professor is a devious, proud, money-hungry eccentric who will kill at a moment's notice if money is involved. Prendergast's Alita is an exotic little gold digger who spends most of the film trying to decide who is going to win the contest between Bromfield and Jory in order to finish on the winning side.

Sometimes writers and directors can defy audience expectations and make a truly creative, interesting film. In this case, however, the screenplay is not imaginative enough to score such a triumph, and audience interest in the characters (and in the film) wanes.

While the color location cinematography is visually pleasing, it does little to create any Poe-inspired mood or atmosphere. And though "The Tell-Tale Heart" serves as part of the film's inspiration, Rose London writes correctly in her book *Cinema of Mystery* that "The imaginary thudding of the betraying heart was translated into the actual bursting of bubbles from an oxygen cylinder attached to a drowned corpse. Out of genius and derangement, crass science!"[63]

Leonard Maltin awards the film a mediocre two stars, and *Video Hound's Golden Movie Retriever 1996* is even more critical, granting only a 1½ bone rating and saying: "The scenes off the Jamaican coast are lovely, but the story fails to take hold. Though there is a star aboard in Chaney, you'll look astern and bow out with a sinking feeling."

El grito de la muerte (1958);
aka *The Living Coffin; Scream of Death*

Young America Productions, Mexico

Credits: Directed by Ferdinand Mendez; produced by Alfred Ripstein, Jr.; American language version directed by K. Gordon Murray; American language version produced by Manuel San Fernando; story and screenplay by Raymond Obon; (suggested by "The Premature Burial" by Edgar Allen Poe); cinematography by Victor Herrera; musical direction by Gustavo C. Carrion; edited by Charles Kimball.

Running time: 72 minutes.

Cast: Gaston Santos (the young man), Mary Duval (Mary Ellen), Carol Barret (Aunt Sarah), Peter D'Aguillon, Charles Ancura.

Story: The young man (he never reveals his name in the film) and his sidekick, Crazy Coyote, ride up to a ranch in Mexico and ask to see a young woman named Mary Ellen. When she arrives home, the young man asks her who carved a statue or idol that she passed on to someone in the city. She says that her Aunt Chloe, now deceased, carved twin statues. The other statue is owned by the village doctor. The statues depict a crying woman, representing death. When the young man expresses surprise at seeing a knife stuck in the face of a clock, Mary, a servant, explains that if a knife is stuck into a clock so that the hands never move from the time of a person's death, that person cannot reenter the house as a ghost. Mary Ellen does not believe in the superstition, but Aunt Sarah does. When the young man and Crazy Coyote leave, Mr. Bigelow, the family executor, brings Aunt Sarah's will to Mary Ellen, tells her that she will inherit everything in the event of Aunt Sarah's death, and complains that Aunt Sarah's neglect of the ranch is causing it to fall into ruin. Many of the villagers who once worked the ranch are now unemployed, and the ranch is becoming worthless. It seems

that Aunt Sarah has her mind on the supernatural and is uninterested in such worldly things.

Aunt Sarah orders her son, Phillip, to take her to the family crypt. There she tests the alarm bell she has installed to save herself from any possible death by premature burial. Mary Ellen, exasperated by all the superstition in the house, pulls the knife from the clock and confronts Aunt Sarah with the deed. Terrified, Aunt Sarah falls to the floor of the crypt, and Tony, a servant, rides for the doctor. It seems that Aunt Sarah fears the return of her sister, Mary Ellen's Aunt Chloe, who died a year ago of grief after the death of her two sons in the swamp. Since Aunt Chloe's disappearance from the family crypt, villagers have reported seeing "the unburied" woman in the swamp, pulling out her hair and killing anyone who comes near the area where her sons died. They call Aunt Chloe "the crying ghost."

Someone shoots Tony in the back as he rides for the doctor, and the young man and Crazy Coyote take him into the village. When told that the doctor is in the saloon, the young man and Crazy Coyote go there to fetch him. In the saloon, the man who shot Tony picks a fight with the young man, and a brawl breaks out. The young man and Crazy Coyote prevail and take the doctor back to the doctor's office where they have left Tony. After patching up the wounded servant, the doctor confesses that he drinks so much because he was in love with the woman now known as the crying ghost. When the young man offers to buy the doctor's statue, the doctor refuses, saying that it means more to him than any amount of money. The young man then explains that the stone Chloe used to carve the statue came from the immediate vicinity of the ranch and swamp, and it contains gold. Someone, he suggests, is committing murder in order to gain control of the property and the gold. Further, he identifies himself as a lawman and offers to solve the case.

Back at the ranch, a trapdoor opens, and a ghostly "woman in white" enters the house. Aunt Sarah, having recovered from her fainting spell, tells Mary Ellen that Chloe blames her for the death of Chloe's sons because Sarah gave the sons permission to go into the swamp that day. When the young man and the doctor arrive, Mary Ellen goes out to meet them, during which time the ghostly woman murders Aunt Sarah. The doctor pronounces Sarah dead. When he goes into another part of the house of find a bottle of brandy, he is murdered by the ghostly woman. The young man discovers the doctor's corpse hanging within the chimney.

The young man decides to investigate the swamp and discovers a band of men in a secluded cabin. They fire on the young man, who falls into quicksand while making his retreat. The young man's horse, which seems to understand human speech, helps the young man extricate himself from the quicksand with the aid of a rope.

Meanwhile, those at the house bury Aunt Sarah in the family crypt and place the alarm buzzer in her grip as she had requested. Later the crypt alarm bell begins to ring, and the young man leads members of the household to the crypt, only to find that the lock on the gate is still intact. After gaining access, the party is surprised to discover Aunt Sarah's body missing. How did she leave the crypt? Crazy Coyote and Mary Ellen, who stayed behind in the house, see a figure they believe to be Aunt Sarah. Is yet another ghost prowling the grounds? Interestingly, because of the doctor's death and subsequent events, there is no legal proof of Aunt Sarah's death. In ten years, however, the guilty parties can file a claim on the land. The young man then announces his belief that Mr. Bigelow is behind the deadly plot, though as yet he cannot prove it. The young

man subsequently discovers a secret panel, and he and Mary Ellen investigate. In the passage, they find the bodies of Aunt Chloe and Aunt Sarah, and it becomes apparent that the criminals had devised a method by which they could enter the crypt from below and remove the bodies.

The criminals surprise the young man and Mary Ellen, and Mr. Bigelow explains that two more murders are now in order. Suddenly and inexplicably, Aunt Sarah sits up in the box where she has been deposited, causing enough distraction for the young man to disarm the criminals. Crazy Coyote then enters to help even the odds. Mary Ellen, meanwhile, subdues the ghostly woman, who turns out to be Phillip under a mask. Having solved the case and having encouraged Mary Ellen to attend to the ranch, the young man and Crazy Coyote ride away.

Production and marketing: Produced at Churbusco-Azteca, *El grito de la muerte* proves that Mexican screenwriters pay no more attention to Edgar A. Poe when adapting his stories than does anyone else. Actually, the credits do not mention Poe, but it is nevertheless obvious that the screenwriters adapted elements from both "The Premature Burial" and "The Murders in the Rue Morgue." Aunt Sarah's fear of premature burial and her installation of the warning buzzer in the crypt is definitely suggested by similar elements in "The Premature Burial," and the discovery of the murdered doctor's corpse hanging within the chimney is suggested by a similar discovery in "The Murders in the Rue Morgue." These flimsy connections are enough for *Video Hound's Golden Movie Retriever 1996* to list *El grito de la muerte* as a Poe adaptation, so I include it in this book.

El grito de la muerte was part of a package of Mexican horror films sold to American television in the sixties.

Critique: Problems with *El grito de la muerte* begin with its English title, *The Living Coffin*, since coffins, as inanimate objects, are neither living nor dead. The first scene, which precedes the title and opening credits, shows a shirtless man staggering in fear through the swamp. He falls on his back, rolls his head to the side, and lies still. Since no further reference is made to the man or to the scene, one wonders why it is there.

The film gives every indication of being badly edited for American television. The dubbing is often wooden, the leading man goes nameless, and the family member masquerading as Aunt Cloey's ghost has only a short scene at the beginning of the film before unaccountably disappearing until the end. When Mary Ellen removes the ghost's mask and gasps "Phillip!" the audience wants to gasp "Who?" Then there is the scene near the end when Aunt Sarah's corpse sits up. Was she actually buried prematurely? That is an unlikely explanation, given the circumstances. Is she rising from the dead? Is her body simply having a spasm? Whatever causes the corpse to rise is never explained, and we hear no more about the incident.

Mexican leading-man Gaston Santos has the handsome look of Guy Madison playing Wild Bill Hickok, and his leading lady, Mary Duval, is suitably dark and attractive. It is difficult to assess their performances, however, because of the unsatisfactory dubbing.

Direction is perfunctory, the cinematography is undistinguished, and the screenplay is uninspired. As a result, the mood, atmosphere, and suspense we would expect in a Poe adaptation never materializes. Only the makeup man, who goes uncredited, deserves a kudo for the eerie, pasty-faced visage of the ghostly woman. The film's many flaws undoubtedly contributed to the decision of *Video Hound's Golden Movie Retriever 1996* to award the film a paltry 1½ bones.

The Tell-Tale Heart (1960); aka *Panic; The Horror Man; Hidden Room of 1000 Horrors*

The Danzigers, Great Britain

Credits: Directed by Ernest Morris; produced by Edward J. Danziger and Harry Lee Danziger; screenplay by Brian Clemens and Elden Howard, based on "The Tell-Tale Heart" by Edgar Allan Poe; cinematography by Jimmy Wilson; music by Tony Crombie and Bill Le Sage; art direction by Norman Arnold.

Cast: Laurence Payne (Edgar), Adrienne Corri (Betty), Dermot Walsh (Carl), Selma Vaz Dias (Mrs. Vine), John Scott (inspector), John Martin (police sergeant).

Story: Edgar Marsh, a librarian and part-time author, lives alone attended only by a housekeeper, Mrs. Vine. He has a slight limp and rarely leaves his study. He spends his evening in a haze of alcohol and other drugs, looking at photographs of nude women.

Through his window, Edgar watches Betty Clare move into the house across the courtyard. He immediately falls in love with her, learns that she is a florist on the square, and attempts to approach her, but he hurries away before introducing himself. That night, able to see into her room from his window, he watches her undress.

Edgar receives a visit from Carl Loomis, one of his only friends. When Edgar asks Carl for advice on how to meet Betty, Carl cheerfully recommends that Edgar simply walk up, introduce himself, and ask her to dinner. When Edgar contrives the meeting, he is awkward. Nevertheless, when he asks her out to dinner, she accepts. At dinner he proves an awkward conversationalist. Presumably because of his limp, he begs off

From the terrifying pages of
EDGAR ALLAN POE **THE TELL-TALE HEART**

LAURENCE PAYNE
ADRIENNE CORRI
DERMOT WALSH
A Brigadier Release

Laurence Payne cradles the heart of his victim in *The Tell-Tale Heart* (1960).

when Betty asks if he would like to dance. Later he agrees to dance, but his dancing is as awkward as his conversation. Later she rebuffs him at the door to her house when he attempts to kiss her in a moment of uncontrolled passion.

The next day Edgar apologizes for his behavior and persuades the girl to give him a second chance. She agrees to accompany him to a restaurant, where the two meet Edgar's friend Carl. Carl inspires feelings in Betty that Edgar was unable to create. In deference to his friend, Carl notices but ignores Betty's obvious interest.

Knowing that Carl and Edgar are to play chess the following evening, Betty uses the pretext of returning a book to join them. As Carl plays the piano, Betty's interest in him increases. What is more, he is beginning to respond. When Betty insists, Carl accepts a dinner date with her and Edgar for the following evening. Although Carl agrees

to walk Betty home, he refuses to make any overtures toward her and leaves her disappointed on her doorstep.

During dinner the following evening, Carl is increasingly drawn to Betty's longing glances. As the threesome prepares to leave the restaurant, Betty asks Carl to come to her later that night. All the while, Edgar suspects nothing. Later, however, as he watches Betty from his window, he is shocked to see Carl walk into her room and engage "his girl" in a loving embrace. In bed, Betty admits to Carl that she went out with Edgar primarily because she was new in the city and had no companions. Carl and Betty confess their love for each other, and Carl promises to break the news to Edgar himself.

Maddened with jealousy, Edgar resolves that Carl must never go into that room again. The next night Edgar requests Carl's presence and, seized by a mad fury, beats him to death with a poker. He then hides the body under the floor of his study, certain that his rival's corpse will never be discovered.

Betty reports Carl missing, but after a brief investigation, the police tell her that he has gone away before as a result of women and gambling debts. Meanwhile, from his unseemly grave, Carl strikes back. Edgar is tortured as he imagines hearing the beating of Carl's heart. He hears it in every rhythmic sound ... the ticking of a clock, the dripping of a faucet, the clicking of a metronome. Near madness, the desperate murderer cuts out the heart and buries it in the garden.

As days pass, Betty begins to suspect that a jealous Edgar may have murdered Carl. When she discovers from Mrs. Vine that Carl visited Edgar on the evening of the former's disappearance, her suspicions intensify. Hoping to gather evidence, Betty enters Edgar's house while he is out and discovers the bent poker hidden in Edgar's closet. Suspecting it might be the murder weapon, she hurries with it to the police station.

When Edgar returns home, he becomes hysterical as he again hears the beating of Carl's heart. As the volume of the beat increases, the killer tears up the floorboards, only to find that the heart has returned to Carl's body.

In utter anguish, Edgar is almost relieved when Betty arrives with a police inspector and his detective sergeant. As the police question Edgar, he breaks down and confesses to the crime: "You know. You know, don't you! You can hear it, can't you ... the beating of his infernal heart!" After confessing, Edgar can no longer hear the tell-tale heart. The beating has stopped.

Suddenly Edgar bolts up the stairs in an effort to escape. Shot by the police, however, he crashes through the second-floor banister and is horribly impaled.

At that moment, Edgar, who is really Edgar Allan Poe, wakes screaming. The ordeal has all been a dream. Carl rushes into the room upon hearing Edgar's cries and tries to comfort his distraught friend. Recovering from the shock, Edgar describes the dream to Carl. Then, walking over to the window, he looks out on the courtyard and, just as in the dream, observes the arrival of the young woman he knows as Betty.

Production and marketing: The Danzigers' apparent goal in producing *The Tell-Tale Heart* in 1960 was to present Poe's American suspense classic in the gruesome style of Great Britain's Hammer Studios. Screenwriters Clemens and Howard, facing the problem of turning a short story into and 81-minute feature film, embellish Poe's tale with a love triangle. As a result, Poe's madman becomes a jealous lover, and the irrational crime motive of the short story becomes one of mundane passion. In an attempt to tie the film a little closer to Poe, though not to "The Tell-Tale Heart," the writers superfluously set the tale in the Rue Morgue in Paris, France.

Realizing Poe's marketability, studio publicists often alluded to Edgar Allan Poe and to unsavory speculation concerning his life, as in this example:

> "The Tell-Tale Heart" ... is based on a horror-filled story by the "master of mystery," Edgar Allan Poe. Written towards the end of Poe's brilliant career, "The Tell-Tale Heart," together with works such as "The Pit and the Pendulum," "The Fall of the House of Usher," and "The Cask of Amontillado," are considered among the greatest mystery stories of all times. Poe's hardships in life resulted in a moral deterioration which made a significant change in his writing technique. Unlike his beautiful (and often melancholy) poetry, he now turned to the macabre. Despite the subject matter change, Poe never fell short in his masterful use of language. The writings were now in prose form although he continued to create moods using language as his vehicle.

This description is, of course, factually incorrect because Poe never gave up his poetry to pursue prose. In fact, he wrote in both mediums simultaneously and considered himself primarily a poet throughout his career.

In a further attempt to hype the film as a literary adaptation, the publicity department created posters employing quotation marks around their catch lines, implying that the quotations were from Poe's story. The one-sheet poster features two such quotations: "He had the pale blue eyes of a vulture ... so horrible, it chilled the very marrow in my bones" and "The beat of his deathless heart ... ripped into my tortured brain." Unfortunately, since the murder victim's pale vulture eye, so prominent in the original story, plays no part whatsoever in the film, this "quotation" is completely dishonest and misleading. It is interesting as well that neither passage appears in Poe's story. The 40x60 poster teased potential patrons with the line: "There in the window I saw my beloved ... framed in the betraying shadow of my best friend." Typically, this "quotation" is just another obvious creation of the publicity department. Consistent with the other pseudo-quotations, this one employs the ellipsis to create an illusion of literal accuracy.

So much for Poe. The attempt to copy the Hammer style is apparent in the scene in which Payne graphically removes a beating heart from Walsh's chest. According to studio publicity, months of planning went into the construction of the heart:

> To begin with, the anatomical structure of the human heart had to be studied. Property men, whose job it was to construct the heart, used medical textbooks and anatomical research works in the planning stages of the recreation. The designs having been completed, the actual physical creation of the heart was begun. One can imagine the difficulties involved in the building of an organ of the body which is never seen by the lay eye and still must appear realistic and must match the viewers' imagination of what the heart looks like! The final (and most difficult) stage was begun. Property men had to construct a heart that would live up to the "tell-tale" description.

While the heart is a passable representation, especially for 1960, publicity hyperbole probably accounts for the pressbook report that the studio physician for Brigadier Films was "awe-struck by the authenticity of (the) human heart used in the film." In the same vein, the pressbook states that Adrienne Corri enjoyed working on the film in all scenes save those in which she appeared with the heart, implying that the gruesome device was too much for her. However, since she and the heart share no scenes, her enjoyment must have been undiminished.

The Danzigers did not release *The Tell-Tale Heart* in the United States until 1963, when Brigadier distributed the property. Apparently, the success of the Roger Corman/AIP series made this British second feature more marketable than it was otherwise considered to be.

Ernest Morris (1915–) made a career directing films for the Danzigers. Among his other second-feature pictures was *The Return of Mr. Moto* (1965), a product that failed to challenge the Peter Lorre film series in quality.

Laurence Payne (1919–) was a leading man on the British stage. Among his other films of note were *Ben Hur* (1959) and Hammer's horror oddity, *Vampire Circus* (1972).

Adrienne Corri (1930–), a British actress of Italian descent, appeared in the British cult film *Devil Girl from Mars* (1954) before going on to carve a small niche in the horror/science fiction genre with *A Study in Terror* (1965, in which Sherlock Holmes meets Jack the Ripper), *Bunny Lake is Missing* (1965), *Moon Zero Two* (1969, a Hammer production), *Vampire Circus* (1972, a Hammer production that reunited her with Payne), and *Madhouse* (1974, with Vincent Price and Peter Cushing). She is probably best known today for her brief appearance in Stanley Kubrick's *A Clockwork Orange* (1971), in which she is raped by Alex and his droogs.

Screenwriter Brian Clemens (1931–) would later write regularly for "The Avengers" television series. He would also generate scripts for such horror/fantasy films as *And Soon the Darkness* (1970), *See No Evil* (1971),

Dr. Jekyll and Sister Hyde (1971, a Hammer production), *Captain Kronos, Vampire Hunter* (1972, a Hammer production which he also directed), and *The Golden Voyage of Sinbad* (1973).

Critique: When *The Tell-Tale Heart* opened in New York in May of 1963, it played second feature on a double bill to the British *Black Zoo* (1963). *The New York Times* wrote: "the first one isn't necessarily better, just less bad."[64] Going on from there, *The Times* savaged *The Tell-Tale Heart* as follows:

> Edgar Allan Poe, in his classic suspense tale, used a telltale heart to seal a murderer's doom, but the thumping noise that is the climax of the second part of the bill sounds more like faulty plumbing. It's a terrible little British job. Now involving a romantic triangle ... Even with the tasteless, messy finale, the film is a dead-earnest force, and yesterday's audience howled at one midtown theater. Apparently the moral is: if you're doing in your best friend, don't board him up under the piano. Use concrete. Poor Poe.[65]

Today *The Tell-Tale Heart* enjoys a spotty reputation. In *Horror and Science Fiction Films*, Donald Willis calls the film "a real bore."[66] Siding with Willis, Leonard Maltin assigns the film two stars, pronouncing it "not sufficiently atmospheric." In *Cinema of Mystery*, Rose London finds it "bloodier than the original and the material prolonged by the voyeuristic obsessions of Payne for Adrienne Corri, and by the need to resurrect the body from under the floorboards, in order to cut out the tell-tale heart and bury it in the garden."[67] On the other hand, *The Overlook Film Encyclopedia: Horror* praises Morris's directorial flair, concluding that though the film is "an otherwise routine thriller ... the sense of growing hysteria is well rendered as various apparently innocent objects such as a clock or a dripping tap echo and intensify the relentless heartbeat invading Payne's world."

In my view, Maltin is most on the mark; the film lacks atmosphere. Someone on the Danzigers' staff obviously sensed the truth, so they desperately inserted the old chestnut of a thunderstorm into the picture in order to evoke some sense of mood otherwise missing. Still, as others suggest, the film has its merits, first of which is Laurence Payne. It is ultimately his film, and as much as could be asked, he carries the part valiantly Adrienne Corri is also effective, though her longing glances at Walsh are at times a bit overdone. Although *The Overlook Film Encyclopedia: Horror* praises the director for the growing sense of hysteria, the dripping faucet and ticking pendulum had all been done before and should have been somewhat expected. It is Payne who takes these elements and creates the hysteria noted by *The Encyclopedia*. Director Morris does do an adequate job with the material, and the cast members turn in distinguished performances, all indicating that the ultimate fault lies with the screenplay. Although Clemens and Howard do a fine job of drawing the main characters, they prove inadequate to the task of spreading the horror of Poe's short story over 81 minutes. As a result, the short features of 1941 and 1953 are superior.

The Fall of the House of Usher (1960)
aka *House of Usher*
American International, U.S.A.

Credits: Directed and produced by Roger Corman; executive producer—James H. Nicholson; screenplay by Richard Matheson, based on "The Fall of the House of Usher" by Edgar Allan Poe; music by Les Baxter; cinematography by Floyd Crosby, A.S.C.; process photography directed by Larry Butler; production design by Daniel

Haller; special effects by Pat Dinga; photographic effects by Ray Mercer; paintings by Burt Schoenberg.

Running time: 79 minutes.

Cast: Vincent Price (Roderick Usher), Mark Damon (Philip Winthrop), Myrna Fahey (Madeline Usher), Harry Ellerbee (Bristol).

Story: Philip Winthrop arrives unannounced at the House of Usher to see his fiancée, Madeline. The land surrounding the forbidding structure is mist-shrouded and bereft of vegetation. Philip knocks on the door but is taken aback when Bristol, the manservant, says regretfully that he may not see Madeline because she is ill and in bed. Alarmed, the young man demands that he be announced to Madeline's older brother, Roderick. Bristol agrees but requests that Philip remove his boots first and replace them with slippers.

After Philip complies with the strange request, Bristol leads him up the creaking stairs to Roderick Usher's door. Before anyone can knock, however, Roderick suddenly confronts them, demanding an explanation for the intrusion. Winthrop has hardly introduced himself when Roderick cries out for him to speak more softly and explains that he has an affliction of the hearing which makes loud sounds cut into his brain like knives. "You must leave this house now," Usher warns. "It is not a healthy place for you to be."

The voices rouse Madeline, who rises from her sickbed and suddenly appears. Although the young lovers, who met and fell in love during Madeline's visit to Boston, are overjoyed at seeing each other again, Roderick hustles Madeline back to bed, after which he explains to Philip why marriage with his sister is impossible. "The Usher line is tainted," Roderick states. Both he and his sister suffer from a morbid acuteness of the senses, though Roderick's case is worse since he is older. "Three quarters of my family have fallen into madness," he continues, "and in their madness have acquired a superhuman strength, so that it took the power of many to subdue them." Philip suggests that

Roderick is exaggerating, admitting only that the Ushers may suffer from certain "peculiarities of temperament." "How diplomatically you put it," Usher responds.

Roderick finally gives up on getting Philip to leave immediately and instructs Bristol to show the young man to a room. As Philip prepares for dinner, the house shakes ominously. Shortly afterwards, a falling chandelier narrowly misses Philip as he is coming downstairs for dinner. Alarmed at the turn of events, Madeline begs Philip to leave, but of course he refuses. "It was probably the trembling of the house that caused that chandelier to fall," Philip rationalizes. "Do you really think so?" Roderick sadly muses. "Do you have a better explanation?" Philip responds. Roderick, Madeline, and their guest pass an uncomfortable dinner, after which Roderick plays one of his own compositions on the lute. When Roderick suggests that they all retire for the night, Madeline expresses the wish to remain up. When her brother insists, however, Madeline reluctantly complies with his wish.

Later, as eerie fog creeps over the land, Philip steals into his fiancée's room and insists that she leave with him in the morning. Their private moment is cut short, however, when Roderick barges in and orders Philip out. Madeline protests that Roderick has no right to rule her life as he does, and even goes so far as to suggest that he hates her. Hurt by the accusation, Roderick protests that he loves her more than anything else in the world. Philip agrees to leave but repeats that he intends to leave with Madeline in the morning.

Later that night Philip is awakened by the opening and closing of a door in the hallway. When he investigates, he finds Madeline's bed empty. As he searches for her, a banister almost gives way beneath his weight—another close call for the increasingly concerned suitor. Finally Philip discovers his fiancée lying on the floor of the family crypt. Bristol arrives and tells Philip not to wake Madeline as the shock might kill her. It seems that since her return from

Boston, the poor woman has taken to sleep-walking down to the crypt. As he says he has done several times before, Bristol lifts Madeline in his arms and carries her upstairs to her bed.

A gloomy morning dawns. At breakfast, Bristol tells Philip of having been the Usher family caretaker for sixty years. As the two men speak, the house again begins to shake, causing a boiling pot nearly to spill its contents on Philip. The butler explains the existence of a fissure in the structure of the house and confides his belief that "When the house dies, I shall die with it."

When Philip goes to take Madeline from the house, she confesses that she wants to leave but cannot. "Very soon," she sighs, "I shall be dead." When Philip objects to such talk, Madeline escorts him to the family crypt and points out seven caskets, each one identified with the name of a dead Usher. There, to Philip's horror, is a coffin designated for Madeline. "It waits for me," she explains. "It does not!" he shouts in exasperation. "Is this your brother's idea?" Madeline absolves Roderick, immediately after which a casket slips from the upper tier, narrowly missing the two. When the oblong box spills its rotting contents onto the floor in front of them, Madeline faints. Roderick then appears and insists that he, and not Philip, carry Madeline upstairs.

Later Usher tells Philip it is time that he truly understand the situation facing them. The whole region, Roderick begins, is plagued by evil. Long ago something crept across the land and blighted it. All flora died. Lakes and ponds grew black and stagnant. That evil was the evil of the Ushers. Pointing to paintings of his ancestors, he identifies each one and his or her crimes. In the rogues' gallery are thieves, swindlers, forgers, drug addicts, blackmailers, murderers, smugglers, slave traders, and mass murderers. They all lived in the abnormal house of Usher, whose evil is rooted in its very stones. With a note of fanaticism in his voice, Roderick continues: "Evil is not just a word; it is a reality ... The pall of evil that fills this house is no il-lusion. For hundreds of years foul thoughts and foul deeds have been committed within its walls." The house itself is evil now. Living evil is the legacy which has been handed down to Roderick and his sister, and its destiny is to destroy them. "If she were to wed and bear children," he continues, "the Usher evil would spread anew—malignant, cancerous."

Philip is aghast and will hear no more. Considering Usher a madman from whom Madeline must be removed, he tells his fiancée to get packed immediately in preparation for a quick departure. As Philip packs, quarreling voices emanate from Madeline's room. Suddenly she screams. When Philip rushes in and finds Madeline dead on the bed, a grief-stricken Roderick declares, "You are the one who killed her ... Her heart could not withstand the strain you put upon her."

Shortly thereafter, Roderick, Philip, and Bristol gather in the chapel for a private funeral for Madeline. While Philip's head is bowed, Usher sees Madeline's hand move. Not wishing Philip to learn the truth, he hastily closes the casket. Then the three men transport the casket to the almost pitch-black crypt. There is a moment of dead silence after the departure of the three—then Madeline's breathing becomes audible and she screams. Madeline Usher has been buried alive.

Seemingly days later, Bristol lets slip that catalepsy runs in the Usher family along with sundry other ailments. Philip quickly picks up on the slip and demands that Madeline be rescued. When he breaks into the casket with an axe, he finds it empty. Charging upstairs, he demands that Usher tell him where she is. "So you know." Usher says. "Where (is she)?" Philip persists. "You cannot find her," Usher answers, admitting that he buried his sister alive but insisting that she is now dead. Still, Philip demands to know where she is and undertakes a frenetic search of the house. Finally he collapses from exhaustion and dreams that he is in the chapel, which is now full of Ushers. Ghostlike, they motion for him to join them. As he walks past their beckoning arms, he

Madeline Usher (Myrna Fahey) attacks her brother Roderick (Vincent Price) in the fiery finale of *The Fall of the House of Usher* **(1960).**

sees Roderick carry Madeline away. He fights free from the leering Ushers but is unable to open the door through which Roderick bore Madeline.

Suddenly he awakens to the sound of Madeline screaming. As a storm rises outside, he goes downstairs to find Roderick strumming discordantly on his lute. "Do you know," Roderick asks, "I could hear every sound she made? That I heard her breathing in her casket, heard her first gasp as she awoke, heard her first scream of terror? Did you know that I could hear the scratching of her fingernails on the casket lid? BE DONE!"

"Is she still alive?" Philip screams repeatedly.

"Yes!" Roderick finally admits. "Even now I hear her. Yes, alive, deranged, infuriate! Can you not hear her voice … below, twisting, turning, scratching at the lid with bloody fingernails, staring, screaming, wild with fury, the strength of madness in her! Can you not hear her voice? She calls my name."

Below, in a secluded part of the crypt, a bloody hand protrudes from a chain-covered casket. Philip rushes down into the crypt. Madeline, who has escaped from her chained casket, is now completely insane. Possessed of superhuman strength, she attacks Philip. He breaks her grasp, but she eludes him and seeks her tormentor, Roderick.

A violent storm shakes the house, causing the fissure to widen. As flames engulf the house, Philip watches helplessly as a ceiling beam falls upon the struggling Madeline and Roderick. Bristol drags Philip to safety and dashes back into the inferno to perish with the last of the Ushers. As Philip staggers sadly to safety, the house disappears in flames "and the deep and dark tarn closed silently over the fragments of the House of Usher."

Production and marketing: By 1960, American International Pictures already had quite a track record for making successful exploitation films. Among their more lucrative double bills were such combinations as *Reform School Girl* and *Rock Around the World* (1957), *The Amazing Colossal Man* and *Cat Girl* (1957), *Motorcycle Gang* and *Sorority Girl* (1957), *I Was a Teenage Werewolf* and *Invasion of the Saucer Men* (1957), *I Was a Teenage Frankenstein* and *Blood of Dracula* (1957), *Attack of the Puppet People* and *War of the Colossal Beast* (1958), and *Dragstrip Riot* and *The Cool and the Crazy* (1958).

One of AIP's most successful directors of such pictures was Roger Corman (1926–). Under his belt were such low-budget moneymakers as *Day the World Ended* (1955), *It Conquered the World* (1956), *Attack of the Crab Monsters* (1956), *Not of This Earth* (1956), *The Undead* (1956), *She-Gods of Shark Reef* (1956), *Viking Women and the Sea Serpent* (1957), *War of the Satellites* (1958), *Teenage Caveman* (1958), *The Wasp Woman* (1959), and *A Bucket of Blood* (1959), all of which became parts of popular horror/science fiction double features.

As the sixties dawned, AIP reportedly approached Corman with the idea of making a pair of ten-day black and white horror films to play as a double feature. According to Corman, he interested AIP in allowing him to make one film in color on a fifteen-day schedule instead. In fact, they let him pick the material. "I had read this story of Poe's in high school," Corman explained years later, "and I always liked it."[68] But, according to Corman, when he suggested "The Fall of the House of Usher," Sam Arkoff wasn't immediately sold on the idea because the story contained no monster. Thinking quickly, Corman supposedly replied, "The house ... it's the house that's the monster."[69] Arkoff later dismissed Corman's version as apocryphal and claimed to have liked the idea immediately.

It is possible that Corman might not have seriously suggested "The Fall of the House of Usher" as a project, however, and that AIP might not have accepted the idea, if it had not been for Hammer Films. Britain's Hammer Studio had recently demonstrated that classic titles in a period setting, well-made and well-acted on a low budget, could rake in a fortune. In 1957 the studio turned a handsome profit with its *Curse of Frankenstein*, a remake of Mary Shelley's 1817 novel. A year later they struck again with the enormously successful *Dracula* (U.S. title: *Horror of Dracula*). Both films starred Peter Cushing and Christopher Lee, who were challenging Boris Karloff and Vincent Price as living icons of the horror film genre.

Roger Corman, however, took a more subtle approach to horror than Hammer did:

> Everything was shot on a stage. I was working on a number of theories that I had developed at that time concerning horror. One of the strongest concepts was that the world of Poe, to a large extent, was the world of the unconscious. Being the world of the unconscious, I thought it could be recreated better within the artificial confines of a stage than it could be in broad daylight. I didn't want to use location shots. I didn't want the film to be shot realistically. Whenever I had to have a shot that called for more scope than a stage afforded, I searched for some sort of landscape that might be perceived as being symbolic. *Usher*'s opening scene had Mark Damon riding a horse through a very desolate landscape toward Usher mansion. There had been a fire in the Hollywood Hills so we shot the scene in this hideously burned out area. It was barren. Foreboding. It fit exactly with the tone of the picture.[70]

Screenplay responsibilities fell to Richard Matheson (1936–), a well-known name in the annals of horror fiction. Besides adapting his own novel *The Incredible Shrinking Man* for the screen in 1957, he had established a successful publication record in such weird fiction magazines as *Fantastic Story Magazine, Imagination, Fantasy and Science Fiction, Worlds of If, Worlds Beyond, Shock, Fantastic, Thrilling Wonder Stories*, and *Galaxy*. Matheson also regularly supplied scripts for the television series *The Twilight Zone*. Although Matheson's screenplay took some minor liberties with the Poe tale, such as adding a love interest and making the house the monster, it was the most faithful Poe adaptation to date.

Matheson recalled his part in birthing *House of Usher*:

> I was called in by James Nicholson in 1959. I met with Roger, Nicholson and Arkoff. They wanted to do an Edgar Allan Poe film. I don't think they had any idea that the movie would actually start a trend. It was just something to do.
>
> I went to work. My outline alone was worth the price of admission. I don't really know why they called me in. I had done *The Incredible Shrinking Man* and some "Twilight Zone" episodes. I would guess that there were, and I suppose still are, only a few names that could handle this kind of material.
>
> I knew I would be working within a limited budget, but I tried not to let that fact affect my writing. The story was simple, anyhow. What could they spend money on? You had a few people stuck in an old house. I tried not to write *The House of Usher* as a "monster" movie (though, according to Corman, that is what Nicholson and Arkoff wanted). For the sake of suspense, I introduced the factor of Usher's sister going mad and having her placed in a casket prematurely. I had a lot of fun with that.[71]

When casting began, Vincent Price (1911–1993) was the first choice to play Roderick Usher. Born in St. Louis, Missouri, Price graduated from Yale and attended the University of London. In 1934, responding to a friend's dare, he auditioned for a stage role in *Chicago* and got the part. After spending several successful years on the stage, he landed his first film role in *Service Deluxe* (1938). In 1960, however, Price was best known as a horror actor, having starred in such successful genre films as *Tower of London* (1939), *The Invisible Man Returns* (1940), *Shock* (1946), *House of Wax* (1953*)*, *The Mad Magician* (1954), *The Fly* (1958), *The Bat* (1959), *The House on Haunted Hill* (1959), and *The Tingler* (1959). Although Boris Karloff was still alive and active in

1960, he was too old for the part of Usher. So AIP got Price, the man considered by many to be Karloff's successor as the "king of horror."

Since the acquisition of Price took a large chunk out of AIP's budget, the remainder of the cast was composed of lesser lights. Cast in the role of Philip Winthrop was young Mark Damon (1935–), a UCLA graduate who had been appearing in routine films since 1956. Myrna Fahey, lovely but virtually unknown, landed the role of Madeline Usher. The role of Bristol, the servant, went to Harry Ellerbe, an elderly veteran of both stage and screen.

Although most of his best work still lay ahead, responsibility for the musical score went to Les Baxter (1922–). Among the composer's credits at that point were the scores for *Hot Blood* (1955), *The Black Sleep* (1956), *Macabre* (1958), and *Goliath and the Barbarians* (1959).

Daniel Haller (1928–), who designed the impressive sets, was reputedly the youngest art director in the industry. Haller worked closely with Corman before handing his work to Harry Reif, who actually assembled the furnishings. The lute played by Price in the film was a museum piece, part of the Lachman collection. It was an original creation by the Viennese craftsman Gregory Ferdinand Wenger, who died in 1760, two hundred years before the film was made.

The eerie paintings of the Ushers were created by Burt Schoenberg, a young West Coast artist commissioned to do the work. Schoenberg knew in advance that his paintings would be damaged or destroyed by the spectacular fire at the end of the picture, as indeed they were.

Shooting commenced without problems. At one point, Vincent Price had to say the line "The house lives! The house breathes!" in hushed, dramatic tones. As legend has it, Price walked over to Corman between takes, pointed to the lines and said, "This doesn't make sense. Why do I have to say this?" "That's the line that allows us to make the movie," Corman said, explaining that Arkoff wanted a monster in the picture, and the house was it. Vincent looked thoughtfully at Corman for a moment and then replied, "Fine. I can bring life to those lines." Incidentally, it was Price himself who had the idea of dyeing his hair white to suggest hypersensitivity to light.

When the time came for the fiery finale, Ken Skerzick, senior inspector for the Los Angeles Fire Department, and his men were on hand to see that things did not get out of hand. Although Skerzick and special effects man Pat Dinga had been doing their jobs for years, things almost did get out of hand. Still-photographer Frankie Tanner, who insisted on getting as close to the scene as possible, got blisters on one lens due to the intense heat. Harry Ellerbe thought he felt the hairs on his hand being singed, and Mark Damon was reportedly almost overcome by smoke. Vincent Price, who lay on the floor amidst the flames with poor Myrna Fahey, was most concerned that her dress not catch fire. Years later Price would still mention in interviews the relative danger of those falling, flaming timbers on the set of *House of Usher*.

Although the full title of the film was indeed *The Fall of the House of Usher*, Corman agreed to shorten the title to *House of Usher* for advertising and marquee purposes. The picture had its world premiere in Palm Springs on June 18, 1960, the proceeds going to the Angel View Crippled Children's Foundation. Most of the film's principals attended the showing. *House of Usher* opened in New York City on September 14. Ironically, though Corman shot the film as a single feature, and though AIP financed it as such, it opened as the top half of a double bill with AIP's *Why Must I Die*. The studio still did not know what it had. As Richard Matheson explains, "The funny thing was that no one at AIP knew what to do with it. They had no idea what was going on. They were running it on a double bill with *Psycho*. It made so much money that they couldn't believe their wallets."[72]

If AIP did not know what it had, it nevertheless knew how to market the film. In fact, the studio launched *House of Usher* with one of its largest horror film ad campaigns ever, beginning with an oversize ten-page campaign manual sporting a full-color cover. The main poster image is that of Price, Ellerbe, and Damon bearing Fahey's casket to the darkened crypt, below which is a cut away side view of the casket with Fahey inside, twisting, scratching, and screaming. The catch line reads "I heard her first feeble movements in the coffin. We had put her living in the tomb." Ads compared the film to *Wuthering Heights* (1939), another immortal tale of forbidden love in a gothic mansion, and to *Diabolique* (1955), Henri-Georges Clouzot's classic of deception and claustrophobic terror.

Interestingly, this ad campaign exploits Poe more tastefully than any before it. Along with its many references to the author as "one of the greatest writers of all time," it includes a lengthy biographical note from the Pocket Library edition of Poe's works, as well as notes on the story from Mabbott's Modern Library edition, both "not to be used for publication." While Universal's *The Black Cat* (1934) and *The Raven* (1935) were little more than vehicles for Karloff and Lugosi, *House of Usher* is clearly more than a project concocted to exploit the drawing power of Vincent Price. In fact, Price and Poe share honors for the film's *raison d'être* throughout. One publicity still of Price "reading the works of Edgar Allan Poe between takes" symbolizes the prominence of both actor and author in the marketing campaign.

The pressbook does contain an interview with Vincent Price on the set of *House of Usher*. The interviewer is obviously quite knowledgeable about horror films; fourteen of the ad's sixteen paragraphs consist of his reflections on the genre. Price's minimal input consists of the following observation: "The gimmick film, in my opinion, is definitely on the way out. We've made the full cycle and now we're going back to the real 'thrillers'—and doing this particular film by the man who started the whole thing." Price was, in fact, correct. The gimmick horror film such as Price's 3-D *House of Wax* and William Castle's *The House on Haunted Hill* (with "Emergo") and *The Tingler* (with "Percepto"), both starring Vincent Price, ended for all practical purposes in 1960.

At year's end, when the *New York Herald Tribune* announced its annual film awards, the winner for best actor was Vincent Price in *The Fall of the House of Usher*. The newspaper thus judged Price's performance superior to that of Academy Award winner Burt Lancaster in *Elmer Gantry*. Perhaps part of the reason for Price's fine performance lies in the joy he took working with Roger Corman. Price later explained: "The *House of Usher* was a very enjoyable experience for me. Partially because Roger worked in all this pseudo-psychological symbolism into the story. I truly think he believed in it. At any rate, it made the film a lot more interesting."[73]

Critique: *House of Usher* opened to generally good reviews. *The New York Herald Tribune* raved (entirely correctly): "Poe's classic horror tale has been fixed on film in fine style. Far above the human gadgetry of most current movies in this category, it concentrates on atmosphere, makes no bones about its necessary artifices and, most crucial, walks conscientiously in Poe's stylistic steps ... Some of the dialogue is not stylistic enough to fit snugly into the atmosphere, but such flaws do not seriously damage the mood set by the art work, the music, the direction and the acting of Price, whose intellectual grasp of this bizarrerie is fine to see.... For afficionados, this is a heartening move in the right direction, a restoration of finesse and craftsmanship to the genre of dread."[74]

Although acknowledging that purists still might object, *Variety* considered Matheson's minor alterations shrewd "since they pursue a romantic course (and) should prove popular with the bulk of modern audiences. It is a film that should attract mature tastes as well as those who come to the cinema for sheer thrills."[75] Turning soothsayer, the reviewer correctly predicted that "Corman has

turned out a go at Poe that is certain to inspire several more cinematic excursions into this author's extremely commercial literary realm."[76]

Almost alone in its bellyaching, the *New York Times* charged that "The 'fall' has been omitted from the film version of 'The Fall of the House of Usher,' but not the pitfalls. American-International, with good intentions of presenting a faithful adaptation of Edgar Allan Poe's classic tale of the macabre ... blithely ignored the author's style, and fell right in."[77] Further, the review charges the producers with "stultifying the audience's imaginations by turning Poe's murky mansion into a cardboard castle encircled by literal green mist" and the "making a horror film that provides a fair degree of literacy at the cost of a patron's patience."[78] Both complaints are baseless Haller's sets are exemplary, especially considering the budget, and while there are a number of expository scenes, to Matheson's and Price's credit, they never drag.

House of Usher has retained its proud reputation since 1960, when its positive critical reception and financial success spawned an entire AIP Poe series lasting into the seventies. Only Carlos Clarens took a dissenting view, calling the film "a ponderous drawn-out movie that seemed the antithesis of [Corman's] earlier work."[79]

More in the mainstream in *Horror in the Cinema*, Ivan Butler writes that the film, "though cheaply made and (apart from the inimitable Vincent Price) stickily acted, was redeemed by its comparative restraint, its welcome period accuracy, its essential fidelity —despite elaboration—to the story, and Floyd Crosby's first rate camera work."[80] Butler also notes the subtle humor "which was not indulged in to the detriment of the horror. ('See to the crypt, will you?' says Roderick Usher to his ancient manservant after a coffin has upset its unpleasant contents on the floor.)"[81]

In *Cinema of Mystery*, Rose London places much of the film's success at the feet of its star: "Vincent Price's first performance in the Corman Poe-cycle has more to do with acting and less with his world-weary *persona* than in his later appearances. He seems more controlled as Roderick Usher, and therefore more truly sinister. His compelling performance is helped by Floyd Crosby's creeping atmospheric camerawork, as well as by the special effects of Ray Mercer."[82]

The Overlook Film Encyclopedia: Horror correctly calls the film "a minor masterpiece, surprisingly faithful to Poe.... Price, in a magnificent performance, gives the film its tone, grand in manner and gesture yet secretly sickening from some inner corruption." The *Encyclopedia* also correctly notes the hints of "incestuous desire (as Crosby's probing, hesitating, incessantly agitated camera subtly suggests) which has communicated itself to the house that has locked them within a familial passion and which is itself crumbling under the same deadweight of decadence." The *Encyclopedia* correctly concludes: "A magnificently *coherent* film that is often dismissed as pure decoration, it shows a remarkable care for detail. When Fahey's suitor (Damon) first enters the room in which Price has virtually imprisoned himself, for instance, he is wearing blue, a splash of vivid life that jars against the crimson worn by Price and echoed throughout the furnishings: the color of blood (and perhaps the guilt that already stains Price's mind) when Fahey returns from the grave to claim him in her bloodstained funeral shroud."

Ultimately, it is hard to argue that other actors could have eclipsed Vincent Price and Harry Ellerbe in their respective roles. Matheson's screenplay masterfully evokes the exterior and interior landscapes of Poe better than any full-length predecessor, save perhaps *The Black Cat* (1934). But, unlike that of the Karloff/Lugosi vehicle, Matheson's screenplay was a relatively faithful Poe adaptation. As in the original, isn't there just a hint of incest present? *House of Usher* set the tone for AIP's Corman/Poe series of the sixties, and as the rest of the series would show, it set a high standard for the succeeding films.

The Pit (1960)
Great Britain

Credits: Directed, produced, and written by Edward Abraham, based on "The Pit and the Pendulum" by Edgar Allan Poe.
Running time: ?
Cast: Brian Peck (the prisoner).

This short feature, made in 1960 but not shown until 1962, had a limited showing in its native England, probably at the National Film Theater. Apparently, it has never been released anywhere else. The only reference book mentioning it is *Horror in the Cinema* by Ivan Butler, who pronounces it "macabre." Butler continues: "Using only one word of dialogue (as Abraham points out, Poe's story has none), it relies on sound effects and silence to underline the terror—and succeeds. Outside one's nightmares, has one even seen anything as nasty as the bottom of this pit?"[83] Critic Dilys Powell described it as "a genuine essay in horror."[84] As I have never seen the film, I can comment no further.

Obras maestras del terror (1961); aka *The Master of Horror; Short Stories of Terror; Masterworks of Horror*

Argentina Sono Film, Argentina

Credits: Directed by Enrique Carreras; produced by Nicholas Carreras; screenplay by Luis Penafiel, based on "The Facts in the Case of M. Valdemar," "The Cask of Amontillado," and "The Tell-Tale Heart" by Edgar Allan Poe; cinematography by Amerigo Haas (or Hoss).

Running time: 115 minutes.

Cast: Narcisco Ibanez Menta (Professor Ekstrom, Jean Samivet, and Thorber), Carlos Estrada (Maurice Fraiport), Oswald Pacheko (Henry Valdemar), Inez Moreno (Teresa Samivet), Narcisco Ibanez Serrador, Mercedes Carreras, Lilian Valmar.

Story: On a stormy night, a bored French maid passes the time by reading the short stories of Edgar Allan Poe. First, she browses through the introduction:

Edgar Allan Poe, the master of horror, advanced with giant steps during the renaissance of literature in this country. He was a genius as a poet and as a writer, and uniting both talents he created a gender [*sic*] that made him forever famous. It is in this light that we have been inspired to offer these stories, trying to leave in them the essence of the witchcraft with which the illustrious American combined the supernatural both in his life and in his stories, steeping them in mystery and intrigue.

The first story, "The Facts in the Case of M. Valdemar," concerns Dr. Ekstrom, a dedicated, expert hypnotist haunted by a botched experiment in mesmerism that ended in the death of an insane young woman. Years after the tragedy, Eckstrom agrees to put his dying friend Valdemar into a trance only moments before the latter's demise. As Valdemar suggests to Ekstrom, the case of M. Valdemar will vindicate Ekstrom and allow the two of them to live forever in the annals of medicine. Unable to find peace after being hypnotized, the poor man, caught in a middle ground between life and death, pleads to be released from the trance so that he may "pass on." The mesmerist, however, is too interested in the experiment to do as the patient wishes. Three months later Ekstrom calls Dr. Chambers and Dr. McCaffrey to witness Valdemar's condition. When they find what they consider to be Valdemar's corpse in perfect preservation, they accuse Ekstrom of embalming and trickery. When Ekstrom elicits from the lips of Valdemar a hideously voiced "I am dead," Chambers and McCaffrey insist that Ekstrom remove the spell. Ekstrom complies, and Valdemar decomposes until nothing is left but a bloodied, desiccated cadaver.

In the second story, "The Cask of Amontillado," Teresa is trapped in an unhappy marriage with her husband Samivet. While Samivet is interested mainly in his wine and his work, Teresa longs for more excitement. She finds that excitement when a handsome young rogue named Maurice descends on the village of Burgundy, performing magical tricks and selling his wares. Samivet invites Maurice to be a guest in his house, and within five days, Maurice and Teresa are involved in an adulterous affair. When Samivet learns of the affair, he lures Maurice into his wine cellar on the pretense of tasting some excellent wine, saying, "You will soon learn the great secret ... of the Samivet family." After the first goblet of wine, Maurice appears slightly drunk or drugged. As they continue to drink, Maurice becomes increasingly drunk. Finally, Samivet offers Maurice "the great secret"— Amontillado from Spain, 1733. Maurice soon passes out and awakens to find himself chained to a wall as Samivet is busily bricking up the area. Samivet shrugs off Maurice's cries of terror, telling him that he and Teresa will always be together. Samivet then raises the drowned Teresa, from within the Amontillado cask, by her hair.

The third story, "The Tell-Tale Heart," involves a young man driven insane by his preoccupation with the eye of an old man with whom he lives. He murders the old man but is driven to confess the crime when he hallucinates the sound of his victim's beating heart.

The maid finishes the third story, goes into the kitchen, sees a mouse, and faints.

Production and marketing: Enrique Carreras was a well-known Argentine commercial director, one of his best-known excursions into horror being *El fantasma de la opereta* (a black comedy version of Gaston Leroux's often filmed classic *The Phantom of the Opera*). Actor Narciso Menta stars in all three segments of *Obras maestras del terror*, as Vincent Price would a year later in AIP's *Tales of Terror*, directed by Roger Corman.

When the film was released in the United States in 1965, Jack H. Harris removed "The Tell-Tale Heart," thereby cutting the film's running time to 61 minutes. It ended up topping a double bill with Harris's *Master of Terror*, a retitled rerelease of *4D Man* (1959). The ads for the double bill promised "TWO CHILLERS to turn your DREAMS to SCREAMS."

Critique: As I have seen only the American release of *Master of Horror*, I cannot comment on "The Tell-Tale Heart" segment, which was deleted. The remaining two stories are somewhat padded adaptations of Poe's original works. Matters get off to a shaky start when the title appears as "Edgar Allan Poe's *Master of Horror*." Poe, who wrote nothing called "Master of Horror," *is* the master of horror referred to in the film's title. Then comes the awful introduction in voice-over as the maid begins reading the Poe book. I cannot believe that the original Argentine introduction is as inept as the babble supplied for American release. We know that Poe did create a new literary genre (the detective genre), but I do not believe he managed to create a new "gender."

Except for the addition of Dr. Ekstrom's botched mesmeric experiment, "The Facts in the Case of M. Valdemar" is fairly true to Poe's original tale. Menta's face glows Svengali-like as he places Valdemar into a trance, and Oswald Pacheko makes a ghastly appearance as the tormented Valdemar.

In "The Cask of Amontillado," Menta is convincing as the vengeful Samivet. While Poe's story does not clarify the point, we know exactly what the victim in the film has done to precipitate his fate. Although the screenplay includes some ironic dialogue, it is less subtle and hence less successful than that written by Poe. Also, the ending of "The Cask of Amontillado" with the dead wife's entombment is more reminiscent of the walling-up scene in *The Black Cat* sequence of AIP's later *Tales of Terror* than it is of Poe's story. Even with one segment missing from the American release, however, the film is at least minimally successful both as a Poe adaptation and as a horror film.

The Pit and the Pendulum (1961)
American International, U.S.A.

Credits: Directed and produced by Roger Corman; executive producers—James H. Nicholson and Samuel Z. Arkoff; screenplay by Richard Matheson, based on "the Pit and the Pendulum" by Edgar Allan Poe; production design by Daniel Haller; cameraman—Floyd Crosby; music by Les Baxter.

Running time: 85 minutes.

Cast: Vincent Price (Nicholas Medina), John Kerr (Francis Barnard), Barbara Steele (Elizabeth Barnard Medina), Luana Anders (Catherine Medina), Anthony Carbone (Dr. Charles Leon), Patrick Westwood (Maximillian), Lynne Bernay (Maria), Larry Turner (Nicholas as a child), Mary Menzies (Isabella), Charles Victor (Bartolome).

Story: In the year 1546, the horrors of the Spanish Inquisition lie only a generation in the past. When hearing that his sister, Elizabeth Barnard, has died under mysterious circumstances, Francis Barnard journeys to Spain in order to learn more. Upon arriving at the castle of Nicholas Medina, Elizabeth's husband, he is met at the door by Catherine, Nicholas's sister, who tells him that Nicholas is resting. Since Catherine has arrived at the castle only a short time before in order to comfort her brother and can therefore tell him little of Elizabeth's death, she offers to show the young man his sister's burial place in the crypt below. As they descend to the burial place, Francis hears a rhythmic, clanking sound and investigates. Suddenly he comes face to face with Nicholas Medina, who emerges from behind a previously locked door and explains that he has been doing upkeep on some machinery that he will not discuss. Since Francis was led to believe that Nicholas was resting, his suspicions about his sister's death increase. When he presses Nicholas for information, the grieving husband reveals only that his wife died of "something in her blood." Nicholas then escorts Francis to the burial room where Elizabeth's casket has been bricked-in behind a wall—a family custom. Francis, however, remains unsatisfied and vows to remain at the castle until he has answers.

That evening Elizabeth's physician and family friend, Dr. Leon, arrives at the castle during dinner. Under Francis's questioning, the doctor reveals that Elizabeth actually died of fright. Brushing aside Nicholas's explanation that he was simply trying to spare Francis the painful details, the young man demands to see the site of his sister's death. Reluctantly, Nicholas leads Francis to the castle torture chamber. He then explains to Francis that his life has become meaningless after Elizabeth's death, that she was the very essence of loving. "She could play the harpsichord like no other woman I have ever known," he adds before breaking down in tears. Upon recovering his composure, he continues his explanation. It seems that his father, Sebastian Medina, was one of the Inquisition's most degraded figures. "I will not dwell upon the history of this blasphemous chamber," Nicholas says. "Suffice it that the blood of a thousand men and women was spilled within these walls ... Limbs twisted and broken ... Eyes gouged from bloody sockets ... Flesh burned black!"

Elizabeth, he says, was too sensitive, too aware of the castle's malignant atmosphere, which eventually destroyed her. Little by little, she lost her appetite and her joy for life. She also began prowling the torture chamber, developing an unhealthy fascination with the instruments of death. One night Nicholas heard "the most blood-curdling scream I have ever heard in my life." Rushing into the torture chamber, Nicholas found his wife inside the iron maiden. As she died, she remained frozen in terror, whispering only the name "Sebastian."

Later Catherine goes to Francis asking forgiveness for Nicholas and telling him of a horrible event in Nicholas's childhood. When Nicholas was a little boy, he was forbidden to enter the torture chamber. But with a child's curiosity, he crept in one day to examine the instruments. Hearing footsteps, he hid and was witness to an awful sight: the murder of his Uncle Bartoleme and his mother Isabella at the hands of his father, for adultery.

The hours pass. As the castle is quiet in sleep, the playing of a harpsichord breaks the silence. Catherine, Francis, and Dr. Leon rush to the music room to find Nicholas, numb with terror, clutching a ring supposedly worn

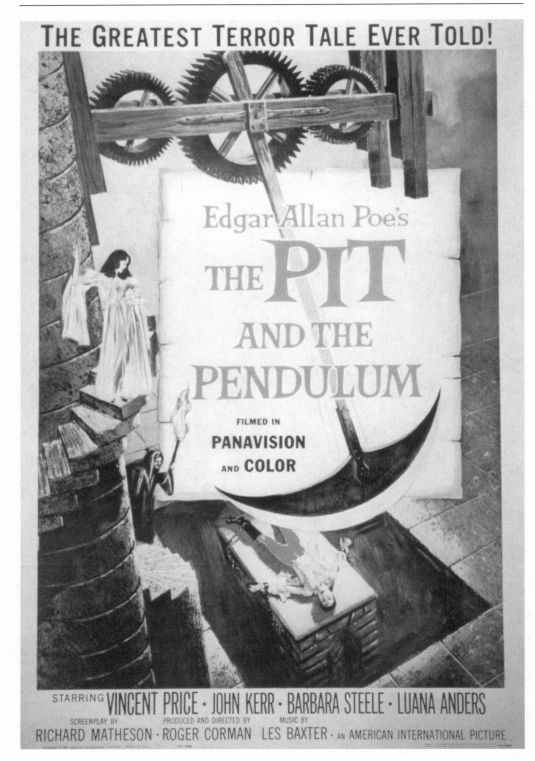

Poster art for *The Pit and the Pendulum* (1961).

by his wife at the time of her interment. No one else in the house can play the harpsichord, and Nicholas confirms that the playing was that of Elizabeth. After Dr. Leon has given Nicholas a sedative and put him to bed, he explains to Catherine and Francis that Nicholas is obsessed with the conviction that he buried his wife alive. It appears that young Nicholas not only watched his father torture his uncle and mother, but he also watched as his father walled his mother up alive. Dr. Leon, however, assures them that Elizabeth was quite dead.

Francis's suspicions are revived when he overhears Catherine tell Dr. Leon that she never liked Elizabeth. He accuses the three of intentional deception but is interrupted by a scream from Elizabeth's room. Running there, they find the maid in a state of hysteria, swearing that she heard Elizabeth call to her. When pressed, however, she admits that the voice was a whisper and therefore hard to identify positively as that of Elizabeth. Nicholas believes the maid, locks the door, and vows that no one will ever enter Elizabeth's room again.

At breakfast, Dr. Leon, Francis, and Catherine hear sounds of destruction coming from Elizabeth's room. Nicholas emerges from his room just as the three hurry upstairs to the locked door. Nicholas unlocks the door to reveal a room in shambles, the shock of which causes him to pass out. Later, as Dr. Leon and Catherine look after Nicholas in his own bedroom, Francis enters Nicholas's room through a secret passage that he says leads to Elizabeth's room. Having discovered the secret passage, Francis accuses Nicholas of being the only person who could have destroyed Elizabeth's room. Dr. Leon, to Catherine's surprise, agrees that the truth must be known in order to free Nicholas from his obsessions.

When the wall is taken down and the casket pried open, it reveals the hideous sight of a contorted, decaying corpse that has fought for air and clawed for release. As Nicholas screams out the fact that his suspicions were true, Dr. Leon swears that Elizabeth showed every indication of being dead when he pronounced her so. Still, Nicholas's mind is beginning to snap at this point, and the others must restrain him from committing suicide with a pistol. Later he simply sits with a fixed stare, proclaiming that he must accept whatever vengeance Elizabeth chooses to inflict on him.

Francis apologizes to Catherine and plans to leave with Dr. Leon in the morning. That night Nicholas is awakened by a woman's voice calling his name. Following the sound, he walks through a spider-webbed secret passage toward the crypt. Meanwhile, Catherine notices Nicholas is missing and asks Francis and Dr. Leon to help find him. The voice draws Nicholas to the burial room, and there he watches as the real Elizabeth rises from her coffin. Fleeing in terror from the pursuing apparition, he finally collapses on the stone floor, apparently completely mindless. At that point, Dr. Leon arrives and hugs Elizabeth, but he chides her for not waiting until Francis had left to complete their plan of driving Nicholas mad for his money. Elizabeth, however, admits that she could not wait and proceeds to gloat over her apparently deranged husband. "Is it not ironical?" she teases. "Your wife an adulteress, your mother an adulteress, your uncle an adulterer, your closest friend an adulterer. Do you not find that amusing, Nicholas?" Her glee changes to concern, however, as Nicholas answers "Yes" and begins to chuckle. Then, rising from the floor, Nicholas takes on the personality of his father and confuses Dr. Leon and Elizabeth with Bartoleme and Isabella. Disabling Dr. Leon, he manhandles Elizabeth over to the iron maiden. "Harlot!" he shouts. "You will die in agony." Then, sneering viciously, he locks her inside the torture device.

In a struggle with the demented Nicholas, Dr. Leon falls to his death in a very deep pit, within which stands a tall slab. When Francis unwittingly enters, Nicholas, believing him to be Bartoleme, ties him to the slab, above which hovers a giant, razor-sharp pendulum. "Do you know where you are?" Nicholas asks. "You are about to enter Hell, Bartoleme. Hell! The netherworld, the infernal regions, the abode of the damned, the place of torture ... (pointing below) the pit, and (pointing above) the pendulum ... the razor edge of destiny."

Nicholas sneers madly as he operates the ropes and gears lowering the swinging pendulum. Upon witnessing the terrifying scene, Catherine summons the aid of the servant Maximillian, who struggles against Nicholas, finally pushing him into the pit. Catherine then stops the descending pendulum shortly before it can slice though Francis's chest.

As the three survivors leave the torture chamber, Catherine locks the door and vows that "No one will ever enter this room again." Still in the iron maiden, however, and unknown to the living, is Elizabeth, her terrified eyes reflecting the horror of her obvious fate.

"The agony of my soul found vent in one loud, long and final scream of despair."

—Poe

Production and marketing: Corman recalls that when *The Fall of the House of Usher* (1960) proved a financial and critical success: "they (AIP) still didn't consider doing a Poe series. They just wanted another movie with a Poe title affixed to it."[85] Sensing another fine opportunity, Corman first considered making "The Masque of the Red Death" before finally deciding on "The Pit and the Pendulum":

> I always considered ["Masque"] to be one of Poe's best stories, and after *House of Usher* it was my original choice for the second film rather than "The Pit and the Pendulum." The reason I chose "The Pit and the Pendulum" over "Masque" is that the hooded figure of Death walking through a plague-stricken country is the essential feature of "The Masque of the Red Death" and also of Ingmar Bergman's picture *The Seventh Seal*, and I didn't want to be in a position of doing a picture based upon a nineteenth-century short story and possibly be accused of taking ideas from a film that was shot in the 1950s.[86]

Years later Corman would express his enjoyment in making the film because it allowed him to experiment with the camera. "There was a lot of moving camera work and interesting cutting in the climax of the film," he explained.[87]

As the project took shape, AIP assembled essentially the same production crew and screenwriter responsible for *The Fall of the House of Usher*. In writing the screenplay, Richard Matheson strayed further from Poe's original source than he had in *House of Usher*. In tact from the original story is the horror of the Inquisition and its machinery of torture. Otherwise, the story is a reworking of *House of Usher*. In both screenplays an unwelcome young man arrives at a house of horror. The death and premature burial of a beautiful woman figure prominently in both scripts, as does the idea of a miasma of evil permeating a house and exerting a destructive influence on those within. Ironically, *The Pit and the Pendulum* owes as much to Poe's "The Fall of the House of Usher" as it does to "The Pit and the Pendulum." Since Matheson could have set the action during the Inquisition itself and thereby have followed Poe's story more closely, some have pronounced him fearful of offending Roman Catholics. In 1961, however, a strong Catholic reaction against the film was unlikely.

Another noteworthy item about *Pit* is that it fully introduces the theme of the dominant female and submissive male that would recur in the AIP Corman/Poe series. The theme, of course, is straight from Poe's short stories. Corman's later films incorporating the theme include *The Premature Burial*, *Tales of Terror*, and *The Tomb of Ligeia*.

Ross Hahn, Jr., was in charge of construction. Of central importance, of course, was the torture chamber and pendulum room. For the latter, art director Haller designed a scenic backdrop of hooded figures amidst twisted, interlocking tree branches. The 40' x 80' mural was carried out in assorted blacks, grays, blues, and greens. Hahn suspended the 18' pendulum from the ceiling of the soundstage and controlled its swath-like movements. Hahn reportedly used 12,000 pounds of plaster in building the sets, one of which was the breakaway wall in the crypt which took six days to construct. Property master Dick Rubin ordered 2,000 candles made for the film, and physical effects supervisor Pat Dinga sprayed over 20 gallons of cobwebbing throughout the castle's subterranean regions.

To maximize the film's box office potential, AIP signed Vincent Price to play the dual role of Sebastian and Nicholas Medina. While no one upstaged Price in *House of Usher,* the actor did face an unexpected challenge on the set of *The Pit and the Pendulum.* During the scene in which Price creeps down a long corridor and down a winding stairway leading to the crypt, a white rat was supposed to dart across his path. During rehearsals, the rat stood still until called upon and then ran on cue. During live filming, however, the rodent moved forward into camera range, eyes blinking, and proceeded to brush its face and whiskers with its paws. In publicity releases, Price sighed, "I leave it to your imagination. WHO will the audience watch in *that* scene."

As an added attraction to Price, AIP signed British actress Barbara Steele (1938–) to her first Hollywood film. The actress had been introduced to the horror film community through her lauded performance as a resurrected witch in director Mario Bava's atmospheric Italian shocker *La maschera del demonio* (1960, aka *Black Sunday*). As Steele testified in a later interview, she made *The Pit and the Pendulum* at a low point in her life:

> I had a contract with Fox.... Finally, I never made a film for them. I was paid. I was bored and suffering a lot not being able to work. The only film I shot in America was *The Pit and the Pendulum* for AIP. My contract with Fox was dreadful. Rank, with whom I was under contract, didn't know very well how to use me. Then, they sold my contract to Fox. In the USA they wanted to change me completely. I was too big. I should

be a brunette or a blonde. And, then, life there is so artificial. I arrived there without much but left with nothing. I was completely demoralized.[88]

While *The Pit and the Pendulum* provided Steele with work, it also gave her the opportunity to work with Vincent Price. In publicity releases, she said she appreciated the opportunity: "I was in awe of him. Our major confrontation where he strangles me was done in one take, with a brief rehearsal beforehand. He really went at me and I had bruises on my throat to prove it. Afterward, he was so concerned he had hurt me—such a gentleman—a truly kind figure in spite of his image."

Further reflecting on Vincent Price, she contrasted their respective acting styles at that time:

> I find that it's very difficult, when one is a young actress, to make this type of film. When one is no longer young, one calls oneself Vincent Price. He can be successful through those very melodramatic effects. For an actress like me, it's terrible because the director always demands some of that "to add more." He's not looking for a shock effects. It's not these roles that suit me the most. It's not that it's more difficult. There are no easy roles and difficult roles. Myself, I prefer "honest" roles.[89]

"Honest" roles would prove in short supply for Steele, however, as the future found her billed as a horror queen in such films as *L'orribile segreto del Dr. Hitchcock* (1962, aka *The Horrible Dr. Hitchcock*) and *La spettro* (1962, aka *The Ghost*). Although she would take a break from horror to appear in Federico Fellini's *8 1/2* (1962) and a few other nongenre features, she would quickly return to terror in *La danza macabra* (1963, aka *Castle of Blood*), her second Poe-inspired film.

Steele aside, as AIP had done in *House of Usher,* it surrounded Vincent Price with two young, relatively inexperienced performers. The male, John Kerr (1931–), made his screen debut in *The Cobweb* (1955), which he followed with performances in the

Vincent Price madly attacks an amused Barbara Steele in *The Pit and the Pendulum* (1961).

successful *Tea and Sympathy* (1956) and *South Pacific* (1958). Younger, and more inexperienced, was Luana Anders (1940–), who had appeared in *Life Begins at Seventeen* (1958). Rounding out the major cast was Antony Carbone, a character actor with stage and television experience.

Inspired by the success of *House of Usher*, AIP launched *The Pit and the Pendulum* with another oversized pressbook and a strong ad campaign. Again, Poe is a central figure in the hype, though to a lesser degree than he was in the *House of Usher* campaign. This time he receives only one large biographical ad to himself but appears prominently as the author of the original short story in all the other ads.

The pressbook cover and posters proclaimed the film "The Greatest Terror Tale Ever Told!" The major art image, of course, was the giant pendulum swinging danger-

ously close to the chest of a prostrate prisoner. Under portraits of the principal characters, AIP placed bogus quotations which appear neither in the film nor in Poe's story.

Vincent Price—"The shrieking of mutilated victims is the music of my life."

John Kerr—"The agony found vent in a long final scream of despair."

Barbara Steele—"As they mourned me ... I was alive ... struggling to be free."

Luana Anders—"Ever since that day ... I have not been able to live as other women."

Among eleven "seat-selling slants" recommended by the pressbook is the following "wonderful gimmick" for extra publicity: "The mystery atmosphere of the picture can be heightened by keeping the theatre dark before 'The Pit and the Pendulum' is screened and having the ushers seat the audience by flashlight. Additional atmosphere can be added by having the Ushers wear black hooded capes."

In addition to the usual marketing strategies, AIP cooperated with Lancer Books in issuing a paperback tie-in written by Lee Sheridan that was based on Richard Matheson's screenplay. Lancer also produced special *Pit and the Pendulum* bookmarks featuring the film's key art image of the descending pendulum. This was the first film tie-in to consist of a screenplay novelization rather than Poe's original short stories. It is a bit disconcerting, however, to see on the book's cover "Poe's horror classic *The Pit and the Pendulum* adapted by Lee Sheridan from the Richard Matheson screenplay," an indication of just how far the film itself had strayed from Poe's original tale.

In 1963, French director and former film critic Alexandre Astruc (1923–) would direct another version of *The Pit and the Pendulum*. Some critics say it is the best Poe adaptation ever made; the film is presently unavailable in the United States.

Before moving on to the critique, I should mention one other item of interest. According to Fred Olen Ray (director of *Haunting Fear* (1989, based on Poe's "The Premature Burial"), Mark Damon, costar of *The Fall of the House of Usher* (1960), claimed that he, *not* Roger Corman, actually directed *The Pit and the Pendulum*. According to Ray, Damon claimed that AIP wanted him so badly to play in *House of Usher* that it promised him the director's chair on *The Pit and the Pendulum*. Damon's name could not appear in the credits because of union regulations, so Corman's name was used instead. I find this claim, if it was actually made, to be unbelievable. No one who worked on *The Pit and the Pendulum* has ever mentioned Mark Damon as playing any role in the technical production. Stills exist showing Roger Corman on the set. The film has all the hallmarks we have come to associate with a Roger Corman/ Poe film. Enough said.

Critique: As was the case with *House of Usher*, the critics were generally favorable. *The New York Times* opined:

Atmospherically, at least—there is a striking fusion of rich colors, plushy decor and eerie music—this is probably Hollywood's most effective Poe-style horror flavoring to date.... If the family is right out of Charles Addams, so is the castle playroom, a torture dungeon. Absurd? No, not exactly. For Richard Matheson's ironic plot is compact and as logical as the choice of the small cast. Against the film's elegant period appointments, ornate furniture, firelit tapestries, a ruby ring on a harpsichord keyboard, director-producer Roger Corman has evoked a genuinely chilling mood of horror.[90]

Time magazine agreed, calling the film "a literary hair-raiser that is cleverly, if self-consciously, Edgar Allan Poetic,"[91] and *Films in Review* pronounced it "even more inventively made and edited than 'House of Usher.'"[92]

Despite dissenting voices, the film today largely retains its reputation as a fine gothic horror picture. In *Horror in the Cinema*, Ivan Butler criticized both the acting and the screenplay's similarity to that of *House of Usher*. In *Cinema of Mystery*, Rose London writes that "There is little of Poe in the film, and even Corman seems weary of the same old style."[93] On the positive side, she does enjoy Price's delivery of the line "*This* room was my father's *life!*"

On a more positive note, in *The Psychotronic Encyclopedia of Film*, Michael Weldon writes that "Barbara Steele is great in her first American role" and notes that "The massive torture chamber, including the fabled razor-sharp pendulum which almost cuts John Kerr in half, provides a visual highlight."[94]

In *The Motion Picture Guide* (Cinebooks, 1985), Jay Robert Nash and Stanley Ralph Ross call *The Pit and the Pendulum* "the best of Roger Corman's Edgar Allan Poe series.... a very entertaining horror film with chills, humor, and a bravura performance by Price who was just beginning to fine-hone his wickedly delightful, villainous characters. Shot in a lush almost garish color by cinematographer Crosby ... the film is filled with some impressive techniques and

vement for a low-budget, quickly
e."[95]

ugh finding fault with the screenplay, *The Overlook Film Encyclopedia: Horror* finds the film only marginally less successful than *House of Usher*. Praising the camera work, the *Encyclopedia* concludes that "From the great sequence in which Steele lures Price down into the crypt to the finale (Steele sealed into an iron maiden, the pendulum in motion, Price tumbling into the pit), its action is terrific."

Finally, Leonard Maltin awards the film 3½ stars and asks the viewer to "bear with the slow first half" in order to witness a "slick horror tale," and *Video Hound's Golden Movie Retriever 1996* throws the film three bones, calling it "A landmark in Gothic horror."

In my view, *The Pit and the Pendulum* falls slightly short of its predecessor, *The Fall of the House of Usher*. First of all, Matheson's *House* screenplay is more faithful to Poe's story, themes, and mood, giving it a more Poe-esque quality. It is true that *Pit* incorporates many of those same Poe-esque themes, but their source is "The Fall of the House of Usher," not "The Pit and the Pendulum." The subplots of infidelity and feigned premature burial, none of which are attributable to Poe, weaken the *Pit* screenplay to a slight extent. While both screenplays are highly literate, a credit to Matheson's ear for dialogue, the *House* screenplay is superior.

While Vincent Price's performance in *Usher* is one of the best of his career, his work in *Pit* is almost as good. In both cases, Corman largely let the actor interpret the roles as he saw fit. The difference is the melancholy consistency of the world-weary Usher, symbolic of the house itself. Nevertheless, in both roles Price exhibits an exquisite vulnerability that many critics have either missed or tended to overlook.

Les Baxter's musical score is appropriately melancholy and uneasy, a perfect complement to the film. As was the case in *Usher*, Daniel Haller's sets triumph over the film's low budget. Particularly effective is the contrast between the castle's elegant living quarters and the cobwebbed subterranean torture chamber and crypt, a contrast that symbolizes the dichotomous mind of Nicholas himself. A similar symbolic contrast is apparent in *House*. Therefore, what we see in *Pit* we have seen before.

Pit has a few superior qualities, however, not the least of which is Barbara Steele. Her wicked sensuality, particularly in the scene in which she taunts the insane, incapacitated Price, is superior to anything executed by Myrna Fahey in *Usher*. Also superior is the ending. While I still shudder at the ending of *Usher*, which is more Poe-esque than that of *Pit*, from the time Steele coaxes Price down to the crypt to the final shot of Steele's frightened eyes within the iron maiden, no Corman/Poe finale is more terrifying or exciting. In those scenes, *Pit's* fluid camera and diverse angles are slightly superior to those of *Usher*,.

Regardless of how critics appraise the relative merits of *Usher* and *Pit*, they must acknowledge that both films capture the aura of Poe and both are effective horror films.

The Premature Burial (1962)
American International, U.S.A.

Credits: Directed and produced by Roger Corman; screenplay by Charles Beaumont and Ray Russell, based on "The Premature Burial" by Edgar Allan Poe; cinematography by Floyd Crosby; art direction by Daniel Haller; edited by Ronald Sinclair; music by Ronald Stein.

Running time: 81 minutes.

Cast: Ray Milland (Guy Carrell), Hazel Court (Emily Gault), Richard Ney (Miles Archer), Heather Angel (Kate Carrell), Alan Napier (Dr. Gideon Gault), John Dierkes (Sweeney), Richard Miller (Mole), Brendon Dillon (minister).

Story: The setting is London in the 1860s. In a neglected public graveyard, Dr. Gideon Gault and medical students Guy Carrell and Miles Archer stand by as graver-obbers Sweeney and Mole busy themselves digging up a recently buried body. As he works, Sweeney whistles the haunting melody "Molly Malone."

When Sweeney passes up the coffin lid, the bystanders are horrified at the sight of a series of long bloody trails, wild scrapings— the frantic efforts of an imprisoned person to gain freedom. The corpse itself offers complete evidence of premature burial. The sight overcomes Guy, and as a result, he breaks off his engagement with Dr. Gault's daughter Emily and shuts himself away from the world.

Unwilling to accept this turn of events, Emily visits Guy to discover why he has called off their wedding plans. She is greeted at the door by Kate Carrell, Guy's sister, who says Guy does not wish to see her. When Emily insists, however, Kate leads her to Guy. It seems that the distraught former medical student still loves Emily but wants to break off their engagement as a result of his morbid obsession with premature burial. Guy takes Emily on a tour of the family crypt and explains the circumstances under which his ancestors met their deaths. "Death has come to the Carrells like an assassin," he says, explaining that his own father died within his coffin "like a single candle in a dark and airless room." Claiming that he too suffers from catalepsy, Guy insists that "I didn't run away (at the cemetery) from what was inside that coffin, but from what I knew to be inside me."

Emily turns on the charm and dissuades Guy from his decision. Soon after, despite the objections of Kate, Guy and Emily become engaged again.

The wedding takes place during a fore-boding thunderstorm. At the reception, Guy becomes distraught when Emily plays "Molly Malone" on the piano, and he goes upstairs to rest. Shortly afterward, Guy hears a cry from outside and discovers that the family dog has been struck by lightning. After saying he will bury the dog, he is astonished and terrified when the animal rises to its feet, alive and apparently recovered— saved by chance from a premature burial.

When time passes without Guy and Emily going on a honeymoon, Miles returns to the house to look after Guy's health. Upon arriving, he is astonished to discover that Guy has constructed a very curious tomb. Within the tomb is a coffin that can be opened from the inside, a rope that rings an alarm bell, a ladder leading to a trapdoor on the roof, sticks of dynamite in case the escape plans fail, and, should the dynamite fail, a goblet of poison.

Kate assures Miles that her and Guy's father was not buried alive, that Guy never really heard the man calling from the crypt. Miles takes no position on whether Guy's father was buried alive, but he does say that Guy probably does not suffer from catalepsy. He also confides in Emily that unless Guy frees himself from his obsession and destroys the strange tomb he has built, the constant fear could have the effect of bringing on a cataleptic condition.

Some time later Guy and Emily are talking out on the lawn when Guy believes he hears Sweeney whistling "Molly Malone." He follows the sound through the fog-shrouded trees, confronts Sweeney and Mole, and lapses into unconsciousness. While unconscious, Guy dreams that he is buried in the tomb. Unfortunately, when he tries to escape, the bell won't ring, the ladder breaks, and the dynamite crumbles. Then, tipping the goblet of poison to his lips, he recoils upon discovering it filled with writhing worms.

When Guy awakens, he explains to Miles that he and Emily have heard and seen the grave robbers, but Emily says she saw and heard nothing. When Guy goes up-

Poster art for *The Premature Burial* (1962).

stairs to rest, Miles explains to Emily that her husband is suffering from delusions. Meanwhile, Guy is awakened by the whistling of "Molly Malone." When he investigates, he is frightened by the sudden appearance of Sweeney outside a window. Kate enters the room to help her brother but sees nothing.

When Emily again pleads with Guy to give up these morbid preoccupations and focus upon their life together, he balks. But when she accuses Guy of already being buried alive by his fears and making her a widow as a result, he reluctantly agrees to destroy the crypt.

With the crypt gone, Guy agrees on a honeymoon but decides to give a party before leaving. At the party, everyone hears a sound coming from behind a wall in the house. When Miles investigates, he finds a trapped kitten, which, of course, reminds Guy of premature burial.

Since Kate insists that their father was really not buried alive, Miles suggests that it might help cure Guy if they reopen his father's grave to prove his fears unfounded. They all go to the crypt, but when it is opened, the corpse is found as though it had been buried alive. It falls out against Guy, who collapses as though dead. After Miles and Dr. Gault mistakenly pronounce Guy dead of a heart attack, he returns to consciousness during the funeral but remains paralyzed within the coffin. As his mind screams for help, he is carried to the cemetery and buried alive.

Directly after the interment, Sweeney and Mole open the grave to steal Guy's body for Dr. Gault. When they lift off the lid, Guy strangles Sweeney and impales Mole, after which he wraps Sweeney's corpse in a blanket and delivers it to Dr. Gault. Guy electrocutes Gault and then visits Emily, taking her from her bed and into the cemetery, where he binds her and buries her alive.

Meanwhile, Miles discovers the bodies of Sweeney and Dr. Gault, guesses what has happened, and rushes to the cemetery where he and Guy engage in a fierce struggle. Suddenly, a shot rings out and Guy slumps to the ground, killed by a bullet fired by Kate. She explains to Miles that she had known all along that it was Emily who used various devices to bring on Guy's attack and inherit the family fortune.

Production and marketing: When Roger Corman and AIP had a disagreement over the division of profits earned from some of Corman's earlier pictures, the director decided to make his next Edgar Allan Poe film for Pathé, the company responsible for AIP's laboratory work. Pathé offered Corman a better financial deal than AIP had, so he accepted and went to work on *The Premature Burial.*

Script responsibilities fell to two authors of considerable reputation, Charles Beaumont (1929–1967) and Ray Russell. Beaumont published horror and science fiction tales from the mid fifties to the early sixties in such places as *Playboy, Rogue Magazine, If Magazine,* and *Amazing Stories.* His short-story collections *The Hunger and Other Stories* (1955), and *Night Ride and Other Journeys* (1960) are held in high esteem by such luminaries as Stephen King and Ray Bradbury. Richard Matheson, author of the *Fall of the House of Usher* (1960) screenplay, wrote that Beaumont's stories are "alight with the magic of a truly extraordinary imagination, shot through with veins of coruscating wit, feather-light and dancing on a wind of jest." Beaumont had also written the screenplay for *Queen of Outer Space* (1958) and contributed many scripts for *The Twilight Zone* television series. He would die in 1967 at the early age of 38 of a strange degenerative illness now known as Alzheimer's disease. Collaborator Ray Russell would serve as a pallbearer at his funeral. Russell was also a well-known author of horror tales, perhaps his best known being "Sardonicus," from which he produced the screenplay for William Castle's *Mr. Sardonicus* (1961).

When Beaumont and Russell returned to Poe's story, they were troubled to discover that it was not a narration easily lending itself to adaptation. Poe's narrator expresses

"WITHIN THE COFFIN
I LIE...ALIVE!"

RAY MILLAND
EDGAR ALLAN POE'S

IN COLOR AND PANAVISION
THE PREMATURE BURIAL

Ray Milland is buried alive in this dream sequence from *The Premature Burial* (1962).

his horror of being buried alive, relates several "historical" examples of premature burial, and concludes with his own shipboard nightmare in which he dreamed himself buried alive. The screenwriters adapted the narrator's obsessive fear of premature burial as the film's premise. Guy Carrell's homemade tomb was inspired by a similar one constructed by Poe's narrator.

I entered into a series of elaborate precautions. Among other things, I had the family vault so remodeled as to admit of being readily opened from within. The slightest pressure upon a long lever that extended far into the tomb would cause the iron portals to fly back. There were arrangements also for the free admission of air and light, and convenient receptacles for food and water, within immediate reach of the coffin intended for my reception. This coffin was warmly and softly padded, and was provided with a lid fashioned upon the principle of the vault-door, with the addition of springs so con-

trived that the feeblest movement of the body would be sufficient to set it at liberty. Besides all this, there was suspended from the roof of the tomb, a large bell, the rope of which, it was designed, should extend through a hole in the coffin, and so be fastened to one of the hands of the corpse.

Poe's narrator dreams that he is buried alive, not in his prepared coffin but in the cold, dank earth. In the film, Guy Carrell dreams that the specially prepared tomb fails in its purpose, and he too later finds himself buried alive in the earth.

In Poe's story, the narrator relates the tale of a lady buried alive:

The lady was deposited in her family vault, which, for three subsequent years, was undisturbed. At the expiration of this term it was opened for the reception of a sarcophagus,—but, alas! how fearful a shock awaited the husband, who, personally threw open the door! As its portals swung outwardly back, some white-appareled object fell rattling within his arms.

It was the skeleton of his wife in her yet unmoulded shroud.

Beaumont and Russell follow suit in their scene in which Guy Carrell opens his father's tomb. When the skeleton tumbles out of the coffin into Guy's arms, it precipitates the spell leading to Guy's own premature burial.

Galvanism is another element appearing in both story and screenplay. In the story, body snatchers remove a "corpse" from its grave and deliver it to a private hospital. Subsequently, medical men are surprised when their galvanic experiments revive the subject who had obviously been buried alive. In the film, Dr. Gault is involved in galvanic experiments, but unlike what happens in the story, Guy Carrell makes him the victim of his own galvanic battery.

Beaumont and Russell also incorporated as much of Poe's language into the screenplay as they could. For some reason, most of it ended up on the cutting room floor, except for one memorable scene. As Guy Carrell gives Emily Gault and Miles Archer a tour of his special tomb, he explains that premature burial involves "the unendurable oppression of the lungs—the stifling fumes of the damp earth—the rigid embrace of the coffin, the blackness of absolute night—and the silence, like an overwhelming sea, and then, invisible in the darkness, but all too hideously real to the other senses, the presence of the conqueror worm." This is, of course, only a slight reworking of Poe's actual words.

Although Corman would later express some disappointment with he screenplay, he would turn again to Charles Beaumont in 1963 when planning what would be his sixth Poe film, *The Haunted Palace*.

As a result of Vincent Price's success in *The Fall of the House of Usher* and *The Pit and the Pendulum*, Corman wanted the actor to play Guy Carrell in *The Premature Burial*. Since Price was under contract with AIP,

Corman's second choice was Ray Milland (1905–1986). Milland had carved himself a nice niche in Hollywood in such films as *The Jungle Princess* (1936), *Beau Geste* (1939), *French Without Tears* (1939), and *Arise, my Love* (1941). Then in 1944 he starred in *The Uninvited*, one of the greatest ghost stories ever filmed, and he followed up the next year with his Academy Award–winning performance in *The Lost Weekend*, which, along with *Leaving Las Vegas* (1996), is one of the most harrowing films about alcoholism ever made. He then turned in fine performances in such films as *Alias Nick Beal* (1949), *The Thief* (1952), and Alfred Hitchcock's *Dial M for Murder* (1954) before getting the call from Roger Corman. The director would be impressed enough with Milland in *The Premature Burial* to use him again in *X—The Man with the X-Ray Eyes* (1963). Unfortunately, though Milland would be able to boast a few good outings as a director, his acting vita would soon include such titles as *The Thing with Two Heads* (1972), *Frogs* (1972), and *Terror in the Wax Museum* (1973), none of which enhanced his reputation.

Hazel Court had attracted Roger Corman's attention in a series of important British horror pictures: *The Curse of Frankenstein* (1957), *The Man Who Could Cheat Death* (1959), and *Dr. Blood's Coffin* (1960). Like several British performers who distinguished themselves in horror films, Court also performed on the Shakespearean stage. For the scene in which she is buried alive, Court was actually covered with several inches of dirt, out of which protruded a small straw that enabled her to breathe. Corman would use her again in his Poe-inspired *The Masque of the Red Death* (1964).

Like Hazel Court, British-born Heather Angel also acted on the Shakespearean stage. She appeared with Ray Milland in the actor's first film *Bulldog Drummond* (1929) and later became a U.S. citizen.

For Guy Carrell's disturbing art work, Corman commissioned Burton Shonberg, the young artist who produced the paintings used in *The Fall of the House of Usher*. It took

Shonberg almost three months to do the four paintings used in the film.

As fate would have it, on the second day of shooting, James Nicholson and Sam Arkoff walked onto the Pathé set and shook Corman's hand, announcing that under threat of losing AIP's lab business, Pathé had sold the rights to *The Premature Burial* to AIP. Corman was back in the fold. Fortunately for Roger, AIP honored all the stipulations of the Pathé contract.

According to press releases, Corman used 2000 pounds of dry ice and over 50 gallons of fog juice to produce the ever-present fogs surrounding the Carrell estate and graveyard. With cinematographer Floyd Crosby and art director Daniel Haller back on the team, *The Premature Burial* would have the professional look expected of a Corman-Poe film.

Upon the film's completion, AIP launched it with another lavish pressbook. Again, the inspiration of Edgar Allan Poe was strongly hyped, though not as much as it had been for the first two films in the series. In one article, the pressbook explains that "It is Poe's years-ahead-of-his-time understanding of human fears and emotions, coupled with his masterful writing, which make his terror tales so gripping and chilling."

Ads and posters for the film emphasized the face of Ray Milland, his eyes whitened in ghostly fashion to emphasize fear as men lower a coffin into an absurdly deep grave. Another poster design had Milland lying, obviously alive, in an open coffin as others prepare him for burial. The ads included these catch-lines:

"Within the coffin I lie ... alive!" "Life remained only in his fevered mind, in his tormented eyes. To those at his graveside ... he was a corpse, the latest victim of a family curse!" "He suffered the worst horror the human mind can imagine—living death!" "As his coffin was laid to rest, his brain screamed—'I am not dead!'"

As was often the case with previous Corman-Poe ads, these lines are obviously meant to resemble quotations from Poe's stories, though none of them is actually from the pen of the master. One ad did use a line from the story, however. It read simply: "Deep, deep, and forever into some ordinary and nameless grave!"

Critique: *The Premature Burial* was and still is considered the weakest of the Corman-Poe series. *Variety* found the film "too familiar to generate much shock.... Not only is the plotting in *Premature Burial* discouragingly predictable, but its gloomy and cavernous interior setting is peculiarly similar to those in the first two pix. By this time, many film fans (and at least one reviewer) are as familiar with Corman's downstairs dungeons as they are with their own basement hobbyshops."[96]

The New York Herald Tribune also condemned the screenplay but added: "Mr. Corman's production group, the only outfit in Hollywood with a spider under long-term contract, has made several handsome horror pictures in the past. *The Premature Burial* is no less attractively designed or tastefully colored."[97]

The New York Times also gave the film a mixed review, finding the screenplay "static, slack and starchily written," while finding impressive its "compelling music, rich color decor and eerie atmosphere ... Donald Stein's rhapsodic treatment of 'Molly Malone' (heretofore a harmless tune) and the handsomely tinted Gothic settings, under the art direction of Daniel Haller. One blue-green nightmare montage is a pip."[98]

In his *Horror in Cinema,* Ivan Butler writes:

> *The Premature Burial* shows little advance (over the first two Corman-Poe films), the mixture being much as before. On the credit side is the atmospheric photography by Floyd Crosby. There are also several imaginative scenes, notably one where the hero dreams he is being buried alive—the start of which, with a black screen and only the sound of loud heartbeats audible, awakens an odd memory of Jekyll's first change to Hyde

in Mamoulian's masterpiece. Ray Milland, an excellent actor, did not make up for the loss of Vincent Price.[99]

Those who scoff at Price's ability as a thespian should take note.

In his *Horrors from Screen to Scream*, Ed Naha, sniping at Beaumont and Russell, writes that "the camera work salvages the script."[100]

In the *Psychotronic Encyclopedia of Film*, Michael Weldon calls *The Premature Burial* "A moody, serious movie."[101]

The Overlook Encyclopedia of Film: Horror judges *The Premature Burial* to be "the third and weakest in Corman's Poe cycle" primarily because Milland could not equal Price's flamboyance and because "Corman relies too heavily on the gloomy graveyards, gothic mansions, swirling ground-fogs, bats, candelabras and opulent spiderwebs that [he had elaborated before]." The *Encyclopedia*, while joining everyone else in praising Milland's nightmare burial, concludes that the film is "superior routine."

Leonard Maltin finds Ray Milland "unconvincingly cast as a medical student." While acknowledging that the film is "lavish," he pronounces it "not one of the director's best." *Video Hound's Golden Movie Retriever 1996* joins Maltin in awarding the film only two stars.

In my view, *The Premature Burial* is a well-sustained horror film. Although Corman had already used many of the film's strongest shock and mood devices, thereby weakening their impact the third time around, he nevertheless successfully experiments. Consider, for example, the widely heralded nightmare sequence. In many ways, Crosby's cinematography alone lifted all three of Corman's first Poe efforts above the ordinary, and in the first two, Vincent Price gave splendid performances. Price's absence in the third film is largely regarded as one of the film's major weaknesses. This, however, deserves some examination. It is true that Price brings a flamboyance and vulnerability to the Corman-Poe films that mesh perfectly with Richard Matheson's conceptions. While Beaumont and Russell's Guy Carrell is squarely in the Matheson tradition, Milland brings a different interpretation to the role. In fact, Milland plays the role much as he did his Academy Award–winning portrayal of alcoholic writer Don Birnam in *The Lost Weekend*. In that film, though Milland is obsessed with alcohol rather than the grave, his struggles against living death are similar. Compare the scenes in which Milland's Don Birnam describes the allure of liquor to a credulous bartender to the ones in which his Guy Carrell describes the devices of his custom-made tomb to two astonished guests.

Although Milland is quite good in the role, would Price have been better? In this particular case, probably yes. But that gets to the real problem of *The Premature Burial*. We have seen so many of its elements in Corman's previous two Poe films that it is ironically the absence of Vincent Price that helps give the film some originality. Aside from the camera work, the most effective element of the film is probably the clever use of the Irish folk song "Molly Malone," in which a young woman peddles a cart of seafood through the streets of the city singing "Alive, alive-o, alive, alive-O." While the words are left unsung in the film, the melody takes on a foreboding life of its own, greatly adding to the mood and suspense.

Tales of Terror (1962)

American International, U.S.A.

Credits: Directed and produced by Roger Corman; executive producers—James H. Nicholson and Samuel Z. Arkoff; screenplay by Richard Matheson, based on "Morella," "The Black Cat," "The Cask of Amontillado," and "The Facts in the Case of M. Valdemar" by Edgar Allan Poe; music by Les Baxter; cinematography by Floyd Crosby; production design and art design by Daniel Haller; special effects by Pat Dinga.

Running time: 90 minutes.

Cast: "Morella": Vincent Price (Locke), Maggie Pierce (Lenora), Leona Gage (Morella), Ed Cobb (driver). "The Black Cat:" Vincent Price (Fortunato), Peter Lorre (Montressor), Joyce Jameson (Annabel), Lenny Weinrib (policeman), Wally Campo (bartender), Alan Dewit (chairman), John Hackett (policeman). "The Case of M. Valdemar": Vincent Price (Valdemar), Basil Rathbone (Carmichael), Debra Paget (Helene), David Frankham (Dr. James), Scotty Brown (servant).

Story: "Morella": Once a handsome, virile man, Locke has lived as a recluse in his mansion for 26 years, mourning the death of his raven-haired wife, Morella. Locke's blonde-haired daughter, Lenora, whom he blamed for Morella's death, returns to the mansion for the first time in 26 years to see her father.

Entering the house, Lenora is shocked to find the rooms covered with spider webs and dust and dismayed to find her father an irritable alcoholic. Locke rebuffs her attempts at friendliness and makes clear his displeasure at seeing her. When Lenora leaves the room, Locke looks at Morella's portrait and muses, "Morella, my beloved wife, your murderer has returned."

Forced to stay overnight in the eerie house, Lenora explores the rooms and finds them all in a state of decay. In her mother's bedroom, she is shocked to find Morella's mummified corpse preserved on the bed.

When confronted with Lenora's discovery, Locke tells her that though he initially buried Morella, he could not bear to consign her beauty to the ground forever. Lenora then has a coughing spasm and admits to Locke that she has only a few months to live, saying, "We're both dead now, Father." Locke, stricken with remorse at his treatment of Lenora, explains to her that 26 years ago, Morella, weakened from giving birth to Lenora, insisted on giving a lavish party. One hour into the party she became ill and took to her bed, blaming the child for her illness and vowing to avenge herself. She died before the doctor could arrive. Locke nearly killed the child that very night and nearly killed himself as well. He settled for sending the child away to boarding schools, however, and locked himself away in the mansion with the body of Morella. Lenora then reveals that her marriage ended in failure, just another failure in a life of failure. Filled with pity and sorrow, Locke embraces his daughter and sighs: "You've come home at last." But, from her bedroom, the corpse of Morella echoes the words "At last!"

That night Morella's ghost rises from its bed and possesses the body of the sleeping Lenora. When the young woman screams, her father rushes in to find her dead. As Locke mourns, the shrouded body suddenly shows signs of life. When he begins to draw back the shroud, he sees black hair instead of blonde. Pulling the shroud further, he is confronted by Morella, alive and beautiful. Confused and terrified, Locke rushes to Morella's bedroom to find Lenora's corpse, mummified as though it had been dead for 26 years. When Morella follows him and announces that she has returned to avenge herself, he drops his candle, setting the house afire. As the apparition of Morella strangles her husband, the mansion is engulfed in flames.

"The wind of the firmament breathed but one sound within my ears, and the rip-

Leona Gage and Vincent Price in the "Morella" segment of *Tales of Terror* (1962).

ples upon the sea murmured evermore ... Morella."

—Edgar Allan Poe

Story: "The Black Cat": Narrator: "And what is it that happens just before death, which leads inexorably to that death? Our second story provides one roguish answer to

that question, in the story of a man who hated a cat ... The Black Cat."

Late one night lovely Annabel Herringbone is awakened by the arrival home of her drunken husband, Montressor. Upon entering the house, he verbally abuses her and vents his anger upon the household pet, a black cat. After stalking about the house in search of money, he finally passes into a drunken stupor.

The next morning Montressor wakes to find the loathed black cat sleeping upon his chest. After threatening bodily damage to the animal, he resumes badgering Annabel for the money he suspects she keeps hidden from him. Although he has not worked for seventeen years, he has the gall to accuse Annabel of hiding away her sewing money. Undeterred by her protests that they must eat, Montressor finally discovers a wad of bills, grins maliciously, and leaves for the tavern.

After running out of money, Montressor is thrown into the street, where he pathetically and humorously tries to weasel money from passersby. Then, to his surprise and joy, he stumbles upon a wine merchants' convention, where famed wine expert Fortunato Luchresi is about to give a wine-tasting exhibition. When Montressor rudely interrupts the proceedings, claiming that he can identify wines by taste better than the expert can, a challenge match quickly ensues. Although Montressor matches Fortunato challenge for challenge, he finally loses when the massive alcohol assault to his brain renders him inarticulate.

Fortunato agrees to see his drunken foe home, where he meets and falls in love with poor Annabel. Shortly thereafter, Montressor finds that his wife gives him all the money he wants and never protests when he goes out each evening to the tavern. But when the bartender asks Montressor how long his wife has been acting that way, the drunkard puts two and two together and immediately heads home. Hiding outside the house, he watches as Fortunato and Annabel embrace on the doorstep. When Fortunato is gone, Montressor enters the house, surprising Annabel before she has had time to remake the bed.

The following afternoon Fortunato accepts a dinner invitation at the Herringbone residence. Montressor there drugs the unsuspecting Fortunato's Amontillado and en-

tombs him alive behind a wall in the basement beside the corpse of Annabel. Not only are Montressor's wife and her lover disposed of, but the murderer then discovers a large stash of cash in one of Annabel's hiding places and treats the entire tavern to drinks. During the libations, however, he fatefully mutters that Annabel will not need the money where she is, spurring a suspicious bartender to notify the police.

That night Montressor has a terrifying, yet humorous, nightmare in which Fortunato and Annabel pull off his head and play catch with it. Upon awakening and finding himself the victim of more alcohol-induced hallucinations, Montressor is soon irritated to find the police at the door wishing to search the house for Annabel. The police want to begin the search in the cellar, and Montressor leads them down with bravado until he hallucinates the ghosts of Fortunato and Annabel beckoning them down. By now the police are quite suspicious of Montressor's odd behavior. Still the murderer keeps talking, asking the police where they think he has hidden Annabel. Behind the very solid basement wall perhaps. At that moment everyone is chilled as an unearthly wail comes from behind the wall. When the police knock a hole in the wall, they see Fortunato dead and the black cat sitting upon the head of Annabel's corpse. The cat Montressor despised had slipped, unknown to the murderer, into the tomb of the victims.

"I had walled the black monster up within the tomb."

—Edgar Allan Poe

Story: "The Case of M. Valdemar": Narrator: "What exactly is it that occurs at the moment of death, especially to a man, who in that moment, is not permitted to die, as in 'The Case of Mister Valdemar'?"

M. Valdemar, an old man nearing the end of his life, suffers from pain in his final illness. Hoping to end his days free of physical pain, he calls upon the services of M. Carmichael, a crafty, unscrupulous mesmerist who uses his skills to ease the sick

Peter Lorre entombs frantic Vincent Price and sedate Joyce Jameson in the "Black Cat" segment of *Tales of Terror* (1962).

man's discomfort, despite the objections of Dr. Elliott James, Valdemar's personal physician. During this difficult period, Valdemar's young wife, Helene, remains faithfully by her husband's side, though she has fallen in love with Dr. James.

At a meeting of all concerned, Valdemar announces that in payment for Carmichael's services he has agreed to let the mesmerist hypnotize him near the moment of his death in an effort to see how long a hypnotic state might stave off the end. What difference will a few more minutes matter? Valdemar reasons, especially if it will help advance Carmichael's knowledge. Helene objects that even though Valdemar does not fear death or a short prolongation of life, he should indeed fear Carmichael, whom she believes revels in the control he exerts over Valdemar during the hypnosis sessions. Valdemar brushes aside Helene's fears and

says that with all his heart he wishes that after his death she will marry Dr. James. Valdemar says he knows that they are attracted to each other and that he will die easier knowing that she will not be alone after his demise. "Your happiness means more to me than anything," he tells her. "I shall not die until that happiness has been assured."

Several weeks later Dr. James tells a physically distressed Valdemar that the end is near. Carmichael soon arrives and places the dying man into a hypnotic trance. Deep in the trance, Valdemar utters the words "No pain ... I am dying. Do not wake me. Let me die ... so." "I will not wake you, Valdemar," Carmichael replies. "Deep sleep ... very deep sleep ... from which there is no waking ... unless I say. You understand?" "Yes," Valdemar answers, "I understand." Dr. James then examines Valdemar, at which point a hideous death rattle begins. When Carmichael orders the poor man to return to his sleep, Helene screams for him to end the experiment and let her husband die. Still Carmichael persists in the experiment.

When Dr. James examines Valdemar, he and Carmichael agree that the patient is dead but still aware. Dead, but unable to pass on. "Darkness ... hovering in darkness," Valdemar moans. When Dr. James again demands that Carmichael end the experiment, the elated mesmerist informs him that though Valdemar is dead, his mind remains in the hypnotist's control. When Carmichael asks what Valdemar sees, the answer is a painful "only darkness."

Seven months later Dr. James pulls a pistol on Carmichael in an attempt to force an end to the experiment. The mesmerist, however, stalls long enough to allow Valdemar to speak. It seems that the entranced man has changed his mind: he now says he wants Helene to marry Carmichael. Although Dr. James objects that Valdemar is simply repeating what Carmichael has commanded him to say, Helene dismisses Dr. James and agrees to marry Carmichael if he will only end the horrible experiment and free her husband. Carmichael, however, states that he is in control and will not be dictated to. Helene, he says, will marry him, and the experiment will continue as before. When Carmichael begins physically to restrain Helene, she cries out for help. At this point, Valdemar literally stirs from the grave, to rise from the deathbed and envelop the evil Carmichael, who dies from fright. The hypnotic spell broken, all that remains of Valdemar is an oozing putrescence enveloping Carmichael's body.

"And there was an oozing liquid putrescence ... all that remained of Mr. Valdemar."

—Edgar Allan Poe

Production and marketing: According to Roger Corman:

I was getting a bit tired of the Poe films by this time, but AIP felt that I should continue. I was exhausted. With *Tales of Terror*, we tried to do something a little different. The screenplay was actually a series of very frightening sequences, dramatic sequences inspired by several of the Poe stories. To break things up a bit, we tried introducing humor into one of them, "The Black Cat."[102]

In turning to the anthology approach, Corman revived a format that had fallen out of favor since Great Britain's masterful *Dead of Night* (1945). Richard Matheson is back as screenwriter, but rather than having to stretch a Poe story into a full-length feature film, this time he has three stories to adapt to the same time frame. Nevertheless, in adapting "Morella," Matheson uses only the broad plot element of the daughter "causing" the mother's death and consequently falling victim to metapsychosis. Unlike Poe's story, which focuses on the relationship between the narrator and Morella, Matheson's adaptation focuses on the relationship between the narrator and his daughter.

For good measure, Matheson throws in elements of his *House of Usher* screenplay (e.g., the hint of incest, the theme of revenge, and, of course, the final conflagration) and lifts most of the ending directly from Poe's "Ligeia," a story somewhat similar in theme. Matheson, however, was ultimately displeased with the final product, largely because of casting. Matheson later referred to the first segment as "Shirley Temple in the Haunted House," complaining that his original script developed a great relationship between the father and daughter. He visualized someone more like Nina Foch playing the daughter and was quite disappointed with the choice of Maggie Pierce. Matheson also claimed that AIP cut a lot of his original script, rendering the final product a failure.

In the second segment, Matheson's synthesis of "The Black Cat" and "The Cask of Amontillado" incorporates the key plot elements of the original tales. The cruel, alcoholic narrator of Poe's "The Black Cat" is injected with some of the black humor and irony employed by Poe's Montressor in "The Cask of Amontillado." For example, the fol-

Vincent Price, "an oozing liquid putrescence," attacks Basil Rathbone in the "Case of M. Valde-mar" segment of *Tales of Terror* (1962).

lowing famous lines uttered during Fortu-nato's entombment are lifted from Poe:

"For the love of God, Montressor."

"Yes, for the love of God."

As Richard Oswald had done in his *Unheimliche Geschicten* (1919), Matheson provides the "Black Cat" narrator with a rival in order to add spice to Poe's tale, which relies upon madness and perversity as an ex-planation for cruelty.

Matheson's treatment of "The Facts in the Case of M. Valdemar" also includes a love triangle not present in the original tale. Otherwise, the basic plot elements and the horrors of mesmeric living death are effec-tively transferred from story to screenplay.

Of course, AIP and Corman wanted Vincent Price for the film, and as Corman explains, "James Nicholson and I really wanted to have Lorre and Rathbone in the cast with Vincent. They were delightful to work with."[103] *Tales of Terror* proved to be

the first Poe vehicle for Lorre. Rathbone had earlier found himself in Universal's *The Black Cat* (1941).

Hungarian-born Peter Lorre (1904–1964) was, of course, an established Holly-wood commodity by 1962. Capable of play-ing both sinister and sympathetic roles, he was and is best known for such films as *M* (1930, in which he plays a pathetic child killer), *The Man Who Knew Too Much* (1933, directed by Alfred Hitchcock), *Mad Love* (1935, a horror tale based on Maurice Re-nard's *The Hands of Orlac*), *Crime and Pun-ishment* (1935, as Raskolnikov), *The Stranger on the Third Floor* (1940), *The Face Behind the Mask* (1941), *The Maltese Falcon* (1941), *The Mask of Dimitrios* (1944), and *The Beast with Five Fingers* (1946). And, in an exam-ple of odd but effective casting, he played the famous Oriental detective Mr. Moto in eight films between 1937 and 1939.

British-born Basil Rathbone (1892–

1967) was also a familiar Hollywood fixture. Particularly adept at sinister and intellectual roles, he appeared in the famous films *David Copperfield* (1935, as Murdstone), *Anna Karenina* (1935, as Karenin), *Captain Blood* (1935), *The Adventures of Robin Hood* (1938), and *Son of Frankenstein* (1939). Of course, his most well-known role was that of Sherlock Holmes, whom he played in thirteen features from 1939 to 1945. Resentful of being typecast as the famous detective, Rathbone later thought he deserved better than many of the roles forced upon him by financial problems. A few such films he never cared to discuss were *Queen of Blood* (1966), *Ghost in the Invisible Bikini* (1966, with Boris Karloff), *Voyage to a Prehistoric Planet* (1967), *Autopsy of a Ghost* (1967, made in Mexico with John Carradine), and *Hillbillies in a Haunted House* (1967, with John Carradine and Lon Chaney, Jr.). Vincent Price later acknowledged Rathbone's mood at the time.

> I think he was very disillusioned, very bitter, because he really had been a great star. People forget that because they think of him as Sherlock Holmes or they think of him as a villain. But he had been a great Shakespearean actor, a great star in the theatre and in movies. And he suddenly found himself— as we all did when Jimmy Dean and Marlon Brando and those people came out, and there was a kind of speaking in the vernacular, and all of us spoke with trained accents and trained English, and theatrically we were different in our approach to acting—that if you wanted to stay in the business, you bloody well went into costume pictures. And Basil rather resented that.[104]

For the female lead in "The Case of M. Valemar," AIP signed Debra Paget (1933–). With such adolescent roles behind her as *Cry of the City* (1948) and *House of Strangers* (1949), Paget garnered major notice when she played James Stewart's Indian love in *Broken Arrow* (1950). She then landed starring roles in such films as *Prince Valiant* (1954), *Love Me Tender* (1956, with Elvis Presley), and *From the Earth to the Moon* (1958). Her exotic blue-green eyes and auburn hair made her a stage presence suited for the Corman-Poe series.

From most accounts, *Tales of Terror* was an enjoyable project. According to Corman, "Everyone had a wonderful time on this film, getting involved with the production as much as possible. Not just the actors, either. The cameraman. The propman. The electricians. Everyone would come up with a great many bits of business on the set. I tried to incorporate as many of these as possible into the movie."[105]

As usual, however, Corman had to compensate for a tight budget. A good example is the scene in which Lorre walks from the tavern to the wine-tasting exhibition. Corman explains: "I built that street on a medium-sized sound stage. It was an example of how to construct a street that's maybe only fifty or sixty feet long. We shot from various angles and hung different street signs to create the impression that Lorre was walking a great distance."[106]

For the dusty, cobweb effects in "Morella," Pat Dinga used almost one hundred gallons of web plastic and over one hundred pounds of an imitation dust called fuller's earth. The result was a mansion that indeed looked as if it had not been touched for twenty-five years. AIP saved money on the final conflagration, however, by using fire footage from the finale of *The Fall of the House of Usher*.

In "The Case of M. Valdemar," Lou La Cava used a gooey mixture of flour, glue, and color to produce Vincent Price's final disintegration. Price had to wear the makeup in progressive stages involving four consecutive changes for successive scenes, all of which culminated in only twenty seconds of screen time. For the scene in which Price appears to levitate from his bed in pursuit of Rathbone, Daniel Haller and production technicians rigged up a pulley and belt arrangement similar to that used in *Peter Pan*, though the result here is not nearly as spectacular.

The two most memorable scenes in the film remain the wine-tasting sequence and the Lorre nightmare sequence, both from "The Black Cat." Vincent Price recalls the preparation for the wine-tasting contest and its shooting:

> A professional wine taster showed us the whole thing about testing the wine and breathing it in and doing all that stuff—then Peter and I just went a little further. I was trying to do it in an exaggerated fashion, which made it so funny. To this day people still talk about that scene. I was doing it the way wine tasters do it, and Peter was doing it the way they didn't do it. But here was an example again where I think Roger (Corman) was so bright—he had two actors who were very inventive, who had this opportunity to see how it was actually done, and we were allowed to "comedy" it up.[107]

For the Lorre nightmare sequence, Floyd Crosby used a special anamorphic camera lens which produces effects similar to trick distortion mirrors. A full-size replica of Lorre's head also figures prominently as the object of a game of catch between Price and Jameson.

In line with others in the Corman-Poe series, the AIP pressbook was large and lavish. One of its high points is a short essay in which Vincent Price defends his horror film portrayals:

> It's time that motion picture critics started taking so-called "terror" or "horror" films seriously—that is the legitimate films of this genre based either on recognized classics or on original stories by our leading writers ... Unlike any other type of motion picture, the terror or horror thriller offers the serious actor an unique opportunity to fully exercise his craft and critically test his ability to make the unbelievable believable. I also believe that such films as "Poe's Tales of Terror" are additionally important to American culture at a time when "method acting" and the sordid stories it usually accompanies, is considered in some quarters as a true reflection of American life. Actually, these "method dramas" are representative of only a very small segment of our people ... As for me, I'd rather take youngsters to see an Edgar Allan Poe thriller anytime than subject them to the amours and perversions of the sick, sick denizens of the backwoods and gutters of America. I think that most decent-thinking Americans feel the same way about entertainment for themselves as well.

Of course, Edgar Allan Poe once again figures prominently in the ads. One titled "Edgar Allan Poe's Works Reflect His Stormy Life": hypothesizes:

> Perhaps nowhere in all the world of fiction are the works of a great writer as stormy and as troubled as that [*sic*] of Poe, but sadly and shockingly the life of the literary genius bears, upon investigation, mute testimony to the accuracy of the fact-fiction relationship ... Poe's unhappy and disjointed biography reveals only a small portion of the torment and mental woe experienced by the brilliant writer. For evidence has been uncovered from Poe's personal letters and from those who knew him that he was constantly bedeviled by the terrifying nightmares and fears which are reflected in the equally unhappy characters of his stories, as those recreated in "Poe's Tales of Terror."

Perhaps the pressbook's oddest content is the passing on of a Black Cat Vanilla Chiffon Pie recipe which reputedly antedates the motion picture, "having originally been concocted for Halloween." "It's so delicious," the ad continues, "and has won so much favor with homemakers from coast to coast that it's worth baking in honor of both the Edgar Allan Poe thriller and your family's pie fans."

Again, in the posters and ads, quotations from the works of Poe accompany key scenes from the film, the most intriguing being the "oozing liquid putrescence, all that remained of Mr. Valdemar." As they had done with *The Pit and the Pendulum* and *The Premature Burial*, Lancer Books marketed a paperback tie-in to coincide with the film's release. Titled *Poe's Tales of Terror*, it featured adaptations by Eunice Sudak rather than Poe's original stories. Joining the Lancer paperback on bookshelves was a Dell comic book tie-in illustrating the trilogy of terror for younger audiences.

Tales of Terror, the fourth Corman-Poe effort, earned AIP slightly less than its predecessors.

Critique: If moviegoers remained enthusiastic about the Corman-Poe series, the same could not be said for critics. Still, while most criticized the concept as tired and repetitive, they could not fault the cast. While *The New York Times* criticized *Tales of Terror* as "absurd and trashy," it nevertheless acknowledged that it was "broadly draped around the shoulders of ... Vincent Price, Peter Lorre and Basil Rathbone."[108] *Variety* wrote that "Corman ... plays his latest entry for all its worth and has assembled some tastily ghoulish acting talent. Vincent Price leers, is mad, is tender, and even laughs straight. Peter Lorre has a madcap time of it and Basil Rathbone is a heavy's heavy."[109]

Critical assessments have changed little since the film's release. In *Horror in the Cinema*, Ivan Butler praises Price, Lorre, and Rathbone and notes that "with less screentime to fill per story, Richard Matheson was able to present more concentrated, less padded versions, and the result was a noteworthy anthology."[110]

In his *Horror and Science Fiction Films*, Donald C. Willis concludes that "The first and third sections have their shock moments, but the first gets too silly and the third gets to be too long. The second is best, hilarious at times, and intentionally so."[111]

In *Horrors! From Screen to Scream*, Ed Naha calls the film "One of the better early Poe-Corman combinations."[112]

The Overlook Encyclopedia of Film: Horror finds the "Morella" episode "in many ways perfection.... It's only fault is that the prowling camera, swirling mists and final conflagration confer a certain sense of *déjà vu*."

Leonard Maltin assigns the film three stars, calling "The Black Cat" sequence "the standout," while *Video Hound's Golden Movie Retriever 1996* awards the film only two bones.

Tales of Terror is an important film in the Corman-Poe series for several reasons. First, it is the only entry in the series to use the anthology format most suited to the Poe stories. As such, the padding so prevalent in the first three films is largely missing. Second, the infusion of intentional humor in the second episode brings something fresh to the series and sets the stage for the next feature, the horror-comedy hit *The Raven* (1963). Third, its successful use of aging horror stars Rathbone and Lorre spurred AIP to team Boris Karloff and Peter Lorre with Vincent Price in Poe's *The Raven* and to use Lon Chaney, Jr., in Poe's *The Haunted Palace* (1963). Fourth, but clearly not least, while the film is not the best in the series, it is a most satisfying outing, largely because of the stellar veteran cast and Corman's willingness to experiment.

Corman explained what he considered the difference between *Tales of Terror* and the first three Poe pictures:

> Most of the Poe short stories were no longer than two or three pages; they were essentially dramatic fragments ... wonderful fragments. The method used in the first Poe pictures was to use the Poe story as the climax, and construct a line of development toward this climax which we tried to make faithful to Poe's quality of imagination. However, not all of the short stories lent themselves to this method. So in this picture I used three stories as the basis and, because I feared being repetitious, added some humor in one story.[113]

Interestingly, Corman's assessment is only partly accurate. *The Fall of the House of Usher* was based on Poe's longest story, and while it resorted to some padding, the result was a very faithful cinematic adaptation. *The Pit and the Pendulum* appears to have most closely followed Corman's stated recipe, while *The Premature Burial* used elements from throughout the story and primarily sought to capture "Poe's quality of imagination." The climax of *Premature Burial* clearly is all Beaumont and Russell and no Poe. Then we come to *Tales of Terror*. Ironically, though the format allows for a faithful rendering of the stories, Matheson follows for "Morella," the philosophy Corman ascribes to the first three films: he essentially adapts the climax of Poe's story and pads the story with effective character development and atmosphere. The segment works, although as Willis points out, it has "a certain sense of *déjà vu*" working against it.

"The Black Cat" segment, on the other hand, contains some of the most memorable footage in the entire Corman/Poe series. Here, if Corman had wished to cast atmosphere to the wind and follow the path of graphic horror blazed by Hammer Films, he obviously had the chance. "The Black Cat" is probably Poe's most gruesome tale: a man gouges out the eye of a cat and buries a hatchet in his wife's brain. Corman, however, plays the segment for a successful mix of horror and comedy, with the emphasis on comedy. For example, the black cat manages to torture Lorre more than he manages to torture it, and even the murder of Jameson is off-camera. Finally, it is Lorre's magnificent performance that one remembers. Although Jameson says of Lorre, "He was so romantic once," we cannot possibly under-stand why the young and beautiful Jameson would have married him in the first place. We can clearly see, however, why she has grown to loathe him over the years. Cruel to the maximum, the besotted Lorre, with his egglike eyes and cold sneer, alternates between sadism and decadent hedonism as he lives only for his next bottle of wine. The wine-tasting contest is a jewel of broad comedy, and his ironic mumblings as he later prepares to dispatch Price are, pardon the expression, priceless.

"The Case of M. Valdemar" succeeds largely because of the sympathetic and pitiable trials of Vincent Price and the coldly villainous machinations of Basil Rathbone. Although it is a trifle slow at times, the performances and sticky climax make it a better than average tale of terror.

While Les Baxter's musical score is slightly less effective than heretofore, the film has no major flaws and should remain one of the most memorable, though not the best, of a very fine series of films.

Horror (1963);
aka *The Blancheville Monster*
AI-TV/Columbus-Llama-Titanus, Spain and Italy

Credits: Directed by Alberto de Martino; screenplay by Jean Grimaud and Gordon Wilson, based on "The Fall of the House of Usher," "Berenice," and "The Premature Burial" by Edgar Allan Poe; cinematography by Alejandro Ulloa; music by Francis Clark.

Cast: Gerard Tichy, Leo Anchoriz, Joan Hills, Iran Eory, Richard Davis, Helga Line (nurse).

Story: The setting is northern France, 1884. Emily returns home to the Blancheville estate after the death of her father. Accompanying her are her best friend, Julie, and Julie's brother John. Upon arriving, Emily's brother Roderick informs her that all the servants she remembers have been replaced. At dinner a scream or howl pierces the night. Shortly afterward, Dr. DeRousse arrives, saying that Count Roderick is expecting him. Roderick then explains to a puzzled Emily that their former family doctor retired.

During the night, Julie is drawn to the tower, where she finds Eleanor, the housekeeper, holding a hypodermic needle over a struggling, disfigured man. When Julie faints, Roderick takes her back to her room and convinces her later that she had a nightmare.

Roderick tells Dr. DeRousse that he intends to end the charade and tell Emily the truth, but, Dr. DeRousse wonders if that is a wise decision. Acting on his own impulse, Roderick informs Emily that their father did not die in a fire at the abbey, as she was first told. Roderick tells her that he actually was horribly disfigured by the fire and that he, Roderick, turned to deceit in order to protect the Blancheville name. Their father escaped when Julie interrupted the administration of a sedative in the tower. Roderick then tells Emily that their father wants to kill her. It seems their father believes an old prophecy that says the house of Blancheville will end with the present generation if a female descendent reaches the age of 21. Emily will be 21 in five days.

That night the disfigured man enters Emily's room, hypnotizes her, and tells her to follow him to her tomb, where she is to die. Dr. DeRousse and a servant intervene at the tomb, the disfigured man escapes, and Emily is taken back to her room. Afterward, Julie tells John that she fears Emily is a victim of hypnosis. She also confesses that she is beginning to fall in love with Roderick. John, who is falling in love with Emily, wants her to leave the estate immediately for her own safety.

Emily later walks downstairs, claiming to feel better. When she goes outdoors, someone pushes a stone from the tower in an effort to kill her. When John finds a male corpse in the forest, he keeps his discovery to himself. That night Emily again goes to her tomb in a trancelike state, followed by the disfigured man. When John tries to save her, the disfigured man bludgeons him senseless. Emily awakens from her trance, runs, and then falls unconscious.

The next day, on her twenty-first birthday, Emily is found "dead" in bed. She is, however, still alive and in a cataleptic state. As she is laid to rest in her tomb, her eyes are closed, but her mind cries out that she is still alive. After the funeral, Dr. DeRousse confesses to Julie his fear that Emily was murdered. He didn't say anything earlier, he says, because he had hoped to trap the killer. He says he knew that Emily's father was not

insane and he also informs Julie that the previous doctor of the Blanchevilles was the first victim. Dr. DeRousse and Julie then discover the body of Emily's father, who has been murdered.

Meanwhile, the disfigured man tries to kill John. When Eleanor tries to intervene, the disfigured man kills her. John pulls off the mask, revealing that the disfigured man is really Roderick. It seems that Roderick, not his father, believed the old prophecy. Dr. DeRousse enters and fires a shot into Roderick's arm. Roderick flees, but is confronted by Emily, who has freed herself from the tomb. Roderick retreats from her, falling to his death in a well.

The film ends with two couples—Dr. DeRousse and Julie, John and Emily—leaving the Blancheville estate to begin their lives together.

Production and marketing: Little is known of the making and marketing of this film. It received a limited American release, if any, and I suspect it was dubbed (sometimes badly) and sold directly to television.

From Poe's "The Fall of the House of Usher," the screenplay borrows the idea of the end of a family line, a brother and sister in a foreboding mansion, the premature burial of the sister, and her subsequent escape from the tomb. From Poe's "The Premature Burial," the screenplay adopts the idea of a person being conscious during his or her own funeral. Finally, traces of Poe's "Berenice" can be faintly sensed in the film's brother/sister relationship.

I know nothing of the careers of the cast members, except for Helga Line, who plays Eleanor the servant. Helga (under the name of Helen Harp) would have a starring role in Amando De Ossorio's fine chiller *Tombs of the Blind Dead* (1971), which was followed by several sequels.

The film's television title was "The Blancheville Monster."

Critique: The film opens in promising fashion. First, the camera focuses on tree branches being tossed in a storm. The jarring horror soundtrack adds to the mood.

The camera moves to the right and focuses on a castlelike building high on a hill. Then the camera moves in and focuses on one of the castle's towers. As the storm continues to unleash its fury, we hear a howl or scream from the tower. The camera approaches the tower's barred window. Suddenly, hands rise up and grasp for the bars. Then the title.

Although the film does not live up to that atmospheric prologue, it does manage an eerie atmosphere throughout. Effective, for instance, are the premature burial scenes in which Emily is carried across the landscape of the ruined abbey to her tomb. Bare tree branches reflect in the glass covering Emily's face. Nevertheless, the premature burial scenes in *The Crime of Dr. Crespi* (1935) and in AIP's *The Premature Burial* (1962) are even more claustrophobic. In the latter, Ray Milland's eyes are open, though unmoving. To point out a flaw in *Horror*, though Emily's eyes are closed, she unac-countably knows which people are looking down at her from above and when.

There are enough long silences and suspicious glances to convince anyone early on that much is amiss in the house of Blancheville. The horror mask worn by Roderick is suitably unsettling, and Emily's late night treks to her tomb number among the film's high spots.

Although the inspiration of Poe is obvious throughout, the scene in which Roderick meets his death is disappointing. We know that Emily has been buried alive, but unlike Madeline's truly terrifying struggles in *The Fall of the House of Usher* (1960), Emily suddenly appears outside the tomb to confront her fleeing brother. Then she simply reaches out to him for help, precipitating the rather contrived ending.

While clearly not among the best Poe adaptations, *Horror* is an average genre film with a few memorable moments.

The Raven (1963)
American International, U.S.A.

Credits: Directed and produced by Roger Corman; executive producers—James H. Nicholson and Samuel Z. Arkoff; screenplay by Richard Matheson, based on "The Raven" by Edgar Allan Poe; music by Les Baxter; cinematography by Floyd Crosby; production design and art direction by Daniel Haller; assistant director—Jack Bohrer; special effects by Pat Dinga.

Running time: 86 minutes.

Cast: Vincent Price (Dr. Erasmus Craven), Peter Lorre (Dr. Bedlo), Boris Karloff (Dr. Scarabus), Hazel Court (Lenore Craven), Olive Sturgess (Estelle Craven), Jack Nicholson (Rexford Bedlo), Connie Wallace (maidservant), William Baskin (Grimes), Aaron Saxon (Gort), Jim, Jr. (The Raven).

Story: The setting is fifteenth-century England. For over two years, sorcerer Dr. Erasmus Craven has mourned the death of his wife, Lenore. One dark night the semiretired magician is roused from his grief by the arrival of a talking raven that demands to be turned back into a man. It seems that the raven was once Dr. Bedlo, a third-rate sorcerer, who was that very night turned into an ebony fowl by a recognized master sorcerer, Dr. Scarabus. Bedlo says he was transformed after challenging Scarabus to a duel of magic.

When Craven agrees to help Bedlo, they journey into the castle basement in search of jellied spiders, dried bat's blood, dead man's hair, and other ingredients necessary for reversing the spell. Unfortunately, the vile drink leaves poor Bedlo a befeathered human. Realizing Bedlo requires more of the potion, they decide to open the coffin of Craven's magician father in order to secure more dead man's hair. After clipping a few locks, Craven is startled when his father momentarily returns to life and delivers an ominous one-word warning: "Beware!" The second batch of potion returns Bedlo completely to his human state. Bedlo then attempts to enlist Craven's aid in returning to Scarabus's castle for revenge. When Craven refuses, Bedlo reveals that he saw a beautiful woman resembling the lost Lenore at Scarabus's castle that very night. Suspecting that the long-running magician's feud between his father and Scarabus may have prompted the latter somehow to take possession of Lenore, Craven agrees to accompany Bedlo to the castle. The pair of magicians are accompanied by Craven's daughter Estelle and Bedlo's son Rexford.

Before they arrive at the castle, however, two attempts are made to stop them. In the first instance, Craven's servant Grimes is possessed by some strange force to attack the party with an axe. Later the same power takes over Rexford as he drives the carriage toward the castle. In both cases, Craven saves the day with his own magical abilities.

When they arrive at their destination, Scarabus greets them with disarming charm and presents a young servant girl as the person Bedlo obviously mistook for Lenore Craven. Bedlo's wine intake at dinner soon causes him to challenge the host to another duel of magic. In the midst of the duel, which Scarabus easily controls, an electrical storm rises and appears to reduce Bedlo to a puddle of liquid.

When Scarabus's guests have retired for the night, the very much alive Lenore Craven reminds the master magician that she agreed to leave Craven because she desired Scarabus's wealth and power. That is why she used a few bits of Scarabus's magic to try to stop her husband from arriving safely at the castle. Scarabus gloats that everything has gone according to his plan. He has Craven's wife, and he has Craven and Estelle in the castle, where he later plans to steal Craven's magical secrets. Bedlo had earlier agreed to be turned into a raven and draw Craven to the castle in exchange for some of Scarabus's occult knowledge.

Shortly thereafter Bedlo returns very much alive and confesses to Rexford and Estelle that he has been part of Scarabus's plot all along but now hopes to help his victims escape. He is, however, deterred by Scarabus, who ties up Craven, Bedlo, Estelle, and Rexford and threatens to torture Estelle if Craven refuses to divulge his deepest secrets of magic. When Bedlo begs to be turned back into a raven and set free rather than undergo torture, Scarabus kindly obliges, especially when Bedlo claims to care nothing for the safety of his friends. So, after embarrassing his son once again, Dr. Bedlo flits out the window into the night.

As Scarabus and his henchman Gort prepare a hot poker for Estelle's face, Bedlo returns unseen through the window and pecks at Craven's bonds, setting him free. As a magical showdown is now necessary, Scarabus suggests a duel to the death, and Craven accepts the challenge. The two men sit opposite each other in chairs and commence a magical battle with only the use of hand gestures. As the magicians engage in a colorful, deadly, and somewhat whimsical battle of magic, Bedlo pecks with his beak at Estelle and Rexford's bonds.

At last, after the duel of magic has set the castle afire, Scarabus slumps in his chair defeated. Realizing that Craven has won, Lenore rushes to his side, proclaiming that she is now free of Scarabus's power. Fully aware now of his wife's greed for riches and power, Craven gathers his party together and proceeds to leave without her. As she runs to join them, however, Scarabus reaches out and detains her, at which point the fire causes the room to collapse in rubble.

The triumphant quartet returns to Craven's castle by carriage, leaving the battered Scarabus and Lenore to argue about their lot in life. "I guess I just don't have what it takes anymore," Scarabus moans, to the obvious disgust of Lenore. Although Bedlo immediately petitions Craven to turn him back into a man, the smiling magician agrees only to take the move under advisement. In the meantime, he orders the bird to sit on a bust of Pallas and to keep its beak shut evermore.

Poster art for *The Raven* (1963).

Production and marketing: Roger Corman's *The Raven* was the third film sporting the title of Poe's poem, the second being the Universal Lugosi-Karloff vehicle of 1935. And as one might expect, Corman's product had no more to do with Poe than Universal's did. Pleased with the comic segment in *Tales of Terror* and sensing that the Poe films were beginning to look alike, Corman and Matheson decided to play *The Raven* largely for comedy, and no one objected. Vincent Price, for instance, thought that trying to adapt Poe's poem into a feature-length film was wrongheaded to begin with. When he realized the extent of comedy inherent in the script, he and the rest of the cast decided to do the film as a parody of the rest of the series.

The film begins in all earnestness as Price reads the first three stanzas of "The Raven" over the backdrop of a castle and crashing waves. Then the story opens in Price's study. The audience gets its first hint that something unusual is going on when Price bumps his head on a telescope as he walks across the room to investigate the tapping at his window. When the raven flits in and perches on the bust of Pallas, Price asks it if he shall ever again hold that radiant maiden whom the angels name Lenore, to which the bird replies, "How the hell should I know. What am I, a fortune teller?" From that moment on the verbal and slapstick comedy is broad, even broader than the original script intended. Much of that extra humor arises from the improvising of Peter Lorre, which sometimes flustered Boris Karloff, as Roger Corman explains:

> Boris was a meticulous actor who would learn his lines to the letter and come in prepared to deliver them just so. Peter would more or less know his lines but constantly improvised on the set. Vincent was somewhat in between—he was as well prepared as Boris but enjoyed improvising with Peter. The two of them drove Boris a little crazy. For example, a convention of the Poe pictures was that the coffin was always buried in a crypt beneath the house—no one was ever buried in a graveyard … so in this pic-

ture, when Vincent said to Peter, "My wife's body is buried in a crypt beneath the house," Peter replied, "Where else?" They continued down the stairs to the crypt, and there was the coffin covered with cobwebs, rats running around and dust all over the place. Peter looked around and said, "Hard place to keep clean, eh?"[114]

Richard Matheson suggested that Lorre might have ad-libbed so much because his memory was starting to fail, but in publicity material Vincent Price suggests otherwise:

> There was one scene in *The Raven* where we had a great deal of exposition…. so Peter was sort of vamping until ready, and carrying on, and I said, "Come on, Peter, for God's sake, say the lines," and he said, "Oh really," and I said "Yes." So he said every line that was in the script. He just got on with it, but he loved to invent. I think that it was part of his training in Germany.

By this time Vincent Price had clearly established himself as the "King of Horror," but later he remembered that his past master costars were having a rather difficult time. Of Lorre, Price recalled "he was a sad little man. He'd put on too much weight; he was not well."[115] Karloff, on the other hand, was in high spirits but suffered from a chronic back problem. In one scene Karloff appears at the top of a flight of stairs and is supposed to walk down. Corman had the camera focus on the actor as he began to descend, then cut away to Jack Nicholson's face. The crew then helped Boris off the stairs, and the camera returned to capture him walking down the last two steps to the floor. Price recalled that Karloff disliked shooting the scenes of the climactic duel in which the magicians levitate in their chairs: "Boris was crippled, and we were both on these wires, floating in the air. It wasn't a pleasant feeling."[116]

Rounding out the main cast were Hazel Court (1926–), Jack Nicholson (1937–), and Olive Sturgess. *The Raven* was Hazel Court's second Corman/Poe picture. Richard Matheson remembered her as a gorgeous woman and a very good actress.

Boris Karloff, Peter Lorre, and Vincent Price in *The Raven* (1963).

Jack Nicholson had worked under Corman's direction in AIP's *The Little Shop of Horrors* (1960) and would linger on the sets of *The Raven* to costar with Boris Karloff in Corman's quickie *The Terror* (1963), of which the actor said, "It was the only movie I ever made that didn't have a plot." Nicholson would, of course, emerge as one of America's top box office draws in such pictures as *Easy Rider* (1969), *Five Easy Pieces* (1970), *Chinatown* (1974), and *One Flew Over the Cuckoo's Nest* (1976), for which he won an Academy Award for best actor.

The career of Olive Sturgess never reached such heights. Before being offered her first film role in *The Raven*, she had appeared on many of the top television shows of the late fifties and early sixties. After *The Raven*, she continued to work steadily but never became a household name.

Once again art director Daniel Haller creates beautiful, ornate sets on little money,

and typical of the entire Corman-Poe series, the costumes are striking. In the film's pressbook, costume designer Marjorie Corso discussed some of the thinking that went into those costumes and pointed out that Peter Lorre presented the greatest challenge:

> Peter Lorre turned out to be my biggest problem, not only because of his height and weight, but due to his role, which calls for him to be half-man, half-raven. His costume had to match both his physical make-up and the grim aspect of the bird.
> My solution was to have Mr. Lorre resemble the bird as much as possible without appearing ridiculous.... It took three men over two weeks, working with me, to properly assemble over ten pounds of feathers (that's almost 50,000 feathers) so that they would look like huge raven's wings and could be used as hands—a tough assignment.

As lavish as *The Raven* looks, it was shot on just a fifteen-day schedule, which was not unusual for Roger Corman and AIP. Again, AIP furnished advertisers with an impressive oversized pressbook. Oddly, the advertising painted *The Raven* as a straight horror picture, completely hiding its strong emphasis on humor. For example, one lead article heralded *The Raven* as the "most terrifying Edgar Allan Poe film of all" and stressed that it "utilizes all of Edgar Allan Poe's famous shock devices—return from the dead, hypnotism, revenge, torture, and more never brought to the screen to make this a classic terror fantasy."

As usual, the pressbook hyped Poe to the hilt, stressing that the poem was written during his wife Virginia's fatal illness and that the poem, "written in sorrow, brought him fame." Posters featured the quote "Take thy beak from out my heart / ... And take thy form from off my door / ... Quoth THE RAVEN: 'NEVER MORE.'"

In addition to a pressbook, AIP also issued a promotional 33 rpm record, protected in a full-color sleeve featuring a portrait of Karloff, Lorre, and Price. The sleeve is actually a booklet of sorts, with ten pages of color and black and white scenes from the film. The great promotional record features Peter Lorre reading selected stanzas from Poe's poem as a narrator adds descriptions of the gruesome horrors explored in the film. Again the approach is designed to sell a horror film. Lorre's half human/half raven creature, for instance, is described as a true monster of horror. A hint of comedy enters at the end of the record, however, as Boris Karloff concludes the promotion:

> Before the picture ends, I guarantee your blood will run cold. You may faint or go into a coma! [Karloff's delivery becomes increasingly excited.] Your hair may turn white! You won't sleep for a week! [In a relaxed tone] What? Have I disturbed you? I didn't mean to. You see, I want you to see Edgar Allan Poe's *The Raven*. I share in the box office receipts.

For the third time in the Corman-Poe series, Lancer Books issued a paperback tie-

in to coincide with the film's release. Eunice Sudak was back at the typewriter working from the Matheson script, which accounts for the fact that Lorre's great ad-libs do not appear in the book. For the second time in the series, Dell issued a comic book tie-in to capture younger audiences. Both the paperback and comic book retold the story as straight horror.

While its $350,000 price tag made it the most expensive of the series to that point, the film racked up $1.4 million in rentals to gross the most money of the first five Corman-Poe pictures. So if the director was tiring of the series, it was obvious that AIP was not. In fact, the company announced plans to make ten more Poe pictures, all starring Vincent Price. The line-up was to be *The Masque of the Red Death, The Haunted Palace, Murders in the Rue Morgue, The Gold Bug, A Descent into the Maelstrom, Ligeia, The Thousand and Second Tale of Scheherazde, The Angel of the Odd, Four Beasts in One,* and *The City Under the Sea.* Of this list, only four would actually be made: *The Masque of the Red Death, The Haunted Palace, Ligeia* (titled *The Tomb of Ligeia*), and *The City Under the Sea* (aka *War-Gods of the Deep*). Roger Corman would direct the first three before moving on to other projects. Vincent Price would, however, star in all four.

Vincent Price and Peter Lorre would do one more film together, *The Comedy of Terrors* (1963), also starring Boris Karloff and Basil Rathbone. When Lorre died in 1964, Price delivered the funeral eulogy. He later recalled the day: "The day of the funeral I was doing the Red Skelton Show. I wrote the eulogy and I went to Red and said, 'You know Peter died yesterday morning. Would you mind if I took an extra hour for lunch, because I'm going to his funeral and read the eulogy?' Red said, 'Peter's dead? We'll all go!' So the entire company went to the funeral, which was marvelous."[117]

Critique: Although some reviewers were caught off-guard by the comedy, most found *The Raven* delightful. *Variety* wrote:

Edgar Allan Poe might turn over in his grave at this nonsensical adaptation of his immortal poem, but audiences will find the spooky goings-on a cornpop of considerable comedic dimensions.... Special effects figure prominently to add sometimes spectacular interest when [Karloff and Price] hurl their talents at each other.... Les Baxter's ... score is another assist in adding an eerie touch. Characterizations are played straight for ... comedy value sparked by ... ridiculous lines.... Price makes his theatricalism pay off. Karloff plays it smooth. Lorre is almost cute.[118]

Time magazine called *The Raven* "a sappy little parody of a horror picture cutely calculated to make children scream with terror while their parents scream with glee.... The real star of the show is scenarist Richard Matheson, who has written three or four of the hoariest lines of the year."[119]

On the negative side, *The New York Times* predictably thought that "Edgar Allan Poe's 'The Raven' might well say 'Nevermore' to appearing in Hollywood films, ... strictly a picture for the kiddies and the bird brained."[120]

Over the years, *The Raven* has remained a subject of mixed opinion. In his book *An Illustrated History of the Horror Film*, however, Carlos Clarens emerges as one of the film's few detractors, writing:

> Corman must have been conscious of the more laughable aspects of his earlier Poe adaptations when in 1963 he directed *The Raven*, a burlesque at the expense of his usual crypt-and-coffin antics. The director—who cannot be said to control his players—brought the Poe ubiquity, Vincent Price, together with Boris Karloff and Peter Lorre to play magicians black, white, and gray, and gave them their heads. Relishing their absurd incantations, improvising their own bits of business, and lampooning their screen images, they emerge as monsters, but of a different kidney. To the sum of its credit, *The Raven* adds acceptable trick camera work and a childish sense of fun that covers a lack of any real wit.[121]

In *Horror and Science Fiction Films*, Donald C. Willis brushes off Corman's

comedy as "Not nearly as funny as the '35 version."[122] In *Cinema of Mystery*, Rose London calls the film "Corman's best travesty of Poe, and in a class with his other gothic parody, *Comedy of Terrors*."[123] Ed Naha calls the film "an enjoyable attempt at horror spoofing.... The production is magnificent, the script semilaughable, but Lorre proves himself a scene-stealer supreme with a charming, off-the-cuff performance."[124] In *The Psychotronic Encyclopedia of Film*, Michael Weldon calls *The Raven* an "enjoyable comedy-fantasy."[125] In *The Motion Picture Guide*, Jay Robert Nash and Stanley Ralph Ross give the film 3½ stars (good to excellent) and say that "Anyone who likes the Corman 'Poe' films, and is a fan of horror greats Karloff, Price, and Lorre will delight in this wonderfully funny send-up of the genre wherein everyone involved looks as if he's having a great time."[126] Leonard Maltin assigns the film three stars, noting that the "Climactic sorcerer's duel is a highlight," and *Video Hound's Golden Movie Retriever 1996* awards the film three bones, calling it "One of the more enjoyable of the Corman/Poe adaptations."

The Raven is indeed a fine picture. The most visually rich and opulent of the first five Corman-Poe films, it benefits from a fine Matheson script, a back-to-form score by Les Baxter, and some magnificently playful chemistry among Karloff, Price, and Lorre, advertised correctly as "The Triumvirate of Terror."

If Vincent Price chewed the scenery a bit in the finale of *The Pit and the Pendulum* and during the second segment of *Tales of Terror*, he virtually feasts on it in *The Raven*. Such acting works in the context of this film, however, since it is a conscious parody. Price, always the possessor of a nice comic touch, uses it broadly and to good advantage in *The Raven*. In one of his most humorous scenes, he nearly turns green as Lorre announces the ingredients (entrails of troubled horse, jellied spiders, etc.) needed for transforming ravens back into humans.

Peter Lorre, who has some truly sinister moments in his partly comedic sequence of *Tales of Terror*, is an inept buffoon in *The Raven*. Still, his hilarious ad-libs and physical comedy steal scene after scene.

Somewhat reminiscent of his Hjalmar Poelzig characterization in *The Black Cat* (1934), Boris Karloff is a sinister, disingenuous malefactor who hides his evil designs behind feigned gentlemanly solicitude. Although hampered with illness, Karloff turns in one of the best performances of his final decade.

Based on *The Raven*, no one could have predicted stardom for Jack Nicholson. Still, like most other young performers in the Corman-Poe series, he adequately fills the bill, as does his love interest, Olive Sturgess. Hazel Court, on the other hand, gives a much more wickedly sensual performance here than in *The Premature Burial*. One can see in *The Raven* why she was one of England's number one pin-up girls during World War II and why she is an intelligent talent deserving of more than the "horror film queen" reputation she earned in some of the finer genre films of the late fifties and sixties.

While the cast and screenplay are outstanding, special effects play a greater part in the success of *The Raven* than in any other Corman-Poe film. Indeed, they make the climactic duel of the magicians an unforgettable experience. Although tame by today's standards, they still succeed in entertaining the children and eliciting nods of approval from adults.

The only noticeable flaw in the film is a long sequence in the middle, beginning after Scarabus's guests have retired for the night and ending when Karloff challenges Price to a duel to the death. Comprised of little horror or humor, this sequence is memorable only for Hazel Court's wicked interchanges with Boris Karloff. On the whole, though, *The Raven* must be considered a commercial and artistic success. I think Poe might even have joined in a chuckle, as long as he never suspected the film of being a self-proclaimed adaptation of his poem.

The Haunted Palace (1963)
American International, U.S.A.

Credits: Directed and produced by Roger Corman; screenplay by Richard Matheson, based on *The Case of Charles Dexter Ward* by H. P. Lovecraft and "The Haunted Palace" by Edgar Allan Poe; cinematography by Floyd Crosby; art direction by Daniel Haller; music by Ronald Stein.

Running time: 85 minutes.

Cast: Vincent Price (Joseph Curwen and Charles Dexter Ward), Debra Paget (Ann Ward), Lon Chaney, Jr. (Simon Orne), Frank Maxwell (Dr. Willet), Leo Gordon (Willet), Elisha Cook (Smith), John Dierkes (West), Milton Parsons (Jabez Hutchinson), Cathy Merchant (Hester Tillinghast), Guy Wilkerson (Leach), Harry Ellerbe (minister), Darlene Lucht (young woman victim), Barboura Morris (Mrs. Weeden), Bruno Ve Sota (bartender).

Story: In the New England fishing village of Arkham, in the year 1765, the villagers are fearfully aware of strange events taking place at the palacelike mansion of Joseph Curwen. One night they follow a young woman who walks as though in a trance to the mansion, where she participates in strange rites performed by Curwen from an occult text called *The Necronomicon*. Curwen is a sorcerer who imprisons young girls from the village and sacrifices them to creatures from another dimension.

Unwilling to put up with such activities in their midst, the villagers question Curwen and his woman, Hester Tillinghast.

When straight answers are not forthcoming, the frustrated villagers seize Curwen, tie him to a tree, and burn him alive as a warlock. Before he dies, however, he curses the villagers, their children and their children's children, and vows to return from the dead.

Over a century later, Charles Dexter Ward and his wife Ann arrive in Arkham by ship. When the descendents of the villagers who burned Curwen notice that Ward, an admitted descendent of Curwen, bears a striking resemblance to the deceased warlock, their hostility is evident. Indeed, they fear that Curwen's curse has been fulfilled and that they will die according to the curse. As the Wards are on their way to take possession of the Curwen mansion, they encounter strangely deformed men, women, and children in the streets of Arkham.

Inside the mansion, the Wards discover a painting of Joseph Curwen and notice its amazing resemblance to Charles. They also meet Simon Orne, who identifies himself as the caretaker and seems strangely familiar to Ward. When Ward looks again at the portrait, his personality and appearance change to resemble that of the warlock. From that time on, Ward wages a battle for his own soul but is often possessed by Curwen's more powerful spirit. Ward/Curwen is soon plotting with Orne and a warlock named Jabez Hutchinson to restore the warlock to full power. These changes, of course, dismay Ann, who does not understand what is going on.

It seems that the mutants in the village were actually the results of the strange mating rites conducted by Curwen a century ago, as well as part of the fulfillment of his curse. The curse continues to fruition as several of the villagers are hideously burned to death. One night while Curwen has taken over Ward, Orne and Hutchinson unearth Hester Tillinghast's coffin and prepare to bring her back to life.

By this time, the villagers decide that they must do what their ancestors did a century ago—destroy the warlock to save themselves. As Ward/Curwen is about to sacrifice

Ann to a horrible creature conjured from a pit, the villagers storm the mansion and set it afire. The villagers rescue Ann, and Ward staggers out of the flaming house, apparently free of Curwen's power. Or is he? As they watch the mansion perish, Charles's and Ann's faces seem to resemble those of Curwen and Hester.

> While, like a rapid ghastly river,
> Through the pale door,
> A hideous throng rush out forever,
> And laugh—but smile no more.
> 　　　　　　　　Edgar Allan Poe

Production and marketing: Although *The Haunted Palace* is advertised as the sixth Corman-Poe film, it is actually based on *The Case of Charles Dexter Ward* by H. P. Lovecraft. The novel concerns eighteenth-century magician Joseph Curwen, who settles in the New World to carry out his experiments in necromancy and eternal life. His neighbors become frightened by his exploits and execute him. In the twentieth century, Curwen's distant descendent, Charles Dexter Ward, discovers that Curwen's associates are still attempting their experiments in Europe. Disaster results when Ward attempts to follow in Curwen's footsteps.

"I fought against calling it a Poe film," Corman said, "but AIP had made so much money with Poe films that they just stuck his name on it for box office appeal."[127] At least Lovecraft is acknowledged in the film credits.

In this latest project, Vincent Price was again cast as the lead, and because of the success of using the horror genre's legendary actors in *Tales of Terror* and *The Raven*, Lon Chaney, Jr. (1906–1973) landed a costarring role. It would be the first and last film in which Price and Chaney would appear together. Chaney, of course, was the son of silent screen star Lon Chaney. Chaney's son actually was named Creighton, but he reluctantly changed his name to Lon Chaney when his film career failed to get off the ground in the thirties. A change of name and a few good roles did wonders, however,

What
was the
terrifying
thing in
the PIT
that
wanted
women?

EDGAR ALLAN POE'S THE *Haunted* PALACE
in PATHECOLOR and PANAVISION

STARRING
VINCENT PRICE
DEBRA PAGET
LON CHANEY

Lon Chaney, Jr., and Vincent Price investigate the contents of a coffin in *The Haunted Palace* **(1963).**

as Lon Chaney, Jr., costarred in the critically acclaimed *Of Mice and Men* (1939, as Lennie) and quickly became Universal's biggest horror star of the forties in such memorable chillers as *The Wolf Man* (1941, as Lawrence Talbot), *The Ghost of Franken-stein* (1942, as the Frankenstein monster), *The Mummy's Tomb* (1942, as Kharis the Mummy), *Frankenstein Meets the Wolf Man* (1943, again as Lawrence Talbot), and *Son of Dracula* (1943, as Dracula). His prolific and often impressive work as a character actor continued in films and television throughout the fifties. Unfortunately, chronic drinking had his career in serious decline by the time of *The Haunted Palace*.

Shortly after making the film, Price remarked for pressbook publicity: "Lon Chaney is one of the most talented actors in films today. He has none of the high-class attitude of today's stars; in fact, he is un-doubtedly one of the most unassuming men

I have had the pleasure of working with." But years later Price divulged the other side of Chaney: "He was very ill at the time. I had admired him enormously and wanted to meet him. He was not really very happy. I didn't really get to know him. I spent a lot of time with him, trying to talk with him and make him cheer up, but I couldn't do it."[128]

AIP tapped lovely Debra Paget (1933–), a veteran from *Tales of Terror*, to costar with Price and Chaney in its sixth "Poe" picture, and a crew of fine veteran character actors signed to play the villagers of Arkham. With Daniel Haller again in charge as art director, the eerie sets associated with the Corman-Poe series return. Quite impressive is the soundstage, measuring 110' long by 115' deep by 50' high, which was known as the "Room of the Beast." Dominating the room is a six-level, wooden-beamed staircase, 40' high; it consists of a total of 80 steps and is lit by eighteen flaming torches. Also part of the "Room of the Beast" is the 8' pit from which the "Beast" begins to emerge in the film's finale.

Although AIP supplies another large format pressbook to help sell *The Haunted Palace*, this one contains about four fewer pages than the others. Again, Poe receives a great deal of attention, but not as much as before. One ad tells us: "*The Haunted Palace* features the weird and terrifying world of Edgar Allan Poe characters which made [the first five films in the series] memorable theatre going experiences. Here the famous shock elements of Poe—return from the dead, revenge, torture and human beings haunted by strange fears and desires—intermingle with the warlock slaves of the black magic of necromancy." Of course, while many of the elements mentioned are indeed typical of Poe, in this context they are clearly the elements of H. P. Lovecraft.

"The Haunted Palace," which appears in Poe's "The Fall of the House of Usher," is critically regarded as a poem symbolic of the deterioration of Usher's reason and the onrush of madness. In the poem, a monarch lived in the greenest of valleys, but evil things in robes of sorrow surrounded him and he died. Vast forms now move beyond the red-lit windows of his palace, and strange sounds come from it. But joy and harmony have fled. The poem's last four lines, quoted at the film's conclusion, have no relationship at all to the film itself other than to justify its linkage with Poe. More relevant to the film are such advertising catch phrases as "What was the hideous thing in the PIT that came to honor her?" and "What was the terrifying thing in the PIT that wanted women?"

It is interesting to compare and contrast Poe and Lovecraft, as well as the cinematic success or failure of adapting these masters of the horror short story to film. Although Lovecraft's early work was strongly influenced by the writings of Edgar Allan Poe (e.g., "The Outsider") and Lord Dunsany (e.g., "The White Ship"), he soon began writing of an ancient race of beings or elder gods, once banished from the earth, who lie just beyond our reality, waiting to reestablish their sovereignty. These stories, which comprise the so-called Cthulhu Mythos, largely account for Lovecrafts' fame today. In his monumental *The Guide to Supernatural Fiction*, Everett F. Bleiler summarizes Lovecraft's literary importance:

> His fiction, while stylistically that of a technical writer working according to smash-ending formulas of the period, has been considered important in stating in clearest form one of the alienation myths of the mid 20th century: the precarious aloneness of man, both the inner world of his psyche and the cosmos, beyond phenomenality.[129]

A difficulty or shortcoming is that characterization is of little importance in Lovecraft; mood and atmosphere are everything. For that reason, screenwriters adapting his work must create interesting characters to accompany Lovecraft's plot and atmosphere. So far, there have been several cinematic attempts to do this, the most successful of which are Corman's *The Haunted Palace* and Daniel Haller's *The Dunwich Horror* (1969). Stuart Gordon's *Re-Animator* (1985) and *From Beyond* (1986) and Brian Yuzna's *Bride of Re-Animator* (1989) are successful black comedies but unsuccessful Lovecraft adaptations. Other Lovecraft films worth noting are *Die, Monster, Die* (1965, based on Lovecraft's "The Colour Out of Space," with Boris Karloff) and the eerie but ultimately unsuccessful low-budget sleepers *The Unnameable* (1988) and *The Unnameable 2: The Statement of Randolph Carter* (1992). It is interesting that the best Lovecraft adaptations were directed by Roger Corman and his art director Daniel Haller. Part of the reason for this is that Haller was responsible for much of the successful atmosphere in the Corman/Poe series, some of which he artfully brings to Lovecraft.

Critique: In January of 1964, *The Haunted Palace* opened to mixed reviews. The *New York Times* dismissed it, of course, saying: "Nothing about it calls for comment, except perhaps the proficient color photography by ... old professional Floyd Crosby. Everyone else, possibly influenced by Mr. Price's sleep-walking routine, seems to be going through the whole thing by rote."[130] On the positive side was Judith Crist of the *New York Herald*:

> The moral is that you can't keep a keen warlock down—and who would want to, when he's so debonair a chap as Price, telling an unwilling but admiring visitor to his torture chamber, "Ah, yes, Torquemada spent many a happy hour here, a few centuries ago," and having so green-faced an assistant necromancer as Lon Chaney, so lovely an 1875 wife as Debra Paget and so sexy a mistress as Cathy Merchant, who gets revivified merely by Price's reciting some fractured Latin over her coffin. The Torquemada line is almost worth the price of admission—but not quite.[131]

The years have not resolved the conflicting critical opinions. Ivan Butler writes:

> The result was a much more closely knit and interesting story than some of the earlier padded-out instances. The production once again showed signs of straitened economy, but Corman demonstrated anew his skill in finding beauty in the conventional misty landscapes, huge baroque rooms, unending stone-flagged passages and the rest of the stock-in-trade... The chief merit of the film, however, is in the subtlety with which Corman and Price ... suggest the change of personality as Charles Dexter Ward's form is gradually taken over by the wicked forebearer.[132]

The Overlook Film Encyclopedia: Horror calls the film "rich but flawed," concluding that "*The Haunted Palace* becomes another of Poe's constructs of the mind. Lovecraft's cosmic vision of domination by evil, altogether more tangible than Poe's nightmarish explorations of guilty fears and desires, perhaps needed to be set in a more demonstrably real world."

Jay Robert Nash and Stanley Ralph Ross award the film 2 1/2 stars (fair to good)

and dub it "not bad."[133] Leonard Maltin also awards it 2 1/2 stars, calling it "good-looking but minor," and *Video Hound's Golden Retriever 1996* seems to make it unanimous by awarding the film 2 1/2 bones.

In my view, *The Haunted Palace* has much to recommend it. With the opening scenes in the fogbound New England village, Corman sustains the dark and brooding atmosphere of his earlier Poe efforts. Ronald Stein's strong musical score is as foreboding as the lightning splitting the sky above Arkham, and Daniel Haller's art direction brings the fog-shrouded village and the "haunted palace" to vivid life. The cast is uniformly effective. In supporting roles, Leo Gordon, Elisha Cook, and Frank Maxwell are particularly impressive. While there are numerous effective horror scenes, the most eerie is that in which Price and Paget are surrounded by mutants on a fogbound Arkham street, where Ted Coodley's realistic makeup work allows the camera some very unsettling close-ups of the menacing mutants.

Ivan Butler is correct in citing the subtlety of Price's personality change, and if there was any sleepwalking being done in regard to this picture, it was done by the reviewer of the *New York Times*, who rarely, if ever, saw a horror film he liked.

Corman respected the reputation of Lon Chaney, Jr., as horror man and used him accordingly. Early in the film, Paget, in close-up, is exploring a room of the mansion when she is shocked by a collision with Chaney. Later Corman employs a similar technique as Price, in close-up, backs into Chaney, who is merely offering him his coat. Finally, Chaney emerges from the shadows to frighten the terrified Paget into a faint as she is making her way through the palace dungeon.

Interestingly, *The Haunted Palace* is the only Corman-Poe film in which evil ultimately emerges victorious. This is, of course, more the influence of Lovecraft than of Poe, although evil does seem to win in Poe's "The Cask of Amontillado," and some other stories clearly leave the conclusion ambiguous.

The Haunted Palace did good business, earning AIP $1.3 million domestically and setting records in Australia, where Lovecraft's writings are very popular. And all of this moneymaking was done without the aid of either a Lancer paperback tie-in or a Dell comic book tie-in; the sixth Corman-Poe film was the first since *House of Usher* to bypass that marketing strategy.

The Masque of the Red Death (1964)
American International, U.S.A. and Great Britain

Credits: Directed and produced by Roger Corman; screenplay by Charles Beaumont and R. Wright Campbell, from "The Masque of the Red Death" by Edgar Allan Poe; production design by Daniel Haller; art direction by Robert Jones; cinematography by Nicholas Roeg; music composed and conducted by David Lee.

Running time: 89 minutes.

Cast: Vincent Price (Prince Prospero), Hazel Court (Juliana), Jane Asher (Francesca), David Weston (Gino), Patrick Magee (Alfredo), Nigel Green (Ludovica), Skip Martin (Hop Toad), John Westbrook (man in red), Gay Brown (Senora Escobar), Julian Burton (Senor Veronese), Doreen Dawn (Anna-Marie), Paul Whitsun-Jones (Scarlatti), Jean Lodge (Scarlatti's wife), Verina Greenlaw (Esmerelda), Brian Hewlett (Lampredi), Harvey Hall (Clistor), Robert Brown (guard).

Story: Prince Prospero, a sadistic Satanist, rules cruelly and tyrannically over the province of Esteban. One day, however, a red-robed stranger gives a blood-red rose to an old woman and tells her that deliverance is at hand. Joyfully, she relays the prophecy to those of her village.

When Prince Prospero rides into the village to invite the people to eat the scraps from his table at a special end-of-harvesting feast which he is holding for his noblemen friends, he hears only murmurs of dissatisfaction and rebellion. Encouraged by the mysterious stranger's prophecy, Gino and Ludovico openly express their distaste for Prospero, throwing the prince into a rage and precipitating their arrest. A beautiful young woman named Francesca, who is Ludovico's daughter and Gino's fiancée, begs Prospero to release them. One man must die, Prospero explains, and he invites Francesca to help settle their fate.

The moment of decision is delayed, however, when Prospero learns that a terrible plague called the Red Death is claiming the lives of the villagers. He quickly orders that all dwellings touched by the disease be burned and sends his couriers to invite his nobleman friends to a masked ball where they will all be safe from the Red Death.

At the castle, Prospero plans to entice Francesca into the rites of Satan worship, but his voluptuous wife Juliana does not approve. Meanwhile, as the guests are being entertained, other intrigues unfold. A dwarf called Hop Toad is angered when his tiny girlfriend is abused by Duke Alfredo. Planning revenge, Hop Toad suggests that Alfredo wear a gorilla costume to the masked ball. The dwarf even volunteers to act as the gorilla's trainer. Delighted with the prospect of stealing Prospero's thunder, Alfredo accepts Hop Toad's suggestion, unaware of the fate that awaits him.

At that point, Prospero orders the mass slaughter of any individuals, royal or peasant, who approach the castle for shelter from the Red Death. The next day at the banquet Prospero brings Ludovico and Gino before the guests and orders the two prisoners to take turns slicing themselves with knives,

Vincent Price faces the Red Death, whom he unfortunately mistakes for Satan, in *The Masque of the Red Death* **(1964).**

one of which is tipped with poison. When Ludovico lunges at Prospero, the prince impales him with a sword. He then orders Gino to leave the castle to face almost certain death from the plague. In the countryside, however, Gino takes the advice of the red-robed stranger and returns to the castle.

Meanwhile, Juliana calls on all the evil spirits to give her strength stemming from total understanding, and she triumphantly announces that she has survived her own sacrifice. Elated, she faces the slow swinging pendulum of the dimly lit clock, from the recesses of which she hears the hollow, echoing voice of Prospero. Suddenly Prospero's bird of prey swoops upon Juliana and with a flurry of talons, kills her. In explaining her death, Prospero simply remarks that Juliana has married a friend of his.

As the masked ball progresses, Hop Toad engineers a fiery death for the gorilla-suited Duke Alfredo on a candlelit chande-

lier. After the flaming corpse and lighting fixture fall to the floor with a crash, Prospero orders his soldiers to reward the dwarf with five gold pieces for providing such delightful entertainment. Hop toad and Esmerelda, however, have already fled the castle.

When the clock strikes midnight, the masked dance begins. Prospero is angered, however, when a stranger enters the ballroom wearing a costume that both alarms and disgusts. His face hidden by a cowl, the red-robed stranger passes among the hedonistic revelers. As he gestures with his hand, the dancers drop to the floor in agony, victims of the Red Death. His ball turned into a grotesque dance of death, Prospero pursues the stranger from one brilliantly hued room to another. Finally, in the farthest room, the stranger turns and confronts Propero. When the prince pulls away the cowl, he finds himself staring into his own face. The prince has met his Satan. Moments later Prospero too falls to the floor in agony, a victim of the Red Death.

Later, on a hilltop, as the Red Death plays a game of cards with a child, other robed figures representing various plagues appear. The Red Death explains that only six survived his coming: a young man and a woman, a dwarf and a tiny dancer, a small child, and an old man in the village. The figures then form a procession through the forest, apparently to continue their endless task of bringing the living eternal rest.

Production and marketing: When a 1964 coproduction deal with Anglo-Amalgamated prompted Arkoff and Nicholson to move their productions to England, Roger Corman was able to plan a bigger production than he had ever been able to engineer in the United States. When AIP asked for a seventh Corman-Poe picture, the director chose "The Masque of the Red Death," the film he had long wanted to make but lacked the resources to undertake. Years later Corman recalled his approach to *The Masque of the Red Death* and his pleasure with the finished product:

This was the biggest and best-looking of the Poe films, the first film we ever did in England. We had a shooting schedule of five weeks, which was ... two weeks longer than our usual shooting schedule. I thought, "Gosh, I'm really going to be able to spread myself out on this thing!" At that time, I didn't realize that English crews work much slower than American ones. So, five weeks in England was, roughly, the equivalent of four in the United States. Still, even a small amount of extra time allowed me to do a lot more stylistically with this production.

We attempted to get a really stylized look on this film. I wanted to film this immediately after the *House of Usher*, but I avoided it because of the haunting figure of death. Death, in our film, is the same representation made famous by Ingmar Bergman in *The Seventh Seal.* I didn't want to be backed into a position of basing one of my movies on a 19th-century classic of literature and then be accused of copying a 1950s film from Scandinavia.

I was quite pleased with the finished film. We tried a variety of different techniques to give this movie a different texture from the rest of the Poe films. Aside from elaborate sets, we choreographed the plague scene during the finale, where Death makes an unscheduled appearance at a masked ball. It gave the entire affair a surreal touch. Death was taking the proceedings out of the realm of the ordinary and into the extraordinary.[134]

In his seventh stint as a Corman-Poe art director, Daniel Haller found himself designing at Elstree Studio on a soundstage adjacent to where Roger Moore was starring in his television series *The Saint.* This time, instead of using all of his skill and imagination to make cheap, small sets appear expansive and expensive—a task he performed admirably—he actually could create expansive and relatively expensive sets. In a break from tradition, however, AIP brought in cinematographer Nicholas Roeg (1928–) to replace Floyd Crosby, who had served admirably in that capacity on all the previous Corman-Poe pictures. Roeg would remain a cinematographer throughout the sixties and then distinguish himself as a director with such films as *Don't Look Now* (1973) and *The Man Who Fell To Earth* (1976).

The screenplay was in the hands of Charles Beaumont and R. Wright Campbell. It was Beaumont's third Corman- Poe screenplay and his best. The Poe story, though quite short, unfolds over a period of several months. The screenplay, on the other hand, condenses the action into a matter of days. Poe describes Prospero as "happy and dauntless and sagacious" as the Red Death devastates the country. Beaumont's Prospero is also happy and dauntless. Poe, however, uses the word sagacious ironically because it is Prospero who wrongly considers himself "gifted with acuteness of mental discernment, having special aptitude for the discovery of truth." Beaumont's Prospero, a devil worshipper, clearly considers himself sagacious, but his errors of judgment lead him to the same crimson fate as Poe's prince. As in Poe's story, Beaumont's screenplay includes a pendulum that swings "to and fro with a dull, heavy, monotonous clang," chambers of varying hues, and revelers who appear as phantasms.

At this point it is probably beneficial to examine the question of how much Ingmar Bergman's *The Seventh Seal* (1957) influenced Corman's *The Masque of the Red Death.* Bergman's film features Max Von Sydow as a disillusioned knight returning from the Crusades. As the Black Death devastates the countryside, the knight searches for some evidence of God in the universe and for some clue as to the meaning of life. In order to win a reprieve from Death, the knight suggests that he and Death play a game of chess. The game is interrupted on various occasions, allowing the knight to continue his search for knowledge. Death finally wins, however, and dances off over the hillside with the knight and a band of people he has come to know.

Both Bergman and Corman explore questions about life's meaning and about whether God and the devil exist. As in Poe's story, these questions are examined against the backdrop of a plague. Both Bergman's Death and Corman's various Deaths dress in robes.

In *The Seventh Seal,* the knight enters a church and participates in the sacrament of penance. Unaware that Death is on the other side of the grille, the knight begins his tortured confession:

> KNIGHT: I want to confess as openly as I can, but my heart is empty. The emptiness is a mirror turned toward my own face. I see myself in it and am filled with fear and disgust. Through my indifference to my fellow man, I have isolated myself from their company. Now I live in a world of phantoms. I am imprisoned in my dreams and fantasies.
> DEATH: And yet you don't want to die?
> KNIGHT: Yes, I do.
> DEATH: What are you waiting for?
> KNIGHT: I want knowledge.
> DEATH: You want guarantees?
> KNIGHT: Call it whatever you like. Is it so cruelly inconceivable to grasp God with the senses? Why should he hide himself in a mist of half-spoken promises and unseen miracles?

Like the knight, Corman's Prospero has isolated himself from his fellow man. In Poe's short story, Prospero's revelers are described as exhibiting "much glare and glitter and piquancy and phantasm," dreamlike qualities the knight associates with his fellow human beings. Like the knight, Corman's Prospero is a seeker after knowledge. Unlike the knight, however, the silence of God has led him to conclude that Satan rules the world. The knight is not sure of the existence of Satan either. These comparisons lead me to conclude that Prospero represents the knight at some later stage of evolution or devolution. Prospero, a thinker, once asked the knight's questions, but unlike the knight, his searching for answers ended when years of witnessing the silence of God and the cruelty of nature and humanity led him to worship Satan. In Bergman's film the knight's squire sings:

> Between a strumpet's legs to lie
> is the life for which I sigh.
> Up above is God almighty
> so very far away,
> but your brother the devil
> you will meet on every level.

Of course, Corman echoes Bergman in the scene in which Prospero unmasks the Red Death, only to peer into his own face. The knight's emptiness acts as a mirror turned toward his own face, implying that ultimately there is only oneself. As the Red Death informs Prospero, "Each man makes his own heaven and his own hell."

Although characters in both films search for meaning, the directors diverge in one important sense. In Bergman's film, neither Death nor God nor any figure of authority provides any answers. Only the knight seems to sense a glimmer of meaning (for himself, at least) while sitting one afternoon, eating, talking, and listening to the soft strings of a lute with his friends under an open sky. Do such moments of peace and sharing constitute the only meaning in life? Bergman doesn't tell us. Corman's Red Death, however, verbally suggests that love might be the ultimate meaning of life and that it might be strong enough to prevail against Prospero. Still, the ambiguities are many, and the film audience is ultimately left to decide for itself.

Finally, both films end with processions. Bergman's film ends with Death leading his victims in a dance over a hill; Corman's ends with the Deaths making their way in a line through a forest. Corman's dance of death came earlier during the macabre masque ball.

In conclusion, it appears that Beaumont and Corman begin with the Poe story and infuse it with Bergman's themes regarding the silence of God. The probability that Bergman was influenced by Poe's story also helps explain similarities in the two films.

Of course, Vincent Price was cast in the starring role as Prospero. In subsequent interviews, though Price pronounced the project a good experience, he related that "There was one moment when I was up on a dais with a long speech and I came down with those long, flowing capes and tripped. I fell down and knocked myself out cold—absolutely out cold [laughing]!"[135]

Price's costars were Hazel Court, making her third appearance in a Corman-Poe film, and Jane Asher (1946–), who was well known at the time for dating Beatle Paul McCartney. Asher made her screen debut at the age of six in *Mandy* (1952) and surfaced regularly thereafter in films and television. After *The Masque of the Red Death*, she would appear in such critically acclaimed pictures as *Alphie* (1966) and *Deep End* (1971) before fading in the mid-eighties.

The supporting cast included a duo of fine British veterans. Patrick Magee (1924–1982), a very capable stage and screen actor, was known primarily for his roles in *The Criminal* (1960) and *Zulu* (1964). After *The Masque of the Red Death*, he continued his stint in sinister cinema with *The Skull* (1965), *Marat/Sade* (1967), *The Fiend* (1971), *A Clockwork Orange* (1971), *Demons of the Mind* (1972), *Asylum* (1972), and other titles in a similar vein. He would appear in one more

Poe film: *Il gatto nero* (aka *The Black Cat*, 1981). Nigel Green (1924–1972) came to public attention through his starring role in the British television series *William Tell* (1957). He later appeared in such films as *Jason and the Argonauts* (1963), *Zulu* (1964, with Patrick Magee), *The Ipcress File* (1965), *The Face of Fu Manchu* (1965), *The Skull* (1966, with Patrick Magee), *Deadlier Than the Male* (1966), *Tobruk* (1967), and *Countess Dracula* (1970).

The pressbook for *The Masque of the Red Death*, almost as lavish as the others in the Corman-Poe series, went from a horizontal to a vertical format. One ad in the pressbook quotes Vincent Price as saying, "It is much more difficult to make unreality real than merely to convey reality. Working as we do, too, from the stories of Edgar Allan Poe, we are able to film the peak of all that is great in horror fiction." While Price had made comments similar to this before, the hyperbole smells of the work of an ad man. Interestingly, however, the same ad expresses what was undoubtedly Price's view that he had made only twelve terror films to date. Depending on what one considers a terror film, Price had appeared in 20 to 23 such films at that point in his career. Like John Carradine, the actor was a bit uncomfortable with being identified as a horror actor. Although Price emphasizes the importance of Poe to the film itself, the rest of the pressbook does not devote nearly as much space to the author as earlier pressbooks of the series did. Perhaps the studio sensed a public awareness that the films were moving further and further from the tales themselves, or maybe they simply wanted to devote more space to their star, Vincent Price. Either way, the neglect of Poe here is a pity because *The Masque of the Red Death*, unlike *The Haunted Palace* and *The Raven*, contained most of the salient elements of its source and presented them in Corman's most stylish format yet.

In another ad, Price repeats his criticism of what he considers the contemporary sacrifice of good cinema on the altar of realism.

It is much more difficult to make unreality real than merely to portray reality itself. We're working with some of the greatest terror fiction ever written—stories by Poe, Guy de Maupassant [Price had recently starred in *Diary of a Madman* (1963), based on Maupassant's "The Horla"]—some of the best things in literature. For this reason, I prefer the term "stories of terror" rather than "horror" which makes most people think of monsters. For me, personally, however, kitchen sink dramas hold the greatest horrors. There's something unspeakably horrific about unwashed characters in sordid circumstances revealing aspects of their squalid lives. I'd run a mile from these dramas of so-called reality.

The same ad also quotes Price on his habits as a traveling art collector. "My nerve ends always tell me when I've made a real discovery. I become nervous, hot, then icy cold—a whole series of physical reactions overtake me when I know that I'm on to something."

The ads and red duo-tone posters for the film featured only the full face of Vincent Price cleverly constructed of images of torture, revel, and death. "Stare into this face," the posters commanded. "Count if you can the orgies of Evil! SHUDDER ... at the blood-stained dance of the Red Death! TREMBLE ... to the hideous tortures of the catacombs of Kali! GASP .. at the sacrifice of the innocent virgin to the vengeance of BAAL!"

As though to express more confidence in *The Masque of the Red Death* than it had in *The Haunted Palace*, AIP once again collaborated to bring out a Lancer paperback book tie-in, this one authored by Elsie Lee, and a Dell comic book tie-in.

While *The Masque of the Red Death* grossed over $1.4 million in North American rentals, it ran into censorship problems in England. There the protectors of the masses threatened to ban the film completely if AIP would not cut the Black Mass scene involving Hazel Court and her conjured demon. When that material was reluctantly consigned to the cutting room floor, *The Masque of the Red Death* opened for business in the country of its birth.

Critique: At the time of the films' release, critics were divided on the quality of *The Masque of the Red Death*. *Time* found it overdone, but *Newsweek* called it a "stylish excursion into demonology."[136] Although its double-billing in New York with the teen exploitation comedy *Bikini Beach* could not have helped, *The New York Times* found it "vulgar, naive, and highly amusing, and it is played with gusto by Mr. Price, Hazel Court, and Jane Asher. As for Mr. Corman, he has let his imagination run riot upon a mobile decor singular for its primary color scheme. The result may be loud, but it looks like a real movie. On its level it is astonishingly good."[137] *The New York Herald Tribune* gleefully praised Vincent Price, adding, "the film is beautifully costumed, the sets are lavish, the props exquisite."[138]

In the years following its release, critical opinion about *The Masque of the Red Death* has remained widely divided. According to Ivan Butler, "This story ... is treated with a combination of beauty and horror which results in a fine piece of *cinéma Gothique*. The magnificent settings, in which the camera seems to take an active delight in recording and passing on to us the loveliness of brilliant colours against grey stone, provide a bizarre contrasting background to the corruption, perversion and self-degradation."[139]

Carlos Clarens, on the other hand, finds it "an over-ornate macabre fable [with] all the flat undimensioned elegance of a well-drawn comic strip. Obviously, Roger Corman is no Ingmar Bergman nor is he Luis Bunuel.... In the long rum, *Masque of the Red Death* is rescued from out-and-out imitation or heavy-handed pretentiousness by the brisk staging of many scenes and the current of irrepressible humor that swells up when least expected."[140]

Donald C. Willis acknowledges "a few good scenes" but finds the film "otherwise ponderous."[141]

Ed Naha calls the film "the acknowledged zenith of Roger Corman's love affair with Edgar Allan Poe ... The finished result is startling, stylish, symbolic and liter-ate."[142]

The Overlook Film Encyclopedia: Horror opines that *The Masque of the Red Death* might not be the best [of the Corman cycle], but it's certainly the most ambitious.... The film is graced by an uncommonly intelligent script which probes the concept of diabolism with considerable subtlety."

Michael Weldon writes, "In what is probably Corman's best all-around serious feature, Vincent Price ... is the ultimate evil character."[143]

Leonard Maltin awards the film 3 1/2 stars (good to excellent), calling it "the most Bergman-like of Corman's films, an ultra-stylish adaptation of the Poe tale. Beautifully photographed in England by Nicholas Roeg; a must in color." *Video Hound's Golden Movie Retriever 1996* is only a bit more restrained, throwing the film three bones.

In my view, *The Masque of the Red Death* is the best of the Corman-Poe series for a variety of reasons. First, its similarities with Bergman's *The Seventh Seal* in no way detract from its effectiveness as a colorful, literate, and sometimes shocking horror film. In fact, the Bergmanesque ambiguities give the film a welcome philosophical depth that is missing from the other Corman-Poe films. Ivan Butler provides examples:

> The gentle dwarf is responsible for the Duke's dreadful death; the tiny, childlike Esmerelda speaks with a husky, sexy voice (not her own); Francesca, the only wholly "good" character is so colorless that one actually begins to long for a glimpse of the old Eve; Prospero kills and tortures with relish, yet treats Francesca with gentleness, and spares, for no personal reason, a little girl from the general slaughter of the villagers. This shifting uncertainty of values adds to the sense of unease, and thus of horror, which the film generates so powerfully.[144]

Although the scenario and underlying ideas are deadly serious, the screenplay allows for just the right amount of black comedy. When Alfredo gets ready to don his ape outfit, he asks Hop Toad, "Won't this thing become uncomfortably hot?" Planning to burn Alfredo alive, Hop Toad calmly answers, "It will become a little warm ... but it won't be for long." Vincent Price gives a performance nearly equal to that of his earlier *The Fall of the House of Usher*. His arched or lowered brow, the ironic, threatening, or tender words rolling like satin from his lips, and his general demeanor strongly suggest a man of almost infinite earthly power, confident that evil rules and that he has positioned himself on the winning side. By this time, some critics were writing Price off as a mere parody of himself, a man who had overacted his way to fame in repetitive horror pictures. Such a conclusion is not substantiated by Price's Corman-Poe films.

The other principals in the cast are nearly perfect. Hazel Court portrays a woman of both beauty and intelligence. Unfortunately, her character Juliana has chosen for herself a precarious role in which only beauty and subservience guarantee survival. Although the screenplay does not allow for a full development of her character, Court skillfully brings to life a flawed, vulnerable woman, difficult to like, but also difficult to despise.

Jane Asher is the embodiment of feminine simple faith. While one cringes to imagine her attempting an intellectual account of Christianity, her soft English complexion, innocent eyes, and ability to project vulnerability make her quite believable. Nevertheless, near the end of the film, in accordance with the persistent theme of ambiguity, she utters a confused, "I don't know" in response to Price's assurance that she will soon understand the real truth. Does her delivery of the line indicate more than confusion? Is her faith faltering? Perhaps the young Christian herself does not know.

David Weston, Patrick Magee, and Skip Martin all turn in solid supporting performances, Martin being particularly effective and memorable as Hop Toad. The revelers at the feast often perform as though under the direction of Fellini, enhancing the nightmare quality of the proceedings.

Cinematographer Nicholas Roeg uses the entire screen as a visual playground, a fact accounting for the film's slightly lesser impact when viewed on television. In charge of production design, Daniel Haller goes all out to create damp horror in the underground torture chambers and sumptuous beauty above. Together Roeg and Haller produce an impression of expanse that is quite different from the equally impressive claustrophobic effect of the earlier films.

Of course, some of the stock horror mechanisms used in *The Masque of the Red Death* were by then predictable elements of any Corman-Poe film. For example, upon hearing distant echoing voices late at night, Jane Asher leaves her bed, wanders slowly through forbidding rooms, opens a strange door, comes face to face with sudden horror, and makes a frantic, screaming retreat. Although the device is familiar, it nevertheless works, and it works as well here as in any of the previous films.

La danza macabra (1964); aka *Terrore*; *La Danse Macabre*; *La lunga notte del torrore*; *Castle of Blood*; *Castle of Terror*; *The Long Night of Terror*; *Tombs of Horror*; *Coffin of Terror*; *Dimensions in Death*

Vulsinia Film/Jolly Film/Leo Lax Film/Ulysee Film
Italy and France

Credits: Directed by Antonio Margheriti (Anthony Dawson); produced by Marco Vicario (Frank Belty) and Giovanni Addessi (Walter Sarch); screenplay by Gianni Grimaldi (Jean Grimaud) and Gordon Wilson, Jr.; cinematography by Riccardo Pallotini (Richard Kramer); music by Roz (or Ritz) Ortolani.

Running time: 87 minutes.

Cast: Barbara Steele (Elisabeth Blackwood), George Riviére (Alan Foster), Margaret Robsahm (Julia), Henry Kruger (Dr. Carmus).

Story: On a foggy night in London, Alan Foster, a reporter for the *London Times,* enters a tavern with the intention of interviewing Edgar Allan Poe. As Foster arrives, Poe is completing a narration of his story "Berenice" for an older gentleman. When Foster introduces himself, a conversation ensues during which Poe insists that all the stories he has written are true and that death is not the end of life, that the grave is merely a resting place from which the spirit still roams the earth. When Foster scoffs at Poe's beliefs, the older gentleman introduces himself as Lord Blackwood and wagers that Foster cannot spend a single night in Blackwood Castle, from which no one has ever returned. Foster accepts the wager, and the three men leave immediately for the castle because tonight is the Night of the Dead (All Soul's Eve).

Alone in the castle, Foster investigates and becomes increasingly convinced that strange forces hover nearby. Suddenly a

George Riviére and Barbara Steele are chained in a haunted dungeon in *La danza macabra* (1964, aka *Castle of Blood*).

beautiful young woman comes to him and identifies herself as Elisabeth Blackwood, sister of Sir Thomas, who believes her dead. She and Foster are strongly attracted to each other.

As they are becoming acquainted, another beautiful young woman enters the room. She is Elisabeth's cousin Julia. The two women argue over Foster, and both leave him in the bedroom, which has been prepared for his visit. It seems that Lord Blackwood persuades someone to spend a night in the castle every year on the Night of the Dead.

Later Elisabeth returns to Foster's room, and they realize they have fallen in love. As Foster rests his head upon her breast, he is shocked to find that she has no heartbeat. Elisabeth confesses that she indeed has no heartbeat and that she has been dead for ten

years. Outside the room, Julia is concerned that Foster will learn the secret of the castle. She then summons Herbert, a young, muscular gardener who loves Elisabeth. Herbert bursts into the bedroom, stabs Elisabeth, and flees. Foster offers hot pursuit and shoots the intruder on the stairs, at which point the murderer disappears before Foster's eyes. Confused, Foster returns to the bedroom to find that Elisabeth has also disappeared.

Mysterious Dr. Carmus, known to Foster as a famous scientist and metaphysician, appears and explains that he rented the castle years ago in order to prove his theory that if life is violently torn from a living thing, its senses sustain its existence. He demonstrates by cutting off the head of a snake, which still threatens to attack even though it has been mutilated. The doctor then explains that Elisabeth and the others in the castle all died violently years ago and are being sustained in a lifelike state by their senses. On this night, Foster will see how each of them died as they reenact their final moments.

Carmus shows Foster a lively scene of long ago when there was dancing and music in Blackwood Castle. Elisabeth's husband has returned from America, interrupting her idyll with Herbert the gardener. Later, when Elisabeth is alone with her husband, Herbert bursts in and strangles his rival. He then attacks Elisabeth but is killed by Julia. Rather than being grateful, Elisabeth hysterically stabs Julia to death. Suddenly all of the participants in the gruesome vision disappear. Foster has seen enough and wants to escape, but his attempt is in vain.

Dr. Carmus then reappears, although in another time dimension. Foster watches as the doctor descends into the catacombs and releases from their tombs the fleshless yet living beings who died violently in the castle. Foster learns that their only means of coming back annually on All Soul's Eve is to drink the blood of their guest. Foster runs and, with Elisabeth's help, manages to escape his pursuers. He tries to take Elisabeth with him, but outside in the half light of dawn, she withers into a long-dead corpse, her face a leering skull. Foster manages to escape the castle grounds but is impaled on the spiked gate and dies.

In the morning, Blackwood and Poe arrive. Blackwood calmly removes the money he has won from the dead man's wallet and promises a decent burial. Poe says that he is afraid no one will believe the story when he finally writes it. Meanwhile, inside the castle grounds, the spirits of Foster and Elisabeth are reunited.

Production and marketing: With AIP's Corman-Poe series raking in profits around the world, it is not surprising that other film companies should seek to cash in. One such attempt was the Italian/French production *La danza macabra*. The film was shot in ten days (Corman would be proud)

using television's three-camera technique. Publicity material and several sources report the film as being based on "Dance Macabre" by Edgar Allan Poe. One report identifies this source as an unpublished tale by Poe. None of this, however, is correct. No record exists of Poe's ever having written a story or poem called "Dance Macabre." This misinformation is probably responsible for the equally incorrect report that one of Boris Karloff's final films, *House of Evil* (1972, aka *Macabre Serenade*) is based on the same nonexistent Poe source, though no such claims are made in the film's credits.

Not only can nothing in the *La danza macabra* screenplay be readily traced to any of Poe's works, but contrary to what the scenario suggests, Poe never traveled to England as an adult. In fact, the Poe connection seems to have been appended to the screenplay simply as a financially inspired afterthought. Although a black cat appears on the castle grounds early in the film and a clock pendulum at one point ticks to and fro, they do not have the same effect as Corman's allusions. On the contrary, Margheriti's use of the black cat and pendulum appear, to be more inspired by their appearance as props in countless earlier horror films, all unrelated, of course, to Poe.

Before openly exploiting Edgar Allan Poe, Antonio Margheriti made *La virgine di Norimberga* (1963, aka *Horror Castle*), an uninspired picture influenced by Roger Corman's *The Pit and the Pendulum* and Mario Bava's *La maschera del demonio* (1960, aka *Black Sunday*). Shortly after completing *La danza macabra*, Margheriti would cast Barbara Steele in *I lunghi capelli della morte* (1964, aka *The Long Hair of Death*). In 1970 he would direct *Nella stretta morsa del ragno* (aka *The Web of the Spider*), an almost scene-for-scene remake of *La danza macabra*.

Barbara Steele undoubtedly came to Margheriti's attention in Mario Bava's highly acclaimed *La maschera del demonio* (1960, aka *Black Sunday*), in which she plays the dual role of a virgin and a sexually seductive witch. Her costarring role one year later in

Roger Corman's *The Pit and the Pendulum* was her first appearance in an Edgar Allan Poe film, and, regrettably, *La danza macabra* would be her last.

Recalling *La danza macabra* in an interview with Michael Caen, Steele said that she regarded one scene in the film as "terrible":

> My partner, Margaret Robsham, didn't want to embrace me. You see, she's the wife of Ugo Tognazzi. She argued with the filmwriter. He wanted her to play the scene, but she said that she just couldn't kiss a woman. Margheriti was angry. He said, "You have only to imagine that it's Ugo you're embracing and not Barbara." I don't resemble him very much, eh? I don't know whether this scene was used. [It does not appear in the U.S. release.] I haven't seen the film.[145]

Critique: Because of its drive-in theater status in the United States, *Castle of Blood* did not receive much critical attention. The *Monthly Film Bulletin* wrote:

> The effectiveness of Riccardo Pallottini's camerawork is vitiated—partly by Ortolani's cliché-ridden score which makes every surprise twist predictable, partly by the heroine's ludicrous Charles Addams make-up, partly by the wooden quality of the dubbed dialogue ("I'm very attracted to you, my dear"). Essentially though, the film's weakness lies in its plot.[146]

Lately the film has garnered more praise than reflected in early reactions. Michael Weldon calls *Castle of Blood* "One of Barbara Steele's best. A great ghost story with some tame (probably cut) lesbian scenes."[147] *The Overlook Film Encyclopedia: Horror* concluded that "Margheriti's direction is wonderfully atmospheric, with long meandering sequence shots and perfectly executed gothic imagery. Unfortunately, the Roz Ortolani score is grossly overemphatic and the English dubbing ruins whatever virtues the spoken word may have had."

In my view, the dubbing and musical score are the two major defects of *Castle of Blood.* The dubbing of the Steele and Riv-

iére bedroom scene is laughable throughout, and this is the scene designed to make audiences care about the fate of the two characters. The musical score is indeed obtrusive, except for the lilting waltz, presumably the "Dance Macabre" of the title, which recurs throughout the film.

On the positive side, Margheriti's direction is indeed atmospheric. Unfortunately, the television techniques used to shoot the film sometimes destroy the light/dark contrast of ill-lit scenes. Also on the positive side is Barbara Steele, without whose presence this film would be most unremarkable. The doe-eyed Steele is physically suited for horror films. While her charismatic presence does not compare with that of a Bela Lugosi, she seems perfectly cut from a gothic pattern and can add a sense of both sensuality and terror simply by carrying out the director's instructions.

Also on the positive side are the scene in which the entombed rotting corpse begins to breathe and those in which the deaths of years past are reenacted. Is it a "great ghost story" as Weldon suggests? Certainly not. It is not nearly in the class of truly great ghost films such as *The Uninvited* (1944), *The Haunting* (1963), *The Innocents* (1963), and *Lady in White* (1988). It is fair, watchable, and enjoyable, but hardly memorable. Although *The Premature Burial* was good, it was the least of Corman's Poe films. This entry, though it apes Corman's long atmospheric walks down darkened hallways, is not as good.

Steele would continue to build a reputation as a horror film star in such features as *I lunghi capelli della morte* (1964, aka *The Long Hair of Death*), *Cinque tombe per un medium* (1965, aka *Terror Creatures from the Grave*), *Amanti d'oltretomba*, (aka *Nightmare Castle*), *La sorella di Satana* (1965, aka *The She Beast*). By 1965, Steele was displeased with being typecast in horror films and unsuccessfully tried to break away. She returned to horror in The *Curse of the Crimson Altar* (1968, with Boris Karloff and Christopher Lee) and continued to do such films into the seventies. She then became a successful producer and reportedly will now talk about her career in horror films without her previous deep disdain.

In the United States, Woolner Brothers released *La danza macabra* as *Castle of Blood*, placing it at the top of a double bill with *Hercules in the Haunted World*. While the pressbook for the film was large, it consisted mainly of just ads and photos, and though the unattractive duo-tone posters and ads read "The living and dead change places in an orgy of terror in Edgar Allan Poe's *Castle of Blood*," the only other place Poe's name appears is in the synopsis as a character.

El demonio en la sangre (1964); aka *Demon in the Blood*
Sergio Kogan, Argentina

Credits: Directed by René Mujica; produced by Sergio Kogan; screenplay by Augusto Roa Bastosa and Tomas Eloy Martinez, based in part on "The Tell-Tale Heart" by Edgar Allan Poe; cinematography by Ricardo Younis and Oscar Nelli.

Cast: Rosita Quintana, Ubaldo Martinez, Ernesto Blanco, Arturo Garcia Buhr, Wolf Ruvinskis, Lidia Lamaison, Graciela Dufau.

Story: This is an omnibus film consisting of three tales which illustrate how people can be drawn into evil. The first involves a mortally wounded black boxer who fantasizes being hypnotized by his manager, after which he is compelled to kill all those who were kind to him. The second story, which is based on Edgar Allan Poe's "The Tell-Tale Heart," chronicles a murdered wife's revenge upon her husband and his lover. The final story relates the arrival of a stranger who seduces a married woman under the nose of her unsuspecting husband.

Production and marketing: René Mu-jica's first film, *El Centroforward Murio al Amanecer* (1959), was a fantasy about a rich man who adds a soccer star to his collection of precious objects, much as one would acquire a painting. Next, probably influenced by the Argentine *Obras Maestras del Terror* (1960), an omnibus including a version of "The Tell-Tale Heart," Mujica filmed his own omnibus film, which also included "The Tell-Tale Heart."

One of the actors, Wolf Ruvinskis, was best known for portraying Neutron, the masked wrestler/super hero in such Mexican films as *Automatas de la muerte* (1961, aka *Neutron vs. The Death Robots*), *Neutron Battles the Karate Assassins* (1962), and *Neutron, el enmascarado negro* (1963, aka *Neutron, the Black-Masked*).

Critique: *The Overlook Encyclopedia: Horror* considered *El demonio en la sangre* a technically competent disappointment with a great deal of ham acting. Since I have not seen the film, the *Encyclopedia* must have the last word.

The Tomb of Ligeia (1965)
American International, U.S.A. and Great Britain

Credits: Directed and produced by Roger Corman; screenplay by Robert Towne, based on "Ligeia" by Edgar Allan Poe; director of photography—Arthur

Vincent Price and Elizabeth Shepherd go to their fiery deaths in *The Tomb of Ligeia* (1965).

Grant; art director—Colin Soutcott; music by Kenneth V. Jones.

Running time: 79 minutes.

Cast: Vincent Price (Verden Fell), Elizabeth Shepherd (Ligeia/Lady Rowena Tevanion), John Westbrook (Christopher), Oliver Johnston (Kenrick), Derek Francis (Lord Trevanion), Richard Vernon (Dr. Vivian), Ronald Adam (Parson), Frank Thornton (Peperel), Denis Gilmore (livery boy).

Story: In 1821, Verden Fell is burying his deceased, raven-haired wife, Ligeia, in an English country churchyard when the local pastor and others object. It seems that since Ligeia was not a Christian, she cannot be buried in hallowed ground. Fell explains that his wife is not really dead—not to him at least. He also quotes Ligeia's philosophy: "Man need not kneel before the angels nor lie in death forever but for the weakness of his feeble will." A black cat leaps upon the

coffin, and Ligeia's eyes spring open. Fell explains with a smile that Ligeia's eyes opened only as a result of a nervous contraction. The villagers leave, and Fell continues with the burial.

A few months later, Lady Rowena Trevanion wanders from a fox hunt with her companion Christopher and is thrown from her horse near Ligeia's grave. She is startled by the sudden appearance of Fell, who carries her into his abbey home. Although Fell is now morose and wears a forbidding pair of dark glasses in the daylight, Christopher recognizes Fell as an old friend. The death of his wife has evidently taken a heavy toll on Fell's personality and mental stability.

As Fell bandages Rowena's ankle, her father, Lord Trevanion, comes in with a dead fox, which Fell identifies as Ligeia's pet. While they talk, the fox disappears, and Fell suggests that the animal was probably taken by the omnipresent black cat that guards

Ligeia's grave and prowls the abbey and its grounds.

A few days later Rowena visits the abbey. Although Fell has been moody and decidedly unfriendly, his heart begins to melt in the presence of his blond-haired visitor. As they are about to kiss, the black cat attacks Rowena and scratches her face. Fell vows to have the cat destroyed, but it lures Rowena into the abbey bell tower, where she is nearly killed before Fell rescues her.

Although Fell is fearful upon discovering that Ligeia's death date has been skillfully removed from the tombstone, he and Rowena soon marry. When both appear happy during the honeymoon, Fell decides to sell the dark abbey and instructs Christopher to make all the necessary arrangements. After the honeymoon, however, Fell learns that since there was no death certificate for Ligeia, the courts still consider her the legal owner of the property. Unless her body is exhumed and she is legally pronounced dead, Fell cannot sell the abbey. Still, he refuses to allow any tampering with Ligeia's grave.

At a dinner party, Fell becomes melancholy and speaks of his interest in hypnosis and the afterlife. When the dinner guests ask for a demonstration, Fell hypnotizes Rowena but is horrified when she begins speaking in Ligeia's voice.

The disintegration of the marriage progresses as Fell begins to absent himself from the abbey at night and Rowena has horrible nightmares about the dead fox, the black cat, and a mysterious black-haired woman. Awakening from one of the nightmares, she finds a dead fox in her bed and a saucer of milk on the floor. Christopher, concerned with Rowena's increasing fear and unhappiness, unearths Ligeia's coffin, only to find a wax effigy inside.

Rowena, now on the brink of madness, sees herself reflected in her bedroom mirror as Ligeia. She smashes the mirror, cutting her wrist, and discovers a secret passage behind it. Following the passage, she comes to an underground room where Fell is sitting

with the preserved body of Ligeia. When Christopher and the abbey manservant Kenrick arrive, the servant explains that the strong-willed and possessive Ligeia had hypnotized Fell shortly before her death and promised that she would not die. She also instructed Fell to visit her every night, which he has done, even after his marriage to Rowena. During the day, Fell drifts into a partial amnesia and forgets the whole affair.

In an attempt to free her husband from the spell, Rowena, pretending to be Ligeia, orders him to disregard her original commands. Ligeia is finally dead, she tells him. At that moment, however, Rowena falls to the floor, having apparently bled to death as a result of her slashed wrist. Fell, in a state of confusion, strangles the black-haired woman he believes to be Ligeia, only to be told by Christopher that he has actually strangled Rowena, who had not really died.

When Christopher and Kenrick carry out the body of Rowena, Fell stays in the room and attempts to kill the black cat. When it eludes him and scratches out his eyes, he knocks over a lantern and sets the crypt afire. As the abbey burns and Fell and the cat (or Ligeia?) die, Rowena opens her eyes and is embraced by Christopher. The spell is broken. Or is it?

"The boundaries which divide life from death are at best shadowy and vague. Who can say where the one ends and where the other begins?"

Poe

Production and marketing: Before AIP had totaled the receipts from *The Masque of the Red Death*, it set to work producing its eighth Corman-Poe film, *The Tomb of Ligeia*.

By this time Roger Corman was tired of directing Edgar Allan Poe films. According to the director, in order to keep himself interested, he decided to experiment still more extensively in *The Tomb of Ligeia*:

> For instance, [in the preceding films] I had never wanted to shoot in real situations. I felt we were dealing with the world beyond the conscious, a closed, somewhat artificial

world, so I tried to shoot everything in studios.... But with *The Tomb of Ligeia* I said, "Okay, I'm gonna show reality." We went into the English countryside and photographed a fox hunt, a wedding at a very pretty English church, a sixteenth-century monastery in ruins, to be used as the exterior of the house. It was very, very interesting. As a result, *Ligeia* had a very different look from the other Poe films, because it was the first and only time the sun ever shone in one of them—I did it just to break the rules. In retrospect, it gave the picture a good look, but I think the original theory was right: it was better to keep it a closed, dark world.[148]

Vincent Price, appearing in his seventh Corman-Poe picture, reported that at least part of the idea for shooting in an actual on-location ruin was his own:

The Tomb of Ligeia was vaguely based on an idea that Roger and I had once. I had said I had always wanted to do a picture in a ruin, but actually using the ruin as an actual place, with real furniture in it and the ruin around it, which I thought would be very effective. Well, this is sort of what he adapted to "The Tomb of Ligeia," which I think was the best one we ever did.[149]

When Corman found the abbey he wanted, he soon discovered that its status as a national monument precluded his moving furniture into it. Corman responded by shooting the exteriors in and around the ruins and by doing the interiors at nearby Shepperton studios.

This time the screenplay was by Corman's friend Robert Towne (1936–), who conceived the tale as a love story. Towne went on to distinguish himself as a screenwriter by producing scenarios for *Chinatown* (1974), *Shampoo* (1974, which he co–wrote), and *Personal Best* (1981, which he also directed).

Poe's tale involves a highly intelligent woman with a powerful will. When she dies, the narrator (nameless in the story, but known as Verden Fell in the film) marries a woman who is the opposite of Ligeia. His second wife sickens and dies, and on her bier the spirit of Ligeia takes over her body.

While the storyline is simple, the tale is both one of Poe's best and most ambiguous. For example, does the story happen just as the narrator tells it, or does the narrator give a very real Ligeia supernatural qualities that no real woman could possess and later hallucinate her return from the dead? Or is Rowena real while Ligeia is a figment of the narrator's imagination? While Towne infuses the screenplay with ample mystery, he clearly writes from the perspective that Ligeia is real. Ambiguity arises largely at the end of the picture when no one is quite sure who is Ligeia and who is Rowena.

Towne wrote the screenplay intending that a young man like Richard Chamberlain play Verden Fell, but AIP would not hear of it. Vincent Price had to star. After all, the response to Ray Milland in *The Premature Burial* (the only film in the Corman-Poe series that did not star Price) had been unenthusiastic, and the studio knew when it had a good thing going. So Price shaved his mustache to appear a few years younger (he was 53 at the time) and again stepped in as star. Of Fell, Price remarked: "He would have probably led a very normal life, except that he married a woman who would not leave life, even after her death. However, the characters are a little off-beat. I mean, who is a man who sleeps with his dead wife? It's a little peculiar."[150] The actor always displayed a good sense of humor.

Costarring with Price was 27-year-old Elizabeth Shepherd, a classical stage actress who had appeared in two films, *The Queen's Guards* (1961) and *Blind Corner* (1963), before coming on board for *The Tomb of Ligeia*. She would go on to add another horror picture to her credits in 1978 with *Damien: Omen II.*

Also appearing was Derek Francis (1923–1984), the portly British actor who generally essayed self-important parts in films such as *Bitter Harvest* (1963), *Ring of Spies* (1964), and *Comedy Man* (1964). He too would lend his talents to the fear genre in one of Hammer's final horror pictures, *To the Devil a Daughter* (1975).

In Price's previous Corman-Poe picture, *The Masque of the Red Death*, he knocked himself unconscious after stumbling and falling from a dais. Filming for *The Tomb of Ligeia* was uneventful, however, until it was time for the fiery finale. Price recalled the near-tragedy:

> They had coated all the walls with a liquid cement that emits a gas after it's been applied. The set was filled with this gas. We were all warned. Don't smoke. Don't light a match. Elizabeth and I were positioning ourselves under the debris. Just before the cameras were supposed to roll, some idiot walked in and lit a match. The whole set went up. I was petrified. I dragged Elizabeth out of there as fast as I could. The whole shot was ruined. The cameras weren't rolling. We had to start over from scratch.[151]

The pressbook for *The Tomb of Ligeia* was similar to that of *The Masque of the Red Death*. Like the posters for *Masque*, those for *Ligeia* were duo-tone and rather drab. The unimaginative design pictures the large head of a black cat over the scene of a woman running through a graveyard. The posters and ads announced that "Even on her wedding night she must share the man she loved with the 'female thing' that lived in the tomb of the cat!" The lobby cards asked, "Cat or woman or a thing too evil to mention? Listen for the scream in the night. Look into the eyes of the creature who rules the land of the living dead."

The pressbook also contains a short piece announcing that "Poe's *Tomb of Ligeia* is terror for eggheads." Corman explains that while general audiences will enjoy the film, those with a knowledge of the philosophy of Sigmund Freud will find their pleasure enhanced:

> I went deeply into Freud when I first began interpreting Edgar Allan Poe stories for the screen. Poe was a writer obsessed with symbolism. In fact, Poe's whole world of ruined sanctuaries, brooding trees, cawing birds, cats, deaths and funerals was a symbolic one. As an American obsessed with Europe's decadence, he was himself symbolic of

America's long, regretful farewell to the Europe it wanted to believe was all evil.

Although Lancer did not cooperate with a paperback tie-in for *The Tomb of Ligeia*, Dell comics provided a handsome tie-in to help boost ticket sales. The cover of the comic, much more attractive than the movie poster, features the grim face of Vincent Price above licking flames and the image of a man carrying the body of Rowena to safety.

When the film garnered a handsome profit, AIP prepared to produce its next Corman-Poe feature, *The Gold Bug*. This time around, however, Corman was simply not interested as he later explained:

> I had a script by Chuck Griffith that was a complete farce. It was set in the South, after the civil war. Vincent Price was a plantation owner who had convinced his one remaining slave, to be played by Sammy Davis, Jr., that the South had won the civil war. Basil Rathbone was a visiting English carpetbagger who comes upon this deserted plantation. It was really very funny, but it was becoming outrageously distanced from Poe, so we decided not to make it.[152]

In fact, *The Tomb of Ligeia* proved to be Corman's last Edgar Allan Poe film for nearly a quarter century. Tired of the series and wanting to move on, he directed six more films, none of them in the horror genre, and then became a producer. In 1989 he would return to Edgar Allan Poe to produce *The Haunting of Morella*, a feature-length version of the tale "Morella," which he had directed as part of *Tales of Terror* in 1962.

Although Roger Corman abandoned the Poe series, AIP was not about to forsake its golden goose. After all, Vincent Price was under contract, and a screenplay was standing by based on Poe's poem "The City in the Sea." The plundering of Poe would march on.

Critique: When the eighth Corman-Poe film arrived at theaters in May of 1965, critics generally received it well. *The New*

York Daily News said: "If you just love being scared, this is the one that will do it.... Roger Corman, director-producer, a veteran of the Poe-Price combination, gets this one off evenly and in short order, building up and sustaining suspense from the beginning to end. Elizabeth Shepherd is an asset, so is John Estbrook ... Needless to say, that old smoothie, Vincent Price, gets under the skin playing a fascinating maniac."[153]

Although the *New York Times* still favored *The Pit and the Pendulum* as the best in the series, it called *The Tomb of Ligeia* "Pretty good, although it goes hog-wild toward the end, and uncorks some familiar horror clichés that not even Mr. Corman can camouflage." The review also acknowledged Corman's "unhealthy and contagious ... climate of evil," as well as the "stunning, ambient use of his authentic setting."[154]

Newsweek allowed that "[it] may not be the best of his [Corman's] series of Edgar Allan Poe divertimentos, but it is the most far-out, and, in the last half hour or so, his most concentrated piece of black magic."[155]

While the years have solidified Roger Corman's reputation as an important director, *The Tomb of Ligeia* shares the critical fate of most of his other Poe films: the reaction is mixed. Ivan Butler wrote that while "the epic sense of grandeur and doom may be missing, and the story reverts to the worn grooves of wax effigies in coffins, ghostly visitations and climactic holocausts, ... the story is treated with seriousness and imagination, and taken on its own without irrelevant comparisons, as it should be, *Ligeia* shows that Corman's increase in stature with *The Masque of the Red Death* may be no freak growth."[156] Butler also drew attention to Corman's beautifully contrasted settings: "The cool greys of the ruined abbey (according to one authority Glastonbury, but to Corman himself an old abbey in Norfolk), the yellows and blues in the huge shadowy house, and the reds and greens of the hunting scenes interplay with and reinforce each other in a kind of colour counterpoint."[157]

Carlos Clarens, no fan of the Corman-Poe series, found the last film of the lot "the handsomest of his [Corman's] color productions, but it polishes off to a glaze the old Corman vigor."[158]

Rose London became impatient with the confusing comings and goings of Ligeia, comparing them to the on-again, off-again tuberculosis of Poe's wife Virginia:

> In Poe's story, Ligeia comes back once from the tomb through the body of the Lady of Tremaine. In Corman's version she rises again and again and again like a farcical Virginia with her broken blood vessels. As if in a black pantomine, Vincent Price has to kill the corpse time after time, as it comes back for more and more and more, even finally changing back to the Lady of Tremaine to provide a silly happy ending.... While it is enjoyable knockabout, it loses Poe's sense of waiting for the evil to come.[159]

The Overlook Encyclopedia of Film: Horror found that the Norfolk abbey setting "gives the film a markedly different tone, a tangible solidity to add to the psychological subtlety: it is as though one were watching Poe filtered through the gothic melodrama of a *Jane Eyre* and reaching—with the perfectly legitimate yet somehow anachronistic dark glasses affected by Price acting as a bridge—forward to the very different kinds of obsession and possession in Hitchcock's *Vertigo*.... Although the final sequence returns a little disappointingly to formula ..., the rest of the film is superbly structured."

Jay Robert Nash and Stanley Ralph Ross awarded the film two stars, concluding: "Though it does have its moments, this is not a very convincing or suspenseful film. Price goes through his role as if he really were hypnotized; he's pretty stiff to say the least."[160]

Finally, *Video Hound's Golden Movie Retriever 1996* and Leonard Maltin both give the film three stars, Maltin calling it "A super-stylish chiller with superb location work."

Joining the critics, Roger Corman and Vincent Price disagreed on the merits of *Ligeia*, Corman arguing that his approach to it was inferior to that of the earlier films, and Price calling it the best of the series. Who was right? I think for the most part that Corman was. The enclosed sets of the earlier films were more consistent with Poe's enclosed world of psychological horror. Corman had made seven Poe films successfully following that method, however, so one should not blame him for wanting to experiment, especially since the experiment is largely, though not wholly, successful.

Butler is correct in his positive assessment of Corman's color combinations and counterpoints. The director had previously employed color symbolically and with striking aesthetic effect, especially in *The Fall of the House of Usher* and *The Masque of the Red Death*. Here the effects are sometimes less subtle, though equally effective.

Ironically, Vincent Price is both a strength and a weakness. He was an undeniable asset in his six previous Corman-Poe films, but here Towne's screenplay truly does call for a younger man. A clean-shaven Price does appear a little younger than he did in the previous films, and the curly black wig helps, but not enough to make him the best match for Elizabeth Shepherd. On the positive side, this is Price's best performance in the entire Corman-Poe series and one of the best of his career. Playing a complex character, Price brings nuances to his portrayal of Verden Fell that he did not bring to Roderick Usher, Prince Prospero, or any of his other memorable Poe roles. The role was not written with Price in mind, and the actor had to make it his, which he does without any of the hamminess mistakenly assigned to him by some critics.

Surprisingly, relatively unknown actress Elizabeth Shepherd gives the best performance by a woman in the entire Corman-Poe series. In the film's opening scenes, she is a strong character with a delightful sense of humor. As her marriage and emotional stability begin to disintegrate, she perfectly executes the changes. No third-rate talent playing second fiddle to Vincent Price here.

The minor weaknesses lie largely with the screenplay and with Corman's direction of the last half hour. The first hour of the film suggests an ominous sense of fate and predestination. Fell, wearing dark glasses symbolizing intellectual and spiritual blindness, is ambivalent toward the prospect of Ligeia's return. In the last half hour, ambiguities accelerate to the extent that confusion results. The screenplay also makes for a rather slow film in places.

Ultimately, the result is a good film, a fine ending for the Corman-Poe series, which has the distinction of being an eight-film series with not a single weak entry. Each chiller is an above average tribute to the skills of Roger Corman and his AIP crew.

Here is my ranking of the Corman/Poe films in order of overall quality:

1. *The Masque of the Red Death*
2. *The Fall of the House of Usher*
3. *The Pit and the Pendulum*
4. *The Tomb of Ligeia*
5. *Tales of Terror*
6. *The Raven*
7. *The Haunted Palace*
8. *The Premature Burial*

I rank the quality of Vincent Price's performances in the Corman/Poe series as follows:

1. *The Tomb of Ligeia*
2. *The Fall of the House of Usher*
3. *The Pit and the Pendulum*
4. *The Masque of the Red Death*
5. *The Haunted Palace*
6. *Tales of Terror*
7. *The Raven*

The City Under the Sea (1965); aka *War-Gods of the Deep*; *Warlords of the Deep*

American International, U.S.A. and Great Britain

Credits: Directed by Jacques Tourneur; produced by Daniel Haller; screenplay by Charles Bennett and Louis M. Heyward, from "The City in the Sea" by Edgar Allan Poe; cinematography by David Whittaker; art direction by Frank White; music by Stanley Black; special effects by Frank George and Lew Bowie.

Running time: 85 minutes.

Cast: Vincent Price (the captain), Tab Hunter (Ben Harris), Susan Hart (Jill Tregellis), David Tomlinson (Harold Tiffin Jones), John Le Mesurier (Ives), Henry Oscar (Mumford), Derek Newark (Dan), Roy Patrick (Simon), Anthony Selby (George), Michael Heyland (Bill), Stephen Brooke (Ted), William Hurndell (Tom), Jim Spearman (Jack), Arthur Hewlett (first fisherman), Walter Sparrow (second fisherman), John Barrett (third fisherman), Barbara Bruce (first woman guest), Hilda Campbell Russell (second woman guest), Bart Allison (first man guest), George Ricarde (second man guest).

Story: Narrator:

Lo! Death has reared himself a throne.
In a strange city lying alone.
Far down within the dim West,
Where the good and the bad and the worst
    and the best
Have gone to their eternal rest....
Resignedly beneath the sky
The melancholy waters lie,...
But lo, a stir is in the air!
The wave—there is a movement there!

A corpse washes ashore on the Cornish coast, the face twisted with fear. Fishermen identify it as the remains of a lawyer who had been staying at Tregathion Manor House, a fifteenth-century manor which is now a hotel inherited by Jill Tregellis, a beautiful young American.

Another American, Ben Harris, goes to the manor house to relay word of the lawyer's death to Jill and her friend, Harold Tiffin Jones, an eccentric artist who is quite fond of a pet rooster. Responding to a commotion in an adjacent study, Ben breaks down the door and finds the room in shambles, with a weird, scaled creature—a gillman—within. The creature attacks him and escapes through a sliding panel which shuts after it.

Later that night Jill walks by candlelight back down to the study and is abducted by the gillman, who leaves a telltale trail of slime and seaweed. When Harold's rooster finds a secret panel, Ben leads Harold and the rooster down a descending passage to an undersea chamber lit by the glow of submarine volcanoes. Suddenly they are swept by a whirlpool to Lyonesse, a legendary golden city that disappeared beneath the waves about a century ago. Soon they come to a place where a trial is being held, after which the condemned man is left to drown as a flood of water cascades down through the fingers of a giant, upturned stone hand.

Unable to help the prisoner, Ben and Harold flee from the water to a well-furnished room and find a seismology book stolen earlier from the manor house study. With the book is a sketch that Harold had made of Jill. When a stranger, later identified as Simon, enters the room, Ben attacks him, demanding to know where Jill is. After Ben knocks Simon unconscious, a man known as the Captain appears and explains that it matters not whether Simon is alive or dead because the man would someday like to take the Captain's place. The Captain then escorts the two intruders to a large glass wall that allows them to observe the legendary underwater city of Lyonesse, whose

Vincent Price stands before a portrait of his deceased wife in *The City Under the Sea* **(aka** *War-Gods of the Deep*)**.**

end is inevitable because of volcanic activity unless some way can be found to halt the eruptions. The Captain says that the people in the city eventually died out, except for the gillmen, strange creatures that are half-fish and half-human. The gillmen, he says, think of him as Death looking down from his tower. The Captain also informs Ben and Harold that they will survive only if they can be useful in saving Lyonesse. Thinking fast, Harold claims that Ben is a famous geologist and seismologist. Momentarily satisfied, the Captain confirms that Jill is alive and well and orders the now recovered Simon to take the intruders to the grotto. There Simon shows them a book of Edgar Allan Poe's poems dated 1847. Ben reads:

No rays from the holy Heaven come down.
On the long night-time of that town;
But light from out the lurid sea

Streams up the turrets silently—
Gleams up the pinnacles far and free—
Up domes—up spires—up kingly halls—
Up fanes—up Babylon-like walls—
...
Up many and many a marvelous shrine
Whose wreathed friezes intertwine.
...
So blend the turrets and shadows there
That all seem pendulous in air,
While from a proud tower in the town
Death looks gigantically down.

Ben and Harold immediately recognize the parallels between the poem and the Captain's city. Also, much to their amazement, an inscription in the book suggests that the Captain is about 200 years old.

In time the men learn that the gillmen kidnapped the lawyer whose body was discovered above. Unfortunately for the scholar, he proved of no use. They also learn that the Captain had found the sketch of Jill, who bore an amazing resemblance to his long-lost wife. He had ordered her capture in the belief that she really was his reincarnated mate. Ben and Harold also learn that life in Lyonesse is eternal or brief, depending on the whim of the mad Captain. Rough justice is served by the gillmen. Some condemned men, it seems, are given a head start in the sea, but none ever escape eventual death at the hands of the creatures.

Aided by the rooster and the mysterious Reverend Ives, who disappeared from Tragathion more than fifty years ago as an old man, they elude the fate of death, rescue Jill, and survive an underwater confrontation with the gillmen. As the fleeing party reaches the shore, volcanic eruptions destroy the Captain and all that is left of his city under the sea.

Production and marketing: When Roger Corman announced that he planned to direct no more Edgar Allan Poe films for AIP, he had completed eight such pictures, all of which were above average to very good. Undeterred by his departure, AIP continued the series with *The City Under the Sea.* As with *The Raven,* the ninth Edgar Allan Poe feature was based on a poem rather than a short story. Poe's moody "The City in the Sea" describes a subterranean deserted city whose former inhabitants are all dead. Inspired by the poem, screenwriters Bennett and Heyward conjured a story allowing Vincent Price to star as the city's captain, whom the gillmen regard as Death. Hence the connection with Poe's "Lo! Death has reared himself a throne." Except for the city itself, which resembles Poe's description, no other connections between the poem and the film are apparent.

Although uncredited, Poe's short story "A Descent into the Maelstrom" also serves as a source to the extent that a maelstrom pulls Hunter and Tomlinson into the bowels of Lyonesse. Otherwise, Poe is left far behind in this adventure story with thematic ties to Jules Verne's *A Journey to the Center of the Earth, Twenty Thousand Leagues Under the Sea,* and *The Mysterious Island* and to

Richard Connell's "The Most Dangerous Game." Lyonesse, by the way, is the lost undersea land mentioned in early English chronicles that is thought to be the scene of the famed Arthurian romances. According to legend, the city flourished on the coast of Cornwall until its sudden and mysterious disappearance beneath the sea.

Without Corman as director, AIP turned to French-American Jacques Tourneur (1904–1977), son of Maurice Tourneur, director of the Poe-based *Le Système du Docteur Goudron et du Professeur Plume* (1912). Although Tourneur was sixty-one at the time, he had successfully directed such atmospheric horror films as *The Cat People* (1942, produced by Val Lewton), *I Walked with a Zombie* (1943, produced by Val Lewton), and *Night of the Demon* (1958, aka *Curse of the Demon*). Daniel Haller, Corman's excellent art director on the Poe films, sat in the producer's chair and turned over his previous role to Frank White.

British cinematographer Stephen Dade (1909–) had been working in films since 1927. Among his credits was the George Sanders horror vehicle *Bluebeard's Ten Honeymoons* (1960). After *The City Under the Sea,* he would serve as cinematographer for Hammer's *The Viking Queen.* Special effects man Les Bowie (1913–1979), known for his use of matte shots, worked many Hammer productions and later distinguished himself on *Star Wars* (1977) and *Superman* (1978).

Of course, since most of the Poe scripts; were being written with Vincent Price in mind, the actor easily walked into the starring role. In later interviews, Price said he was dissatisfied with Bennett's screenplay, so executive producer Sam Arkoff sent Heyward to England to do a rewrite. Heyward, who would produce most of Price's remaining AIP films, claimed that a power play was going on between Tourneur and Haller, himself an aspiring director. To bring in the film on budget, Heyward took control of production. Later he criticized what he saw as AIP's slipshod approach to the Poe films after Corman's departure:

What we were doing in those days at AIP was hit-and-run. Do the picture—people are gonna come anyway. If you excised a scene before you shot it, to save a day's shooting, nobody really knew the difference, because you didn't have to give the explanation of the logic of an illogical situation. So there'd be a credibility gap, and nobody would notice or care, because you would get the same audience.[161]

Price shared Heywood's assessment:

War-Gods of the Deep was just a disaster. Nobody knew what it was about. It was a badly produced picture. Jacques was a marvelous director. When we did *Comedy of Terrors* [1963, a non-Poe film directed by Roger Corman and starring Price, Boris Karloff, Peter Lorre, and Basil Rathbone] he was just wonderful, but he just couldn't get around the script.[162]

With Vincent Price was veteran British actor David Tomlinson (1917–), who had played both leading men and comedians. Some of his most well-known appearances were in *Miranda* (1948), *The Chiltern Hundreds* (1949), *Three Men in a Boat* (1955), and *Tom Jones* (1963). His most memorable film, however, was clearly *Mary Poppins* (1964). There he plays the father into whose household Julie Andrews brings a sense of what is really important in life.

The male romantic lead was played by American Tab Hunter (1931–), a teenage rave of the fifties best known for *Track of the Cat* (1954), *Battle Cry* (1955), and *Damn Yankees* (1958). He also distinguished himself on television, winning an Emmy for his performance opposite Geraldine Page in a *Playhouse 90* presentation titled "Portrait of a Murder." Although no longer a teen heartthrob, Hunter was still a very handsome 34-year-old at the time of *City Under the Sea*. Susan Hart had appeared with Bob Hope in *A Global Affair* (1964, directed by Jack Arnold), as well as in the AIP teenage exploitation flicks *Pajama Party* (1964) and *Ride the Wild Surf* (1964). In 1966 she would reunite with Vincent Price in *Dr. Goldfoot*

and the Bikini Machine, a send-up of AIP's films, including the Corman-Poe series.

British exploitation material for *The City Under the Sea* prominently featured Poe's name on all ads and posters. Strangely, the American pressbook for *War-Gods of the Deep* made no mention of the author. Instead, it hyped Vincent Price as Hollywood's "Merchant of Menace," provided information on the legend of Lyonesse, ran lengthy articles on Hunter, Tomlinson, and Hart, and drew attention to the gillman. Regarding AIP's latest monster, one ad included what is almost certainly a fabricated quotation attributed to Vincent Price: "So far, there have been only four really great screen monsters—Frankenstein, Dracula, The Werewolf and The Mummy—but now The Gillman bids for a place with these. A hideous, marrow sapping horror, I believe The Gillman may join the ranks of the monsterously great." Actually the gillman ripped off the monster of Universal-International's *The Creature from the Black Lagoon* (1954), an amphibious horror that had already entered the ranks of the great monsters. That creature appeared in two sequels, while the gillman of *War-Gods* was never heard from again.

Dell comics produced a tie-in sporting a colorful cover that featured Vincent Price, Susan Hart, and the Minoa-like architecture of Lyonesse. In a move clearly not designed to lend the picture prestige, AIP double billed it in New York with the latest Frankie Avalon and Annette Funicello surf party, *Beach Blanket Bingo*.

Critique: Upon its release, *War-Gods of the Deep* garnered uniformly poor reviews. For example, the *New York Times* ridiculed the plot, criticized the gillmen's "mangy-looking diving suits," and stated the obvious—that Tourneur's earlier *The Cat People* was far superior.[163] More recently, Michael Weldon called *War-Gods* "A dull and unconvincing adventure,"[164] and Jay Robert Nash and Stanley Ralph Ross also found it "Dull."[165] Leonard Maltin was a bit more generous, awarding it 2 1/2 stars and noting that "establishing menace, [the] first half has

[an] odd, almost poetic feel to it, but [the] second half deteriorates with [the] shoddy underwater city."

Maltin's appraisal is generally accurate. Enhanced by the crashing waves of the Cornwall coast, Price's opening narration from Poe's "The City in the Sea" sets a mood of loneliness and dread. The mood is heightened when the fishermen discover a corpse and speak in foreboding tones of the lost city of Lyonesse, and Tab Hunter arrives at Tregathion House during an ominous thunderstorm. The carefully established mood is all but destroyed, however, with the introduction of David Tomlinson's intrusive comic relief. Tomlinson is a fine actor, but the timing of his humor nearly destroys the gothic atmosphere established in the opening scenes. Still, there are several dark and suspenseful moments in the ransacked study, including the gillman's late night abduction of Susan Hart.

After the film's uneven beginning, we follow Hunter and Tomlinson to the underwater city and meet Vincent Price. To the seasoned filmgoer, Price is becoming overly familiar in such roles, but even for a novice, the suspense of the film at this point begins to lapse. Although Price infuses his character with the proper mix of cruelty, devotion, and singlemindedness, and though some of Stephen Dade's photography in what serves as a courtroom and execution chamber is reminiscent of Mario Bava's atmospheric use of red hues, and though George and Bowie's special effects are convincing, the story becomes somewhat confusing and slow until the climactic chase scenes. While John Lamb's underwater photography is adequate, shots of the characters' faces in diving helmets were clearly filmed on dry land and clumsily edited into Lamb's footage.

As the romantic leads, Tab Hunter and Susan Hart are no weaker than many other young lovebirds in the AIP Poe series. Still, the talents of the perky Hart were better suited for the light juvenile fare that AIP cast her in both before and after *War-Gods of the Deep*.

Finally, the fact that AIP found it necessary to inject monsters into the Poe series indicated waning creativity, and as Heyward noted, the push to get the film in on budget at the expense of quality betrayed the studio's cynicism toward its loyal audience.

The Black Cat (1966)
Hemisphere/Falcon International, U.S.A.

Credits: Directed by Harold Hoffman; produced by Patrick Sims; screenplay by Harold Hoffman, based on "The Black Cat" by Edgar Allan Poe; assistant director— George Costello; art direction by Robert Dracup; cinematography by Walter Schenk; edited by Charles Schelling; makeup by Beverly Gilbert; special effects by Manuel De Aumente, Clifton Barr, and Shields Mitchell.

Running time: 77 minutes (another source says 91 minutes).

Cast: Robert Frost (Lew), Robyn Baker (Diana), Sadie French (Lillith), Scotty McKay, George Russell, Tommie Russell.

Story: Lew and Diana are celebrating their first wedding anniversary, and Diana gives Lew a black cat as a present. As champagne flows, he introduces that cat to his preexisting menagerie of monkeys and parrots. At first, Lew pays so much attention to the cat that he neglects his wife. Then, after an evening of hard drinking at a nearby bar, Lew is scratched by his beloved animal. Jumping to the conclusion that the cat is the reincarnation of his hated father, Lew cuts

out the animal's eye. Diana becomes concerned as her husband's nearly psychotic
feelings about his father make him progres-
sively more distraught. After another drinking bout, Lew returns home and attempts to
strangle Diana. Lillith, the housekeeper, rescues Diana, and they both leave the house
but return the next morning. The next night
Lew hangs and electrocutes the black cat,
accidentally burning down the house. Lew
and Diana go to their lawyer to inquire
about insurance. Enraged to find that the
house is uninsured, Lew attempts to strangle the lawyer. Diana knocks her murderous
husband unconscious with a book end; he is
then hospitalized and given psychiatric
treatment.

After Lew returns from the hospital,
he and Diana resume married life in their
new home. Lew tries to refrain from drinking but finds it difficult. One day, finding no
whiskey in the house, he goes to a bar. After
drinking all day, he discovers a one-eyed
black cat in the street and takes it home.
Some days later Diana, needing something
from the cellar but afraid to go alone, asks
Lew to accompany her. Going down the
stairs, Lew trips over the black cat, becomes
enraged, and tries to kill it. When Diana
tries to stop him, he buries an axe in her
brain. Lew then creates an opening in the
cellar wall and conceals the corpse behind it
with cement.

Lillith, who has been out of the house,
returns looking for Diana. Lew tells her that
his wife has left him and has gone to visit
her mother. Unconvinced, Lillith gets the
police, who insist on searching the house.
As they are looking through the basement,
the overconfident Lew gestures and hits the
wall where Diana is entombed. The startled
police shudder to hear the cry of a cat behind the wall. The police break down the
wall and find the black cat atop the head of
Diana's corpse. His charade over, Lew escapes, gets into a car, and races away with
the police close behind. He turns off into a
side road to evade the chase, and, thinking
he is safe, smiles. Suddenly he sees a black
cat in the middle of the road and jams on
his brakes. The car overturns, killing the
murderer.

Production and marketing: Hemisphere Pictures was notorious for distribut-
ing poor quality, low-budget horror pictures,
of which *The Black Cat* was one. With a relatively unknown director (whose previous
work included *Love and the Animals*, a documentary showing how animals mate) and
an unknown cast, the film relied on lurid advertising and on Poe's popular name to draw
an audience. Examples of lurid advertising
included the back cover of the pressbook,
which features a bloody hand holding a cat's
eye, and the one-sheet poster that offered
the black-and-white image of the one-eyed
feline atop the head of Robyn Baker's rotting corpse. Dubbing *The Black Cat* "the
most terrifying story ever filmed," publicity
material asked, "What force drives him to
commit acts against nature … to terrify …
to torture?" Of course, the label "Edgar
Allan Poe's immortal classic" adorns every
poster and ad.

Universal Pictures made two films
"based on" or "suggested by" Poe's "The
Black Cat," one in 1935 and the other in
1941, neither of which followed Poe's story
at all. Interestingly, though Harold
Hoffman's low-budget entry is padded, it is
surprisingly true to Poe's storyline. It even
opens with lines from Poe's poem "Alone":

Then—in my childhood, in the dawn
Of a most stormy life—was drawn
From every depth of good and ill
The mystery which binds me still:
From the torrent, or the fountain,
From the red cliff of the mountain,
From the sun that round me roll'd
In its autumn tint of gold—
From the lightning in the sky
As it pass'd me flying by—
From the thunder and the storm—
And the cloud that took the form
(When the rest of heaven was blue)
Of a demon in my view.

Critique: This third feature-length
film inspired by Poe's "The Black Cat" did

Ad art for *The Black Cat* (1966).

not garner much critical attention, but what attention it got was unfavorable. The *St. Louis Post-Dispatch*, for instance, withheld the names of the cast so as not to embarrass them further. *The Overlook Film Encyclo-* *pedia: Horror* proclaims it "cheaply made and indifferently acted," adding that "the Poe atmosphere, frayed by Hoffman's uncertain direction and pacing ... is finally dissipated by explicit gore." Jay Robert Nash and Stanley

Ralph Ross give the film 1 1/2 stars but offer little critical commentary.

The Black Cat is probably the most histrionic Poe film since the inept exploitation shocker *Maniac* (1934), which also revels in overacting and tasteless violence. Director Hoffman pads the picture with a seemingly interminable nightclub scene, then allows Frost to overact shamelessly as if to make up for it. The actor's melodramatics in the lawyer's office and psychiatric hospital are laughable and clearly destructive of mood. To my knowledge, the film has not been shown on television.

Still, screenwriter Harold Hoffman does try something interesting. True to Poe, he has Lew's wife tell him that sometimes witches turn themselves into black cats. Poe lost his mother when he was three; Lew's mother and father also died when he was three years old. Like Poe's parents, they were considered trash. Lew is adopted, and his adoptive father beats him when he is kicked out of school for gambling. The allusions to Poe and John Allan are unmistakable. Considering his father a demon, Lew turns to writing as a profession and to alcohol as an avocation. In a borrowing from Poe's theme

of perverseness, Lew says that he does things he doesn't want to do. Some urge seems to overwhelm him.

The film adds an odd but interesting touch when Lew, who has cut out his cat's right eye, goes to the bar and sees a band, all of whom wear right eye patches, singing "Sinner man, where you gonna run to?" In the mental hospital, Lew begins writing a story about a black cat. When the doctor asks how the story will end, Lew tells him that he hasn't finished the story yet, that there are a few more pages to go. Again, the identification between Poe and Lew is unmistakable. The demon of Poe's "Alone" is obviously Lew's adoptive father. In the film, Lew identifies the black cat with the demonic father. At the end of the film, Lew lies dead in the wreckage of his car, his right eye demolished.

Other positive aspects include the realistic axe murder and the grisly scene of the cat's eyeball in Lew's palm. However, though *The Black Cat* has the right idea, it unfortunately does not have a cast talented enough to carry it out, nor do covers from Bo Diddley and Chuck Berry help establish an atmosphere suggestive of Poe.

Die Schlangengrube und das Pendel (1967); aka *The Blood Demon*; *The Torture Chamber of Dr. Sadism*; *Blood of the Virgins*; *Torture Room*; *The Snake Pit and the Pendulum*; *Pendulum*

Constantin, West Germany

Credits: Directed by Harold Reinl; screenplay by Manfred R. Kohler, based on "The Pit and the Pendulum" by Edgar Allan Poe; cinematography by Ernst W. Kalinke and Dieter Liphart; art direction by Gabriel Pellon and W. M. Achtmann; music by Peter Thomas; special effects by Erwin Lange and Theo Nischritz.

Running time: 90 minutes.

Cast: Lex Barker (Roger), Karin Dor (Baroness Lilian), Christopher Lee (Count Regula), Karl Lange (Anatol), Vladimir Medar (Fabian), Christine Rucker (Babette), Deiter Eppler (coachman).

Story: For having murdered twelve virgins, the infamous vampire Count Regula is

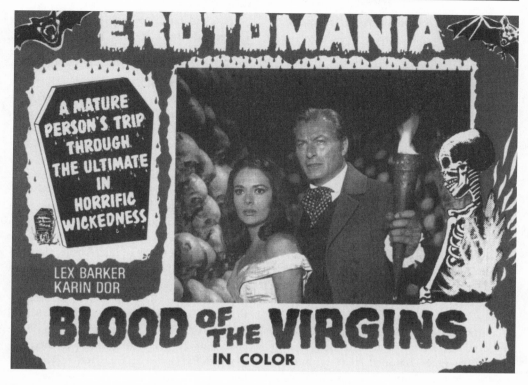

Karin Dor and Lex Barker explore a chamber of horrors in *Die Schlangengrube und das Pendel* (1967, aka *Blood of the Virgins*).

sentenced to be quartered rather than beheaded. Before he dies, he swears vengeance on those responsible.

Thirty-five years later, Baroness Lilian and her attorney, Roger, are invited by a mysterious messenger to the legendary Blood Castle (former home of Count Regula). Since Roger hopes to learn the secret of his birth and Lilian hopes to receive an inheritance, they accept. While looking for the castle, Roger runs into "ignorant" villagers who fear the name of the castle, and he observes Roman Catholic processions designed to drive the evil out of the valley.

On the way, Lilian and Roger are joined by Fabian, a strange and rather worldly monk who is subsequently revealed to be a highwayman in disguise. Fabian offers to guide Roger and Lilian to the castle. The journey to the castle is fraught with danger and foreboding. Roger and Fabian rescue Lilian from apparent highwaymen

but are too late to prevent the abduction of her maid Babette. The rest of the ride takes them through a forest of gnarled trees and hanging corpses. Three black crows also appear on Good Friday, a definite sign that things are amiss. Upon their arrival, the travelers find that the castle to which they were invited is a ruin. A green-blooded supernatural being named Anatol greets them, however, and the journey goes on. When the carriage driver dies, Anatol takes the reins and delivers Roger and Fabian to a gloomy castle.

Babette, who is already at the castle, is in a drugged state and acting as royalty. Anatol explains that he drugged her because of her emotional distress, but that she would recover before the arrival of Count Regula.

Finally, the travelers meet Count Regula, who has been existing in a state of suspended animation under glass. With drops of his own green blood, Anatol revives the evil Count on Good Friday. It seems that Count Regula had hoped to achieve immortality through the blood of thirteen virgins. His plan was thwarted, however, when the thirteenth virgin escaped and brought the authorities. Lilian discovers that she is the daughter of that thirteenth virgin and that she is to meet the fate intended for her mother. Roger, it turns out, is the son of the man who had condemned the Count thirty-five years before. For his father's offense, Roger is put to torture under a swinging, slowly descending, razor-sharp pendulum. Meanwhile, Lilian is subjected to mental torture in a snake pit. Roger manages to break free and rescue Lilian with the aid of Fabian. Fabian leads Roger and Lilian to a braided, blonde woman soon to be lowered onto a bed of spiders. They rescue her without a moment to spare and discover that she is Lilian's kidnapped maid, Babette. When Babette flees, Anatol accosts her. Fabian shoots the green-blooded creature, but the wounds repair themselves immediately. Anatol is "undead."

When Roger confronts Regula and Anatol with a diamond-studded cross, they immediately disintegrate, breaking the monstrous spells that have held the castle and forest in thrall.

Production and marketing: In 1967, West German filmmakers could not resist entering the Edgar Allan Poe sweepstakes. For inspiration, they returned to Poe's "The Pit and the Pendulum," which Richard Matheson had scripted for AIP in 1961. The Matheson script took the element of a prisoner subjected to the pendulum and built around it a plot completely unrelated to Poe's story. West German Harold Reinl's screenplay took the same approach, building a story completely unrelated to Poe around the image of a deadly descending pendulum.

The film's leading man, American Lex Barker (1919–1973), played Tarzan in five films and went on to appear in such diverse fare as *Battles of Chief Pontiac* (1952, with Lon Chaney, Jr.), *Terror of the Red Mask*

(1959), and *La Dolce Vita* (1959, directed by Federico Fellini). In 1967 he was the number-one leading man in European films, the most popular star in postwar Germany. German leading-lady Karin Dor (1938–), the wife of director Reinl, earlier costarred with Lex Barker in *Winnetou II* (1964) and with Christopher Lee in *The Face of Fu Manchu* (1965). She would also appear with Roger Moore in the James Bond epics *You Only Live Twice* (1967) and *Live and Let Die* (1973). Sandwiched between those 007 outings, she would also act under the direction of Alfred Hitchcock in *Topaz* (1969).

If the West Germans could not get Vincent Price for the villain's role, they acquired someone who was probably second best in 1967—Christopher Lee. Lee rose to prominence in the Hammer Film productions of *The Curse of Frankenstein* (1958) and *Dracula* (1958, aka *Horror of Dracula*), both costarring Peter Cushing. In the former, Lee played a Frankenstein monster largely of his own invention, a creature not so much evil as lacking personal control. While Lee's monster pales in comparison to that of Boris Karloff, it does evoke sympathy as a sort of caged and confused wounded animal. In the latter film, Lee delivers one of the screen's great interpretations of Count Dracula, sometimes a restrained aristocratic gentleman and other times an athletically powerful, snarling, and sexually magnetic fiend. *The Curse of Frankenstein* and *Dracula* made Hammer Films internationally synonymous with horror and launched Lee's career as one of the screen's most sought after bogeymen.

Sometimes Lee played important supporting roles, as in *Doctor of Seven Dials* (1958/1962, aka *Corridors of Blood*, with Boris Karloff), *The Hound of the Baskervilles* (1959, with Peter Cushing), *The Man Who Could Cheat Death* (1959, with Anton Differing), *The City of the Dead* (1960, aka *Horror Hotel*), *The Two Faces of Dr. Jekyll* (1960, aka *House of Fright*), and *The Curse of the Crimson Altar* (1968, aka *The Crimson Cult*, with Boris Karloff and Barbara Steele). At other times, he starred as a legendary character of mystery and horror, as in *The Mummy* (1959, as Kharis the Mummy), *Sherlock Holmes und das Halsband des Todes* (1962, aka *Sherlock Holmes and the Deadly Necklace,* as Sherlock Holmes), *The Face of Fu Manchu* (1965, as Fu Manchu), *Dracula, Prince of Darkness* (1965, as Dracula), and *Rasputin the Mad Monk* (1965, as Rasputin).

Since Lee had become synonymous around the world with Dracula, the script cast him as a vampire of sorts. His character's name, Count Regula, is a combination of Dracula and Alexander Dumas's *The Man in the Iron Mask.*

Today critical opinion on Lee is divided. While most pundits do not consider him as good an actor as his countryman and frequent costar Peter Cushing, many consider him one of the top six or seven actors associated with horror films, a performer whose considerable skills improved over the years and who now deserves serious consideration and recognition. Others characterize Lee as a relatively untalented actor whose physical presence and ability to appear stern and authoritative carried him much further than he deserved. Having seen most of Lee's films, I tend to side with the kinder critics. Lee would go on to do one more film that was officially, but not really, based on a story by Edgar Allan Poe—"The Oblong Box" (1969, with Vincent Price). That film, unfortunately, did not then and does not now enhance his reputation.

Years after the fact, Lee said that he agreed to play in *Schlangengrube* for a number of reasons.

I was asked to go and do a picture in Germany, at the studios outside Munich in 1967. It was a top set-up.... It was at the height of [Lex Barker's] fame and popularity, that I was asked to co-star with him with a top director, a top star, and one of the top leading ladies. The whole idea was absolutely Number One in Germany, and (as everyone knows) I believe the more one internationalizes oneself, the more important it is to an actor.[166]

In his autobiography, *Tall, Dark and Gruesome,* Lee devoted a few derogatory words to *Schlangengrube:*

In *Blood Demon,* a perfectly dreadful composite of *The House of Legends, Eternal Life, The Hunchback of Notre Dame,* and *The Pit and the Pendulum,* I was chastised by having a gold mask driven into my face with spikes attached to it, so that my face resembled a green at the end of a major tournament.... The conclusion, when I vanish like a pantomime king in a cloud of green smoke, can hardly have persuaded the audience that I was dead enough to stay away from their jugular veins when they put the cat out for the night.[167]

In his autobiography, Lee also cites *Schlangengrube* in rebuttal against those who claim films incite people to unsavory actions: "Erotica was a genre I did not fancy. It was true that in *The Torture Chamber of Dr. S* I was surrounded by a sea of nude women, and the effluvium that rose from their bodies as the lights grew hotter was like a marsh gas, but I could not believe the film incited to erotic indulgence."[168]

Die Schlangengrube und das Pendel was distributed in the United States under several terrible titles, notably *The Torture Chamber of Dr. Sadism, Blood of the Virgins* and *Blood Demon.* The titles and publicity campaigns sought out the drive-in crowd with lurid advertisements and silly gimmicks. *Blood Demon,* for instance, played at the bottom of a Hemisphere Pictures double bill topped by an awful Philippine atrocity titled *Mad Doctor of Blood Island.* In reference to the undead Anatol of *Blood Demon,* the campaign manual for the double bill asked: "Do you have the GUTS to come and join the WEIRD RITES of GREEN BLOOD? ... FREE: Mystic potion given to all patrons!" According to the manual, *Mad Doctor of Blood Island* was made in "Blood dripping color," while *Blood Demon* came in "Blood curdling color." I'm sure the difference is subtle. Unaccountably, in none of the American campaigns for *Schlangengrube* was Poe used to lure customers.

Critique: Since *Schlangengrube* played mostly at hinterland drive-ins in the United States, we must look to Europe for contemporary reviews. According to *Today's Cinema* (London), the film was

> a surprise packet of deadpan humour deriving from the contrast between the lavish supply of corpses, snakes, rats, tarantulas, scorpions and buzzards and the tongue-in-cheek banality of the English dialogue. The name of Christopher Lee provides box office appeal ... weird and wondrously camp ... to provoke more laughs than screams. Enormous fun.[169]

Cine Weekly (London) agreed:

> The producer of this film really piles on the agony ... but it never really achieves its object. This is largely due to such episodes as his mist-laden forest festooned with countless hanging bodies all most obvious dummies, and a tendency to overdo the obvious ... lines of dialogue which cannot fail to bring laughs.... That master of the horrific, Christopher Lee, adequately fills the role of the count and Lex Barker proves himself a formidable rival.[170]

Although more recent critics enjoy the film, they too find flaws. Michael Weldon advised that while "This is supposed to be based on Poe's 'The Pit and the Pendulum,' ... forget that and enjoy the outrageous story.... Lee really looks dead and there are some striking visual treats like an impressionistic forest full of corpses."[171] *The Overlook Film Encyclopedia: Horror* found that "Just enough elements of the plot and characters of the Poe story are retained to keep this film commercially viable. Eerily lit tableaux and nightmarishly disjointed scenes set in caves, secret passages, a forest garlanded with hanging corpses and hands emerging from trees, a chamber of horrors populated with the frozen bodies of naked, bloodless women, all combine to achieve a powerful sense of delirium." *The Encyclopedia* concluded that "the narrative collapses under the pressure of the accumulations of images.... [Still] memorable moments are achieved in the imagination of the less savory desires and fantasies mobilized by the cinematic spectacle itself."

Both *Video Hound's Golden Movie Retriever 1996* and Leonard Maltin award the film 2 1/2 stars or bones, the latter pronouncing it "Atmospheric, but not for the squeamish."

I view *Schlangengrube* as a very enjoyable, though flawed, film. Naturally I shuddered when the English credits incorrectly said the film was based on Poe's *novel.* Moments into the film, however, I was engrossed. Lee's execution is effectively grisly. Shortly afterward, however, Barker's coach drives through the countryside to ridiculously bouncy music, a sign that the film might soon collapse into typical Euro-trash (European films with bad dubbing and atrocious sound tracks). As the coach nears the castle itself, the music is appropriate to the mood and never again lapses until the credits roll. As the film pays homage to its roots, we are treated to the typical scenes of "superstitious and "ignorant" villagers. We even hear Lee ominously intone "The blood is the life," words reminiscent of Browning's *Dracula.*

Still, certain original touches are executed effectively. For example, the coach ride through the forest, with its blues and plush greens, is the film's highlight. The impressive scenes of deadly animalia inhabiting the castle serve their purpose and harken back to Poe's story. The swinging pendulum, though not as professional as Corman's, is impressive enough to carry the banner of the film's German title.

Christopher Lee is a presence more than a person. His deep voice and menacing cold stare aid him greatly in embodying the vampiric Count Regula. Only at the film's conclusion does he express emotions of pain and fear related to his own imminent destruction. Baxter is indeed a formidable foe, and Dor effectively comes across as a Barbara Steele *sans* the Steele aura of menace.

Overall, *Die Schlangengrube und das Pendel* is a worthy entry in the Poe filmography. It delivers as gothic horror, and it definitely rises above the tasteless titles with which it was saddled during its American releases.

Histoires extraordinaires (1967); aka *Spirits of the Dead; Tales of Mystery*

Films Marceau/Concinor/Pea Cinematografica

Italy and France

This film comprises three separate stories by three different directors.

Credits: "Metzengerstein": Directed by Roger Vadim; screenplay by Roger Vadim and Pascal Cousin; cinematography by Claude Renoir; edited by Helene Plemianni-kov; art direction by Jean Andre; music by Jean Prodromides. "William Wilson": Directed by Louis Malle; screenplay by Louis Malle, based on the story by Edgar Allan Poe; cinematography by Tonino Deli Colli; edited by Franco Arcalli; music by Diego Masson. "Never Bet the Devil Your Head" or "Toby Dammit": Directed by Federico Fellini; screenplay by Federico Fellini and Bernardino Zapponi; cinematography by Giuseppe Rotunno (Mario Bava?); music by Nino Rota; art direction and wardrobe by Pierro Tosi; special effects by Joseph Nathanson.

Running time: 123 minutes; U.S. version, 117 minutes.

Cast: "Metzengerstein": Jane Fonda (Countess Frederica), Peter Fonda (Baron Wilhelm), Carla Marlier (Claude), Rancois Prevost (friend of Countess), James Robertson Justice (Countess's adviser), Annie Duperrey (first guest), Philippe Lemaire (Philippe), Serge Marquand (Hughes), Andreas Voutsinas (second guest), Audoin de Bardot (page), Douking (du Lissier). "William Wilson": Brigitte Bardot (Giuseppina), Alain Delon (William Wilson), Katia Cristina (young girl), Umberto D'Orsi (Hans), Daniele Vargas (the professor), Renzo Palmer (the priest). "Never Bet the Devil Your Head" or "Toby Dammit": Terence Stamp (Toby Dammit), Salvo Randone (priest), Fabrizio Angeli (first director), Ernesto Colli (second director), Marina Yaru (child), Anna Tonietti (television commen-

tator), Aleardo Ward (first interviewer), Paul Cooper (second interviewer).

Story: "Metzengerstein": When Countess Frederica inherits the Metzengerstein estate at the age of 22, she engages in a life of sexual promiscuity, debauchery, and cruelty. Next door to her lives Baron Wilhelm, a young man absorbed in his love of horses. Frederica and Wilhelm have never met because of an ancient family feud. One day Frederica steps into a leg trap in the forest and is freed by Wilhelm. She tries to beguile Wilhelm, but he condemns her conduct and resists her. Haunted by his eyes, she longs to see him again.

Furious at being rejected, she sets Wilhelm's stables afire and learns later that he perished trying to save his horses. Shortly afterward, a horse that presumably escaped from the burning stables comes to Metzengerstein castle. The horse acts as though it were mad, and Frederica's servants have difficulty restraining it. Frederica sets out to tame the horse, and a strange, subtle contest of wills begins. At the same time, Frederica becomes obsessed with a damaged tapestry featuring a black charger identical to the one she now rides day and night. She demands that the tapestry be repaired immediately, and an artisan begins the laborious process. One day during a thunderstorm, lightning strikes the heath and the black horse carries Frederica into the flames. Like Wilhelm, Frederica perishes by fire.

Story: "William Wilson": The time is the nineteenth century. The place is northern Italy, which is occupied by Austrian forces. A young officer rushes into a church and demands to confess. He tells the reluc-

Jane Fonda strikes a pose in the "Metzengerstein" segment of *Histoires extraordinaires* (1967, aka *Spirits of the Dead*).

tant priest that his name is William Wilson and that he has committed murder. The priest listens as Wilson tells his story.

The son of an Englishman, William Wilson has become an Austrian citizen. Even as a youth, Wilson is cruel. At prep school, while overseeing the torture of a classmate, he is confronted by another youth, a new student also named William Wilson, who commands him to stop. That night Wilson goes to the new student's bed and tries to strangle him. Both are expelled. Years later Wilson enters a school of medicine. While he is torturing a young woman whom he and his friends have kidnapped, the other William Wilson enters and intervenes on the woman's behalf. Before she can escape, however, the cruel Wilson stabs her to death. Wilson later leaves medical school and joins the Austrian army. While in the army, he continues his dissolute and evil

ways. During a game of cards, he humiliates his lovely opponent, Giuseppina. When he literally wins her in the final hand, he takes a whip to her back rather than taking her to the bedroom. At that point, the other William Wilson enters and proves to everyone that officer Wilson cheated at cards. Disgraced, Wilson flies into a rage and stabs to death his other self—his conscience. William Wilson leaves the priest, climbs to the top of the church tower, and leaps to his death.

Story: "Never Bet the Devil Your Head" or "Toby Dammit": Englishman Toby Dammit, a former Shakespearean actor whose career is drowning in a sea of alcohol, agrees to make a Western in Italy. A race car enthusiast, he is interested in making the film only to secure the Ferrari promised him by the producers. At the airport, a ball rolls to his feet. Toby picks it up

Brigitte Bardot faces Alain Delon's challenge in the "William Wilson" segment of *Histoires extraordinaires* (1967, aka *Spirits of the Dead*).

and returns it to a little golden-haired girl, who thanks him with a smile so strange that he experiences a premonition and falls into a fit of anguish. During a car ride from the airport with the producers, Toby continues to have visions of the little girl chasing her ball. At the awards ceremony, Toby is awarded his Ferrari. In a desperate effort to escape the lights, crowds, and inane questions, the drunken Toby flees the ceremony in his Ferrari. On the road, in front of a fallen bridge, some workmen frantically attempt to stop his speeding car. Toby pauses, then guns the car, forcing it across the ravine to the other side. Inside the car, Toby lies headless, and a wire across the ravine drips blood. The golden-haired girl with the strange smile cradles something in her arms—something the shape of a ball.

Production and marketing: The idea of hiring three internationally acclaimed European directors to adapt three stories by Edgar Allan Poe to the screen was both intriguing and promising. French writer/director Roger Vadim (1924–) was best known for bringing Brigitte Bardot to world attention in his film *And God Created Woman* (1956). Among his other critical successes were *Les Liaisons Dangereuses* (1959), *Blood and Roses* (1960, based on Sheridan Le Fanu's vampire classic "Carmilla"), and *Warrior's Rest* (1962). Vadim would soon direct his wife, Jane Fonda, in the science-fiction satire *Barbarella* (1969) based on a comic strip featuring a forty-first-century space adventuress.

The screenplay by Vadim and Cousin for the "Metzengerstein" segment makes several changes in Poe's original story. In the story, Frederick of Metzengerstein is an 18-year-old young man. In the screenplay, he becomes Countess Frederica, a 22-year-old

Terence Stamp drives to his doom in the "Toby Dammit" segment of *Histoires extraorinaires* **(1967, aka** *Spirits of the Dead***).**

woman. In the story, Wilhelm, Count Berflit-zig, is an "infirm and doting old man." In the screenplay, he becomes an attractive, reclusive youth obsessed with horses. Otherwise, the screenplay stays close to Poe's main themes of revenge and transmigration of souls (reincarnation).

The cinematographer for "Metzenger-stein" was Claude Renoir (1914–1993), one of Europe's best. There was critical praise for his camera work in such films as *Une Partie de Campagne* (1936), *The River* (1951), *The Golden Coach* (1953), *Elena et les Hommes* (1956), and *Blood and Roses* (1960, directed by Roger Vadim). Renoir would be Vadim's cinematographer for *Barbarella*, and he would score a James Bond credit for *The Spy Who Loved Me* (1977).

The "Metzengerstein" segment marked the first (and, to my knowledge, the last) joint appearance of Jane Fonda (1937–) and

Peter Fonda (1939–). High points of Jane's early film career included *Walk on the Wild Side* (1961), *Cat Ballou* (1965), *Hurry Sundown* (1967), and *Barefoot in the Park* (1967). After *Histoires extraordinaires*, her career would hit high gear with *Barbarella* (1968), *They Shoot Horses, Don't They?* (1969), *Klute* (1971, for which she won an Academy Award), *Julia* (1977, for which she won a British Film Academy Award), and *The China Syndrome* (1981, for which she won a British Film Academy Award). In 1981, she would costar with her famous father, Henry Fonda, and film legend Katharine Hepburn in *On Golden Pond*. Today Jane is known not only as an actress but also as a notorious Vietnam War protester of the early seventies. She later tossed her counterculture values aside, however, to become the wife of millionaire Ted Turner, owner of the CNN network and the Atlanta Braves baseball team.

When Jane's brother Peter came to the "Metzengerstein" segment, he had starred in such diverse fare as *Tammy and the Doctor* (1963), *The Victors* (1963), *Lilith* (1964), *The Wild Angels* (1966, probably the best motorcycle gang film of the sixties), and *The Trip* (1967, an LSD exploitation film). After *Histoires extraordinaires*, however, he would produce, cowrite, and costar in *Easy Rider* (1969), the critically acclaimed and financially successful trendsetter of the sixties counterculture. Unfortunately, his career would decline after *Easy Rider*, and unlike costars Dennis Hopper and Jack Nicholson, he would soon find himself in such lesser films as *Dirty Mary, Crazy Larry* (1974), *Open Season* (1974), and *Race with the Devil* (1975)

Also appearing in the "Metzengerstein" segment is respected Scottish character actor James Robertson Justice (1905–1975), who had received enthusiastic notices for performances in *Scott of the Antarctic* (1948), *Whiskey Galore* (1949), *Doctor in the House* (1954), *Very Important Person* (1961), and *The Fast Lady* (1962).

French new wave director and *auteur* Louis Malle (1932–1995) both directed and wrote the screenplay for the "William Wilson" segment. He was best known for such groundbreaking films as *The Lovers* (1958), *Zazie dans le Métro* (1961), and *Le Feu Follet* (1963). He would go on to enhance his reputation by directing the acclaimed *Souffle au Coeur* (1971, for which he won an Academy Award for best screenplay), *Atlantic City* (1980, for which he won the British Film Academy Award), and *My Dinner with Andre* (1981).

Malle's screenplay for the "William Wilson" segment stays close to Poe's story, the best interpretation of which conceives William Wilson as a man at war with his own conscience. The original story has Wilson go from Bransby to Eton to Oxford and finally to Italy. In the screenplay, the travelogue is not so precise. Still, we get the impression of a man pursued by his conscience in a variety of places. In the original story,

Wilson is revealed as a card cheat while playing with a number of his male acquaintances. In the screenplay his opponent is the sensuous and bright prostitute Giuseppina. In the original story, Wilson is a debauchee with many acts of evil to his credit, but he commits no murders until he murders himself (his conscience). In the screenplay, he is even more a villain than in the story, murder numbering among his acts. The original story ends with Wilson discovering that he has killed his conscience and by extension himself (or the best part of himself). The screenplay extends the theme to include Wilson's literal suicide.

French leading man Alain Delon (1935–) and French sex-kitten Brigitte Bardot (1933–) provide the key acting talent in the "William Wilson" segment. Among Delon's credits were *Rocco and His Brothers* (1960) and *The Leopard* (1962), both directed by Luchino Visconti. He would later enhance his reputation in such films as *Borsalino* (1970), *The Assassination of Trotsky* (1972), and *Swann in Love* (1984). The pulchritudinous Bardot, while only an adequate actress, helped many a film turn a profit in the fifties and sixties. Among her most notable credits are *The Light Across the Street* (1955), *And God Created Woman* (1956), *En Cas de Malheur* (1957), *The Truth* (1961), *Vie Privée* (1961), *Love on a Pillow* (1962), *Contempt* (1964), and *Viva Maria* (1965). She has recently become known as a militant animal rights activist.

Italian director Federico Fellini (1920–1995) was probably the most fashionable and influential of the three directors working in *Histoires extraordinaires*. Among his most acclaimed films were such masterworks as *La Strada* (1954), *La dolce vita* (1959), *8½* (1963), and *Juliet of the Spirits* (1965). He would go on to enhance his reputation with *Satyricon* (1969, which I consider one of the greatest films ever made), *The Clowns* (1970), *Fellini Roma* (1972), and *Ginger and Fred* (1985).

The music for "Never Bet the Devil Your Head" was composed by Nino Rota

(1911–1979). Rota had received international praise for having scored all of Fellini's films, adding to their success significantly. But he also composed successful scores for such films as *The Glass Mountain* (1948), *War and Peace* (1956), *Rocco and His Brothers* (directed by Luchino Visconti), and *Romeo and Juliet* (1968, directed by Franco Zefferelli). He would go on to score *Satyricon, Waterloo* (1970), *The Godfather* (1972, for which he won an Academy Award), and *Death on the Nile* (1978).

Michael Weldon, author of *The Psychotronic Encyclopedia of Film*, reports that Mario Bava was the actual cinematographer and second unit director. This may have been true for scenes added to the American release because some of the cinematography in the segment is obviously consistent with Bava's style and use of color.

British actor Terence Stamp (1940–) came to the "Toby Dammit" segment on the strength of strong leads in such films as *Billy Budd* (1962), *Term of Trial* (1962), *The Collector* (1965), and *Far from the Madding Crowd* (1967).

Poe's "Never Bet the Devil Your Head" is an example of the author's theory of humor as "the witty exaggerated into the burlesque." It is a satire on transcendentalism (particularly that of *Dial* magazine) and literary pedanticism. In a letter, Poe denies such aims, stating, "The tale in question is a mere Extravaganza levelled at no one in particular, but hitting right and left at things in general." In Poe's story, Toby Dammit and his friend are crossing a bridge when they come to a turnstile. Dammit's friend passes through the turnstile, but Dammit insists on jumping over it. In fact, he bets the Devil his head that he can. He leaps, and his headless body falls on the other side of the turnstile. It seems that while jumping the turnstile, Dammit's neck encountered something unexpected. Poe writes:

About five feet just above the top of the turnstile, and crossing the arch of the footpath so as to constitute a brace, there extended a flat iron bar, lying with its breadth horizontally, and forming one of a series that served to strengthen the structure throughout its extent. With the edge of this brace it appeared evidently that the neck of my unfortunate friend had come precisely in contact.

Fellini takes the core event of the Poe story, creates new characters, creates new situations, updates the tale, and makes it all his own. This is indeed Fellini's "Toby Dammit," not Poe's. It is also the only segment in the film to be released separately.

For American release, American International added a voice-over by Vincent Price to the opening of the film that does not appear in the original European print: "Thy soul shall find itself alone 'Mid dark thoughts of the gray tomb-stone."

These are the opening lines of Poe's poem "Spirits of the Dead," from which we get the film's misleading American title. The film, of course, adapts nothing from the poem. This was American International's way of making American audiences believe that *Histoires extraordinaires* was somehow a continuation of its earlier Poe series. It is so in name only.

The posters and advertising for *Spirits of the Dead* were unimpressive. American International issued a substantial pressbook with a black, white, and purple cover. Prominently featured are Jane Fonda, Brigitte Bardot, and Terence Stamp. Ads proclaimed the film "Edgar Allan Poe's ultimate orgy! An adventure in terror beyond your wildest nightmares." Another ad announced: "You may not believe in ghosts but you cannot deny terror! Edgar Allan Poe opens forbidden doors to lead you beyond your wildest nightmares!" Other ads teased readers with lines never written by Poe: "Where unseen hands reach out for the warmth of human flesh and icy breaths disturb the silent dust … where Terror walks on tiptoe, and the Dead cannot rest." In the same vein, we get "Who will satisfy them, soothe those strangled sobs, those screams of panic pain that make no sound at all?"

Pressbook exploitation tips included

this reminder: "Don't overlook the use of the Edgar Allan Poe name. In this vein use 'Shock' displays at book stores, libraries, etc." Otherwise, publicity focused on Bardot, the Fondas, Delon, Stamp, and the three world-famous directors.

Critique: *Spirits of the Dead* opened in the United States to mixed reviews. Most pronounced the film uneven, savaged Vadim, shrugged off Malle, and praised Fellini. Today the film's reputation remains shaky. Numbering among the film's biggest supporters, Leonard Maltin awards it 3 1/2 stars, calling it "Three separate Poe tales, impossible to describe, delightful to watch, done with skill and flair by three top directors."

Michael Weldon devotes an unusual amount of space to the film in his *Psychotronic Encyclopedia of Film*, his overall conclusion being that "'Toby Dammit' ... by Fellini is brilliant. All of Fellini's usual grotesque characters (and his humor) are present in this unforgettable horror story ... The other two segments pale by comparison."[172]

According to *The Overlook Encyclopedia of Film: Horror*:

> Three more unlikely allies on an anthology of Poe stories than Vadim, Malle, and Fellini are difficult to imagine, and the results are predictably uneven (and remote from Poe). Adapting *Metzengerstein*, Vadim's imagination seems to have exhausted itself on the teasing perversity of casting Jane and Peter Fonda as the decadent countess and the object of her frustrated passions. Shot with ugly reliance on zooms, the episode is little more than an excuse for some titillating orgies and a bit of demonic galloping by the black stallion.... Malle's version of *William Wilson* ... is not uninteresting. The elaborations to the story are both telling and precise (Bardot redoubling in a dual role; the card game with the players in masks to conceal their dissembling), but it finally emerges as too skeletally brief to be really persuasive. The best episode is Fellini's version of *Never Bet the Devil Your Head* ... the episode is pure Fellini.

Rose London also found the film uneven:

The result was not successful.... Fellini largely ignored Poe to enter his own private world of bizarre images.... Yet if Fellini gave a dazzling display in "Toby Dammit," Vadim shamelessly misused Poe's terrible story of the mythical death-horse in "Metzengerstein" as a vehicle for his wife of the time, Jane Fonda, and his own bizarre tastes. Miss Fonda appears in a succession of costumes that seem left over from a medieval Barbarella and plays a debauched countess in love with her brother, whom she burns to death, but who returns as a black stallion to rape her to death.... [In Malle's "William Wilson"], Delon plays the split-minded Wilson with an elegance and a sadism that is true to the spirit of Poe. His breakdown into paranoia is believable and the story is told with economy. Unfortunately, the inclusion of Bardot ... is superfluous and rather ridiculous, while some of the images of horror are more Hammer than Edgar—a scalpel in a corpse, the torture of a schoolboy by rats, and a knife-edge stroking a girl's face.[173]

I agree that the film is uneven, but that is to be expected when three independent directors contribute to an omnibus. I agree, too, that the best segment is Fellini's. Although he leaves Poe far behind, Fellini allows us a glimpse of modern Rome through the eyes of a liquor-sodden actor, played convincingly by Terence Stamp. As Toby fields inane questions and looks into the faces of Rome's admiring grotesques, he tries to explain that his film represents the myth of redemption in western style. The theme of redemption as myth permeates this little masterpiece. Although Toby has been a Shakespearean actor, he has slipped from the heights of the Bard to the level of a spaghetti western. The sights and sounds of Rome suggest that modern civilization has likewise slipped. To emphasize the point, Fellini gives us haunting visions of human beings mistaken for mannequins and mannequins mistaken for human beings. A victim of modern materialism, Toby sells out for a Ferrari. The fact that he is a hopeless drunk underscores the painful defeat that he both accepts and hates. At one point Toby recites the famous soliloquy from Shakespeare's *Macbeth*:

And all our yesterdays have lighted fools
The way to dusty death. Out, out, brief can-
dle!
Life's but a walking shadow, a poor player,
That struts and frets his hour upon the
stage
And then is heard no more. It is a tale
Told by an idiot, full of sound and fury.
[He pointedly forgets and omits the last
line: "Signifying nothing."]

In Shakespeare's play, when Macbeth utters these lines, he has just learned of his wife's death, he is weary, and his world is crumbling around him. Toby evidently identifies with the tragic hero.

Toby denies that he was a great actor. "I could have been," he says. "My last director said I was drunk. Why did you make me come here? What do you want from me?"

All of this makes the "Toby Dammit" segment an unnerving companion piece to Fellini's earlier *La dolce vita* (1960), in which Marcello Mastroianni plays a tabloid reporter who accepts his existence in spiritually barren modern Rome as meaningless, but can't change. Other things lift the segment beyond the ordinary as well. Nino Rota's dotty musical score has all the modernistic qualities of a piece of plastic abstract art. The cinematography of Giuseppe Rotunno (and Mario Bava) is constantly engrossing as the camera focuses on subtle and jarring images of cultural decadence. The whole segment is dreamlike (or nightmarelike), exactly what the world according to Toby Dammit would dictate. And finally, the image of the pale, silver-haired, red-lipped child as Satan will haunt viewers for a very long time.

Although I believe the "William Wilson" segment is slightly underrated, I agree with the less-than-enthusiastic assessment of the episode offered by critics. Thanks largely to the torture scenes, to Delon's fine performance, and to some deliciously wicked lines in the screenplay, Malle's William Wilson emerges as significantly more despicable than Poe's. Bardot obviously holds audience attention as she coolly taunts Wilson and then engages him at cards for "high

stakes." With her cigars, her dark eyes, and her forbidding beauty, she makes an intriguing adversary for Delon. On the negative side, in the premonition scene that opens the segment, the body plunging from the bell tower is an obvious dummy. More damaging, however, is the fact that Malle's screenplay and direction never quite achieve the disturbing atmosphere of the other two segments.

For years I had considered Roger Vadim's segment the weakest in the film. After recent repeated viewings, however, I now consider it quite fine—definitely the second-best segment. Poe's original story is usually considered a burlesque of the German gothic tale. Vadim and cousin inject some humor into the opening scenes as Fonda and her court ride up to her childhood home. As she surveys the scene, which includes the jarring note of a corpse hanging from a tree, Fonda gushes, "God, I love this place!" Although the narration is always serious and somber, Fonda's excesses are just excessive enough to carry an undercurrent of dark humor. While Fonda's outfits are outlandish, male viewers will be compelled to savor what they reveal. This, the sexual orgies, and even some implied lesbianism add levels of eroticism to the film completely missing from Poe's story. It seems that earlier critics have assumed incorrectly that Vadim saw the segment as little more than an excuse to exhibit and promote his wife. Although Vadim misses no opportunity to do so, the segment has many strengths to recommend it beyond the positives mentioned above. First of all, though Jane Fonda was not yet the fine actress she would soon become, her performance here is engaging. Her eyes and pouty mouth enhance her performance as the spoiled, undisciplined "rich bitch." The theme of the segment appears to be that character is fate. Fonda's immorality, capped by the murder of her cousin, successfully underplayed by Peter Fonda, supernaturally seals her doom. She knows that Wilhelm's soul inhabits the black charger, and as she watches the weaver repair the tapestry of the black horse, she senses that he is, with a fatal logic, weaving her own doom. In finishing the tapestry, the weaver makes the horse's eyes the color of fire. Shortly afterward, as the charger carries Jane Fonda into the flames, she appears to welcome death. In fact, as the heat intensifies, her facial expressions and physical reactions are indistinguishable from those of love making. Finally, Jean Renoir's beauti- ful cinematography and the moody medievalism evoked by Prodromides's dreamy flutes and strings aid Vadim in weaving a cinematic tapestry of great merit.

Everything considered, *Spirits of the Dead* is a memorable film that deserves better than the reputation it now generally holds.

Torture Garden (1967)
Amicus/Columbia, Great Britain

Credits: Directed by Freddie Francis; produced by Max J. Rosenberg and Milton Subotsky; screenplay by Robert Bloch, based on his stories "Enoch," "Terror over Hollywood," "Mr. Steinway," and "The Man Who Collected Poe"; cinematography by Norman Warwick, D.S.C.; edited by Peter Elliott; music by Don Banks and James Bernard.

Cast: Jack Palance (Ronald Wyatt), Burgess Meredith (Dr. Diablo), Beverly Adams (Carla Hayes), Peter Cushing (Lancellot Canning), Robert Hutton (Paul), John Standing (Leo), Barbara Ewing (Dorothy), David Baur (Charles), Michael Ripper (Gordon).

Running time: 93 minutes (television print, 100 minutes).

Story: Visitors to a carnival sideshow are dared by the sinister Dr. Diablo to see what is in store for them if they permit the evil in their natures to rule their lives. First to accept Diablo's challenge is Colin Wilson, who finds that his lust for his uncle's money will lead to murder. Carla Hayes is faced with the prospect of being turned into an automaton or meeting death. Dorothy Endicott, Carla's cousin, finds her future holds the promise of a love affair with a famous pianist, but the spirit of his possessive mother, using his grand piano, will menace her life.

When Poe enthusiast Ronald Wyatt accepts Dr. Diablo's challenge, he is shown a future in which he comes to covet the superb Poe collection of third-generation collector Lancellot Canning. Accepting an invitation to see the entire Canning collection, Wyatt travels to the collector's home in America. Once there, Wyatt comes to understand what Canning meant in saying "My whole life is centered around Edgar Allan Poe in every respect." After an evening of cordial but heavy drinking, Canning invites Wyatt to see what Canning says must remain a secret between them. Wyatt follows Canning into the basement, where the former is astonished to find a number of previously unpublished Poe stories such as "House of the Worm" and "The Further Adventures of Arthur Gordon Pym." Canning then shows Wyatt a box said to contain the dust of Edgar Allan Poe, stolen from the cemetery by Canning's grandfather. When Wyatt opens the box and finds it empty, he accuses Canning of lying. He also argues that the watermarks on the unpublished Poe manuscripts prove that they are also hoaxes of recent origin. Wyatt then demands that Canning show him what lies behind a locked door. When Canning refuses, Wyatt kills him. Using Canning's key to open the door, Wyatt enters a secret chamber and discovers the resurrected body of Poe, who is still writing stories because he sold his soul to the devil and was resurrected. Wyatt begs Poe to teach him the secrets of the unknown

Jack Palance and Peter Cushing take Poe collecting too far in *Torture Garden* (1967).

and agrees to give the devil his own soul in exchange for Poe's release. Poe explains that fire is the means of his release, and Wyatt obliges by setting the basement afire, only to be trapped there himself.

Production and marketing: Apart from its connection with Edgar Allan Poe, *Torture Garden* is an important film because together with *Dr. Terror's House of Horrors* (1964), it laid the foundation for Amicus's wildly successful *Tales from the Crypt* (1972). All of these productions are distinguished omnibus films, compilations of several terror tales in one picture. This format had been successful only sporadically in the past, the most notable English-language entries being *Flesh and Fantasy* (1943) and *Dead of Night* (1945).

This omnibus film owes what success it can claim largely to two sources. The first is screenwriter Robert Bloch (1917–1995).

Bloch, a protégé of horror-literature giant H. P. Lovecraft, cut his teeth on the legendary terrorzine *Weird Tales*. Although he published three top-notch short story collections—*Sea Kissed* (1945), *The Opener of the Way* (1945), and *Pleasant Dreams* (1960)—he did not burst into the national consciousness until Alfred Hitchcock adapted his novel *Psycho* (1959) to the screen in 1960. From then on, the author became known as Robert "Psycho" Bloch, and his work was in constant demand by filmmakers. Bloch wrote an original screenplay for *The Cabinet of Caligari* in 1961 and adapted his novel *The Couch* to film in 1962. He followed up with original screenplays for *Strait-Jacket* (1963, directed by William Castle, starring Joan Crawford), *The Night Walker* (1963, directed by William Castle, starring Robert Taylor and Barbara Stanwyck), *The Psychopath* (1966, directed by Freddie Francis), and *The*

Deadly Bees (1966, based on *A Taste for Honey* by H. L. Heard and directed by Freddie Francis). *Torture Garden* was thus the third Robert Bloch screenplay directed by Freddie Francis.

The Poe-related story written and adapted by Bloch, "The Man Who Collected Poe," appeared first in *Famous Fantastic Mysteries* (October 1951) and was anthologized widely thereafter. Bloch's original story alludes more directly to Poe than does the screen treatment. For example, the first paragraph of the story obviously alludes to the first paragraph of Poe's "The Fall of the House of Usher." Bloch writes: "During the whole of a dull, dark and soundless day in the autumn of the year, when the clouds hung oppressively low in the heavens, I had been passing alone, by automobile, through a singularly dreary tract of country; and at length found myself, as the shades of evening drew on, within view of my destination."

In Bloch's story, Poe escapes from his basement imprisonment much as Madeline Usher does in Poe's "The Fall of the House of Usher." Bloch writes:

"Wait!" he cried. "Have you not heard his footsteps on the stair? MADMAN, I TELL YOU THAT HE NOW STANDS WITHOUT THE DOOR!" ...
There without the doors there *did* stand a lofty and enshrouded figure; a figure all too familiar, with pallid features, high, domed forehead, mustache set above the mouth. My glimpse lasted but an instant, an instant during which the man—the corpse, the apparition, the hallucination, call it what you will—moved forward into the chamber and clasped Canning to its breast in an unbreakable embrace. Together, the two figures tottered toward the flames, which now rose to blot out vision forever.

All such allusions to Poe's "The Fall of the House of Usher" are missing from the film. Bloch complained later that Amicus used only about 60 or 70 percent of what he had written, so the screenplay for "The Man Who Collected Poe" may have been significantly altered from Bloch's original concept. Although to add clarification to the

film, the television print is seven minutes longer than the theatrical release, Bloch remained unsatisfied.

British Freddie Francis (1917–) began as a cinematographer. Although turning to directing with less distinguished results, his work with the camera included such fine films as *Mine Own Executioner* (1947, with Burgess Meredith), *Room at the Top* (1959, directed by Jack Clayton), *Sons and Lovers* (1960), *The Innocents* (1961), *The French Lieutenant's Woman* (1980), *The Elephant Man* (1981), and *Dune* (1985). Other horror films directed by Francis include *Paranoiac* (1963), *Nightmare* (1963), *The Evil of Frankenstein* (1964, starring Peter Cushing), *The Skull* (1965, based on a story by Robert Bloch, starring Peter Cushing), *They Came from Beyond Space* (1966), *Dracula Has Risen from the Grave* (1968), *Tales from the Crypt* (1972, starring Peter Cushing), *Asylum* (1972, based on stories by Robert Bloch, starring Peter Cushing), *Tales That Witness Madness* (1973), and *Legend of the Werewolf* (1974, starring Peter Cushing).

The film's pressbook contains the following account of the Poe props used during production:

For a manuscript supposedly "written" by Edgar Allan Poe for a sequence in "Torture Garden," ... 88-year-old Tom Addicks, a calligrapher, was employed. Yellowed by strong tea, the manuscript was indistinguishable from authentic documents of the period concerned.
Other Poe memorabilia in the film ... included Victorian furniture and bric-a-brac, even a small drug cabinet ... and trinkets of the era. Dozens of other leatherbound books also were genuine and valued at a total of £1,000.
A portrait of Poe was reproduced from an authenticated likeness which appeared in William F. Gill's biography of Poe published in 1878.

Unfortunately, the ad also states that "Poe not only was a heavy drinker but also a drug addict." This is clearly an overstatement because Poe rarely had the money to indulge in such excesses, but it is typical of publicity written by those ignorant about Poe's actual life. Poe may have been an alcoholic, but an alcoholic must have money in order to drink heavily, and Poe rarely had it. While Poe did occasionally indulge in drug use, he was clearly not an addict.

Jack Palance (1920–) and Peter Cushing (1913–1995), the stars of "The Man Who Collected Poe," came to the film with strong reputations. Palance was a leading man with stage experience who became known as a screen villain. Among his best outings were *Panic in the Streets* (1950), *Shane* (1953), and *The Big Knife* (1955). He would go on to star in a number of horror films, including *The Strange Case of Dr. Jekyll and Mr. Hyde* (1968), *Dracula* (1973), *Craze* (1973), and *Without Warning* (1980). He would play Fidel Castro in *Che!* (1969). Since winning an Academy Award for best supporting actor in the film *City Slickers*, Palance has become known as a man over seventy years old capable of doing a series of one-armed push-ups and for saying in a television commercial, "Confidence is very sexy; don't you think?" Although he ends up committing murder, Palance plays a soft-spoken, pipe-smoking English gentleman in *Torture Garden*. Responding to a question about this role in which he played apparently against type, Palance said:

> I chose to play an English gentleman in "Torture Garden" because it's the kind of role I've wanted to play for a long time. I get sick and tired of answering the same question all the time: "Are you really a tough guy?" I am not the violent type—and never have been. I boxed a great deal in my youth, but it was purely for the sport. Now I'm not so sure it's such a sport.

Peter Cushing came to *Torture Garden* as one of the great horror film stars of his era, his most notable films being *The Curse of Frankenstein* (1957, as Dr. Frankenstein), *Dracula* (1958, aka *Horror of Dracula*), *The Revenge of Frankenstein* (1959), *The Hound of the Baskervilles* (1959, as Sherlock Holmes), *The Mummy* (1959), *Brides of Dracula* (1960), and *Dr. Who and the Daleks* (1965). Cushing

would continue to star in the horror/science fiction genre for the next twenty-eight years preceding his death, his major films being *Frankenstein Must Be Destroyed* (1969), *Tales from the Crypt* (1972), and *Star Wars* (1977).

Ads for the film asked: "Do you dare see the 100 horrors of Dr. Diablo? Enter his 'Torture Garden' and take the screen's most astonishing journey into the unknown! See the amazing 'hundred horrors' that are like nothing ever seen before."

The most interesting marketing slant was the following: "Free to every patron! A package of "Fright-Seeds" for your own "Torture Garden!" *Plant at your own risk!*" The packets featured a skull and crossbones. Vincent Canby of the *New York Times* reported that the forbidding packets actually contained innocuous timothy grass.

Critique: Critics generally received *Torture Garden* favorably. According to the *New York Times*, "'Torture Garden,' based on a script by Robert Bloch ('Psycho'), is a simple-minded forthright horror movie, made without condescension." The *Times* called *Torture Garden* "a very superior horror film (no shamefacedness about it this time)…. The film resolves itself then into four episodes, dealt with very well in suitably contrasting styles by … director … Francis. The cast is really excellent."[174]

The years have not dimmed the film's overall reputation. Although *Video Hound's Golden Movie Retriever 1996* awards the film only two bones, Leonard Maltin gives *Torture Garden* 2 1/2 stars, saying "Good cast and production, but stories uneven; first and last tales best." According to *The Overlook Film Encyclopedia: Horror*:

> As a gothic exercise with ex-cameraman Francis creating four enjoyable variations in style, from the shocker with the cat to the moody atmospherics of the mother-obsessed pianist … the film works well. Palance is particularly impressive as the manic collector, excitedly fondling the treasures he cannot buy and chuckling with delight at each new horror as he finds himself becoming part of the Poe legend—even a character in Poe's "last" story.

Deborah Del Vecchio and Tom Johnson, authors of *Peter Cushing,* assess the acting a bit differently:

> Cushing performs extremely well—despite co-star Palance's exaggerated portrayal of Ronald Wyatt—and gives the more credible performance. Palance hams it up too much to be taken seriously. Subotsky's initial choice for Wyatt [Christopher Lee] might have elevated the story somewhat. At best it might have made Cushing's job a little easier.[175]

From my perspective, "The Man Who Collected Poe" must be considered a parody. I love Palance's breathless performance. Del Vecchio and Johnson are right, of course; Cushing gives a very fine performance, while Palance is over the top. Still, Palance adds smiles to a segment that I don't think could be taken seriously by most viewers anyway. The title itself is ironic, and the story is full of macabre humor. How many serious memorabilia collectors can't see a bit of themselves in Palance's Ronald Wyatt?

The film itself still holds up well. It is uneven, as Maltin reports, but it provides some chills and chuckles along the way. As far as the cinema of Edgar Allan Poe is concerned, it is a mere, but welcome, trifle. My only complaints involve the depiction of the real (not resurrected) Poe himself. Palance, while admiring a portrait of Poe, exclaims that "no one ever equaled his knowledge of the secrets that lie beyond the grave." While Poe read very widely, he was not a student of the occult. The casual viewer of the film could therefore be easily led astray. On another occasion, Cushing excuses himself for drinking too much, saying, "If I go on drinking like this, you'll think that I'm Poe himself." Here I must restate that Poe did drink heavily at certain times, but his drinking has been greatly exaggerated. Because of his metabolism or possibly because of brain lesions, only a few drinks would make him tipsy. *Torture Garden* continues the popular culture exaggeration of Poe as a man addicted to the bottle.

Witchfinder General (1968); aka *The Conqueror Worm*
Tigon and American International, Great Britain

Credits: Directed by Michael Reeves; produced by Louis M. Heyward; executive producer—Tony Henser; screenplay by Michael Reeves and Tom Baker, based on the novel *Witchfinder General* by Ronald Bassett and the poem "The Conqueror Worm" by Edgar Allan Poe; production manager—Ricky Coward; assistant director—Jim Morahan; sound—Paul Le Mare; edited by Howard Lanning.

Running time: 98 minutes.

Cast: Vincent Price (Matthew Hopkins), Ian Ogilvy (Richard Marshall), Rupert Davies (John Lowes), Hilary Dwyer (Sara Lowes), Robert Russell (John Stearne), Wilfrid Brambell (horse dealer), Michael

Beint (Captain Gordon), Nicky Henson (Trooper Swallow), John Trenaman (Trooper Harcourt), William Maxwell (Trooper Gifford), Tony Selby (Salter), Beufoy Milton (priest).

Story: The year is 1645; the place is England. After Cromwell's victory at Naseby, the country is torn apart by civil war. Army deserters roam the land, looting and raping. Taking advantage of the lawlessness and disorder is Matthew Hopkins who, with his henchman John Stearne, travels from village to village torturing and executing accused witches for money.

Richard Marshall, a young Cornet in Cromwell's army earns a leave of absence to

Witchfinder Matthew Hopkins (Vincent Price) and his brutal henchman Stearne (Robert Russell) prepare to defend themselves in *Witchfinder General* (1968, aka *The Conqueror Worm*).

visit his betrothed, Sara Lowes, who lives with her uncle, John Lowes, a priest in the village of Brandeston in Suffolk. When he arrives, he finds that the vicarage has been pillaged and John Lowes tortured and executed as a warlock by Hopkins and Stearne. In a vain effort to save her uncle, Sara has submitted sexually to Hopkins. Richard takes Sara into the ruined church, makes her his wife without aid of clergy, and vows to kill Hopkins.

When Richard finds that Hopkins has moved on, he sends Sara to stay with friends at Laveham and deserts the army in order to find Hopkins. He accidentally runs into Stearne at a wayside inn and fails in an attempt to kill him. Stearne escapes with his life, and Richard returns to Cromwell's army. Captain Gordon pardons him for desertion because he earlier saved the captain's life at the battle of Naseby. Richard is promoted to

the rank of captain and given an audience with Cromwell himself. Cromwell gives Richard the special assignment of taking a small troop in search of the fugitive king.

Although Richard wants to pursue Hopkins, his friends talk him out of it. At Aldeburgh, however, Richard learns that the king has already escaped England by boat and that witch burnings are in progress in Laveham. Relieved of his obligation to find the king, Richard rides his troop straight for Laveham. Expecting that Richard will show up in search of Sara, Hopkins uses her for bait in order to trap the young soldier.

When Richard reunites with Sara, Stearne and a group of villagers take them captive. In a castle dungeon, Hopkins tortures Richard in an attempt to extract a confession of witchcraft, which will make "legal execution" possible. When Richard refuses to confess, Hopkins threatens to torture Sara.

Meanwhile, Richard's troops discover a half-dead husband who has just watched Hopkins burn his wife to death as a witch. The man tells them that Richard has been taken to the castle. In the torture chamber, Hopkins prepares to burn a cross into Sara's back with boiling grease if Richard will not confess. All the while, Sara pleads with Richard not to give in. In the nick of time, the troopers break in and free Richard. With insane fury Richard then attacks Hopkins with an axe. To spare Hopkins any further torture, one of the troopers shoots the dying witchfinder. Richard screams in anger that Hopkins has been taken from him, and Sara, now quite insane, begins screaming uncontrollably.

Production and marketing: The actual source for *Witchfinder General* is the 1966 novel by Ronald Bassett of the same name. Hopkins, of course, was a historical character. With his accomplice John Stearne, he put to death some 300 "witches" in East Anglia. Historical accounts of Hopkins's death differ. In one version, the witchfinder was taken by a mob to Mistley Pond and subjected to his own witchcraft test. If he drowned, he would be considered innocent, but if he swam, he would be found guilty of witchcraft. When Hopkins swam, he was either hanged or banished forever from East Anglia. The most likely account, however, is that Hopkins died in bed of tuberculosis. Preferring the first account, Ronald Bassett has Hopkins hanged at the end of the novel. Screenwriters Reeves and Baker resort to artistic license and have Hopkins meet a much more grisly death than historical fact supports.

When Reeves and Baker completed the script, Louis Heyward of American International made a deal with Tigon of England to coproduce the film and handle American distribution. Vincent Price was nearing the end of his contract with AIP, AIP was short on funds, and Heyward was able to buy the property for less than $150,000 and cast Price in the lead role.

Slotted to direct was the film's screen-

writer, Michael Reeves (1944–1969). Reeves, part American, was from an early age obsessed with films. After finishing school, he joined his parents in Boston, took a flight to California, and went directly to the home of his idol, Don Siegel, who had directed the classic *Invasion of the Body Snatchers* (1956). Siegel was impressed enough to give the young man a job as dialogue director for a project he was doing at Paramount. Reeves later returned to England and worked his way up to assistant director for television commercials. Paul Maslansky then invited Reeves to work on some scripts in Italy and hired him as assistant director on the Italian/French production *Le Chateau Des Morts Vivants*, aka *Castle of the Living Dead* (1964, with Christopher Lee). Reeves then went on to stylishly direct *La sorella di satana*, aka *The She Beast* (1965, with Barbara Steele), and *The Sorcerers* (1967, with Boris Karloff).

Trouble began when Reeves was unhappy with the casting of Vincent Price as Matthew Hopkins. Fearing Price would give a performance of self-parody, Reeves wanted Donald Pleasence to play the witchfinder. When Price arrived in England, sparks began to fly. Price later recalled:

> Reeves hated me. He didn't want me for the part. I didn't like him either. It was one of the first times in my life that I've been in a picture where the director and I just clashed…. Michael Reeves didn't really know how to deal with actors. He really got all our backs up…. We didn't get on at all. He would stop me and say, "Don't move your head like that." And I would say, "Like what? What do you mean?" And he'd say, "There—you're doing it again. Don't do that." He was only 24 years old when he did that film. He had only done two others. He didn't know how to handle actors.[176]

Reeves persevered, however, and got from Price probably the finest performance of the actor's career. After the fact, Price agreed. "Afterwards," Price said, "I realized what he wanted was a low-key, very laidback, menacing performance. He did get it, but I was fighting with him almost every step of the way. Had I known what he wanted, I could have cooperated. I think it's one of the best performances I've ever given."[177]

Besides Price, Reeves had a fine cast for *Witchfinder General*. Ian Ogilvy (1943–) had previously worked for Reeves in *La Sorella Di Satana* and *The Sorcerers*. His career would later include strong roles in such gothic tales as *Wuthering Heights* (1970) and *And Now the Screaming Starts* (1972, with Peter Cushing). He would also appear regularly in the television series "The Return of the Saint" (1978) and on the British stage.

Rupert Davies (1916–1976) was one of Britain's most respected character actors, having appeared in such films as *Sapphire* (1959), *The Spy Who Came in from the Cold* (1965), *Brides of Fu Manchu* (1966, with Christopher Lee), and *House of 1,000 Dolls* (1967, with Vincent Price).

Hilary Dwyer (1946–) was a relative newcomer to the acting field. Executive producer Tony Tenser and Michael Reeves chose her for the part of Sara.

Johnny Coquillon, Reeves's cinematographer, had figured prominently in adding atmosphere to the otherwise mediocre *Curse of the Crimson Altar*, aka *The Crimson Cult* (1968, with Boris Karloff, Christopher Lee, and Barbara Steele). He would be cinematographer for such genre efforts as *Scream and Scream Again* (1969), *The Oblong Box* (1969), and *The Changeling* (1980).

Back at AIP, Jim Nicholson decided that *Witchfinder General* would do better if it could be sold as another in the Edgar Allan Poe/Vincent Price series. So, after consulting the works of Poe, Nicholson changed the film's American title to *The Conqueror Worm* and had Price recite lines from Poe's poem of the same name over the opening and closing of the film. That was Poe's sole contribution to the finished product.

Poe first published "The Conqueror Worm" in *Graham's Magazine* in 1843. He later included it in the short story "Ligeia." The poem consists of five stanzas, of which the film uses only the first and fifth. Ac-

cording to Poe specialist T. O. Mabbott, most critics read the five stanzas as symbolic of the acts of a tragedy, and clearly the film is a legitimate tragedy if it is anything.

AIP produced an eight-page pressbook for *The Conqueror Worm*. The green, white, and black cover features the rotting face of a corpse and Hopkins wrestling with a scantily clad girl against a backdrop of burnings and hangings. "Leave the Children at Home!" the posters and ads warn, "… and if you are squeamish stay home with them!" Posters and ads also featured part of a stanza from Poe's poem not recited in the film itself:

A crawling shape intrude!
A blood-red thing that writhes from out
The scenic solitude!
It writhes!—It writhes!—with mortal pangs
The mimes become its food,
And the seraphs sob at vermin fangs
In human gore imbued.

These lines, which make little sense out of context, tend to conjure up visions of a fifties-style giant worm on the rampage. The publicity stories within the pressbook focus on Price and on production anecdotes. For example, we are told of a close call involving actress Gillain Alden, who is burned as a witch:

With the flames roaring twelve feet high and half a dozen movie cameras whirring busily, the ropes were slowly lowered away. Suddenly Jill's simulated screams took on a new note and she gave the pre-arranged signal to stop. She was hastily hauled back while firemen standing by doused the flames. But not before some harrowingly realistic shots had been obtained.

Of course, the "seat selling slants" included the exploitation of Edgar Allan Poe: "The name of Edgar Allan Poe and his popularity as an author make a tie-up with your local public library a MUST. Arrange for displays, imprint bookmarks and distribute to all library users. Declare Edgar Allan Poe Week to coincide with your run of the picture."

Critique: When *Witchfinder General* was released in 1968, the critical reaction was generally unfavorable. Dilys Powell of London's *Sunday Times* called it "Peculiarly nauseating."[178] The *Hollywood Citizen News* called it "A disgrace to the producers and scriptors, and a sad commentary on the art of filmmaking…. A film with such bestial brutality and orgiastic sadism, one wonders how it ever passed customs to be released in this country."[179] The *New York Times* grudgingly acknowledged the film's appeal, saying that "Vincent Price has a good tone as a materialistic witch-hunter and woman-disfigurer and dismemberer, and the audience at the dark, ornate New Amsterdam seemed to have a good time as well."[180] On a more positive note, London's *Times Saturday Review* wrote:

> [*Witchfinder General*] is quite happily and deliberately a horror film; that is to say, it has no particular pretensions to being anything else…. There is much in [it] which would win Michael Reeves an important reputation if he were dealing with some more pretentious, but fundamentally no more serious subject…. In particular, the unexpectedly downbeat ending of the film…. has an all-out passion and intensity…. Mr. Reeves is no longer merely promising. He already has real achievements behind him: not merely good horror films, but good films, period.[181]

Interestingly, while calling *Witchfinder General* "a very frightening film," *Films and Filming* disagreed profoundly with the *Times Saturday Review*, saying that "*Witchfinder General* is emphatically not a horror film; it is, however, a very horrifying film."[182]

The first truly perceptive critical appraisal of *Witchfinder General* appears in *A Heritage of Horror* by David Pirie. Originally published in 1973, the book considers Reeves a major British genre director and praises *Witchfinder General* for its thematic complexities. Pirie especially explicates scenes in which the personalities of Richard and Hopkins become blended. For example, he writes:

The devoted *mise-en-scène* of *Witchfinder General* is matched by a structure of some thematic complexity. The two superficially opposing poles of the story are represented by Matthew Hopkins, the cruel and ruthless Witchfinder, and Richard Marshall, the soldier/hero, whose paths cross both metaphorically and literally throughout the film, until finally their personalities become indistinguishable and inseparable."[183]

Pirie draws attention to the scenes in which Richard first rides to Brandeston to be with Sara:

> At first sight, this is an utterly conventional situation which could be found within the pages of any hack historical novel, the hero returning to claim his bride; but the scenes which follow have an oddly disturbing quality. To begin with, Reeves has organized matters so that Richard's return to Brandeston comes immediately after he has killed one of the enemy for the first time (and there is a held close-up on his face to reveal doubt and uncertainty). When he appears in Brandeston, and the priest agrees to their marriage, he steps forward to embrace Sara but she suddenly pulls herself away in pain saying "the army has taught you rough manners": the violence and chaos is *inside* the couple as well as around them.[184]

Pirie explains how "Richard initially harmonizes with the English landscape as he rides over the fields, but gradually he loses empathy with it and, after he has sworn vengeance on Hopkins and set the machinery in motion, his alienation is demonstrated by a prolonged long shot in which he rides blindly through the country, scattering sheep on both sides of his horse."[185]

Before I had read Pirie's book, I published "A Defense of *Witchfinder General*," the first critical article written on the film in America.[186] In that article, I recognized some of the positive elements first discovered by Pirie, identified some elements he missed, and missed some he found. Specifically, I defended the film against three general criticisms: (1) that it fails as a continuation of the AIP Poe series, (2) that the cast is inadequate, and (3) that the film is artless and tasteless. Of course, the first charge is groundless because the film is not a continuation of the AIP Poe series. Still, I would argue, the insertion of stanzas from Poe's poem is contextually sound.

As the film opens, Price recites the first stanza of "The Conqueror Worm":

Lo! 't is a gala night
    Within the lonesome latter years!
An angel throng, bewinged, bedight
    In veils, and drowned in tears,
Sit in a theatre, to see
    A play of hopes and fears,
While the orchestra breathes fitfully
    The music of the spheres.

Then, as a minister reads monotonously from the Bible a witch is dragged, begging and pleading, to her place of execution. When she is dead, the camera zooms to a nearby hillside where Price sits astride his horse overseeing the execution. Although Poe's poem has no connection with witch-finding, the first stanza of "The Conqueror Worm" works in context. If there are angels, then they must watch sadly as Hopkins commits his atrocities, all of which are part of the tragic play of humanity. This theater is that in which all human beings act their parts. This extremely grim introduction is a bleak foreshadowing of what is to come.

At the film's conclusion, when the camera freezes on the screaming face of Hilary Dwyer, Price recites the last stanza of Poe's poem:

Out—out are the lights—out all!
    And over each quivering form,
The curtain, a funeral pall,
    Comes down with the rush of a storm,
And the angels, all pallid and wan,
    Uprising, unveiling, affirm
That the play is the tragedy, "Man,"
    And its hero the Conqueror Worm.

Both film and poem are portraits in hopelessness. Both explore worlds in which human life is ultimately meaningless. Still, Reeves is not making a Poe film, and the final product must be judged in that light.

The second charge, that the cast is in-

adequate, also fails. Price heads the cast as Matthew Hopkins, a role reminiscent of his 1959 portrayal of Richard III in Roger Corman's *Tower of London*. In both, he plays historical characters as horror monsters who enjoy human suffering. His performance in *Tower of London* was hammy, but his performance in *Witchfinder General* is not. Reeves insisted on restraint, and he got it. In fact, Price gives what is probably the best performance of his career. Robert Russell, Rupert Davies, and Ian Ogilvy are more than adequate in their respective roles, and Hilary Dwyer is as good as most other menaced heroines, especially evoking sympathy in the scene in which she reveals to Marshall what the witchfinder has done to her.

The third charge, that the film is artless and often lacking in good taste, can be dismissed upon consideration of the film's purpose and construction. *Witchfinder General* was filmed on location in Suffolk, an area of beautiful forests and rolling green meadows. Against this background of natural beauty, Reeves unleashed the excesses of an unnatural monster. The historical background provided by the film's narrator describes a time in which "The structure of law and order has collapsed…. Justice and injustice are dispensed in more or less equal quantities and without opposition."

The idea of justice and injustice being dispensed in more or less equal quantities emerges as one of Reeves's major themes. While Hopkins's acts of torture and murder are deplorable in themselves, they are even more so because he realizes the innocence of his victims as he callously collects his witchfinder fees. Hopkins always cloaks his work in a mantle of holiness while on the job, but sometimes he even seeks to do so when speaking privately to Stearne. His assistant, however, sarcastically exposes Hopkins's true motives, as illustrated by the following conversation:

STEARNE: How much farther, Matthew?
HOPKINS: You'll not call me Matthew! I'm not one of your drinking cronies, carousing and wenching in the taverns!

STEARNE: Aye, you're not that, sir.

HOPKINS: It's the Lord's work, a noble thing.

STEARNE: You call it work?

HOPKINS: Remember, John Stearne, you ride with me only because you help in my work.

STEARNE: The good Lord paying in silver for every hanging!

HOPKINS: That is blasphemy, Stearne. Hold your tongue!

STEARNE: I'm merely an honest man who helps you get your confessions.

HOPKINS: The law has prescribed you methods of interrogation.

STEARNE: An I have been blessed with the skills to carry them out.

HOPKINS: Oh, stop your gabbling. We have work to do in Brandeston.

STEARNE: Who is it this time?

HOPKINS: The message tells of a priest, one who worships Satan and calls him Lord.

STEARNE: Hmmm. With the priest himself a witch there will be others corrupted too, I'm thinking (smiling).

HOPKINS: You enjoy torture, don't you Stearne?

STEARNE: And you ... (sarcastically) ... Sir?

The very idea of a devil like Hopkins executing the innocent for witchcraft provides a certain irony. In fact, Reeves artistically weaves irony throughout the film. When asked what he, a lawyer, would want in Brandeston, Hopkins replies in reference to a priest, "A man who may not be what he appears to be." Ironically, of course, the description applies perfectly to Hopkins himself. Later in the film, again in reference to the priest, Hopkins says, "Men sometimes have strange motives for what they do." Again, Hopkins is ironically describing himself. We find one of the greatest instances of irony interwoven with the justice and injustice theme. For example, when explaining to Sara that her uncle must die, Hopkins righteously states, "Justice must be done, my dear." In calling for justice, Hopkins ironically signs his own death warrant. As will be explained, it is the canceling of injustice through justice (and vice versa), the bring-ing of order out of chaos (and vice versa), and the general theme of balance that most concerns Reeves in this film.

Cromwell's England during the Civil War is a picture of social upheaval, fear, and superstition. Matthew Hopkins is both a product and a creator of chaos, out of harmony with the natural order symbolized by the natural beauty of Suffolk and the love between Sara and Richard. This being the case, *Witchfinder General* exhibits the theme of humanity in conflict with itself and nature. Just as in Shakespeare's *Macbeth, King Lear,* and *Hamlet,* chaos arises when the social and natural order is upset. In *Horror in the Cinema,* Ivan Butler writes "The atmosphere of menace, cruelty, and general nastiness during the English Civil War is well suggested, but the film collapses into an absurd, gratuitously disgusting axe-hacking, blood-spattering welter."[187] But Butler misses the point. Hopkins's excesses are shown not to exploit violence but to draw a visual contrast between the natural and unnatural. Considered as such, the vivid depiction of a witch burning, which upsets some critics, can surely be seen as quite purposeful. The "blood-spattering welter" in which Richard hacks up Hopkins with an axe is necessary to balance visually the preceding excesses, such as the witch burning, with justice. Only an excess can balance an excess, and as Hopkins has ironically stated, "Justice must be done, my dear." Here Reeves creates his own fictional ending for the sake of art. The theme of imbalance and justice was earlier handled by Reeves in *The Sorcerers,* which with *Witchfinder General* marks the culmination of a promising career cut short by the director's tragic death at the age of 26.

Last to be considered against the charge of artlessness is the manner in which Paul Ferris's moving musical score augments the contrast and lifts the film to the category of cinematic poetry. The main musical theme occurs five times throughout the film. Since the theme is sweeping and beautiful, it is never heard when Hopkins is on screen. It occurs first as Richard is riding across the lovely meadows on his way to see Sara before the arrival of Hopkins. Its second occurrence is when Richard rides again over the meadows, this time in hopes of comforting Sara after he hears of her uncle's execution. Its third occurrence is when Richard rides off in pursuit of Hopkins as an instrument of justice The theme is played quite tenderly later in the film when Richard and Sara, now married, are reunited in Laveham, shortly before being taken prisoner by Hopkins and Stearne. This time, too, it is played connection with the love bond between Richard and Sara. Its final occurrence is at the film's conclusion after Sara's screams have risen from the dungeon of carnage shortly after her rescue. The film having ended, the main theme is played softly and mournfully on single strings as the viewer reflects upon what has transpired. This is a touching moment. Ferris's score serves the same purpose as Maurice Jarre's score in Franju's horror masterpiece *Les Veux sans Visage,* aka *The Horror Chamber of Dr. Faustus* (1959). In Franju's film, Jarre's beautifully haunting score combines with the visual beauty of Edith Scob's eyes without a face and the film's eerie black and white photography to produce an effective contrast to the bloody, unnatural horror scenes. With Franju, we have science in contrast with the natural order. Ferris's sweeping score combines with the sweeping color photography of beautiful Suffolk to form an effective contrast to Hopkins's unnatural evil. Rather than science, we here have greed and superstition in contrast with the natural order. In both films, we have horror transformed into cinematic poetry.

In 1975, Ed Naha commited a critical fumble in dismissing the film as "an exercise in sadism ... tasteless.... A particularly gory climax leaves much to be desired."[188] More recently, *The Overlook Film Encyclopedia: Horror* is critically on the mark:

> The colours of death and decay imbue the movie with a muted but eerie intensity, relentlessly building up to the explosion of unconscionable violence.... The film aroused an outcry about violence, but rarely has violence been used so legitimately: Reeves shows a man who sets out to rid society of a deeply ingrained evil that has become an accepted part of daily living. He has himself become so infected by it that the purging process duplicates the insanity against which it is deployed.

Most recently, Peter Hutchings supplies the inevitable politically correct interpretation that is, nevertheless, off the mark. According to Hutchings, the film deals with "the difficulties involved in the maintenance of a male authority that is largely dependent upon female submission in the face of an increased female resistance to this submissive role."[189] He also claims that "there is an even more powerful and wide-ranging investigation of issues relating to gender, particularly in its representation of a violently repressive denial of female subjectivity."[190] But enough of that.

Today, though its relationship with Poe is purely accidental and superficial, *Witchfinder General* is rightly considered an important film by an important director.

The Oblong Box (1968)
American International, U.S.A. and Great Britain

Credits: Directed and produced by Gordon Hessler; executive producer—Louis M. Heyward; screenplay by Lawrence Huntington, based on "The Oblong Box" by Edgar Allan Poe; additional dialogue by Christopher Wicking; cinematography by John Coquillon; music by Harry Robinson.

Running Time: 101 minutes.

Cast: Vincent Price (Julian), Christopher Lee (Dr. Neuhartt), Alastair Williamson (Sir Edward Markham), Hilary Dwyer (Elizabeth), Peter Arne (Samuel Trench), Harry Baird (N'Galo), Carl Rigg (Mark Norton), Maxwell Shaw (Tom Hackett), Michael Balfour (Ruddock), Godfrey James (Weller), Rupert Davies (Joshua Kemp), Sally Geeson (Sally Baxter), Ivor Dean (Hawthorne).

Story: It is the nineteenth century. During a frenzied African ceremony, a tribal witch doctor crucifies and facially disfigures Sir Edward Markham. Julian Markham takes his half-insane brother back to England and keeps him locked in an upstairs room at their mansion. Julian tells his beautiful fiancée, Elizabeth, that Edward has a tropical disease requiring complete isolation. Brooding and moody, Julian will not answer Elizabeth's questions about what really happened in Africa.

The family lawyer, Samuel Trench, and his colleague, Mark Norton, promise to help Sir Edward escape. They go to a disreputable lodging house in London where the owner, Tom Hackett, leads them to the room of a strong-faced African witch doctor, N'-Galo, who is preparing a drug that will make Sir Edward appear dead so that his body can be taken from the house.

Meanwhile, Elizabeth regretfully informs Julian that she can no longer resist her father's efforts to send her to Italy. That night someone tosses N'Galo's drug to Sir Edward. When Julian's servant, Ruddock, finds Sir Edward's prostrate body, he assumes the tortured man is dead and calls Julian. Julian tells Trench that another body must be substituted for Edward's for the villagers to see. Trench refuses to produce a body because the penalty for grave robbing is hanging. When Julian produces proof that Trench has been engaged in forgery and embezzlement, crimes also punishable by hanging, the lawyer decides to cooperate.

Obeying Trench, N'Galo kills innkeeper Hackett with a poison dart to the neck, after which the dead man lies in state as Sir Edward Markham. The real Sir Edward is buried, and Hackett's corpse is thrown into

the river. Elizabeth returns to Julian, and they resume their wedding plans.

Meanwhile, Dr. Neuhartt, a local surgeon who needs bodies for his anatomical experiments, receives just such a corpse from Weller, a bodysnatcher. To his surprise, the "body" rises from the coffin and tells the terrified doctor that he plans to stay in the house until certain debts have been repaid. The "body," of course is Sir Edward, who plans to kill those who left him buried alive. Sir Edward dons a crimson mask, and Dr. Neuhartt agrees to tell the servants that the newcomer is a badly burned relative who prefers not to frighten people with his appearance. Shortly afterward, Joshua Kemp, a local painter, discovers the discarded body of the innkeeper and later sketches the dead man's face.

The hooded Sir Edward tracks down Norton and cuts his throat. He then beds Dr. Neuhartt's servant girl. When the doctor is outraged, an argument ensues that ends with the servant being fired. When a local prostitute seduces Sir Edward and her boyfriend tries to rob the confused masked man, Sir Edward knocks the man unconscious and cuts the prostitute's throat after she sees his hideous face. In his panic, he leaves behind his cloak. Police officer Hawthorne traces it back to Neuhartt's laboratory. The doctor has an alibi that clears him, and later he tells Edward he knows of the murder he committed.

Sir Edward kills Trench and asks N'-Galo to help restore his face to normal. He also asks the witch doctor why the natives performed such atrocities on him. N'Galo relates that a white colonist named Markham ran down and killed a native boy while out for a horseback ride. Sir Edward realizes that the real killer was Julian. When N'Galo fails to restore Sir Edward's face, a fight ensues during which the disturbed nobleman suffers a knife wound and tosses a cauldron of boiling water into the witch doctor's face.

The wounded Sir Edward returns to Dr. Neuhartt's laboratory and asks the doc-

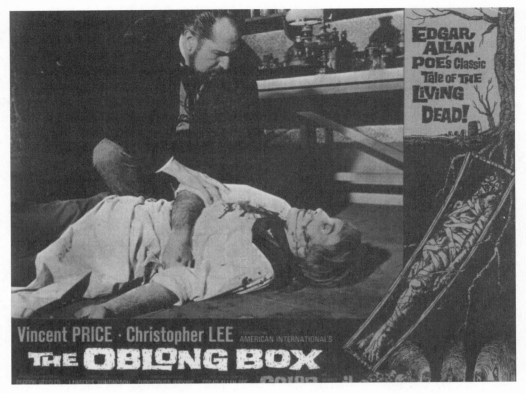

Vincent Price discovers the corpse of Christopher Lee in *The Oblong Box* (1968).

tor for something to help him continue living for a while longer because he has further work to do. When Neuhartt gives Sir Edward a liquid concoction to drink, the wounded man suspects the drink is poison and cuts the doctor's throat.

Meanwhile, Julian learns that his brother was buried alive and apparently resurrected. He also learns from Dr. Neuhartt's former maid that the murderer with the crimson hood is staying at the doctor's home. Julian quickly rides to Dr. Neuhartt's' laboratory and finds the doctor with his throat cut. Before dying Dr. Neuhartt reveals that Sir Edward has gone to Julian's manor. Sir Edward abducts the maid and takes her into the country. Julian follows and shoots his insane brother. Before he dies, however, Sir Edward bites Julian on the wrist.

At Markham Manor, Julian has returned to Edward's old room at the top of the house. Elizabeth enters to call him to

dinner. "This is Edward's room, isn't it?" she asks. Turning to her, his face becoming hideously disfigured like Edward's, Julian answers, "No. This is my room." Elizabeth screams.

Production and marketing: So pleased was AIP with the success of *Witchfinder General*, aka *The Conqueror Worm*, that the company rushed three of its stars, Vincent Price, Hilary Dwyer, and Rupert Davies, into its next Edgar Allan Poe picture, *The Oblong Box*. The executive producers, having posters already designed for something to be titled Edgar Allan Poe's *The Oblong Box*, presold the film based on those graphics. They then scheduled Michael Reeves, director of *Witchfinder General*, back at the helm. Unfortunately, the production would soon be beset by difficulties.

The first difficulty was the loss of director Michael Reeves. AIP replaced Reeves when it became clear that the young man's repeated suicide attempts, emotional and mental problems, and shock treatment therapy rendered him too great a financial risk. Reeves was engaging in heavy drug use and experiencing setbacks in his love life. Finally, Reeves did commit suicide via barbiturates and alcohol in 1969. AIP assigned directorship to Cy Endfield. But when the shooting location was changed from Ireland to England's Shepperton Studios, AIP replaced Endfield with Gordon Hessler (1930–), who began his career as story reader for the *Alfred Hitchcock Presents* television show and later worked himself up to associate producer and finally producer before the series ended.

The screenplay was written by Lawrence Huntington (1900–1968), the veteran director of routine thrillers and horror films such as *Tower of Terror* (1941) and *The Vulture* (1966). When the script arrived from the United States, Reeves, and later Hessler and Vincent Price, considered it too difficult to follow. By the time Hessler arrived, AIP had brought in veteran screenwriter Christopher Wicking to help Reeves readapt it. Ironically, while someone seems to have lifted elements form Rudyard Kipling's "The Mark of the Beast," during all of this writing and rewriting, no one bothered to consult Edgar Allan Poe's short story, the film's nominal inspiration.

Far removed from British colonialism, premature burial, and revenge, Poe's "The Oblong Box" is a mystery set aboard a ship bound from Charleston, South Carolina, to New York. On board, a newly married man keeps a mysterious oblong box in his cabin. Each night the woman identified as his wife retires to an adjacent empty cabin purchased by the man, leaving him alone with the box. When a storm hits and the ship is abandoned, the man refuses to leave the box, which contains the remains of his actual wife, recently deceased. Because he knew the passengers on the ship would never sail with a corpse on board, the man hired his maid to impersonate his wife in an effort to transport his beloved's body quietly to her par-

ents for burial. Refusing to leave her aboard the sinking ship, he ties himself to the coffin and disappears with it into the sea. The Huntington/Wicking screenplay, set in nineteenth-century England and featuring themes of British colonialism, premature burial, and revenge, has *nothing whatever* to do with Poe's tale. In fact, *The Oblong Box* is the first AIP-Poe film that both completely ignored the original Poe plot and failed to include even a single line from Poe in the film itself to justify the title.

Even though Wicking provided additional dialogue, he could do little to save the screenplay, especially given AIP's expectations of what the film should be. So, with a budget of only about $175,000 and with only three weeks to shoot, *The Oblong Box* went before the cameras with a script disliked by the producer and director and the star. Hessler explained that "Vincent [Price] was concerned, and he had a right to be, with the scripts that were whipped up. He had a contract to make three pictures, and I had to make four. So you had to make it. They'd already sold the picture from the poster, so the script came and you worked on it. All you could go for was the melodrama and try to be interesting with camera angles."[191]

In an effort to make the film interesting, Hessler, unlike Michael Reeves on *Witchfinder General*, allowed Vincent Price to lapse back into certain familiar mannerisms typical of his later horror film performances. A little hamminess, he reasoned, could not hurt.

Appearing with Price, apparently for marquee value only, was Christopher Lee, who with frequent costar Peter Cushing, was challenging Price for the title of contemporary horror-film king. Of *The Oblong Box*, Lee said:

> That's really only important as the first film I ever made with Vincent Price. I played an anatomist. I play him as a man who is driven by this demon, partly for decent reasons. Everything gets out of hand, out of control, because he couldn't stop. He's a man who, in the interests of science, wants to learn about the human body, and is reduced to dealing

with graverobbers and resurrectionists. He becomes a bad character. I did the picture because I wanted to do a picture with Vincent Price.[192]

Unfortunately, Lee and Price share only one scene, a scene that Lee recalls was filmed with some humorous difficulty:

It was not in fact till I was dying, with my throat cut, that my story intersected with Vincent's, so that it was a hail and farewell meeting, as I lay expiring in his arms, with him asking me, "Which way did they go?" and I glugged in answer with a severed artery. He was swathed in a coat like a tent, and by mistake rolled me on to it so that the camera could relish my death agony to the full, and kept hissing, "You're lying on my train!" as I gurgled.[193]

Later Price remarked of Lee:

We're great friends, you know. We both find each other hysterically funny. Before we met, I had heard he was very pompous, and I was really a little worried about meeting him. Well, we took one look at each other and started laughing. We spend our lives screaming and laughing at each other, and having a wonderful time. I'm really devoted to him. I think he's one of my very few friends in the business.[194]

Although Lee would play a cameo in Price's starring vehicle *Scream and Scream Again* (1970), the two would share no scenes. A true, though disappointing, reunion would have to wait until *The House of Long Shadows* (1983), a horror film spoof starring not only Price and Lee, but also John Carradine and Peter Cushing.

When *The Oblong Box* was released, its pressbook reflected the decline of the AIP-Poe series. Gone were the large, lavish pressbooks of films like *The Fall of the House of Usher, The Pit and the Pendulum,* and *The Premature Burial.* In their place was a reduced eight-page book with only one page of publicity. On the rather unattractive green, white, and black posters appeared false phrases linking the film to Poe: "Edgar Allan Poe's classic tale of the restless dead

and their subterranean world of horror and the unspeakable!" and "The Living Dead whimpers an unspeakable curse and claws with bony hands to free its evil from *The Oblong Box* ... Edgar Allan Poe's horror classic!" Ads placed the following sentence in quotation marks to incorrectly imply Poe's authorship: "Deep beneath the dank ground where vile things crawl among the slime a pale hand twitches and a beatless heart still hungers for revenge."

Although publicity releases largely ignored Poe, one did call *The Oblong Box* "typical Edgar Allan Poe terror- territory, where the atmosphere is one of impending doom, where every awful happening is the harbinger of something worse." Since in reality the film's plot, atmosphere, and mood are strikingly untypical of Poe, most publicity stressed the teaming of Price and Lee, calling them the "terror kings of two nations."

One exploitation suggestion exhorted theater owners to hype the author of the film's title. "Sell Poe!!!" it shouted. "Sell the name of Poe—it is a winner with movie going patrons ... Have a local radio station stage a Poe Contest for Oblong Box ... Award passes to the winners who can most correctly list the names of Edgar Allan Poe's writings." Obviously, the publicity department was not working overtime to produce creative seat-selling slants.

The film's disappointing gross of $1.2 million in the United States and Canada demonstrated a waning audience interest in pseudo-Poe pictures. But AIP was not deterred. It still had Vincent Price and Gordon Hessler under contract, and it would drag the name of Poe through the mud and onto two more marquees before finally letting matters rest.

Critique: As described above, *The Oblong Box* was a troubled production, and troubled productions rarely result in good films. Predictably, this AIP-Poe picture proved no exception. Calling the film "quaint, laughable, and unconvincing," *The New York Times* wrote that Christopher Lee plays Dr. Neuhartt in "grumpy fashion," and "Mr.

Price, broadly portraying the jumpy lord of the manor from memory, is obvious even if the plot is unnecessarily convoluted.... All things considered, ... *The Oblong Box* (the coffin in this cheerless charade) might have been better left interred."[195]

In later reviews, Ed Naha simply stated the obvious, that as "The eleventh film of the American International series, this contrived entry has absolutely nothing to do with the aforementioned master of terror,"[196] and Michael Weldon pronounced the film a "lame Poe adaptation."[197] On the positive side, *The Overlook Encyclopedia of Film: Horror* concluded that the film "is surprisingly effective, though overly elaborate, and is excellently photographed by Coquillon."

Jay Robert Nash and Stanley Ralph Ross awarded the film one star (poor) and drew attention to its fuzzy plot, while Leonard Maltin conceded it two stars, called it "a boring treatment of a halfway interesting situation," and criticized its "hammy performances, long drawn-out narrative, and lackluster direction."

In my view, *The Oblong Box* can be considered "surprisingly effective" only if one approaches it with low expectations. In an interview given to coincide with the film's release, Gordon Hessler said, "I agree with Hitchcock that logic in thriller and horror movies is not that important. If audiences are continuously keyed up to a full pitch, as they should be, then the logic of a scene or a character's behavior doesn't matter that much."[198] The trouble is, however, that *The Oblong Box* has a convoluted plot so littered with superfluous characters that Hessler's "full pitch" is never achieved. At one point, Hessler further stalls the already slow action by inserting a long scene of tavern revel apparently just to pass the time while two characters make love upstairs. Had the camera played voyeur instead, perhaps those scenes would have elicited something other than a yawn.

As far as the acting is concerned, Hilary Dwyer, who gave a strong performance in *Witchfinder General*, has little to do here

other than occasionally walk by Price's side. Worse, since the 57-year-old actor, with a full beard, looks even older than he did in *Tomb of Ligeia*, 26-year-old Dwyer makes a very unlikely fiancée. Not helping matters any, Price, who gave one of the best performances of his career in *Witchfinder General*, gives a singularly undistinguished performance here. Rupert Davies, also outstanding in *Witchfinder General*, serves only to clutter affairs with his few minutes of screen time. Christopher Lee maintains the demeanor of an irritable, harried surgeon, but since the character allows him little to do, he understandably delivers what is required and goes on his way.

Some critics, including David Pirie, author of *A Heritage of Horror: The Gothic English Cinema 1946-1972*, found the photography interesting. Said Pirie:

> [Hessler's] audacious technique, evolved in documentary and newsreel work, resulted in a camera-style which probed his characters and sets as though they were under some kind of visual interrogation. For the first ten minutes his fluid journalistic camera prowled Markham's (Vincent Price) somber mansion, using subjective effects to convey the alienated animal-like existence of strange (and unseen) Sir Edward—a deformed nobleman imprisoned by his brother. By keeping Sir Edward behind the camera for so long Hessler exaggerated his evil presence enormously, giving him a kind of sub-human aura long after the device had been discontinued.[199]

I must protest. Crucified and mutilated by a witch doctor, driven nearly insane, and chained as a prisoner in his brother's house, Sir Edward is not an evil presence. If Hessler's subjective camera has any effect, it serves to establish an identification between this tragic figure and the audience. Even Sir Edward's killing rampage is precipitated by a sense of betrayal at being buried alive. Yes, he was a British nobleman engaged in African colonialism, but the film makes clear that if there is an evil presence in the film, it is Vincent Price, or possibly English society itself. Ultimately, Hessler's photography, highlighted by in-your-face close-ups, is more disconcerting than enlivening.

The Oblong Box is what it is because AIP no longer cared to make quality Poe pictures. Just throw a premature burial into the script, put Vincent Price's name on the marquee, and presto! A new Edgar Allan Poe film magically appears. Unfortunately, beginning with *The Oblong Box*, the magic would become more scarce with every film.

The Oval Portrait (1969)
Northwest Motion Picture Corporation and Apple Leaf International Pictures
Mexico and the United States

Credits: Directed by Rogelio Gonzales, Jr.; produced by Enrique Torres Tudelo; screenplay by Enrique Torres Tudelo, based on "The Oval Portrait" by Edgar Allan Poe; cinematography by Leon Sanchez; music by Les Baxter; edited by Dick Legrand and Sigfrido Garcia.

Running time: 89 minutes.

Cast: Wanda Hendrix (Rebecca), Barry Coe (Joseph), Gisele Mackenzie (Mrs. Warren), Maray Ayres (Lisa Buckingham), Barney O'Sullivan (Major Huntington), Doris Buckinham (Mrs. Buckingham).

Story: The time is shortly after the American Civil War. Mrs. Buckingham and her daughter Lisa arrive on a stormy night at the Huntington mansion. The carriage driver tells them that the mansion is reputedly haunted. While waiting at the door, Lisa is frightened to see the spectral figure of a pleading young woman. Once inside, Mrs. Buckingham and Lisa find Mrs. Warren, the housekeeper, a woman disliked and distrusted by Mrs. Buckingham. Lisa is intrigued by an oval portrait of a beautiful woman named Rebecca, who once lived in the house and whose ghost she saw earlier in the evening.

That night Lisa is awakened by harpsichord music. She goes downstairs to find a young handsome man named Joseph Hudson playing music for his Rebecca. The next day Lisa again sees Rebecca's ghost. It seems that Mrs. Buckingham and Lisa have arrived at the house for the reading of the will of Rebecca's recently deceased father, Major Alexander Huntington. Other relatives are expected soon. Lisa meanwhile has become obsessed with the oval portrait.

As Lisa studies the portrait, Rebecca's ghost emerges and swoops down on her, causing her to faint. Mrs. Warren says that a doctor cannot help Lisa and that Lisa should leave the house at once. Upstairs, as Lisa rests in bed, she asks Mrs. Warren how Rebecca and Joseph originally met, and Mrs. Warren responds with this story:

Rebecca is the beautiful daughter of the brutally strict Major Alexander. The major rants to Rebecca that her mother was a whore who left with another man. One night Union soldiers come to the house looking for a wounded Confederate soldier. Alexander, a Union major, convinces the soldiers that the wounded man is definitely not in his house. Rebecca, however, discovers the fugitive hiding in the house, and she and Mrs. Warren decide to hide him in Mrs. Warren's room until he recovers.

Major Alexander soon leaves for the war, but before going, he tells Rebecca that if he ever catches her with a man he will kill the man and make sure that she ends up no better than her mother. With the major gone, Rebecca and Mrs. Warren get to know the soldier. His name is Joseph, and he wears a medal around his neck that is of interest to Mrs. Warren. He explains that he got the medal from his mother, who died when he was very young. As the days pass, Joseph and

Video box art for *The Oval Portrait.*

Rebecca fall deeply in love. Joseph vows that he will never leave Rebecca, and she says that if he ever must, she will wait for his return. When Joseph has regained his health, he paints an oval portrait of Rebecca that seems to capture the very depths of her soul. Joseph and Rebecca attempt to marry secretly, but Union soldiers enter the house and capture Joseph.

The war ends. When Major Alexander returns to find Rebecca very ill and carrying the child of a Confederate soldier, he makes good his word and evicts her from the house, after which she dies. The major then suffers a stroke and joins his daughter in death.

When Joseph returns, he finds Rebecca in her coffin. After the funeral, he digs her up and takes her to the Alexander mansion, where he resides with Mrs. Warren.

By the time Mrs. Warren concludes her story, Lisa is asleep.

The other relatives presently arrive, and the reading of the will commences. Mrs. Warren comes forward and proclaims that the major left a new will before he died. Mrs. Warren inherits the house, which no one else really wants, and the other relatives are pleased to divide the rest of the estate.

When the relatives have left, Joseph plays the harpsichord and talks to the oval portrait. Then he goes to the part of the house where he keeps Rebecca's rotting corpse. As Mrs. Warren watches in horror, Joseph dances with the corpse, kisses it, and whispers words of love. Suddenly he cries out to Rebecca that the Union soldiers are returning for him. Mrs. Warren ends his life with a bullet. "This world is not for you," she says, and reveals that she is actually Joseph's mother. She created the new will that sent the relatives away happy so she could share the house with her son. His growing insanity, however, has made his mercy-killing necessary.

At last, Rebecca and Joseph are reunited, and their ghosts walk the grounds of the Alexander estate.

Production and marketing: Coming at the end of sixties Poe mania, *The Oval Por-*

trait hoped to cash in with the Poe name and with a name star, Gisele Mackenzie. Mackenzie, however, was a popular fifties singer, not a film star. The only other "name" involved in the production is Les Baxter, who had scored the music for Poe's *The Fall of the House of Usher* (1960), *The Pit and the Pendulum* (1961), *Tales of Terror* (1962), and *The Raven* (1963). He adds *The Oval Portrait* to his résumé.

Other than the title itself and the presence of an oval portrait, Tudela's screenplay borrows very little, if anything, from Poe's short story. Poe's story is not set during and immediately after the American Civil War since Poe died twelve years before the war broke out. Poe's narrator is a wounded man accompanied by a valet, but they seek shelter in a chateau in the Apennines. While recovering from his wound, the narrator becomes interested in an oval portrait that hangs near his bed. Finding a short account of the portrait's creation, he reads that as the painter gave life to the portrait, his subject, his beautiful young bride, declined in health and died. Of course, no such thing happens in the screenplay.

In Poe-like fashion the screenplay flirts with the idea of a deceased woman returning to possess the living, a theme reminiscent of such Poe tales as "Morella" and "Ligeia," but not of "The Oval Portrait." The theme, however, is left undeveloped. Also suggestive of Poe is the theme of necrophilia, though that theme is addressed in other Poe stories, not this one. The grief of one having lost his true love to death is clearly a Poe theme, but again, that theme is only at best barely suggested in "The Oval Portrait."

Advertising for the film's video release called "The Oval Portrait" Poe's "most popular short story," although at least a dozen other Poe stories obviously surpass it in popularity.

Critique: *The Oval Portrait* is not a very impressive film. Most of the wooden performances are aggravated, I am sure, by stiff dialogue. From the general cliché of the screenplay, we get such tired effects as shaking chandeliers (à la *The Fall of the House of Usher* [1960]), doors slamming shut by themselves, and ghostly, sardonic laughter. Leon Sanchez attempts some artsy cinematography to no positive effect, and Legrand and Garcia attempt some artsy quick cuts, also to no positive effect.

Despite its flaws, however, the film's pace rarely invites boredom, and the relationships among the main characters are mildly interesting. Les Baxter's musical score, though far from his best, adequately punctuates the scenes of pathos and shock. The mood, however, is not that of Poe. It is as though William Faulkner, while drinking heavily, tried to write a screenplay based on the last half of *Wuthering Heights*. Some things work, and some things do not. The result is a mediocre film that does not do justice to its source. *The Video Hound's Golden Movie Retriever 1996* obviously agrees, as it assigns the film only 1 1/2 bones.

Cry of the Banshee (1970)
American International, Great Britain

Credits: Directed and produced by Gordon Hessler; executive producer—Louis M. Heyward; first assistant director—Ariel Levy; screenplay by Tim Kelly and Christopher Wicking; cinematography by John Coquillon; art direction by George Provis; edited by Ossie Hafenrichter; production supervisor—Clifford Parks.

Running Time: 87 minutes.

Cast: Vincent Price (Lord Edward Whitman), Elisabeth Bergner (Oona), Essy Persson (Lady Patricia), Hugh Griffith (Mickey), Hilary Dwyer (Maureen), Sally Geeson (Sarah), Patrick Mower (Roderick), Pamela Farbrother (Margaret), Marshall Jones (Father Tom), Carl Rigg (Harry), Michael Elphick (Burke), Stephen Chase (Sean), Andrew McCullouch (bully boy), Robert Hutton (guest), Godfrey James (rider), Terry Martin (brander), Richard Everett (Timothy), Quin O'Hara (tavern witchgirl), Jan Rossini (tavern wench), Peter Forest (party man), Joyce Mandre (party woman), Gertan Klauber (landlord).

Story:

In the startled ear of night
  How they screamed [sic] out their affright!
Too much horrified to speak
  They can only shriek, shriek
Out of time....
           —Edgar Allan Poe

"England in the 16th century ... a dark and violent time. Witchcraft and the ghosts of the old religion still hold sway in minds of people, pre-occupying both the law and the church."

Lord Edward Whitman, an influential person in the community and a harsh magistrate, leads a raid on a witch's temple as pagan rites are in progress. Whitman's soldiers massacre most of the worshippers, but Whitman spares Oona, the high priestess, and a few of her followers. She places a curse on Whitman, saying that he will pay for the massacre until he, his wife, and the last of his bloodline are dead. She then conjures a sidhe (pronounced "see-hee"), a spirit from beyond the grave, in the form of young Roderick, who becomes Whitman's stud groom.

Years after the massacre, Whitman's son Harry arrives home from his schooling at Cambridge to find that an atmosphere of cruelty and madness has settled over his family. His mother, Lady Patricia, suffers from a mental disorder, and his brother Sean is as evil as their father. Only his sister Maureen, who is having an affair with Roderick, is both kind and emotionally well balanced.

Accompanying Harry home is Father Tom, the new parish priest. When Roder-

Vincent Price as the cruel magistrate in *Cry of the Banshee* (1970).

ick saves the life of a little girl by calming a mad dog, Father Tom is intrigued by the young man's power over animals. He also notices the strange medallion Roderick wears. Roderick says he knows nothing of its meaning and has always had it.

Oona, meanwhile, performs mystical religious rites with her followers during which she calls for her sidhe to begin its work of revenge. The wind starts to howl, and banshees cry in the distance. After a cruel revel at a local tavern, Sean hears the cry of the banshee as he heads home. Moments later he is found dead, killed by "an animal." Although the villagers whisper about the power of witchcraft and Oona's curse, Whitman asserts that his son was killed by the mad dog earlier calmed by Roderick. A hunting party soon tracks and kills the animal, and Whitman proclaims the trouble finished. Privately, however, he begins to suspect witchcraft.

Oona again conducts a revenge ceremony, and the banshees begin to howl. That night Lady Patricia is the sidhe's victim. Later, when Whitman opens her coffin, he finds that her body has aged horribly. He now strongly suspects witchcraft, regrets having spared Oona's life, and commands his henchmen to find her. After burning a villager to death in an attempt to get information on Oona's whereabouts, Whitman returns home to find Maureen and Roderick making love in Maureen's bedroom. Whitman beats Roderick and has him chained in the dungeon. Oona performs another ceremony, however, and Roderick turns into a beastlike monster and attacks Maureen.

Meanwhile, Father Tom and Harry interrupt Oona and her coven. Oona tells Father Tom and Harry that Roderick is her sidhe and that he will destroy the Whitman family. Harry then steps forward and slits her throat. Father Tom and Harry return to the Whitman estate and find Maureen injured but still alive. Roderick is nowhere to be found. A short time later, when Roderick reappears as the monster and attacks Whitman, Maureen fires a bullet into the attacker's face.

As Whitman, Harry, and Maureen leave the estate by coach, Whitman stops by the cemetery, only to discover that Roderick's coffin is empty. Returning to the coach, Whitman finds Harry and Maureen murdered. The coach, with the Whitmans inside, then plunges into the forest, driven by Roderick.

Production and marketing: *Cry of the Banshee*, the third Gordon Hessler/Christopher Wicking collaboration, is considered by executive producer Sam Arkoff to be the last of American International Pictures' Poe series (though *The Murders in the Rue Morgue* [1971, directed by Gordon Hessler] would follow). Its connection with Poe, however, is tenuous at best. According to Hessler, AIP gave him "the worst script I have ever worked on."[200] Hessler brought in Wicking and they began to rewrite the script. AIP then informed them that for legal reasons they could change only ten percent of the script. "All we could do with the film," Hessler said, "was try to make it cinematically interesting; strange angles, moving camera, that sort of thing."[201]

Poe never wrote anything titled "Cry of the Banshee." He never wrote a story about a banshee or a sidhe. Nor did he ever write anything about the European witchcraft persecutions, though after *Witchfinder General* (aka *The Conqueror Worm*) and *Cry of the Banshee*, anyone unfamiliar with Poe's writings could easily assume witchcraft was one of his main themes. Actually, *Cry of the Banshee* was based on an original story designed to cash in on the success of *Witchfinder General*. The only connection to Poe in the film is the insertion of lines from the third stanza of Poe's poem "The Bells" after the introductory film credits. In Poe's lines, it is the alarm bells that "scream out their affright" and "shriek." In the film, however, we are led to believe that the shrieking is that of pagan revelers.

When the film wrapped, Sam Arkoff threw a party for Vincent Price, celebrating what Arkoff said was the actor's 100th picture. Hessler had to talk Price into attending, however, since the actor was not speaking to Arkoff because of the scripts the producer was forcing on him. When Price was supposed to cut the cake, Hessler could not find the knife. Price then suggested that they "take the knife that's in my back."[202]

Vincent Price was obviously angered over the treatment he was getting from AIP. Under contract, he was at the mercy of any script the studio sent his way. Although Arkoff wanted Price to renew his contract, the actor was reluctant. While going on to appear in such genre standouts as *The Abominable Dr. Phibes* (1971), *Dr. Phibes Rises Again* (1972), *Theater of Blood* (1973), and *Edward Scissorhands* (1990), he would make no more theatrical films based on the work of Edgar Allan Poe. He would, however, star in the AIP television production of "An Evening with Edgar Allan Poe." Said Price: "I did four Poe stories—absolutely pure Edgar Allan Poe, without a word by anybody else, no changing the plot, just as monologues—with action and with sets and with costumes. It's probably the best thing I ever did."[203] Ironically, the television executives were disappointed because they evidently knew Poe only from film adaptations. According to Price, "They said, it's too serious—it isn't the real Edgar Allan Poe.' But it *was* the real Edgar Allan Poe."[204]

As usual with AIP films relying on British actors, the supporting cast of *Cry of the Banshee* is strong. Hilary Dwyer, who turned in an equally fine performance in *Witchfinder General*, is impressive as the strong yet vulnerable Maureen.

German-born Elisabeth Bergner (1898–1986) made a career of playing fey young women in such critically acclaimed films as *Der Traumende Mund* (1932), *Catherine the Great* (1934), and *Escape Me Never* (1935). As Oona, she is quite believable in a role far removed from her accustomed fare. Also a strong addition to the cast is the Swedish Essy Persson, who had appeared in *I A Woman* (1967) and the controversial lesbian drama *Therese and Isabelle* (1968).

Lex Baxter's musical score was good enough to be released as a record album. Actually, he produced two important genre soundtrack albums in 1970, the other being *The Dunwich Horror*. While the *Cry of the Banshee* soundtrack is good, it does not have the otherworldly quality and relentless intensity of *The Dunwich Horror*, which many rightfully consider one of the best horror film soundtracks ever composed.

The posters and ads for *Cry of the Banshee* featured such catch-lines as "Edgar Allan Poe probes new depths of terror! ... A tale of terror and torture and a thing that never learned to die!" One poster even included lines of poetry on the face of a tombstone:

> Who spurs the Beast
>   the corpse will ride,
> Who cries the cry that kills?
> When Satan questioned,
>   who replied?
> Whence blows this wind
>   that chills?
>   Who wanders 'mongst these
>   empty graves
> And seeks a place to lie?
> 'Tis something God had
>   ne're planned.
> A thing that ne're had
>   learned to die.

While the poster implies that the lines are by Poe, they are not.

The pressbook contains the following exploitation tip: "Sell the name of Poe—it's a sure winner with movie patrons. Have a local radio station stage a POE contest for CRY OF THE BANSHEE.... Award passes to the winner who can most correctly list the names of Edgar Allan Poe's writings."

While such devices are common, it might have proved embarrassing in this instance had such lists turned up the fact that Poe never wrote "Cry of the Banshee." Refusing to let Poe lie, another exploitation tip

suggested: "Arrange a promotional tie-in with your local library. Have them set-up an EDGAR ALLAN POE book corner with all of Poe's books in this area. For this purpose, give your library a selection of stills as well as one-sheet posters. DON'T FORGET BOOK STORES TOO!"

While Poe was featured prominently in the posters, ads, and exploitation tips, the publicity for the film focused almost solely on Vincent Price. In a pressbook interview, Price makes an incredible statement: "This is my one-hundredth movie, but only about 15 of them have been in the macabre mold. In the rest of them, I've played straight." Once can only wonder how Price defines "macabre," since a conservative estimate would place Price in at least 25 horror films. When asked why he has made so many horror films, Price replies, "I have a stomach to feed. I've got ex-wives and wives and mothers-in law, all with their eyes on me. And besides, making these horror jobs is fun."

Rather unbelievably, the publicity also reports Price as being so interested in the history of the Tudor-style country home used as the main location background in the film that he researched the house's history. Finding that it was once owned by W. S. Gilbert (of Gilbert and Sullivan), Price relates that Gilbert was swimming with two attractive young women in the lake when one of the swimmers got into difficulty. Gilbert dived in and made the rescue, but died of a heart attack while extracting the woman from the water.

Price also supposedly drove to his local library to find out what a sidhe is. Considering the fact that Price was anything but happy about making *Cry of the Banshee*, such interest and dedication on his part are doubtful.

Interestingly, Price would not be the only horror film star to suffer as a result of the success of *Witchfinder General*. In 1972, Christopher Lee would be dragged into a "historical" witchcraft drama called *Night of the Blood Monster*, in which he plays a sadistic magistrate. Unfortunately, its quality even manages to fall short of that of *Cry of the Banshee.*

Critique: Reviews for *Cry of the Banshee* were uniformly negative, and time has not improved its reputation. Giving the film 2 1/2 stars, Leonard Maltin writes that "confusion sets in half way." Michael Weldon dubs the film "unsatisfying [and] confusing."[205] *The Overlook Encyclopedia of Film: Horror* calls *Cry of the Banshee*

the weakest of the collaborations between Wicking and Hessler.... Only in the location scenes does Hessler create a sense of haunting evil. Elsewhere the film exploits whatever opportunities for violence are provided by its theme: women are stripped, one is burnt alive, a head is blown off, there is a massacre, and so on. Dwyer ... is effective as the magistrate's daughter ... Price performs with professional aplomb and only those who remember Berner's sugary performances of the late twenties and early thirties will appreciate the nicely sacrilegious aspect of casting her as Oona and cutting her throat.

I see no reason to dispute conventional opinion regarding *Cry of the Banshee.* All the aspects that the critics point out as flaws are indeed flaws. In addition to Dwyer's good performance, however, I would also like to add that of Essy Persson, who brings out all the qualities of an unhinged woman who has put up with and seen too much. Price is Price. As *Variety* remarked, "It is a measure of Price's image that he can enjoin a banquet room full of guests, 'drink, dance, and be merry,' and the line comes out ominous."

Price has one effective moment of ironic black humor when he seeks the villagers' aid in helping him find Oona. "Now hear me, all of you," he intones to the assembled villagers. "I must know Oona's whereabouts. She is a danger and a menace to all of you. To protect you I must destroy her. To find her, I will kill as many of you as I need to."

To Hessler's credit, he has the beastly sidhe photographed mainly in shadows, its makeup being none too impressive. The film does manage a certain amount of formulaic suspense and an occasional chill when the wind picks up and the banshees howl, but the mood usually falls short of what the production requires. A Poe adaptation in name only, *Cry of the Banshee* is a mediocre, forgettable film.

Nella stretta morsa del ragno (1970); aka *Dracula Im Schloss des Schreckens*; *Prisonnier de L'Araignée*; *In the Grip of the Spider*; *Web of the Spider*; *Edgar Poe Chez Les Morts Vivants*; *E venne l'alba ... ma tinto di rosso*

Produzione DC7/Paris Cannes Productions; Terra Filmkunst, Italy, West Germany, and France

Credits: Directed by Antonio Margheriti; produced by Giovanni Addessi; screenplay by Bruno Corbucci and Giovanni Grimaldi; cinematography by Sandro Mancori and Memmo Mancori; edited by Fima Novek; music by Riz Ortolani.

Running time: 94 minutes.

Cast: Anthony Franciosa (Alan Foster), Michele Mercier (Elizabeth Blackwood), Klaus Kinski (Edgar Allan Poe), Peter Carsten (Dr. Carmus), Karen Field (Julia).

Story: See *La danza macabra,* aka *Castle of Blood* (1964). Because *Nella stretta morsa del ragno* is an almost scene-for-scene remake of *La danza macabra,* directed by the same director, there is no need to repeat the synopsis. All the characters in the remake retain their names from the original.

Production and marketing: In 1970, Antonio Margheriti chose to remake his *La danza macabra.* He retained the same musical director from the original and made no noteworthy changes. For information on Margheriti, see *La danza macabra.*

The major changes, of course, involve the cast, three of whom are important. In the remake, German Klaus Kinski (1926–1991) assumes the role of Edgar Allan Poe. Kinski began his acting career in Germany, where he performed one-man poetry recitals, sometimes re-creating and altering the texts of Rimbaud, Villon, Shakespeare, and Goethe. When critics tossed endless barbs at his interpretations, he fought back, sometimes with his fists, but he finally moved to Italy. There he turned down film offers from Fellini, Pasolini, and Visconti because he felt the internationally acclaimed directors did not pay enough. "They expected me to work for love," Kinski explained. He agreed to play in "popular" films, though, if the price was right. That attitude eventually led him to play Clint Eastwood's nemesis in *For a Few Dollars More* (1965) and to appear in David Lean's monumental *Dr. Zhivago* (1965). Money led Kinski to accept roles in horror films, and he appeared in such exploitation films as *Circus of Fear* (1967, with Christopher Lee), *Count Dracula* (1970, with Christopher Lee), and *Slaughter Hotel* (1971). During this time he would tell producers, "Don't send me the screenplay, just the money."

Kinski's preference for money over artistic promise would melt somewhat after a move to Paris, where he met director Werner Herzog. Under Herzog's direction he would win international acclaim for his starring performance in *Aguirre: Wrath of God* (1972). He would again answer Herzog's call in 1978 to star in a remake of the silent German horror classic *Nosferatu.* In the film, Kinski delivers an effective, repulsive, ratlike interpretation of Dracula. He would further establish himself in the horror genre with intense performances in *Jack the Ripper* (1976), *Android* (1982), *Venom* (1982, with Oliver Reed), and *Crawlspace* (1986). As Kinski once remarked, "Making movies is better than cleaning toilets."

Replacing Barbara Steele, the femme fatale of the original, is French leading-lady Michelle Mercier (1939–). Mercier made her acting debut at the age of eight in the corps de ballet of the Nice Opera. She later danced in the Ballet Company of the Eiffel Tower. Before *Nella stretta morsa del ragno,* her film credits included *Retour de Manivelle* (1957), *Aimez-vous Brahms?* (1961), and *A Global Affair* (1963, with Bob Hope). She also costarred with Boris Karloff in Mario Bava's atmospheric horror film *Black Sabbath* (1963).

Replacing George Riviére, the leading man of the original, is Italian leading-actor Anthony Franciosa (1928–). Before *Nella stretta morsa del ragno,* he appeared in such acclaimed films as *A Hatful of Rain* (1957, in which he reprised his stage role), and *The Long Hot Summer* (1958), as well as in many other popular films of the late fifties and sixties. He also starred in several television series, the most notable being *The Name of the Game* (1968–1970). In 1982 he would appear in *Tenebrae,* a horror film directed by Dario Argento.

Critique: The only reason I can see to reshoot *La danza macabra* almost scene-for-scene six years later was to film it in color. Alas, color does not elevate *Nella stretta morsa del ragno* over its predecessor. According to *The Overlook Encyclopedia of Film: Horror:*

Ortolani's score is as intrusive as in the original version and the presence of Kinski doesn't compensate for the absence of Steele, but the camerawork is pleasant, and helps make the film one of Italy's last classic gothic movies before gore and sex drastically changed the genre, as in Margheriti's own *Dracula Sangue di Vergine e ... Mori di Sete* (1973).

I concur with that assessment. Kinski, with high forehead, thin mustache, and wild hair, plays a high-strung, almost frenzied Edgar Allan Poe. The opening scene is his best when he paraphrases the last two paragraphs of Poe's "Berenice" as part of a storytelling finale in the tavern. Later in the film, he is depressed and resigned. Mercier is lovely and clearly competent, but she lacks Steele's sepulchral magnetism. Since Kinski's scenes are many fewer than Mercier's, one must conclude in favor of the original cast. At least the film has the smooth cinematography of the original. Although mediocre, it is worth watching once, but, as was the case with the original, it is *not* based on an unpublished story by Poe as the publicity claims. Consequently, it is a mere trifle in the cinema of Edgar Allan Poe.

Murders in the Rue Morgue (1971)
American international Pictures,
United States and Great Britain

Credits: Executive producer—James H. Nicholson and Samuel Z. Arkoff; directed by Gordon Hessler; produced by Louis M. Heyward; associate producer—Clifford Parkes; production supervisor—Roberto Roberts; screenplay by Christopher Wicking and Henry Slesar; cinematography by Salvador Gil; edited by Max Benedict; art direction by Jose Luis Galicia; makeup by Jack Young; sound by Wally Milner.

Running time: 86 minutes.

Cast: Jason Robards, Jr. (Cesar Charron), Herbert Lom (Marot), Christine Kaufmann (Madeleine), Adolfo Celi (Vidocq), Lilli Palmer (Madeleine's mother), Maria Perschy (Genevre), Michael Dunn (Pierre), Jose Calvo (hunchback), Peter Arne (Aubert), Werner Umburg (theater manager), Luis Rivera (actor), Virginia Stach (Lucie), Dean Selmeir (Jacques), Marshall Jones (Orsini).

Story: At the Rue Morgue Theatre in Paris, Madeleine, the theater owner's wife, who also appears in the company's horror plays, is plagued by repeated nightmares that resemble elements of the current play. She dreams she is pursued by an axe-wielding masked man. In the real play, which is Poe's "Murders in the Rue Morgue," her husband, Cesar Charron, is beheaded by an ape.

At a performance of the play, the actor who was to portray Erik the Ape is killed, his face scarred by acid. The killer, dressed in the ape suit during the play, escapes via rooftops and streets. Inspector Vidocq takes command of the case. Soon, Genevre, an employee, is also found dead and disfigured by acid. The people killed are employees of Charron or his coworkers. Evidence indicates that the killer is Marot, a former employee and former coworker with Charron. Marot was thought to have died twelve years ago after Madeleine Charron's mother, an actress in the Rue Morgue company, accidentally threw acid into his face during a performance. He had been in love with Madeleine's mother and was jealous of the fact that she even worked for Charron; he was accused of having killed her.

Believed dead at the time, Marot was actually still alive. With the help of Pierre, a dwarf, Marot returns from the grave using a carnival stunt he learned from Orsini, another of Charron's acting troupe.

Orsini has himself buried alive as part of a carnival show. When his coffin is dug up three days later, Marot rushes out of the crowd and kills the performer with acid.

Seeking the truth about her mother's death, Madeleine goes to her mother's chateau and finds herself in rooms reminiscent of those in her nightmares. On a small stage once used by Madeleine's mother, Marot confronts Madeleine and tells her that it was Charron who killed her mother and then convinced the rest of the acting troupe to testify against him. Charron and Marot fight, and it appears that Charron kills Marot with Madeleine's help. They bury Marot in a mausoleum and return to the theater, believing that the terror is over.

Marot, however, is still not dead. With Pierre's help, a revived Marot lures Charron and Madeleine back to the stage of the chateau. There Marot kills Charron, and Madeleine escapes and returns to the Rue Morgue Theatre.

At the next performance of a horror play at the Rue Morgue Theatre, Vidocq deploys his police around the auditorium to capture Marot. Marot again dons the ape costume and is chased by the police into a street carnival, where he succeeds in killing several of his pursuers.

Marot doubles back to the theater, where Madeleine has been left alone. When Marot attempts to get to Madeleine by swinging from a rope to the stage, she cuts the rope with the axe, and Marot falls to his death.

But later Madeleine is awakened by footsteps on the stairs, her door knob slowly turns, and Marot's voice intones: "The will— the will lives on!"

Production and marketing: *Murders in the Rue Morgue* is the last film in the AIP Poe series. Back at the helm is director Gordon Hessler, who directed *The Oblong Box* and *Cry of the Banshee.* Hessler admitted problems in adapting Poe's "The Murders in the Rue Morgue" to the screen:

The problem was that the Poe story, which is a mystery where the monkey did it, was not the kind of story you could do any more. So, we used *Murders in the Rue Morgue* as a play-within-a-play; the Poe story was being done on the stage, and we developed a mystery that was going on around the Poe play.[206]

The film was shot in Spain on a budget of about $700,000. Then in a predistribution move, AIP reedited it. According to the director: "They took out a whole end sequence and made the film unintelligible! I almost begged them to put back that end sequence, but they never did. Our original finish was a wonderful twist ending, but they took it all out and I was very unhappy."[207]

Heading a cast of strong performers is Jason Robards, Jr. (1920–), whose father was a fine stage and film actor. Considered probably the greatest interpreter of the plays of Eugene O'Neill, Robards received considerable acclaim for his work in such dramas as *The Iceman Cometh* and *Long Day's Journey into Night.* Before accepting the lead role in *Murders in the Rue Morgue,* he had scored with critics in such films as *Tender Is the Night* (1961), *Long Day's Journey Into Night* (1962), *A Thousand Clowns* (1965), *The Hour of the Gun* (1967), *The St. Valentine's Day Massacre* (1967, directed by Roger Corman, with Robards as Al Capone), and *Julius Caesar* (1970). He would go on to enhance his career with performances in such films as *Pat Garrett and Billy the Kid* (1973), *All the President's Men* (1976, for which he won an Academy Award), and *Something Wicked This Way Comes* (1983, based on the novel by Ray Bradbury). Concerning *Murders in the Rue Morgue,* Gordon Hessler remembered that "Jason realized after we started that he had taken the wrong role—he suddenly realized he should have been playing Herbert Lom's role. But he realized that a little bit too late [laughs]!"[208]

Czech actor Herbert Lom (1917–) moved to Great Britain in 1939 and built a solid film career. Among his notable films were *The Young Mr. Pitt* (1941, as Napoleon), *The Seventh Veil* (1946), *Dual Alibi* (1947), *State Secret* (1950), *The Ladykillers* (1955), and *War and Peace* (1956, as Napoleon). Lom

Axe-wielding Herbert Lom prepares an attack on Lilli Palmer in *The Murders in the Rue Morgue* (1971).

had also ventured into the horror/science fiction genre with performances in *The Mysterious Island* (1961, as Captain Nemo), *The Phantom of the Opera* (1962, as the Phantom), and *Dorian Gray* (1970). After *Murders in the Rue Morgue,* he would contribute to such horror entries as *Count Dracula* (1970, with Christopher Lee and Klaus Kinski), *Asylum* (1972, with Peter Cushing), and *And Now the Screaming Starts* (1973, with Peter Cushing). He would also gain fame as the exasperated police chief of Peter Sellers's *Pink Panther* series.

A German leading lady and the former wife of actor Tony Curtis, Christine Kaufmann (1944–) had turned in performances in such varied fare as *The Last Days of Pompeii* (1960), *Town Without Pity* (1961), *Taras Bulba* (1962), *Wild and Wonderful* (1964), and *Tunnel 28* (1964).

Austrian leading actress Lilli Palmer

(1911–1986) came to *Murders in the Rue Morgue* on the strength of a fine stage and film career, her most notable film performances being in *Thunder Rock* (1942), *The Rake's Progress* (1945), *My Girl Tisa* (1947), *The Pleasure of His Company* (1961), and *Oedipus the King* (1967). Later she would add a few more horror films to her credits, namely, *Night Hair Child* (1971) and *The Boys from Brazil* (1978). According to Gordon Hessler, AIP's reediting of *Murders in the Rue Morgue* left most of Lilli Palmer's work on the cutting room floor: "Lilli Palmer had a marvelous role in the picture—she was the catalyst for the film to shift into a new gear, and her role made the whole story make sense—but it was almost all cut out! ... They cut it down so she was almost an extra. I don't know what she must have thought when she saw the film."[209]

For their Poe series swan song, AIP

produced posters and a pressbook featuring some lurid imagery. Prominent on the one-sheet poster and insert posters is the image of a gorilla's arm hovering over the body of a young woman, her black-stockinged legs and garters prominently displayed. No wonder the pressbook cover suggests that "Murder Means Money on the Rue Morgue." One ad is incredibly strange. The art is that of Rackham—of an eight-legged creature with beastlike claws and a head, half skull and half monster. Above this abomination appear the following lines from Poe:

> ... and much of madness
> and more of sin ...
> and horror the soul
> of the plot.
> —Edgar Allan Poe, 1839

Those lines are from Poe's poem "The Conqueror Worm," first published seperately in 1843 in *Graham's Magazine* and earlier inserted in the short story "Ligeia," published in 1838. So either way, the date of 1839 attached to the quoted lines in the ad is wrong.

Other ads proclaimed:

> "The Rue Morgue is a one-way street that winds and twists its way into the world of the once human!"
> "A sigh of Passion! A scream of Terror! And the scratch of claws on the cobblestones. These are the sounds of Murder in the Rue Morgue!"
> "Love and Murder are the two consuming passions of the Rue Morgue!"
> "Rue Morgue ... where sighs of passion end in screams of terror!"
> "A sigh ... a gasp ... a scream! Night has fallen on the Rue Morgue."

As usual, the exploitation angles included a Poe pitch:

> As with all of Edgar Allan Poe subjects, a tie-up with your local book store is a natural. "Murders in the Rue Morgue" is one of Poe's most famous classics and new generations of kids have yet to be introduced to its thrills. Arrange for window displays with paperbacks of the novel and have local library set up bulletin board and counter displays featuring the works of Poe.

Interesting, the pressbook cover reports that the film is "based on the novel by Edgar Allan Poe." Obviously, "the Murders in the Rue Morgue" was a short story, not a novel. But, as often was the case throughout the cinema's long flirtation with Poe, I'm sure no one cared.

Critique: When *Murders in the Rue Morgue* opened in New York City, it shared a double bill with *The Return of Count Yorga.* The *New York Times* noted, "This is the third go at this Poe we know of ... [and] it's the most interesting, at least artistically.... The entire film is a gorgeous eyeful in excellent color, with lavish period costumes and some perfectly beautiful dream montages."[210]

The *Times* does criticize the ending, which it calls "sound but fairly predictable.... The picture reaches into 'Phantom of the Opera' pasture for an old hat showdown."[211] Still the review concludes that "even minus Poe and our favorite ape next to Kong, see it."[212]

According to Rose London, this 1971 version, "While arguably the best of the versions ... is still as far from the eerie suggestibility and subtlety of Poe as Hollywood Boulevard is from the Boul' Mich."[213]

Ed Naha notes the film's debt to *The Phantom of the Opera* and suggests, "This Poe abortion offers a tale of mild, but colorful content.... There is an unmasking scene and everything in between bursts of nightmarish action."[214]

Michael Weldon notes the film's debt to *The Phantom of the Opera* and pronounces it "A totally confused movie with flashbacks and dream sequences galore."[215]

Leonard Maltin awards *Murders in the Rue Morgue* only 1 1/2 stars but doesn't offer a rationale for the low rating except to call the film "sensationalistic." *The Video Hound's Golden Movie Retriever 1996* is more generous, throwing the film 2 1/2 bones.

The Overlook Film Encyclopedia: Horror offers a positive, thoughtful critique:

Boundaries between fantasy and reality are totally blurred, suggesting they cannot be distinguished since each is shaped under the determining pressures of the other. Perhaps the film's greatest achievement is that it manages to convey this fundamental insight without falling into the paranoid delirium of *Scream and Scream Again* [another Hessler/Wicking film]. This allows the film's final sequences to be lifted to the level of surrealistic poetry.

Unable to understand Leonard Maltin's 1 1/2 star rating, I consider Hessler's *Murders in the Rue Morgue* one of the best horror films of the 1970s. While agreeing with the positive points made in the above reviews, I want to add some additional insights of my own.

Although the film was shot in Spain, the Parisian atmosphere is convincing. As the credits roll, we see a series of colorful Lautrec-like paintings used to advertise the Rue Morgue Theatre. In addition, the street carnivals are bright and evocative of turn-of-the-century Paris.

One of the most interesting aspects of the film is the way Hessler pays homage to the previous two versions of *The Murders in the Rue Morgue*. In the opening scenes, the actors are putting on a play very reminiscent of the 1932 version. Robards is performing an experiment on a woman, and the ape, which resembles the humanoid in *Trog* (1970), attacks him. This echoes the scene in the 1932 version in which Bela Lugosi is beginning an experiment on Sidney Fox when the ape intervenes. As in the 1932 and 1954 versions, Hessler gives us scenes of the phantom killer escaping over the rooftops. Incidentally, in both the 1932 and 1971 versions, the ape is named Erik.

A positive aspect of the 1954 *Phantom of the Rue Morgue* is the gaiety of Paris street carnivals that give the film a period atmosphere. Hessler successfully uses street carnivals to the same end. During the murder of Genevre, the camera cuts from the screaming, acid-scarred woman to a colorful performance of the can-can and back

again, juxtaposing entertainment and death much as Poe does in "The Cask of Amontillado."

Hessler, as Corman before him, adds other touches to the film reminiscent of Poe's writings. For example, Hessler tips his hat to Poe's recurrent theme of premature burial three times in the film: first, when Marot rises from the grave; second, when Orsini is buried alive for three days; and third, when Marot survives the mausoleum. In addition, Lom's "The will—the will lives on!" echoes Poe's "Ligeia," and a scene involving mesmerism may also have been inspired by Poe.

Hessler learned not only from Corman, however. He also learned from Alfred Hitchcock. As a Hitchcock employee, Hessler worked on the *Alfred Hitchcock Presents* television show, climbing the ladder from story reader to associate producer. He also directed a handful of episodes. Although Hessler denies being a Hitchcock protégé, he does say that he watched Hitchcock's films with more care than he would watch those of most directors. Anyway, Hessler pays homage to Hitchcock in the scene in which Robards and Kaufmann "murder" Herbert Lom. Although the murder is not nearly as gruesome and detailed, it appears inspired by similar scenes in which Paul Newman and Julie Andrews murder Wolfgang Kieling in Hitchcock's *Torn Curtain* (1966).

The greatest strength of the film is its exploration of dream and reality. In fact, *Murders in the Rue Morgue* thematically most resembles the last lines of Poe's poem "A Dream within a Dream":

All that we see or seem
Is but a dream within a dream.

Madeleine's Freudian nightmares symbolize a reality she is unable to understand; so what is more real, what she sees or what she dreams? Characters in the film place emphasis on the words "it seems." In fact, much in the film is not what it seems. The opening scenes depicting the ape's beheading of

Charron are quickly revealed to be part of a play. Marot seems to be dead, but he is not. Charron seems to be the protagonist, but he is not. The stylish dream sequences are in-deed nightmarish—adeptly mixing illusion and reality—a credit to both Hessler and cinematographer Salvador Gil.

The Sabbat of the Black Cat (1971)
Ralph Lawrence Marsden, Australia

Credits: Directed and produced by Ralph Lawrence Marsden; screenplay by Ralph Lawrence Marsden, based on "The Black Cat" by Edgar Allan Poe.

Running time: 80 minutes.

Cast: Ralph Lawrence Marsden, Barbara Brighton, Tracey Tombs, David Bingham, Jim Fitch, Babylkon Dance Troupe.

Story: A young man accidentally stumbles upon a witches' sabbat and is persecuted by a black cat.

Production and marketing: Ralph Lawrence Marsden began as a director of television commercials and later worked for Australian television before emigrating to Great Britain. His *Sabbat of the Black Cat* is apparently important as the first attempt at indigenous Australian gothic cinema. Mars-den created the 16 mm *Sabbat* on a part-time basis with about 7,000 Australian dollars donated by the Experimental Film and Tele-vision Fund. Marsden's Melbourne-based production used as its location an abandoned gold-mining settlement in Victoria. The film received a brief public run at the Mel-bourne Coop Cinema in 1973.

Critique: I have not seen *The Sabbat of the Black Cat*. The information I present here is gleaned from an entry in *The Overlook Film Encyclopedia: Horror*, which itself does not appear to be based on a viewing. It would appear that the film is only loosely based on Poe's story. But loose adaptations are the rule, not the exception, in the cinema of Edgar Allan Poe.

La mansion de locura (1972); aka *Dr. Tarr's Torture Dungeon; House of Madness; The Mansion of Madness; The System of Dr. Tarr and Professor Fether*
Producciones Prisma, Mexico

Credits: Directed by Juan Lopez Moc-tezuma; screenplay by Juan Lopez Moc-tezuma and Carlos Illescas, based on "The System of Dr. Tarr and Professor Fether" by Edgar Allan Poe; cinematography by Rafael Corkidi; music by Nacho Mendez; edited by Federico Laderos.

Running time: 88 minutes.

Cast: Claudio Brook (Dr. Maillard), Arturo Hansel (Gaston LeBlanc), Ellen Sherman (Eugenie), Martin Lasalle (Cuvier), David Silva, Robert Dumont.

Story: The setting is eighteenth-century France. Journalist Gaston LeBlanc travels by coach with his former schoolmate, Cuvier, and Cuvier's niece, Julia, to Dr. Maillard's mental sanatorium. Maillard is celebrated for his "soothing system," an inventive treatment of mental illness, and Gaston wants to write an article on the subject because his father died in a mental asylum. As the coach approaches the sanatorium grounds, armed guards block the path.

Upon gaining clearance, the travelers ride through a forest toward the sanatorium itself. Along the way, they see strange individuals dancing grotesquely and a man in a robe shouting the various names of Satan. Since Cuvier is frightened of madmen, he and his niece leave Gaston at the sanatorium entrance and decide to leave. Gaston then enters alone.

Unknown to Gaston, Cuvier and his niece are attached in the forest by madmen. Meanwhile, Gaston meets Dr. Maillard, who talks of the "soothing system" and of the kingdom in which he watches over his "children." He explains to Gaston that the system was devised by the learned Dr. Tarr and advanced by the celebrated Professor Fether. The system consists of allowing the inmates great freedom to act out their mad fantasies. "We do our best to comply with every humanitarian argument," Maillard says. Not lost on Gaston, however, is Maillard's tendency to babble poetic absurdities and to laugh inappropriately.

Maillard introduces Gaston to Mr. Chicken, a patient who eats raw corn and walks and clucks like a fowl. Maillard then leads Gaston to the dungeons, where a chained figure claiming to be Dante exhorts them to "Abandon all hope, ye who enter here." Gaston objects that what he sees in the dungeons is inhumane, but Maillard explains that such restraints are necessary under certain circumstances.

Leaving the dungeons, Maillard and Gaston come upon a lovely young woman playing a harp. The woman's name is Eugenie, and she claims that it is indecent to rest when one can dance. She dances a dance that originated in "a remote region of Java." Later Gaston drinks drugged wine and is visited by Eugenie, who instructs him to meet her in the garden that night. Gaston is roused from his drugged state by a scream. He leaves his room in time to see Eugenie being restrained by some of Maillard's madmen. Maillard says that she is to be prepared for the ceremony. He explains to Gaston that when she is enraged she is like a wild boar. Having seen enough, Gaston accuses Maillard of being an impostor. Maillard laughs hysterically and orders his madmen to lead Gaston back to his room. Later Gaston escapes, overcomes several guards, and rescues Eugenie from the sanatorium's winery, where an inmate has her covered with grapes. Eugenie explains that her father was the head of the sanatorium before Maillard, who escaped from Devil's Island and incited the inmates to riot. Eugenie has survived by pretending to be mad. Her father and all the other sane individuals associated with the sanatorium are being held prisoner in the dungeons.

In the forest, Gaston and Eugenie discover Cuvier, who has escaped from his captors. Through a joint effort, Gaston, Cuvier, and Eugenie humorously overcome several of Maillard's guards in the forest. Unfortunately, Maillard and more of his guards intercept them and return them to the sanatorium. Cuvier is placed in the dungeons, and Gaston and Eugenie are forced to attend a "Roman orgy from Hell" during which one female patient rides by as Lady Godiva. Maillard, who wants to apply his "soothing system" to the entire world, explains that he is a new religious leader and eventually his "children" will become missionaries of his new religion. A heap of celery is then carried into the large "dining hall." Under it is Eugenie's father, who is taunted and then removed. The inmates

Claudio Brook as the madman who takes over an asylum in *La mansion de locura* (1972, aka *Dr. Tarr's Torture Dungeon*).

then initiate a musical interlude of completely discordant noises.

Maillard and the inmates decide that Gaston and Eugenie must go to the dungeon as punishment for their criminal rebellion. A cry then goes up to "Burn them! Fire purifies everything."

Meanwhile, the prisoners in the dungeons overcome a guard and escape. Above, "chicken people" dance before Gaston to the stimulus of tribal music. A shot rings out and a chicken man falls. The rebellion of those formerly confined to the dungeons is underway. Gaston and Maillard fight. Eugenie fires a pistol, ending Maillard's life. The asylum is back in the hands of the sane.

Production and marketing: The screenplay by Moctezuma and Illescas draws upon key elements of Poe's "The System of Dr. Tarr and Professor Fether." Poe's story begins with two riders arriving on horseback at the grounds of Dr. Maillard's mental sanatorium. In the film, they arrive by coach with the friend's niece. As in Poe's story, the friend refuses to go inside because of his "feelings on the subject of lunacy." When Poe's narrator enters, he meets a young woman whom he assumes to be mad, and later he encounters a chicken man, all of whom are in the Mexican screenplay.

Poe's Dr. Maillard is "a portly, fine-looking gentleman of the old school, with a polished manner, and a certain air of gravity, dignity, and authority which was very impressive." Claudio Brook's Dr. Maillard is tall and handsome. Although he carries himself with authority, he sometimes babbles poetic absurdities and laughs inappropriately. No love interest develops in Poe's story, and the narrator's friend plays no role in the story after the opening paragraphs.

In both story and film, Dr. Maillard has

decided to dispense with the "soothing system" and to return to the old ways. In both story and film, the narrator is treated to a lavish banquet which includes a discordant concert. Both story and film include the insane locking the sane in underground cells, and in both versions, the sane eventually escape and restore order. People are tarred and feathered in the story, but not in the film. On the whole, the Mexican screenplay is a faithful adaptation of Poe's satire.

Director Juan Lopez Moctezuma began as a theater and television director and as a radio presenter of jazz programs. As a lover of comic strips and surrealism of the type evident in Peter Weiss's *Marat-Sade* (1966), he brings those influences into his films. Using Claudio Brook, one of director Luis Bunuel's favorite actors, is Moctezuma's tip of the hat to that Mexican surrealist filmmaker. In 1971, Moctezuma produced Jodorowsky's surrealistic fantasy masterpiece *El Topo.* In 1974, Moctezuma would direct his wife Christina Ferrare in *Mary, Mary, Bloody Mary,* a disappointing tale about a bisexual vampire pursued by her vengeful father, played by John Carradine. Moctezuma's next foray into the fearful would be *Alucarda* (1975), a routine exploitation film of religious obsession and lesbianism, with Claudio Brook in a triple role as doctor, warlock, and hunchback. Unfortunately, none of his later films would live up to the promise shown in *La mansion de las locura.*

Critique: *Dr. Tarr's Torture Dungeon* received limited release in the United States. Although usually ignored in books covering the horror film, it garnered praise in *The Overlook Film Encyclopedia: Horror*:

> Moctezuma handles the shifts between gothic horror—the mysterious apparitions in the castle's grounds—and the humorously sinister and erotic chaos in the asylum with considerable skill…. The cinematography effectively situates the picture in a no man's land between the comic and the uncanny.

In direct contrast, *Video Hound's Golden Movie Retriever 1996,* without explanation, gives the film its lowest rating (Woof!).

I must agree with the *Encyclopedia.* First of all, the film is one of the finest Edgar Allan Poe adaptations, expertly transferring to the screen the horror and satire of Poe's story. The cinematography is atmospheric. Fog crawls ominously through slants of light, giving the film a dreamlike (or nightmarelike) quality. The sound effects are unnerving; inmates scurry about, creating the sound of rats or bats on the move. Humorous xylophone and flute music punctuates Cuvier's hopping escape attempt. In effective contrast, during Gaston's phantasmagoric drug-induced nightmare, the camera creeps along the corridors of the sanatorium, stopping briefly at times to peep into the cells of the inmates. All the while the soundtrack recites disturbing stanzas from Part II of Coleridge's "The Rime of the Ancient Mariner":

> The very deep did rot: O Christ!
> That ever this should be!
> Yea, slimy things did crawl with legs
> Upon the slimy sea.
>
> And, about, in reel and rout
> The death-fires danced at night;
> The water, like a witch's oils,
> Burnt green, and blue and white.
>
> And some in dreams assured were
> Of the Spirit that plagued us so;
> Nine fathoms deep he had followed us
> From the land of mist and snow.
>
> Ah! Well a-day! What evil looks
> Had I from old and young!
> Instead of the cross, the Albatross
> About my neck was hung.

The lines reinforce in Gaston the knowledge that Christ has here been displaced by some other spirit. In this madhouse, slimy things indeed creep and crawl, not the least among them being Maillard. It is he who must carry the albatross around his neck in place of a cross. It is he who must answer for his sins. Moctezuma infuses this film with religious themes and motifs that he would develop with less success in *Alucarda.*

The cast is exemplary. As the journalist Gaston, Hansel is appropriately curious, then credulous, then outraged. Brook is very impressive as Dr. Maillard. He delivers his lines emulatory of the voice and delivery of Criswell, who introduces *Plan Nine from Outer Space* and *Night of the Ghouls*, films directed by Ed Wood, Jr. I doubt that anyone familiar with Criswell's delivery could distinguish it from that of Brook in *La mansion de la locura*. The big difference of course, is that Brook could act and Criswell could not. When her character is struggling to act mentally ill to insure her own survival, Ellen Sherman is intelligent, sexy, and vulnerable. After her escape and during the final rebellion, she is strong and vengeful. What a delightful performance! Finally, Martin Lasalle is appropriately humorous as the rather cowardly and ineffectual Cuvier, who manages to rise to the occasion when the situation demands.

Like Poe's story, this film can accommodate a variety of interpretations. Obviously, the main theme is that of the inmates taking over the asylum. "Do as thou wilt!" is the informing sentiment Dr. Maillard proposes as the foundation of his new religion. As a Southerner of his time, Poe may have been warning against abolition. Viewing the film from the perspective of an American very familiar with the days of 1972, I prefer to interpret the film as a warning against the "Do as thou wilt!" attitude of the late sixties and early seventies. During those years, acting on impulse was elevated to a sacrament, and officials bowed to the pressures of an undisciplined rabble demanding to "do its own thing." When institutions adopted their own version of the "soothing method," they invited the kind of chaos conjured artistically by Moctezuma in *La mansion de la locura*.

Il tuo vizio è una stanza chiusa e solo io ne lo la chiave (1973); aka *Your Vice Is a Closed Room and Only I Have the Key*; *Excite Me*

Lea Film, Italy

Credits: Directed by Sergio Martino; produced by Luciano Martino; screenplay by Ernesto Gastaldi, Adriano Bolzone, and Sauro Scavolini, based on "The Black Cat" by Edgar Allan Poe; cinematography by Giancarlo Ferrando.

Cast: Edwige Fenech, Anita Strindberg, Luigi Pistilli, Ivan Rassimov, Franco Nebbia, Riccardo Salvino, Angela la Vorgna, Enrica Bonaccorti.

Story: In an old mansion on the Cornish coast, a high-strung couple engages in marital warfare. Caught in the crossfire, several servants and mistresses become murder victims. The enraged wife uses a pair of scissors to gouge out the eye of her husband's beloved cat. She also discovers that he plans to murder and bury her, at which point she kills him first and places the cadaver in the place initially planned for her. Later, the crying of a cat behind the cellar wall reveals the whereabouts of the corpse and leads to her undoing.

Production and marketing: Director Sergio Martino, apparently impressed by countryman Dario Argento's *L' uccello dalle piume di cristallo* (1970, aka *The Bird with the Crystal Plummage*) would turn from soft core

Edgar Allan Poe to female murder and mutilation with his *I corpi presentano tracce di violenza carnale* (1973, aka *Torso,* aka *The Bodies Bear Traces of Carnal Violence*), somewhat anticipating the success of *The Texas Chainsaw Massacre* (1974) and the slasher cinema in general.

Critique: According to *The Overlook Film Encyclopedia: Horror,*

> Fenech, who had worked with Martino before, tries to give some credibility to the maniacal wife but the inane script, with its crude introduction of a bisexual hippy (Strinderg) to underline the protagonists' degeneracy as she beds both partners, as well as some facetious references to the women's movement, makes this a crassly exploitative effort. The sledgehammer style of direction, with repetitive shots of the cat and the main characters relentlessly emoting in closeup, reduces the proceedings to a tiresome domestic drama larded with Grand Guignol effects.

I have not seen this film. Apart from my desire to be an Edgar Allan Poe completist, I am not sure, based on the above description, that I want to.

The Tell-Tale Heart (1973)
American Film Institute, U.S.A.

Credits: Directed and produced by Steve Carver; music by Elmer Bernstein; cinematography by Steve Carver and Irv Goodnoff; makeup by Bob Stein and Doug Kelly.

Running time: 26 minutes.

Cast: Alex Cord (young man/narrator), Sam Jaffe (old man), Ed Binns (officer #1), Dennis Cross (officer #2), Dan Desmond (officer #3).

Story: A young man shares a house with an old man. The two are reclusive. Although the old man has done him no harm, the young man decides to murder him because of his "vulture eye." The young man at first had turned from the vulture eye in shame, and later the shame turned to loathing. In the days before the murder, the young man continues to smile fondly at the old man, all the while planning to kill him.

At midnight, the young man mounts the stairs to the old man's room, stabs the old man to death, dismembers the body, and conceals the remains beneath the floor boards. When three officers investigate the report of a scream, the young man invites them in and explains that the scream was the result of his own nightmare. The young man then confidently places his chair over the very spot where he concealed the body and continues a conversation with the officers. At length, however, his head begins to ache, and he fancies a ringing in his ears. Wishing the officers gone, he becomes agitated. Then he hears the beating of the old man's heart, like a watch wrapped in cotton. "Villains!" he shrieks, "Dissemble no more! I admit the deed!—Tear up the planks! Here, here!—It is the beating of his hideous heart!"

Production and marketing: *The Tall-Tale Heart* is a short subject made by the American Film Institute Center for Advanced Film Studies. Producer, director, and cinematographer Steve Carver, apparently taking his inspiration from Daniel Hoffman's *Poe Poe Poe Poe Poe Poe Poe* (1972), cleverly combines narration from Poe's "The Black Cat" and "The Tell-Tale Heart" to tell his story. Taking his cue from Hoffman, Carver has his narrator say that he first recoiled in shame from the old man's vulture eye, only later to come to loathe it. Hoffman writes:

> The Evil Eye is a belief as old and as dire as any in man's superstitious memory, and it usually signifies the attribution to another of a power wished for by the self. In this particular case there are other vibrations emanating from the vulture-like eye of the

benign old man. Insofar as we have warrant —which I think we do—to take him as a father-figure, his Eye becomes the all-seeing surveillance of the child by the father, even by The Father. This surveillance is of course the origin of the child's conscience, the inculcation into his soul of the paternal principles of right and wrong. As such, the old man's eye becomes a ray to be feared. For if the boy deviates ever so little from the strict paths of rectitude, *it will find him out.*[216]

It is easy to see why loathing follows. Carver borrows lines directly from Poe's "The Black Cat" in giving the narrator a "rational" explanation of the crime. Preparing the murder, the narrator relates that perversity plays a role in his decision to kill the old man. The narrator quotes from "The Black Cat": "Yet I am not more sure that my soul lives, than I am that perverseness is one of the primitive impulses of the human heart— one of the indivisible primary faculties, or sentiments, which give direction to the character of Man." Indeed, the narrator concludes that he wants "to do wrong for the wrong's sake only." Of course, in "The Black Cat," Poe's narrator attributes the cutting out of his pet black cat's eye to perversity, and in the film, the narrator attributes the murder of the old man to the same impulse. Interestingly, Carver has his film narrator kill the old man with a knife, while Poe's narrator resorts to suffocation. Why the change? Perhaps to convey the fury of the narrator in "The Black Cat" as he dispatches his wife with a hatchet, or possibly to link more closely the murder of the old man with a blade's removal of the black cat's eye.

After the old man is dead, Carver returns to "The Black Cat," having the narrator ponder various ways of disposing of the body. Then Carver returns to "The Tell-Tale Heart" for a description of the dismembering of the corpse and its concealment beneath the floor boards. The deed done and hidden, the narrator expresses his relief with

lines from "the Black Cat": "Once again I breathed as a freeman…. I looked upon my future felicity as secured." Of course, the murderer's felicity is short-lived, as both Poe's "The Tell-Tale Heart" and "The Black Cat" make clear.

For the part of the young man/narrator, Carver secured the talents of Italian-American leading man Alex Cord (1931–). Cord had scored in *Synanon* (1965), a film about the famous (and later infamous) center for drug addiction treatment. He also appeared in the genre film *The Dead Are Alive* 1972. Cord is probably best known for his television work in *Castle and Company* (1962) and *Airwolf* (1984–1986).

Performing as the old man is Sam Jaffe (1891–1984), an American character actor of eccentric appearance who gained critical attention in *The Scarlet Empress* (1934), *Lost Horizon* (1937, as the high Lama), *Gunga Din* (1939), *The Asphalt Jungle* (1950, for which he received an Academy Award nomination), and *Ben Hur* (1959). He also appeared in the science-fiction classic *The Day the Earth Stood Still* (1951) and the made-for-television *Night Gallery* (1969), and he costarred in *The Dunwich Horror* (1970, based on a story by H. P. Lovecraft). He is probably best known for his role as Dr. Zorba in the television series *Ben Casey* (1960–1964).

Critique: Carver's decision to mesh Poe's "The Tell-Tale Heart" and "The Black Cat" into a 26-minute short subject proves successful. Cord's narration is from Poe sources. Jaffe has little to do as the old man, but what he does is effective as his peculiar appearance catches the eye. Cord does a fine job as the young man/narrator, especially in his heart-wrenching (no pun intended) scene in which he falls to the floor and painfully utters the last lines of Poe's short story.

The Spectre of Edgar Allan Poe (1974)
Cintel Productions, U.S.A.

Credits: Directed and produced by Mohy Quandour; screenplay by Mohy Quandour, based on an original story and treatment by Kenneth Hartford and Denton Foxx; cinematography by Robert Birchal; music by Allen D. Allen.

Running time: 86 minutes.

Cast: Robert Walker, Jr. (Edgar Allan Poe), Cesar Romero (Dr. Grimaldi), Tom Drake (Dr. Forrest), Carol Ohmart (Lisa), Mary Grover (Lenore), Mario Milano (night nurse), Dennis Fimple (Farron), Paul Bryar (Mr. White), Frank Packard (Jonah), Marsha Mae Jones (Sarah).

Story: Poe's friend Dr. Forrest narrates: "To some people, Edgar Allan Poe was a profound man of letters. To others he was the incarnation of evil itself. Yet others wondered helplessly why his morbid tales had to be written…. There are always many explanations of his work and his actions, but all conflicting, all confusing." Dr. Forrest proposes to explain why Poe wrote the stories and poems he did, and the main narrative begins.

Poe is warned by the editor of the *Southern Literary Messenger* to temper his critical reviews. When he refuses, his fiancée Lenore is concerned. She suggests he concentrate on writing poems and stories. Poe says he would like to, but he must earn his keep.

Lenore and Poe romp happily in a blooming field until Lenore becomes ill as though overcome by the fragrance of the flowers. She is pronounced dead, but at the funeral Poe refuses to believe she is *really* dead. Leaping into the grave, he opens the coffin and rescues Lenore, who is now insane, her hair turned white from the horrors of premature burial.

Poe and his friend Dr. Forrest take Lenore to an asylum run by Dr. Grimaldi. While there, Poe asks to remain for a few nights in order to study Jonah, one of the asylum's violent madmen, in preparation for

a story he plans to write. The agitated Jonah insists that he is not insane, and Dr. Forrest confides to Poe that he has seen the man before somewhere. That night, his suspicions aroused, Poe finishes off a bottle of whiskey and investigates the dark corridors of the asylum. Suddenly someone knocks him unconscious.

Grimaldi and his assistant Joseph are conducting experiments on patients in order to find a cure for Grimaldi's insane wife, Lisa, who usually appears quite sane, but regularly experiences fits of murderous madness.

Meanwhile, Poe regains consciousness only to find himself chained to a raft of wood in the cellar as jets fill the area with water. Complicating matters is the presence of many snakes that swim about as the waters rise. When Poe cries out for help, Grimaldi rushes in, chloroforms him, and returns him to his room.

Later Grimaldi explains Poe's stories about snake-infested water as the hallucinations of a chronic alcoholic. Forrest believes Poe's story but takes Poe away in order to allay Grimaldi's suspicions. That night, as a storm brews, Dr. Forrest and Poe return to the asylum in search of the truth. Jonah, who actually is Lisa's brother, escapes from his cell as Grimaldi prepares to operate on Lenore. After killing a servant, Jonah attacks Poe and Dr. Forrest in the asylum's torture dungeon. Grimaldi fights off Jonah, but Lisa hits him with an axe. Lisa then knocks Jonah into the water with her axe, and the snakes finish him off.

Dr. Forrest shoots Lisa, but she manages to escape. Meanwhile, Grimaldi recovers enough to aid in Poe's rescue. The wounded Lisa murders Joseph and enters the operating room, where Lenore lies unconscious. Poe arrives just in time to witness Lisa repeatedly chopping Lenore with the axe.

As a result of Lenore's death, Poe be-

Robert Walker, Jr., as Edgar Allan Poe and Mary Grover as his lost Lenore in *The Spectre of Edgar Allan Poe* (1974).

comes obsessed with death, decay, and madness.

Production and marketing: *The Spectre of Edgar Allan Poe* is not the first film to offer a fictional explanation of Poe's inspiration or to use Poe as a character in a fictional scenario. The film proposes a fictional explanation for Poe's interest in "the lost Lenore," as well as suggesting the origin of his interest in madness, premature burial, and horror. Although the narrator offers a few dates, the whole tale is obviously fiction. Still, when Poe cradles his fallen Lenore at the beginning of the film, the soundtrack treats us to lines from Poe's "Alone":

From childhood's hour I have not been
As others were—I have not seen
As others saw—I could not bring
My passions from a common spring—
From the same source I have not taken

My sorrow—I could not awaken
My heart to joy at the same tone—
And all I loved—I loved alone.

At the film's conclusion, as Poe sits with his child-bride Virginia, the soundtrack offers us a stanza from "The Raven"—

Ah, distinctly I remember it was in the
	bleak December;
And each separate dying ember wrought its
	ghost upon the floor.
Eagerly I wished the morrow;—vainly I had
	sought to borrow
From my books surcease of sorrow—sorrow
	for the lost Lenore—
For the rare and radiant maiden whom the
	angels name Lenore—
		Nameless *here* for evermore.

The film's cast contains names familiar to those knowledgeable about the horror genre. Robert Walker, Jr. (1941–), came to *The Spectre of Edgar Allan Poe* having appeared in two genre films: *The Ceremony* (1964, with Elizabeth Taylor) and *The Road to Salina* (1970, with Rita Hayworth). He had also appeared with John Wayne in *The War Wagon* (1967) and with Peter Fonda, Dennis Hopper, and Jack Nicholson in *Easy Rider* (1969). Although he would make more films, he would never gain the level of distinction earned by his father, Robert Walker.

Cesar Romero (1907–1994), best known as a handsome Latin-American leading man, appeared in the genre films *Lost Continent* (1951) and *Latitude Zero* (1970). Tom Drake (1918–1982) had appeared with Lon Chaney, Jr., and John Carradine in *House of the Black Death* (1967). With more pride, I'm sure, he also appeared in such films as *Meet Me in St. Louis* (1944, with Judy Garland), *The Green Years* (1946), and *The Sandpiper* (1965, with Richard Burton and Elizabeth Taylor). Carol Ohmart (1928–) had costarred with Vincent Price in the delightfully chilling *House on Haunted Hill* (1959) and with Lon Chaney, Jr., in the also delightfully chilling *Spider Baby* (1964).

The pressbook for *The Spectre of Edgar Allan Poe* featured an announcement that "Photographs of Edgar Allan Poe were used by the producers ... to create the makeup for Robert Walker, Jr. His resemblance to the real Poe was designed to give the film a startlingly realistic feeling." Another ad suggested that theater owners exploit the reputation of "The Master Story-Teller":

> Edgar Allan Poe has been acknowledged to be the master teller of horror-suspense stories. Among his most famous writings were "The Tell-Tale Heart," "The Fall of the House of Usher," "The Raven," "The Murders in the Rue Morgue," "The Gold Bug," and "The Pit and the Pendulum." Now the new film "The Spectre of Edgar Allan Poe" takes the audience into Poe's own bizarre world that fed his strange imagination.

One element of the showmanship campaign suggested the following to theater owners:

> You can build and develop promotions and contests geared to the famous Edgar Allan Poe stories. Which is your town's favorite Poe story? Favorite Poe film? How many Poe titles can you list? Find a double for Edgar Allan Poe. (Many young men today have the Poe mustache). Offer possible two-for-one admissions to anyone appearing at the theater with a copy of a Poe book. Precede your engagement of "Spectre of Edgar Allan Poe" with a Festival of Poe film classics.

Another campaign item suggested the "Basic Sell"—

> The film will have its major appeal to the horror-suspense audience and the Edgar Allan Poe fans. The key art and the key approach in the radio-TV spots is [*sic*] based on the atmosphere of terror and madness. The campaign begins with references to famous Poe titles. "What drove him down into the bizarre world of madness and murder?" Then, the payoff is the scene in which Poe is shackled to a table in a pit.

The posters for the film featured Robert Walker, Jr., tied to a wooden raft in a pit filling with water as snakes threaten and a woman stands above with an axe. The wording reads: "He wrote MURDERS IN THE RUE MORGUE ... THE FALL OF THE HOUSE OF USHER ... THE RAVEN ... THE PIT AND THE PENDULUM. What drove him down into the bizarre world of madness and murder?"

Critique: *The Spectre of Edgar Allan Poe* depicts little of Poe's actual life, but rather uses him as a fictional character to spin out a relatively mild horror film. According to *The Overlook Film Encyclopedia: Horror,*

> *The Spectre of Edgar Allan Poe* bears little relation to the facts of his life; unfortunately, however, it's not especially interesting as a fantasy either, except for the scenes in a flooded cellar infested with snakes. Production values are relatively high, but direction, script and acting (especially that of woefully miscast Romero) are dull. Indeed so unhorrific was the film that it was awarded a PG rating in the United States.

The Spectre of Edgar Allan Poe actually

is somewhat reminiscent of *The Black Sleep* (1956), a low-budget yarn starring Basil Rathbone as a ruthless brain surgeon who experiments on patients to find a cure for his comatose wife. *The Black Sleep,* however, featured a fine cast and managed some gothic suspense. An actor of Rathbone's demeanor would have proven a better choice to play Dr. Grimaldi than was Romero. Walker bears a passable resemblance to Poe, but he brings little else to the role. Carol Ohmart and Tom Drake provide the best acting performances, though that is not a strong recommendation in this case. Ohmart does

provide some chills as the emotionless axe murderess.

Allen's musical score is unintrusive, except for a rather embarrassing song about the lost Lenore, and Birchall's cinematography is unremarkable. The film's failure must finally rest with Mohy Quandour, who produced, directed, and scripted the film. Such one-man efforts are difficult and require a breadth of talent that Quandour apparently lacked. Therefore *The Spectre of Edgar Allan Poe* ranks as one of the more disappointing entries in the Poe cinema.

Il gatto nero (1981); aka *The Black Cat*
Selenia Cinematografica, Italy

Credits: Directed by Lucio Fulci; produced by Giulio Sbarigia; screenplay by Lucio Fulci and Biagio Proetti, based on "The Black Cat" by Edgar Allan Poe; music by Pino Donaggio; special effects by Paolo Ricci.

Cast: Mimsy Farmer (Jill Travis), Patrick Magee (Mr. Miles), David Warbeck (Inspector Galli), Dagmar Lassander, Daniela Doro, Al Cliver, Bruno Corazzari, Geoffrey Copleston.

Story: In an English village, a black cat hypnotizes a man and guides him to commit suicide. The cat then returns to its home, the mansion of Mr. Miles, an eccentric psychic who frequents graveyards to tape messages from the dead. The cat attacks Miles, who appears to fear it.

Jill Travis, an American photographer, arrives in the village to take cemetery photos. When the black cat arranges the deaths of two young lovers in an unventilated boathouse, Inspector Galli is called in from Scotland Yard to investigate their disappearance.

As a result of public talk and gossip, Jill

wants to meet the eccentric Miles. As a pretext for her visit, she returns to him a microphone he left in the cemetery. She asks him if he is a medium who can truly communicate with the dead. "Death is not the end of everything, " he replies, "just the beginning, a new journey." Miles expresses his interest in understanding the secrets of death and the afterlife, and Jill expresses her fear that he will not know when to stop. At that point, the black cat attacks Miles, who explains that the cat attacks him whenever it can. "We need each other," he says. "We are bound together by hatred. He wants to kill me."

The black cat's next victim is a cowering drunk. Inspector Galli calls on Jill to photograph the death scene because she is the only professional photographer in the village. While photographing the gruesome scene, she notices on the corpse's hands claw marks that resemble those the black cat inflicted on Miles.

The mother of the girl killed in the unventilated boathouse calls on Miles to use his psychic ability to find her daughter. Her efforts result in the discovery of the bodies, and Inspector Galli again enlists the photographic expertise of Jill Travis. Miles sees cat prints at the scene, and Jill becomes increasingly suspicious that Miles's black cat is the killer. When Jill relays her suspicions to Miles, he confirms that the cat is indeed the killer. Jill believes, however, that the whole scenario is so absurd that no one will believe her.

Miles decides to end the horror by hanging the cat. After he is apparently successful, psychic disturbances erupt in Jill's room, and she sees the shadow of the hanging cat on her wall. When Miles goes to throw away the cat's food bowl, a fire breaks out, leaving the image of the hanging cat on his wall.

When crime scene reports show the paw print of a cat on the shut-down air conditioner at the boathouse, Jill becomes convinced that Miles has been using his psychic powers to control the cat. Meanwhile, the black cat returns to Miles—apparently risen from the dead.

When the black cat nearly kills Inspector Galli, Jill confronts Miles, who claims that he has buried the cat. Jill returns later to Miles's house in search of evidence. There she comes face to face with the black cat. Miles returns and admits that the cat's will was more powerful than his and that the creature forced him to obey the evil side of his nature. Bats attack Jill, and Miles knocks her unconscious. Afterward, he walls her up alive in his cellar. Meanwhile, Inspector Galli reveals that he was hypnotized by the cat and leads police to the home of Miles. There they hear the cry of a cat and follow the sound into the cellar, where they break down the wall, rescue Jill, and free the black cat that is walled up with her.

Production and marketing: The credits state that the film is loosely based on Poe's "The Black Cat." "Loosely" is right. The action is given a contemporary setting, and except for a few scenes obviously derived from Poe's story, the rest is all Fulci and Proetti. At least this time the black cat figures prominently in the plot, which is more than it did in Universal's 1934 version, but in the original story the black cat is no murderous creature. Patrick Magee's Mr. Miles is as close as we get to the narrator in Poe's story. Miles loathes the cat and hangs it without success, as does Poe's narrator. As in the story, the cat's shadow returns to haunt its owner. As Miles is not married, he has no wife to assault and to inter in the cellar as does Poe's narrator. Therefore Mimsy Farmer's Jill Travis must suffice. But in the film, Miles hits Jill with a club and walls her up alive with the cat. In Poe's story, the narrator uses a hatchet with more deadly results. The endings in both story and film are essentially the same: the cat's cries lead police to uncover the crime.

The first noteworthy film of Lucio Fulci (1920–1996) was *Una lucertola con la pelle di donna* (1971, aka *A Lizard in a Woman's Skin*, aka *Schizoid*), in which he unsuccessfully attempts to follow in the crime/sex/horror footsteps of director Dario Argento. He then directed *Sette note in nero* (1977, aka *The Psychic*), a dull tale of clairvoyance that inspires few shudders and is, with few exceptions, visually listless. Fulci earned international notoriety, however, with his *Zombie 2* (1979), fallaciously promoted as a sequel to George A. Romero's *Dawn of the Dead* (1978). In that film, Gianetto de Rossi's special effects and Elisa Briganti's screenplay provide Sergio Salvati's camera with enough visceral gore to shock any audience. The groundbreaking aspects of the film, however, cannot for the most part be convincingly attributed to Fulci, who simply directs the camera to shoot the gore that is in front of it. Fulci's follow-up effort, *Paura nella citta dei morti viventi* (1980, aka *City of the Living Dead*, aka *The Gates of Hell*) was a clumsy, over-the-top attempt to capitalize on his superior *Zombie 2*. Although claiming the Lovecraftian setting of Dunwich, the film bypasses Lovecraftian mood and atmosphere and goes for the cheap gross-out thrill. After directing *Il gatto nero*, Fulci somewhat dismissed the film by claiming he directed it only to keep his hand in.

Fulci would continue to direct in the horror genre with *E tu vivrai nel torrore! L'Aldila* (1981, aka *And You'll Live in Terror! The Beyond*) and *Quella villa accanto al cimitero* (1981, aka *The House by the Cemetery*). The first is another attempt to exploit the zombie subgenre, and the second is a haunted-house drama carried by gruesome cinematography.

American actress Mimsy Farmer (1945–) made her screen debut in *Spencer's Mountain* (1963), a popular film that inspired television's "The Waltons." She then appeared in *Bus Riley's Back in Town* (1965) and the adolescent-oriented *Hot Rods to Hell* (1967) and *The Devil's Angels* (1967). Her career took a turn toward the macabre when she played an incest-obsessed young woman in an excellent psychodrama/horror film called *The Road to Salina* (1969, with Ed Begley and Rita Hayworth). Ironically, the object of her desires in that film is Robert Walker, Jr., who played Edgar Allan Poe in *The Spectre of Edgar Allan Poe*. Farmer entered deeper into the depths of cinematic horror by costarring in *Four Flies in Gray Velvet* (1971, directed by Dario Argento) and *Autopsy* (1978). British actor Patrick Magee (1924–1982) made a career out of playing sinister roles. Among his most notable genre films are *The Masque of the Red Death* (1964, starring Vincent Price, directed by Roger Corman), *The Skull* (1965, with Peter Cushing), *The Fiend* (1971), *A Clockwork Orange* (1971, directed by Stanley Kubrick), *Demons of the Mind* (1972), and *Asylum* (1980). I once was astonished to walk out of a London subway in 1971 and pass Patrick Magee on the sidewalk. In the late seventies, my wife and I were privileged to attend an avant-garde performance of *Faust* in which Magee played Satan. And a good Satan he was. In fact, a little bit of Satan tended to creep into many of his macabre performances, making him an ideal candidate to portray characters suggested by Edgar Allan Poe.

Critique: If Fulci agreed to direct *Il gatto nero* only to keep his hand in, his lack of interest shows. On the other hand, given his previous work, one wonders if he is capable of successfully directing a film requiring the subtlety and atmosphere necessary for a successful Edgar Allan Poe adaptation. *The Overlook Film Encyclopedia: Horror* zeroes in on the film's defects:

> With the exception of a few atmospheric crane shots and high angles, Fulci's direction is uninspired, with an over-reliance on tight shots of eyes.... The film shows that he is basically a realist director whose work derives its impact from what others put in front of Salvati's camera (gore and gruesomely made up figures)

While I generally agree with the *Encyclopedia*'s assessment, the film does have other positive elements. First of all, it is not dull. Although the relationship to Poe is quite stretched, the screenplay moves at a brisk pace and focuses on interesting characterizations. Close-ups of the black cat also make it look demonically purposeful throughout. During one effective scene, a terrified woman mistakes the glowing eyes of her child's doll for the predatory orbs of the cat. The cinematography and editing of the cat attacks are successfully disturbing and realistic, and, typical of Fulci's films, the corpse makeup is stomach churning.

The characterizations are believable, particularly those of Mimsy Farmer and Patrick Magee. As required by the scenario, the latter's facial expressions strongly reflect the struggles of a tortured soul.

While the film ultimately disappoints, it fares well when compared with most other cat-on-the-prowl tales. Missing the claustrophobic atmosphere of *The Shadow of the Cat* (1961), it nevertheless manages to rise above such pedestrian efforts as *Eye of the Cat* (1969) and *The Uncanny* (1977), both of which fail to produce felines up to the task.

The Haunting of Morella (1989)
New Horizons, U.S.A.

Credits: Directed by Jim Wynorski; produced by Roger Corman; screenplay by R. J. Robertson; associate producers—Alida Camp and Rodman Flender; music by Fredric Ensign Teetsel and Chuck Cirino; edited by Diane Fingado; director of photography—Zoran Hockstatter; production designer—Gary Randall.

Running time: 82 minutes.

Cast: David McCallum (Gideon), Nicole Eggert (Morella/Lenora), Christopher Halsted (Guy), Lana Clarkson (Coel Deveraux), Maria Ford (Diane), Jonathan Farwell (Dr. Gault), John O'Leary (Quintis), Brewster Gould (Miles Archer), Gail Harris (Ilsa), Clement Von Franckenstein (Judge Brock), R. J. Robertson (Reverend Ward), Debbie Dutch (serving girl).

Story: The film opens with a "quotation" from Poe that has been modified for this purpose: "And the ghostly winds whispered but one sound upon my tortured ears—Morella … evermore."

Morella is crucified as a witch, blasphemer, and murderess. As she suffers, she curses her husband Gideon and vows to return in the body of their daughter. A masked executioner puts out her eyes with a hot poker.

Seventeen years later, lawyer Guy Chapman pays a visit to Gideon, who is now blind. He informs Gideon that his daughter Lenora will upon her eighteenth birthday come into a financial inheritance set up for her by Morella's parents. When Guy wishes to speak with Lenora, however, Gideon orders him out.

It appears that the young Lenora has never been allowed to leave the estate, where she is looked after by Coel Deveraux, her governess, who was also present at Morella's execution. Deveraux gives Lenora a beautiful gown in anticipation of her eighteenth birthday, but her demeanor indicates that she is not to be trusted.

While playing chess with Dr. Gault, Gideon takes laudanum and indicates that he has become quite dependent upon Deveraux, who reminds him of his former wife, whose name he has not uttered for seventeen years.

Lenora discovers her father's diary and reads of the events leading up to her mother's death. Gideon writes of marrying Morella, who soon lapses into ill health and takes up the Black Arts in an effort to pursue eternal life. After the birth of her daughter Lenora, she sacrifices a servant girl and bathes in her virgin's blood as a means of achieving her quest. When Gideon arrives home early, he finds the body of the servant girl and, with several townspeople, interrupts Morella's Black Arts ceremony and executes her.

It soon becomes apparent that Deveraux is engaged in a lesbian relationship with Diane, Gideon's sexy nurse. Diane wants some time with Deveraux, but the latter is preoccupied with other matters such as necromancy. When a storm arises, Deveraux engages in a Black Arts ceremony in Morella's tomb in an effort to resurrect the deceased sorceress. As the heavens thunder above, light appears in the decayed eye sockets of Morella's remains.

Soon Lenora is awakened by someone whispering her name. With a tripart candelabra in hand, she walks trancelike through the shadowy corridors outside her bedroom and finally stands before her mother's eerie portrait. She is suddenly awakened from her trance by Gideon, who is upset to learn that she has been reading about Morella in his diary. When Gideon refuses to let Lenora go into town to meet with Guy about her inheritance, she rebels and insists that she will go wherever she wishes once she attains her inheritance.

The next day Deveraux arranges a lakeside meeting between Guy and Lenora. The two are immediately drawn to each other and soon are holding hands during a secluded walk. When they arrive at the cemetery, they embrace and kiss within sight of Morella's tomb. After the lawyer leaves, Lenora examines the tomb, apparently for the first time. She discovers her mother's corpse, attempts to flee, but is restrained by Deveraux, who compels her to look into Morella's eyes. Morella's spirit enters the body of Lenora. As Lenora's spirit attempts to regain control of her own body, Morella fights to dominate. "I can feel her," Lenora says. "She struggles within me." Morella invites her true love, Deveraux, to enter into immortality with her. To do what is necessary, however, she says that her consort must continue working to resurrect her corpse because Lenora's spirit is too strong-willed for possession to remain a long-term option.

Following Morella's instructions, Deveraux murders Ilsa, a servant girl, and pours her blood over Morella's corpse. The hideously decayed corpse is revived, but more sacrifices are required to return Morella to her full beauty.

When Lenora confides to Guy that she fears something is wrong, he dismisses her concerns. Morella's spirit takes over Lenora's body, however, and quickly tells him to disregard her previously expressed fears. Morella, possessing Lenora's body, passionately comes on to Guy, and they make love during a rainstorm.

About that time, a young blacksmith from the village asks and receives permission from Gideon to search the grounds for Ilsa, his missing girlfriend. Shortly afterward, Lenora returns home, still possessed by Morella. Gideon recognizes the voice of Morella in Lenora and realizes that Morella's curse is being fulfilled.

While standing before a mirror, Lenora returns to possess her own body, but sees Morella's corpse reflected in the glass. Suddenly the young woman is drawn into the glass where she has several nightmarish experiences, including a vision of Morella's decaying corpse making love to Guy.

In an effort to revive herself further, the still corpselike Morella draws the life from the young blacksmith and immediately assumes a young appearance. She notifies Deveraux that one more sacrifice will return her to a completely revitalized state. Now absolutely committed to Morella, Deveraux murders her lesbian lover, Diane, and prepares for the final sacrifice.

Because he has sensed the return of Morella in Lenora's body, Gideon begs Guy to marry Lenora and take her away immediately. He also expresses his fear that the recent disappearances are related to Morella's return. Guy is worried for Gideon's mental health and rides toward town to consult Dr. Gault. Before reaching town, he discovers Ilsa's body. Upon examining the corpse, Dr. Gault admits that the girl's severed jugular vein reminds him of the human sacrifices that occurred nearby seventeen years ago. At Guy's insistence and because he fears that Gideon and others could be in danger, the doctor departs for the estate.

Meanwhile, Lenora is in the cemetery searching for Deveraux when she hears a voice calling her name from Morella's tomb. As lightning parts the night sky, Lenora answers the summons. Quintis, the butler, follows and is brutally murdered by Deveraux. Inside the tomb, Morella confronts Lenora and reveals a plan to become completely revitalized by killing Gideon. Guy arrives at the tomb and is attacked by Deveraux, who is shot from behind by Dr. Gault.

Morella invites Lenora to become immortal through participation in the Black Arts, but the girl refuses and flees from the tomb. Morella follows, beckoning to Lenora. Suddenly Gideon appears, holding a lantern, and announces that he is the one Morella wants, not Lenora. When the blind man and his resurrected wife embrace, Gideon drops the lantern at their feet, consigning them both to a fiery death. As they drop to the ground, a bolt of lightning demolishes the tomb. Then Lenora, realizing she is pregnant, senses a message from beyond the grave—"I still live."

Production and marketing: Director Jim Wynorski (1950–) had already filmed *Transylvania Twist,* a spoof on Hammer films, on the Corman-Poe series, on the Universal horror series, and on just about everything else, when he approached producer Roger Corman with an idea. Since they had already filmed a Poe spoof, why not return to Poe's "Morella" and film a straight horror film in the tradition of the Corman/ Poe series? Corman, who had directed a version of "Morella" as part of his *Tales of Terror* (1962), considered the suggestion favorably. Because he believed that Poe films do not work in a contemporary setting, Wynorski opted to direct a period film in the Corman tradition.

Corman, Wynorski, and New Horizons filmed *The Haunting of Morella* for about one million dollars. Corman, of course, directed in the sixties some of the cinema's best-known and most financially successful Poe adaptations. One of his best, *The Haunted Palace,* though based more on a story by H. P. Lovecraft than on a poem by Poe, serves as the most identifiable cinematic inspiration for *The Haunting of Morella* (see Critique).

R. J. Robertson's screenplay incorporates the broad outlines of Poe's original story, but of course, embellishes them immensely in order to flesh out a full-length feature film. Present is the disturbed father who watches as his daughter appears to take on the characteristics of his deceased wife, a probable former student of magic. There are some striking differences that occur in the process, however. For example, in Poe's tale the narrator displays an apparent jealousy of his wife's immense knowledge, simultaneously absorbing the fruits of her intellect while withdrawing from her his love. Consequently, the narrator plays the role of "psychic vampire" as Morella pines away. In the screenplay, Morella plays the vampire role, quite literally absorbing the life force of her victims in order to regenerate her corpse. In Poe's tale, Morella possesses the body of her daughter, who then dies and is buried by her father. In the screenplay, Morella is depicted

as an unsympathetic horror monster bent on gaining immortality through human sacrifice. As one might expect, most of Poe's subtlety is sacrificed to elements of "gross horror" common to eighties horror films. Interestingly, Robertson gives most of the characters names from previous Corman/ Poe films. For example, the names of Guy and Dr. Gault derive from characters' names in Corman's *The Premature Burial.*

The film's Scottish star, David McCallum (1933–), played the juvenile lead in films of the fifties and sixties, among his earliest being *The Secret Place* (1956), *Robbery Under Arms* (1957), *Violent Playground* (1958), and *The Long, the Short and the Tall* (1961). He got good reviews in the fine Peter Ustinov film *Billy Budd* (1962) and followed up with a good performance in John Huston's troubled production of *Freud* (1962). McCallum scored again in John Sturges's critically acclaimed *The Great Escape* (1963), in which he formed part of an all-star cast with Steve McQueen, James Garner, Richard Attenborough, Charles Bronson, and James Coburn. From 1964 to 1967, McCallum costarred with Robert Vaughn in the popular television series *The Man from U.N.C.L.E.,* a campy spy drama inspired by the success of Sean Connery's James Bond films. In the television series, Vaughn appealed to the more sophisticated college audience, and McCallum became the idol of the teen set.

After costarring in the mediocre science-fiction film *Around the World Under the Sea* (1965), McCallum began to appear with increasing regularity in genre films. First came two made-for-television efforts. In the first, *She Waits* (1971), McCallum and Patty Duke star in a tale of ghostly possession somewhat reminiscent of *Back from the Dead* (1957). Second was *Frankenstein: The True Story* (1973), a bit of a misnomer because of its distance from the original Mary Shelley novel, but nevertheless a fine film. McCallum then starred in *Dogs* (1976), a rather weak low-budget shocker about killer canines on the loose, and joined Bette Davis in the atmospheric *Watcher in the Woods*

(1980). He returned to science fiction television in 1975 as star of the short-lived series *The Invisible Man*. McCallum's name recognition and acting competence made him an attractive choice for the starring role in *The Haunting of Morella*. According to Wynorski, McCallum was "an interesting guy who was always on the set and who always knew his lines."

Nicole Eggert came to the film fresh from a television sitcom. According to Wynorski, because acting in a sitcom is so much different from acting in a dramatic film, he had a difficult time getting Eggert to "really act." "I tried to get a performance with more depth than she was used to giving," he said. "I'm not sure I succeeded."

Exteriors for *The Haunting of Morella* were filmed partially at the Fox Ranch near Malibu Creek, west of Los Angeles. "We wanted to use a waterfall at the Fox Ranch for the waterfall scenes, "Wynorski said, "but the owners wouldn't let us use it because they had stocked the water with baby bass. They were afraid that the perfume from the women's bodies would get into the water and poison the fish."[217] The waterfall used in the film was a three-story contraption built on the parking lot of Corman's studio. It faced a bus depot, and during the filming of the nude scenes, bus drivers gathered to get the best possible view. "We filmed in the winter," Wynorski said, "And the wind threatened to blow down our outdoor sets, but at night, with the fog, everything looked great. We built the graveyard set near Malibu Creek. The temperature was thirty degrees or lower, and everybody was freezing out there!"[218]

The Haunting of Morella received limited distribution on the West Coast and in New York, but turned a profit largely because of brisk video sales.

Critique: As a film, *The Haunting of Morella* is highly derivative of *The Haunted Palace* (1963), directed by Roger Corman. The rousing and foreboding musical score echoes that of Ronald Stein, and the screenplay borrows heavily from that of Charles

Beaumont. For instance, the idea of a Black Arts master possessing the body of a look-alike relative borrows more heavily from the previous Corman film than from Poe's "Morella." Also derivative is the mesmerizing wall portrait evident in both films. The ending, while borrowing somewhat from *The Haunted Palace* in that an evil spirit may yet live on, more fully derives from *The Dunwich Horror* (1970), directed by Daniel Haller, Roger Corman's former art director. In other words, Corman's influence permeates *The Haunting of Morella*. Also present are the omnipresent candles of the Corman/Poe series and a number of other subtle touches reminiscent of Corman's earlier work. Interestingly, most highly derivative films fall flat for that very reason, but in this case, the derivative influences are also some of the film's saving graces.

Had it been produced, directed, and scripted by lesser talents, one could easily imagine a much less successful film than *The Haunting of Morella*. The primary influences of the post-Corman/Poe era are the lesbian elements which hark back to Hammer Studios' Karnstein vampire series of the early seventies and the heavier emphasis on nudity and semiexplicit sex that had been generally creeping into films since the late sixties. According to director Wynorski, Corman would have liked to use nudity in his Poe series, but the times simply would not allow it. Considering that Poe is the source, Corman's films are probably better for their absence of nudity.

Wynorski grew up watching Roger Corman's films, and those experiences clearly influenced his direction of *The Hunting of Morella*. While he sometimes allows or encourages Lana Clarkson to overplay her wicked intentions, his command of the actors is generally sure. Although he repeats such tired horror clichés as the "hand on the shoulder" technique, which is always guaranteed to make an audience jump, he pulls off the film successfully.

To turn to the cast, David McCallum is believable as the bedraggled, blind, and half-insane Gideon, and young Nicole Eggert is surprisingly versatile as Morella and Lenora. As already indicated, Lana Clarkson is sometimes allowed to overact on the sinister side, but otherwise she is a striking presence who brings an added dimension of sensuous evil to the film. The remainder of the cast is adequate.

Interestingly, Poe was not allowed to speak for himself in the opening quotation. The correct quotation from the tale itself is "The winds of the firmament breathed but one sound within my ears, and the ripples upon the sea murmured evermore—Morella." And, one last regret as we leave "Morella" is that no cinematic rendition of the story has yet captured the flavor of these evocative words of Edgar Allan Poe: "But one autumnal evening, when the winds lay still in heaven, Morella called me to her bedside. There was a dim mist over all the earth, and a warm glow upon the waters, and, amid the rich October leaves of the forest, a rainbow from the firmament had surely fallen."

Buried Alive (1989)
Breton Films, South Africa

Credits: Directed by Gerald Kikoine; produced by Harry Alan Towers; screenplay by Jake Clesi and Stuart Lee, based on "The Premature Burial" by Edgar Allan Poe; cinematography by Gerald Loubeau; special effects by Scott Wheeler and Bill Butler; music by Frederic Talgorn.

Running time: 89 minutes.

Cast: Robert Vaughn (Gary), Donald Pleasence (Dr. Schaeffer), Karen Witter (Janet), John Carradine (Jacob), Ginger Allen (Debbie), Nia Long (Fingers), Bill Butler (Tim), Janine Denison (Shiro), Arnold Vosloo (Ken Wade), Ashley Hayden (Boze), Roslynn Farrell (Tina).

Story: Late at night at the Ravenscroft Medical Facility for women, Fingers gives her friend Tina a switchblade to help her escape. Tina leaves the facility but before she can reach the highway, is attacked by an assailant wearing a Ronald Reagan mask. A chute opens in the ground, and Tina slides into the basement of Ravenscroft. There she is again attacked by the masked assailant and buried alive behind a wall of bricks.

The next day a pretty blonde named Janet arrives at Ravenscroft to begin work as a teacher. She was inspired to apply for the job after being favorably impressed by Dr. Gary Julian, the head psychologist at Ravenscroft. Gary's writings focus on the superego—the internalization of external authority. Gary's father ran the facility as an asylum until his death, when Gary took over and implemented his own more liberal theories.

During her first night at Ravenscroft, Janet imagines hearing a man pleading for help behind a brick wall. Dr. Schaeffer, however, demonstrates to Janet that her experience was not real.

On her first day as a teacher, during which she teaches about ants, Janet finds the girls of Ravenscroft crude, violent, and generally unruly. She manages, however, to finish the day successfully. When she asks about the rebellious Yvonne, Dr. Schaeffer explains that "Yvonne sees reality as a warped projection of her own superego." Shortly afterward, Yvonne is murdered and recorded as missing. Gary says Yvonne ran away as Tina did, and he wonders if her action casts doubt on the validity of his theories. Janet assures Gary that his theories are sound.

Meanwhile, Janet's own hallucinations are becoming more pronounced. She imagines seeing ants all over her legs, after which she falls down a chute and finds a young woman buried alive. At the same time, Gary becomes increasingly interested in Janet because she was reared by a strong father. Gary makes a pass at Janet, but she tactfully refuses his advance by excusing herself for the evening.

During an initiation, the girls lock Janet in a bathroom, where she hallucinates being attacked by an arm that reaches out from an ant-covered commode.

When Cheryl is next to rebel, the masked assailant attacks her and buries her alive in the basement. Fingers becomes suspicious and investigates the basement, finding the switchblade she earlier gave to Tina. Fingers shares her fears with Janet, who suspects that the unruly Debbie is frightening off girls with the threat of physical violence. Nevertheless, Janet investigates the basement and imagines an elderly man reaching through a brick wall behind which he was buried alive. She runs away and tries unsuccessfully to convince an incredulous Dr. Schaeffer.

Debbie complains to Gary about Janet's teaching, and Gary tells Janet he is going to have Debbie transferred to a more structured environment. While speaking to Gary, Janet discovers from a photograph that the old man she thought she saw in the basement was Gary's father, Jacob. Gary tells her, however, that Jacob is dead and that she is probably suffering from anxiety.

That night Debbie has a rendezvous with her boyfriend Tim. The masked assailant kills Tim outright and buries Debbie alive.

Janet discovers that Dr. Schaeffer was once a patient of Gary's father, but that Gary cured Schaeffer and put him on the staff. Gary confirms that Schaeffer was his first major success and proposes marriage to Janet. "If you don't get better," he tells Janet, "it looks like my methods are a failure … I'm a failure."

Janet goes through Gary's files and finds that Debbie "ran away" and was never transferred as Gary had claimed. "They need to think about things," Gary says. "That is the only way they will get well … to be alone … to think. The method works. I know it does. That's how my father made me better."

When Janet says that Gary's methods are insane, he briefly explodes but quickly regains his composure. Later Janet calls Ken, a policeman she knows, and asks to meet him in town regarding strange happenings at Ravenscroft. As she leaves, however, Gary stops her and repeats his proposal of marriage. Janet flees and Gary pursues her into the basement of Ravenscroft. When Dr. Schaeffer tries to intervene on Janet's behalf, Gary kills him with a prolonged dose of electroshock. Gary then sedates Janet and attempts to bury her alive in the same room where Gary's father sent him for solitude and punishment. Janet manages to thrust a pin into Gary's eye and escape. Gary then sees his father emerge in a wheelchair from behind a wall. "We'll need a little punishment," Jacob suggests, laughing hysterically. An explosion rocks the basement of Ravenscroft, sending rubble down upon the heads of Gary and Jacob. Only Janet escapes from the basement alive.

As the police report finding a number of bodies buried in the rubble of the basement, Janet leaves Ravenscroft in search of a new life. In the basement, however, Gary and Jacob show signs of life as their arms push up through the rubble.

Production and marketing: *Buried Alive* was one of three Edgar Allan Poe films produced by Breton Films and Harry Allan Towers in 1989 and 1990, the others being *House of Usher* and *Masque of the Red Death*. Towers made his mark in horror films as the producer of a series of low-budget quickies directed by Jesus Franco (see *Il gatto nero*, 1981).

Screenwriters Clesi and Lee credit Poe's "The Premature Burial" as their source, but the film is neither thematically nor atmospherically reminiscent of that particular Poe story at all. In "The Premature Burial," the narrator fears being accidentally buried alive. He fears the closeness of the coffin and the horrors of lonely suffocation in deep darkness. Murder is not a theme in "The Premature Burial." Instead of constructing a screenplay based on factors present in "The

Premature Burial," Clesi and Lee opt for the horror of being walled up alive. We find this particular approach, of course, in Poe's "The Cask of Amontillado" and "The Black Cat," both of which appear to have influenced this film more than did "The Premature Burial," especially since a black cat conspicuously roams the Ravenscroft environs and since the burials are clearly intentional. Vaughn also attacks Witter with a axe in a scene more reminiscent of "The Black Cat" than "The Premature Burial."

Beyond the theme of premature burial, the appearance of a black cat, an axe, and problems distinguishing illusion from reality, nothing else in *Buried Alive* is clearly reminiscent of Poe.

Robert Vaughn (1932–) came to *Buried Alive* with an established reputation in American television, largely based on *The Man from U.N.C.L.E.* (1964–1967), a very popular spy series. His film career, however, never landed him in the big time. Although appearing in the critically acclaimed *The Magnificent Seven* (1960), he usually labored in such celluloid ephemera as *One Spy Too Many* (1966), *The Venetian Affair* (1967), and *The Helicopter Spies* (1968). Vaughn was no stranger to the horror/science fiction genre, however, having starred in *Teenage Caveman* (1958, directed by Roger Corman), *Starship Invasions* (1978, with Christopher Lee), *Battle Beyond the Stars* (1980), and *Superman III* (1985).

Buried Alive marked the first of two appearances by Donald Pleasence (1919–1995) in a Breton-produced Edgar Allan Poe film. The second would be *House of Usher.* Pleasence was also a veteran of the horror/ science fiction genre, having worked in *Mania* (1959, with Peter Cushing), *Dr. Crippen* (1962), *Fantastic Voyage* (1966), *Eye of the Devil* (1967), *Tales That Witness Madness* (1972), *The Mutations* (1972), *Land of the Minotaur* (1976, with Peter Cushing), and *The Uncanny* (1977, with Peter Cushing). In 1978, Pleasence appeared as the character for whom he will probably be best remembered: Dr. Sam Loomis in John Carpenter's highly

successful shocker *Halloween* (1978). Pleasence's Dr. Loomis is a rather unorthodox psychiatrist leading the search for Michael Myers, his criminally insane patient whom he believes to be evil incarnate. The film also launched the career of Jamie Lee Curtis. So successful was *Halloween* that *Halloween II* (1981) followed. Less successful than its predecessor, its fiery finale seemed so thoroughly to destroy both Loomis and Myers that the plot of *Halloween III: Season of the Witch* (1983) was unrelated to the first two entries. In the motion picture business, however, the smell of money can revive the deadest of the dead. Opening with one of the most ludicrous explanations ever to justify a sequel, *Halloween IV: The Return of Michael Myers* (1988) resurrected Myers and Loomis for yet another confrontation. The results were about what a cynical onlooker might expect. In any case, it was Pleasence's work in the horror genre, as well as his fine reputation as a mainstream actor (don't miss his moving performance in an episode of *The Twilight Zone* called "Changing of the Guard") that landed him a costarring role in *Buried Alive.*

Significantly, *Buried Alive* was John Carradine's last film. Carradine (1906–1991), who began his acting career as Richard Reed Carradine, appeared very briefly in three of Universal's classic horror films of the thirties: *The Invisible Man* (1933), *The Black Cat* (1934), and *Bride of Frankenstein* (1935). In the forties, he gained recognition as a horror film star by playing Dracula in *House of Frankenstein* (1944, with Boris Karloff and Lon Chaney, Jr.) and *House of Dracula* (1945, with Lon Chaney, Jr.). Although Carradine's physical appearance closely resembled Bram Stoker's description of the vampire, the actor was never given a script worthy of the character. In the fifties, Carradine found himself in such low-budget horror entries as *Half Human* (1955), *The Black Sleep* (1956, with Basil Rathbone, Lon Chaney, Jr., and Bela Lugosi), *The Unearthly* (1957), and *The Cosmic Man* (1959). The sixties saw a marked decline in the quality of Carradine's horror films with such clunkers as *Invasion of the Animal People* (1962), *Billy the Kid vs. Dracula* (1966, as Dracula), *Hillbillies in a Haunted House* (1967, with Basil Rathbone and Lon Chaney, Jr.), *The Fiend with the Electronic Brain* (1967), *The Astro-Zombies* (1968), and *Bigfoot* (1969). In the seventies, Carradine continued to step up the pace and scale down the quality with such horror films as *The House of the Seven Corpses* (1973), *Silent Night, Bloody Night* (1974), *The Sentinel* (1970), *The Bees* (1978), and many, many more. Although suffering from arthritis, Carradine appeared in a large number of horror films throughout the eighties. Usually receiving top billing, the actor actually contributed little more than cameos to most of those productions.

All his life, Carradine brushed off his career in horror films. Considering himself first and foremost a stage actor, he often told interviewers that he acted in horror films only to finance his Shakespeare company and other thespian projects. In the last decades of his life, the horror films kept him active and supplied an income. Indeed, it would be unfair to see John Carradine as a "horror man" only. After all, he turned in fine starring or costarring performances in such acclaimed films as *Prisoner of Shark Island* (1936), *Five Came Back* (1939), *Stagecoach* (1939), *The Grapes of Wrath* (1940, probably his best film performance) and *Bluebeard* (1944), along with fine supporting performances or cameos in such first-rate productions as *Captains Courageous* (1936), *The Ten Commandments* (1956), *The Last Hurrah* (1958), *The Man Who Shot Liberty Valance* (1962), *Cheyenne Autumn* (1964), *The Shootist* (1976), and *Peggy Sue Got Married* (1986).

In addition to being a fine actor, Carradine was a character in his own right. An eccentric self-promoter, he walked the sidewalks of Hollywood drawing attention to himself by quoting lines from Shakespeare. Producer Oliver Drake recalled an occasion when Carradine got drunk at a party and drove up and down the street naked, gloriously shouting lines penned by the Bard.

Actor Robert Quarry (see *Haunting*

Fear) told me that Carradine would often leave his son David alone for long hours while attending to his acting career. On one occasion, Quarry went and made soup for David. When John came back demanding to know where the soup came from, Quarry exploded and dumped the soup on the negligent father. Quarry also said that Carradine was not above going to sleep on camera during live television productions.

I twice had the pleasure of seeing John Carradine on stage: once in a poetry reading at Southern Illinois University in 1969 and again at the Muny Opera in St. Louis in the 1979 production of *A Funny Thing Happened on the Way to the Forum*. He was always thoroughly professional and always effective, whether giving voice to the greatest poets or drawing laughs in comedy.

In the end credits of *Buried Alive*, the producers ran the following tribute: "With fond remembrance of John Carradine and his distinguished film career spanning six decades."

Buried Alive saw only limited distribution in the United States, reverting quickly to the video rental shelves. Still, Towers remembers it as the favorite of his Poe films: "Maybe it's because it's the first of them, and because it's Carradine's last picture. But it's really quite a good movie. I was also more linked to it than to the other two because I'm doing more pictures and couldn't be around so much for them."[219]

Critique: Leonard Maltin gives *Buried Alive* 1 1/2 stars, explaining that while the film is based on elements from Edgar Allan Poe stories, it "juices them up with sex and gore." *The Overlook Encyclopedia of Film: Horror* calls *Buried Alive* "a trite old-dark-house movie," and *Video Hound's Golden Movie Retriever* throws the film two bones. All are basically correct.

Edgar Allan Poe's tales rarely translate well to the screen when given modern settings. *Buried Alive* is no exception. For example, the presence of automobiles and crude young women does little to evoke the claustrophobic atmosphere of Poe. A black cat does prowl the grounds, but it plays no important part in the scenario. Corman would frequently add small touches from various Poe tales to his Poe pictures, but these touches were usually not included to add Poe presence to a film that otherwise has little connection to Poe. In addition, *Buried Alive* is derivative to a fault. The opening scenes of the masked assailant's assault on Tina are like so many others in the slasher genre, which was already becoming tiresome when this film was made. When a policeman awakens Karen Witter in her car, he leans forward in dark glasses to startle her momentarily—an effect lifted from Alfred Hitchcock's *Psycho* (1960). The influence of *Psycho* insinuates itself further as Robert Vaughn plays a murderer shaped by the destructive influence of his overly strict father—an echo of Anthony Perkins's problem with his mother in *Psycho*. Almost "becoming" his father as Perkins "becomes" his mother, Vaughn assumes the destructive characteristics of his father, even to the extent of trying to bury Witter alive in the very room where his father punished him with solitude. Interesting, too, is Vaughn's choice of a Ronald Reagan mask, as the fortieth president was considered a diabolical "father figure" by some liberal critics. While most horror films are derivative to some ex-

tent, that alone is usually not a valid criticism. In this case, however, director Kikoine is no Alfred Hitchcock.

The major problem of *Buried Alive* is its fractured and confusing point of view. Kikoine shows us bulging walls, armies of ants, and other strange events from Witter's perspective. No one else in the film can confirm her visions, which the film reveals as hallucinations, suggestions of Witter's own psychological problems. Is Witter mentally ill? Is John Carradine's ghost really trying to reach her, or is she indeed manufacturing the ghost from a photograph she saw? What is really going on here? Sometimes ambiguity works, as in Jock Clayton's *The Innocents* (1961), in this case it merely confuses. At the end of the picture, beyond Witter's vision, the arm of the ghostly father rises from the rubble. Is it real? At that point, since the audience thinks the director is not playing fair, who cares?

On the positive side, the cast is engaging. Robert Vaughn, an accomplished actor, brings Dr. Gary Julian to life as a troubled and dangerous human being. Witter is adequate as Janet, and Donald Pleasence creates a curious, though somewhat ridiculous, character as Dr. Schaeffer, a mild-mannered, eccentric former mental patient who gobbles food as a substitute for sex.

The House of Usher (1989)
21st Century/Breton, Great Britain and U.S.A.

Credits: Directed by Alan Birkinshaw; produced by Harry Alan Towers; executive producer—Avi Lerner; associate producer—John H. Stadel; screenplay by Michael J. Murray, based on "The Fall of the House of Usher" by Edgar Allan Poe; director of photography—Jossi Wein; production designer—Leonordo Coen Cagli; edited by Michael J. Duthie; special prosthetic effects—Scott Wheeler.

Cast: Oliver Reed (Roderick Usher);

Donald Pleasence (Walter Usher); Romy Windsor (Molly); Rufus Swart (Ryan); Norman Coombes (Mr. Derrick); Anne Stradi (Mrs. Derrick); Carol Farquhar (Gwen); Philip Gadewa (Dr. Bailey); Leonorah Ince and Jonathon Fairbirn (the children).

Story: The time is 1987, the place London, England. Ryan Usher and his fiancée, Molly, are driving through the English countryside in search of the estate of Ryan's uncle, Roderick Usher, when two children appear in the road before them. Ryan swerves to avoid hitting the children and crashes into a tree. Seeing that Ryan is bloody and unconscious, Molly locks the car door and runs to the House of Usher for help. She is admitted by the butler, Mr. Derrick, who informs her that the police have already been called. The maid, Mrs. Derrick, tells her not to worry, that her husband will take care of everything. In the meantime, Mr. Derrick makes his way to the car, tries to open the locked door, and smashes the window with an iron bar. Mr. Derrick later tells Molly the obvious lie that Ryan is in the hospital with superficial wounds.

Later Molly meets Gwen Derrick, the friendly deaf-and-dumb daughter to the butler and maid. When alone, Molly hears the giggling of children behind her bedroom wall. When Molly dresses for dinner, Mrs. Derrick informs her that she will have to change into a more tasteful dress and remove her perfume. Seeing that Molly is slightly offended, the maid explains that Roderick Usher suffers from a terrible sensitivity to bright colors and strong scents, both of which cause him migraine headaches.

On the way down to dinner, Molly sees a portrait of two children and tells Mrs. Derrick that they are the two children who caused the accident on the road. Mrs. Derrick informs her that she must be mistaken because the two children in the portrait have been dead for one hundred years. At that moment, the house shakes and shifts. The maid explains to the surprised Molly that the House of Usher was built upon marshland and is slowly sinking.

At dinner Molly meets Roderick Usher. He shows her a portrait of his mother and remarks that his nephew Ryan has very good taste. He inquires about the health of Molly's parents and seems satisfied when she tells him that she comes from good stock. Roderick then informs her that, unfortunately, the same cannot be said for the Ushers.

That night, awakened by thunder and lightning, Molly calls for the maid, but there is no answer. Startled once again to see the

two children, she rises from her bed, secures a candle, and follows the spectres along a dark hallway. When she comes to what appears to be a subterranean catacomb, she finds Ryan lying on a stone slab. Roderick appears and tries to explain to the shocked, grief-stricken girl that Ryan had lost so much blood as a result of the accident that calling for medical attention had been deemed useless. Anyway, he says, the Ushers take care of their own. Molly thinks Usher is mad, but allows herself to be escorted back to her bedroom. Soon she realizes that she is Usher's prisoner.

That night the house again shifts, rumbles, and sinks. Molly runs from her room just in time to see young Dr. Bailey preparing to leave. She pleads with him to take her with him, only to discover that the doctor is loyal to the Ushers. He tells her, however, that Roderick did everything possible for Ryan and that the Usher family suffers from a rare blood disease. Molly is hardly consoled, however, especially when Roderick makes her submit to a complete physical examination. The doctor pronounces her fit, after which Roderick explains to Molly that he wants to mate with her in order to continue the Usher line. Predictably, she vows no cooperation whatever. When Molly has left, Dr. Bailey half-seriously quips that he will serve in Roderick's place if the need arises. The mentally deteriorating Usher is not amused and arranges the doctor's death at the paws of a starving rat.

The grieving and angry Molly soon finds herself at a memorial service for Ryan, during which she picks up a carelessly placed set of keys. Unfortunately, she has to drop the keys into Ryan's coffin to avoid their being seen. At the end of the service, the house again rumbles, forcing open a vertical coffin. Its mummified corpse lurches forward and embraces the terrified Molly. Roderick takes advantage of the moment to place the corpse's necklace around Molly's neck.

That night Molly returns to the crypt to retrieve the keys, but she cannot force Ryan's coffin open. To her shock, she hears movement from within the coffin and concludes that Ryan has been buried alive. At that moment, the phantasmic children reappear, and once again Molly follows them. To her surprise, she stumbles upon a physically and mentally deteriorating prisoner in an otherwise deserted part of the house. Identifying himself as Roderick's brother, Walter Usher, he says that Roderick has not visited him for fifteen years. Walter is convinced that Roderick does not want to see him because Walter is a mirror of what Roderick will soon become himself. To occupy his time, Walter sculpts small objects with a drill that is attached to his arm. Molly does not know what to think, but when Walter says that he saw Roderick kill Ryan, Molly agrees to a mutual escape plot.

Later, as part of Roderick's mating plan, Derrick renders Molly unconscious with a shot from a hypodermic needle. A dream sequence follows in which Molly makes love to Ryan in the shower and is then sexually assaulted by Roderick. Still dreaming, she participates in a fog-shrouded, macabre wedding ceremony with Roderick.

Upon waking, she sprays herself with strong perfume in order to repulse Roderick. In the meantime, Walter strangles Mrs. Derrick and kills young Gwen with the prosthetic drill. Mr. Derrick is beside himself with grief and anger, and Roderick goes in search of his deranged brother. Before they can escape, Walter attacks Molly with the drill. Roderick encounters the fleeing girl down below, where Molly has run in an effort to escape Walter and free Ryan. As the walls sway and the house threatens to crumble, Roderick accuses Molly of agreeing to marry Ryan in an effort to acquire some nonexistent Usher fortune. Roderick further admits to burying the boy alive as punishment for his stupidity.

Walter then enters, claims that he is Ryan's father, and vows that all the Ushers will die this night. Roderick and Walter engage in hand-to-hand combat which soon sets the house afire. Molly desperately returns to Ryan's coffin and succeeds in freeing him.

As Molly attempts to help Ryan to safety, Mr. Derrick attacks Ryan, raving that the boy's father murdered his daughter. Molly knocks Derrick down, but as she and Ryan try to escape, Roderick grabs Ryan and forces him back into the fire so that the last of the Ushers can die together. As timbers fall and flames engulf the house, Molly escapes and gulps the fresh air outside.

Suddenly, as though nothing has happened, Ryan and Molly are back in their car searching for the House of Usher as they were at the film's beginning. They see the two children, but this time Ryan simply turns the car in the opposite direction and drives away.

Production and marketing: *House of Usher* was filmed in South Africa. In an attempt to make the film marketable, Breton Films signed two actors with name recognition in the horror genre: Oliver Reed (1938–) and Donald Pleasence (see *Buried Alive* for background on Pleasence). Both actors were also established talents in mainstream cinema. Born in Wimbledon, England, Oliver Reed was a young, rugged six-foot athlete when he ran away from home at the age of 17 after an argument with his stepmother. Settling in London, Reed used his physical attributes to land a job as a nightclub bouncer. After unsuccessfully pursuing a prizefighting career, he worked for six months as a hospital orderly and put in a stint with the British Army Medical Corps. When the acting bug bit the handsome young man, he approached his uncle, Sir Carol Reed, and asked if the venerated director could help him break into the business. Refusing to engage in nepotism, Sir Carol urged Oliver to join a repertory company and get some experience. Oliver ignored his uncle's advice and joined the ranks of film extras instead.

After a short time, Reed auditioned for and got a part in a television series. This led to parts in films such as *The Rebel* (1960) and *No Love for Johnnie* (1961). Fortune smiled when he was cast in several Hammer Film productions directed by Terence Fisher: *Sword of Sherwood Forest* (1960), *The Two*

Faces of Dr. Jekyll (1961), and his first starring vehicle, *The Curse of the Werewolf* (1961). Hammer was riding a wave of international notoriety as a result of its horror film remakes *The Curse of Frankenstein* (1957) and *Dracula* (1958), which launched the genre careers of Peter Cushing and Christopher Lee. The company added *The Man Who Could Cheat Death* in 1959 and stood poised to fulfill its promise as the horror studio successor to Universal Pictures. Oliver Reed would be part of those early years.

The American pressbook for *The Curse of the Werewolf* heralded Oliver Reed as the "successor to Lon Chaney." As fate would have it, he would actually become the successor to Lon Chaney, Jr. Both would become notable horror stars as a result of starring in excellent werewolf films. Both would eventually branch out from horror films to play a wide variety of roles; both would develop reputations as hard drinkers, and both would eventually find themselves the denizens of poor exploitation films.

The qualities that would make Reed an international success were all present in *The Curse of the Werewolf*: the burly demeanor, the flaring nostrils, the brooding and moody persona, and the animal magnetism. In the film's British pressbook, Director Terence Fisher is quoted as saying of Reed's performance: "It is absolutely haunting, unforgettable. Were I invited to predict sure stardom for an unknown young actor today, and asked to back that prediction with a heavy bet, the youngster I'd pick would be 22-year-old Oliver Reed." Anyone seeing the film in 1961 would be hard pressed to disagree.

One year earlier Alfred Hitchcock had fathered a new horror film subgenre as the director of *Psycho,* and Hammer sought to jump on the bandwagon with *Scream of Fear* (1961), *Maniac* (1962), and *Paranoiac* (1963), the last of which starred Oliver Reed as a mentally deranged murderer. Having scored in Hammer's small but effective science-fiction thriller *These Are the Damned* (1962) and in its historical drama with horror overtones, *Captain Clegg* (1962), Reed returned

to a starring role in *Paranoiac.* As the paranoiac Simon Ashby, he turns in one of his finer performances. A tense screenplay by Jimmy Sangster, creative direction by Freddie Francis, and fine work from the general cast make *Paranoiac* one of Hammer's most underrated pictures. Interestingly, at the time of the film's release, Reed reflected back on *The Curse of the Werewolf,* dubbing it his "debut in corn."

Also in 1963, Reed earned good reviews in *The System,* Michael Winner's intelligent portrayal of a pack of young hoodlums at a seaside resort. This freed the young man from indelible horror-film typecasting and allowed him to undertake important roles in such critically acclaimed films as *The Trap* (1966), *The Jokers* (1966), and *Oliver!* (1968).

About this time, Reed began a professional association with Director Ken Russell, who would soon shock audiences and critics with his frontal assaults of cinematic excess. First Reed portrayed poet Dante Gabriel Rossetti in Russell's BBC production "Dante's Inferno." He then costarred in Russell's smash hit of D. H. Lawrence's *Women in Love* (1969), in which he and Alan Bates engage in a memorable nude wrestling scene. In Russell's autobiography *A British Picture,* the director recounts the difficulties in actually filming the nude wrestling scene. It appears that each star was fearful that the other's penis would win the battle of the yardstick, and both therefore found ways to delay the shooting of the scene. Russell eventually realized what was going on and arranged for both men to go to the restroom at the same time, allowing both to realize that their respective organs were about of equal length. The scene was then immediately shot without difficulty.

After appearing in several minor films, Reed returned to Russell's stable in the director' awesome *The Devils* (1971). Reed was cast as Father Grandier opposite Vanessa Redgrave's Mother Jeanne in Russell's film version of Aldous Huxley's *The Devils of Loudon* and John Whiting's derivative play. Almost every conceivable blasphemy is portrayed on screen as Jeanne accuses Grandier of the demonic possession that turns her nuns into wild women. Actually, political intrigue and sexual repression account for the deadly antics.

In 1973, Reed gave what might be remembered as his greatest performance in Michael Apted's *The Triple Echo.* In the film, actor Richard Deacon portrays a young man who masquerades as a woman to avoid being arrested for military desertion. When Reed, as the rough sergeant, is sexually attracted to Deacon, the stage is set for both sensitive character portrayal and nail-biting suspense. By 1989, Reed was appearing in both awful European exploitation films and major American television productions. Always known as a "serious drinker" and "bully-boy," he has had a very successful career. Still, Reed failed to make the big time for the same reasons that Lon Chaney, Jr., failed. Just as the latter's fame in the horror genre never reached that of Karloff and Lugosi, so Reed's fame never reached that of Cushing and Lee. Among Reed's other horror/science fiction films were *The Shuttered Room* (1966), *Z. P. G.* (1972), *Burnt Offerings* (1976), *Venom* (1981), and *The Brood* (1979). He would have another brief foray into Poe in *The Pit and the Pendulum* (1991).

New Zealand–born Alan Birkinshaw was a rodeo rider before becoming a film director. Before taking the helm on *House of Usher,* Birkinshaw directed several British films, including *Killer's Moon,* the story of four psychotic killers who escape from a mental hospital where they are undergoing LSD dream therapy. When they escape, they still think they are in a dream, and they have been told by their psychiatrist to act out all their evil thoughts in dreams.

Screenwriter Michael J. Murray came to *House of Usher* on the strength of an earlier script titled *The Lightning Field,* a reworking of the *Rosemary's Baby* theme. Murray describes his first contact with Towers:

> I'd never met Harry, and I got a call from him at 12:30 a.m. He was on location in Africa [filming *Buried Alive*], and he was

calling to ask if I'd be interested in working on *Fall of the House of Usher.* Before I knew it, he was telling me what he wanted in terms of story, and then he said, "I'll be in Los Angeles in three days. Put a treatment together. See you then." I had never worked under that kind of pressure before, but it was good. It was practical. It was real nuts and bolts, and I appreciated that.[220]

Murray explains the key theme that guided his treatment:

> In Poe's "Usher," it's a relationship between a brother and a sister. In ours, it's two brothers. In terms of contemporary storytelling, Poe didn't really exploit the possibilities of the story, and since horror's an exploitative medium, we did. This woman thinks she's marrying into a proper British family, and that she'll become Lady Usher. But she finds out the *last* thing she wants to become is Lady Usher.[221]

Other Poe themes Murray taps are those of premature burial and illusion versus reality (dream within a dream).

So far unseen in the United States, *Zanik domu Usherii* (1981, aka *The Fall of the House of Usher*) was directed in Czechoslovakia by Prague native Jan Svankmajer (1931–). The director, known for his cinematic creations of an absurdist universe, would employ subjective camera techniques in the Poe-inspired *Kyvadlo, jáma a naděje* (1983 aka *The Pit, the Pendulum, and Hope*).

Critique: Almost everyone associated with *House of Usher* should be ashamed. Gone is the Poe universe, completely destroyed by the modern setting. Gone is most of the Poe plot as Usher becomes an aging lecher who buries alive his nephew (not his sister) in an attempt to continue the family line. Gone are the sinister elements of the house itself, as no attempt is made to capture Poe's association of the house with the Ushers. Roderick Usher is therefore depicted as a living alone in a 118-room house for no apparent reason. Gone is everything one would hope for in a Poe adaptation, and present is everything one jaded by inept late seventies and eighties horror films would fear.

The screenplay insults Poe by taking just enough of the most exterior aspects of the basic plot to justify use of the title. The director puts the cast through their paces, but there is hardly a creative scene in the entire picture. The situation arouses a flutter of interest with the question of Ryan Usher's actual physical condition, but since Ryan and Molly are characterized as little more than sexually active youngsters in the tradition of most heroes and heroines of late seventies and eighties horror films, their sparse character development fails to build real sympathy for their survival. In terms of the larger plot, sublime aspects of family and fate are driven away by a marked emphasis on puerile hormones run wild that in no way suggests a Poe theme.

As far as the cast is concerned, Oliver Reed is Oliver Reed. He is still too good for this painful travesty. The same can be said of Donald Pleasence. Romy Windsor is completely undistinguished as the heroine, and Rufus Swart is equally forgettable as her beau. On the positive side, Anne Stradi gives a sympathetic performance as the degraded Mrs. Derrick, and Norman Coombes is appropriately nasty as her butler husband.

All considered, *House of Usher* is a disgrace not only to Poe but to the cinematic Poe tradition, degrading both author and tradition with its mindless pilfering and pillaging of a classic horror tale. Leonard Maltin gives the film only 1 1/2 stars, but *Video Hound's Golden Movie Retriever 1996* is closer to the truth in awarding it only one bone.

Masque of the Red Death (1989)
Concorde, United States

Credits: Directed by Larry Brand; produced by Roger Corman; screenplay by Daryl Haney and Larry Brand, based on "The Masque of the Red Death" by Edgar Allan Poe; cinematography by Edward Pei; music by Mark Governor; edited by Stephen Mark; associate producers—Sally Mattison and Adam Moos.

Running time: 83 minutes.

Cast: Adrian Paul (Prospero), Patrick MacNee (Machiavel), Clare Hoak (Julietta), Jeff Osterhage (Claudio), Tracy Reiner (Princess Lucretia), Kelly Ann Sabatsso (Ornelia), Maria Ford (Isabella), Paul Michad (Benito), Michael Leopard (Paulo), Daryl Haney (Fabio).

Story: As a child, Prince Prospero is warned by his teacher Machiavel not to rule cruelly as his father had done. As a young man, however, Prospero has nightmares involving Machiavel's words and finds himself in conflict about his proper role as a prince and as a man. Alternately resolved, confused, and resigned, he ponders the great questions of life—death, power, and privilege—and his place in the vast scheme of things.

Outside the castle walls, a stranger garbed in red spreads a plague known as the Red Death. Those stricken become disfigured, blood pours from their faces, and they die a quick but painful death. Frightened that the plague, which is responsible for thousands of deaths across countryside, will spread to the castle, Prospero fortifies himself and his sister/wife behind impregnable walls. Before locking the castle doors, however, Prospero invites a group of his aristocratic friends and a bevy of maidens from the village to join him. He also forbids everyone in the castle to wear red.

Prospero's attentions quickly turn to Julietta, one of village maidens. A woman of virtue, she resists his advances, saying that he can force her body to the bedroom, but he cannot force her to love him. The Prince's lieutenant, Claudio, becomes disgusted when Prospero orders the maidens (except for Julietta) to dance naked before the revelers.

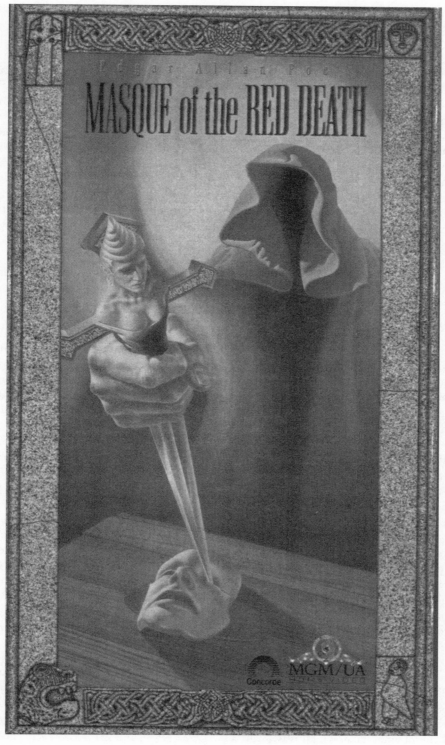

Video box art for *The Masque of the Red Death* (1989).

Jealous Princess Lucretia shows Julietta a secret egress from the castle, but Prospero stops Julietta before she can escape and sends her to the dungeon.

When a band of peasants (including Julietta's father) arrives at the castle begging entry, Prospero refuses and scalds two of the peasants to death with boiling water hurled from atop the castle wall. This so enrages Claudio that Prospero has him restrained and sent to the dungeon.

At the masked ball that follows, the man in red appears. Prospero orders the man to remove his mask so that he can see who he is about to put to death. The man removes his mask, revealing himself to be Prospero's old teacher Machiavel. Prospero's mood quickly lightens as he realizes that the newly arrived Machiavel could not possibly have heard of the order against wearing red. Machiavel then removes his red gloves and begins to dance with the revelers, all of whom quickly succumb to the Red Death. As the Red Death approaches him, Prospero commits suicide, and Julietta and Claudio escape from the castle through Lucretia's secret egress. Free from the castle, Julietta and Claudio are joined by a small band of surviving children from the village.

Production and marketing: Never quite able to leave the works of Edgar Allan Poe behind, Roger Corman chose in 1989 to produce a new version of Poe's "The Masque of the Red Death," the story he directed in 1964. For director, he chose Larry Brand, who had directed and played a cop in a Corman production called *The Drifter* (1988). Brand recalled accepting the challenge: "I thought, 'Oh well, it's probably another one of those movies he made in five minutes, and I'm going to make the remake look terrific. Then I got to town and looked it up in this book I have on Roger's movies and I said, 'Geez this is his *classic!*'"[222]

Brand had never seen Corman's classic, and he refused to see it before embarking on his own version. Said Brand: "I wanted to avoid the obvious take, which was to do a campy version or a fun homage to the orig-

inal. I wanted something that was deadly serious in its own right, something that would stand or fall on its own merits."[223]

Corman assigned Daryl Haney to write the script. Haney had scripted and starred in the Corman-produced *Daddy's Boys, Friday the 13th, Part VII* (1988), and the Corman-produced *Crime Zone* (1988). He was working as an actor in the Corman-produced *Lords of the Deep* when he received the assignment to script *The Masque of the Red Death.* Corman was unhappy with Haney's original draft because it did not include enough of the Bergmanesque quality the producer wanted. Corman finally gave the draft to director Brand for a rewrite. The screenplay captures the essence of Poe's parable and weaves a pageant incorporating ideas important both to the Middle Ages and to all times.

Production designer Stephen Greenberg, who also worked on Corman's *The Drifter,* created a castle quite different than that of the 1964 original. This castle is not opulent; it is in decay—much more in tune with a low budget. Taiwan-born Edward Pei made his debut as a cinematographer in *The Masque of the Red Death.*

Winning the role of Prospero was Adrian Paul, who starred in the popular eighties science-fiction television series *The War of the Worlds* and the even more popular nineties adventure series *Highlander.* The role of Lucretia went to Tracy Reiner (the daughter of Rob Reiner and Penny Marshall), who had just appeared in the successful *When Harry Met Sally* (1989). Claire Hoak (the daughter of former professional baseball player Don Hoak) landed the role of Julietta. Screenwriter Haney appears in the film as one of the nobles recruited by Prospero.

The important role of Machiavel (the Red Death) went to British veteran Patrick MacNee (1922–). Although MacNee had appeared in films since the early forties, probably most notably in *Hamlet* (1948), *Les Girls* (1957), and *A View to a Kill* (1985), he was best known for his starring role in the long-running television series *The Avengers* (1960–1968). Based on his popularity in *The Avengers,* he landed starring roles on television in the less successful *The New Avengers* (1976), *Gavilan,* (1982), and *Empire* (1984). Horror film fans and those conversant with psychotronic cinema would remember his appearances in *The Howling* (1980), *Waxwork* (1988), and *Lobster Man from Mars* (1989). He would go on to appear with Christopher Lee in *Sherlock Holmes and the Leading Lady* (1991) and in *Waxwork II: Lost in Time* (1991).

The Masque of the Red Death was filmed at Concorde's Venice, California, studios, with additional scenes shot in the California desert. It received limited release in the United States and eventually was released in video with the ad line "An engrossing tale of power, paranoia and sexual taboo."

Critique: Although *Masque of the Red Death* (1989) was largely ignored when it was released, it subsequently received some attention in the usual film review books. Leonard Maltin awarded the film two stars and ventured this opinion: "Roger Corman produced this remake of one of his best films. Poe's Prince Prospero (Paul) is still dissipated, but this time more thoughtful and troubled. Despite an interesting approach to the figure of the Red Death and a literate (if talky) script, overall cheapness and very slow pace cripple this medieval melodrama."

The Overlook Film Encyclopedia: Horror proved hardly more kind, praising Reiner's performance but concluding, "The grandeur and elegance of Corman's earlier film are missing: in their place is plentiful dialogue about the cruelty of God and Death and the behavior of princes."

In my view, *Masque of the Red Death* (1989) is one of those rare horror films that successfully rises above the conventions of the genre while at the same time delivering what mature genre fans expect. It rises above the conventions of the genre by addressing ideas of perennial importance to humanity. Among them are aristocracy, duty, fate, God, good and evil, justice, life and death, nature, punishment, and wealth.

The idea of plutocracy, central to Poe's story, is transferred successfully to the screen. Plutocracy is rule by the wealthy. We quickly discover that Prince Prospero's father ruled on the strength of wealth and property, not virtue. In the opening scenes, Prospero has a dream in which Machiavel tells young Prospero that "Not even death can look on your father's excesses with approval." Machiavel teaches that there must be more mercy and less "justice." "I will not disappoint you," Prospero replies. "It is you yourself you best not disappoint," Machiavel warns. When a hanged man threatens Prospero in the dream, the prince awakens in fear. "They're only dreams," Lucretia says. "We live in dreams," Prospero replies uneasily. "Something has been following me, Lucretia. It always has. I can't see its face. There's no face, only the face of imagination." These scenes raise the issue of aristocracy from Poe's story and also introduce a recurrent theme in Poe's work—that life is a dream within a dream. However, unlike films such as *Murders in the Rue Morgue* (1971), this film does not continue an exploration of the latter theme.

When the Red Death breaks out in the countryside, Prospero asks, "Do you suppose God has a sense of humor? All smiles are measures of our mortality. We have brought this on ourselves. We have brought death to us." Prospero seems to sense that the excesses of his own administration have called death to the countryside to punish him. When Prospero shudders at the number of sins he has committed, he is reminded that a prince is his own measure and that all men sin. Prospero states: "A man must be more than an animal. A prince must be more than a man." One of the key conflicts raging within Prospero's psyche is that of the role of the prince. Prospero has power and means to keep it. To keep it, he feels he must rule harshly. Fate made him a prince. Has not fate then dictated his cruelty? As he says, "Man thinks he has a choice. He has *none.*"

He senses that a prince's virtue should be the foundation of his rule, not his power born of wealth and property alone. Yet he lacks the courage to be that kind of prince, and the conflict torments him deeply.

The meaning of death also preys upon Prospero's mind. At one point he kneels in the dungeon and watches carefully as a prisoner dies as a result of torture. When the man has died, Prospero confides to Lucretia, "Do you know what changed? Absolutely nothing. He just stopped moving, that's all." Prospero then makes love to Lucretia in the dungeon as the dead man hangs above them. This juxtaposition (passion and life/pain and death) is symbolic of existence itself, as well as symbolic of the war within Prospero's soul.

Claudio is a questioner too, but not a tortured one. He basically accepts life as it is and simply resolves to be the best human being he can be under the circumstances. When Prospero sends Claudio and some soldiers out to bring a number of village maidens to the castle, the men find a victim of the Red Death. One soldier touches the corpse before Claudio can warn him of the consequences. Claudio immediately draws his sword and kills the soldier, explaining that if he had not killed the man, "he would have died much worse." Upon hearing of Prospero's request for maidens, the villagers protest that when the previous ruler made such requests, the maidens were often never seen again. Claudio simply reminds them that "Prince Prospero rules as his father, and his father before him. It is the way of things." In other words, princes will act like princes and subjects must act like subjects. That is fate. Later, when the revelers have passed out and Prospero and Claudio have a quiet moment, they have a heart-to-heart talk:

CLAUDIO: The castle is secure, my lord.
PROSPERO: Look at them, sleeping in the land of the dead. Do you suppose God tests man past his capacity to endure?
CLAUDIO: I don't know, my lord.
PROSPERO: There is no balance, and there

is no equity. Death is winning his war against men.
CLAUDIO: No. He wins every battle, but never the war.
PROSPERO: Perhaps he's never had such able accomplices. Why do you suppose it is I have no children?
CLAUDIO: I can't say, my lord.
PROSPERO: Could it be God's punishment?
CLAUDIO: I don't know that God punishes us, my lord. You remember our first campaign? We were hardly boys. On the first night of battle I fell asleep and dreamed I had been killed and stood before God. And it was I who stood in judgment of Him. I demanded to know why He acted so harshly against his children. God just looked at me and laughed. "Stupid boy," He said. "God no longer acts in creation. He simply watches."

Lucretia is involved in an incestuous relationship with her brother. Perhaps it is for love, perhaps for power, or for both. When Prospero turns his attention to Julietta, Lucretia plunges a knife into her own hand in a possible suicide attempt. When Prospero finds her, she says: "You wanted to remove the color red, my lord. See how easy that was. I've removed it from my veins. You always believed that sin was in the blood. Your father and your father's father—all the way back to Adam. You've ended the bloodline. I see that now. But have you ended sin, Prospero? This is a small world you've created here within these walls. And you may be a god, but you're a terribly small one." This tortured observation, with all its focus on fate, sin, and God makes the audience recall an earlier scene in which Prospero discovers that a nobleman has tortured one of Prospero's prisoners to death just for sport. Prospero explodes with anger and orders the dungeon keeper to lop off the hand of the nobleman. At the last second, he orders the dungeon keeper to halt. Then he says to the nobleman, "There is only one voice that speaks for life and death within these walls. How do you like the acts of a capricious god?" These scenes establish Prospero as a small god, one of earth's petty stand-ins. He accepts his role, yet questions the morality of his position. Is it all the will of God and fate?

The answers come when the Red Death enters the castle walls in the form of Prospero's former tutor Machiavel. As the *Overlook Film Encyclopedia: Horror* suggests, the resemblance of the name is irony only. Machiavel is *not* Machiavellian, but Prospero is. And as the Red Death, Machiavel enters the castle walls and offers some answers to the questions raised by the film. Before Prospero knows that Machiavel is the Red Death, the tutor poses a riddle: "When man invades death's domain, where is death to go?" The implication, lost on Prospero, is that the Prince (not death or God) has chosen to decide who lives and dies. Death then comes to the domain of the prince. "I hope you won't judge me without a trial," Prospero jests. "No more than would you," Machiavel solemnly answers. "Shall we dance?" Prospero asks the revelers. "It's long overdue," says Machiavel, the Red Death. Machiavel removes his gloves and the dance of death begins.

As the Red Death, Machiavel explains to Prospero the reason for the plague:

MACHIAVEL: How do you like the face of your tutor, Prospero? I had a dream, dear pupil. The minute I died, the first victim of the Red Death, I entered the realm of the dead and came face to face with the master himself. Death wouldn't let me rest and sent me back to the realm of the living to be his messenger. And it seems, my pupil, that you are fouling his name.

PROSPERO: How can the name of death be fouled?

MACHIAVEL: There is only one fairness in life, and that is the fairness of death. Death doesn't choose between rich and poor, young and old, man and woman. But you, dear pupil, have taken upon yourself to decide who lives and who dies, and there is no fairness in that. When you invade the domain of a neighbor, isn't it to be expected that the neighbor will retaliate?

PROSPERO: You treated me too well, old friend.

MACHIAVEL: Not well enough.

PROSPERO: There are no ghosts, and na-

ture is the only instrument of death. You're but a man.

MACHIAVEL: Very good, dear pupil. Do you recognize my face, Prospero? Have you seen it in the mirror?

The point is that Prospero's role as prince has caused him to contradict himself (and the order of things) by regarding himself as the deliverer of what only nature (or death) can ethically deliver. Order of things, indeed? Although Machiavel leaves plenty of mystery in his wake, he clarifies the role of the prince in the order of things, and his explanations are not Machiavellian. Invading the land like an Old Testament prophet, the Red Death offers people choices and then strikes down those who refuse him bread. In this role he is a Christ figure. Benito goes door to door as a Noah, warning people of the coming plague, but the people do not listen. Prospero is the prince who in biblical terms worships Mammon, but Mammon is a false god. Significantly, all of these themes are present to a greater or lesser extent in Poe's parable. Claudio tries to accept necessary suffering (a part of the human condition) along with unnecessary suffering (as often engineered by Prospero). His negative reaction to the enforced dance of the naked maidens is symbolic of his position that human beings can rise above their animal natures. Even the revelers eventually fall silent in shame as they uncomfortably gaze at the travesty of the betrayed dancers. The message seems to be that the degradation of human beings is a shameful act and that while the human body can be exploited, the human spirit cannot. In fact, the relationship between Julietta and Prospero is a study in this very reality.

Critically, the 1989 version of *Masque of the Red Death* has suffered by comparison with its 1964 predecessor. But are such conclusions justified? The 1964 film stands as one of the best film adaptations of Poe's work, but the 1989 version, though different in execution, is definitely of equal quality. The most obvious differences are in the depictions of Prospero himself. In the 1964

Masque, Vincent Price is a devil worshipper (unlike Poe's Prospero), and the dénouement makes it clear that he worships a false god. Price's Prospero does not question the order of things. He is a zealot on the side of evil. In contrast, Paul's Prospero is a multifaceted human being, a prince who questions the order of things and, Hamlet-like, cannot reconcile what ought to be with what is. Paul's Prospero is much more emblematic of the human condition as experienced by thinking, sensitive human beings. This is not to imply that everyone who dislikes the 1989 *Masque* is a simpleton. It is to imply that genre expectations and taste itself can influence to some extent critical judgments. My purpose here is to show that the 1989 version can be defended as a fine film.

The 1964 *Masque* is clearly more visually attractive and stylish. Contrast, for example, the masques themselves. The 1964 masque is beautifully choreographed, majestic even as death wipes out the participants. The 1989 masque is simpler, definitely not majestic, but more earthy in its horrible depictions of death. Both films can boast en-hancing musical soundtracks, but the 1989 version is at least equal to its predecessor because of the more simple, tragic medieval flavor that matches the more simple, tragic proceedings reflective of the period.

The main criticism of the 1989 *Masque* is its "talky" script. Evidently some critics prefer that genre conventions be more strictly followed. Both the 1964 and 1989 screenplays are literate, but the 1989 *Masque* is much more significant in its realistic handling of important ideas. Unfortunately, too many genre films play by the numbers and avoid confronting the audience with intellectual dichotomies that transcend the genre. Interestingly, the 1964 *Masque* relied heavily on Ingmar Bergman's *The Seventh Seal* for its intellectual roughage, and *The Seventh Seal*, like most of Bergman's films, is very "talky" and "uncinematic." The 1989 *Masque* is actually more Bergmanesque than the 1964 version that pays obvious homage to the Swedish director. Critics can't have it both ways, and the position they should take is that the 1989 *Masque* is a masterpiece equal to, if not slightly superior to, the 1964 original.

Il gatto nero (1990); aka *Edgar Allan Poe's The Black Cat*; *De Profundis*; *Out of the Depths*
World Picture/21st Century, Italy

Credits: Directed by Lewis (Luigi Cozzi) Coates; produced by Lucio Lucidi; story and screenplay by Luigi Cozzi; art direction by Marina Pinzuti; cinematography by Pasquale Rachini; music by Vince Tempera; edited by Piero Bozza; production manager—Piero Amati; special effects by Antonio Corridori and Armando Valcauda.

Running time: 85 minutes.

Cast: Florence Guerin (Ann), Urbano Barberini (Mark), Caroline Munro (Nora), Brett Halsey (Levin), Luisa Maneri, Karina Huff, Alessandra Acciai, Giada Cozzi, Michele Marsina, Jasmine Maimone, Antonio Marsina.

Story: Actresses Ann and Nora are working on a film based on Edgar Allan Poe's "The Black Cat." Meanwhile, Ann's husband, Mark, and Nora's husband, Dan, are collaborating on an upcoming film project called *Levana*. With Mark set to direct and Dan working on the screenplay, they seek the funding of Leonard Levin, an embittered producer confined to a wheelchair.

Mark has Ann tabbed to play Levana, a witch appearing in Baudelaire's "Suspiria de Profundis." According to Mark, director Dario Argento featured Levana in his film *Suspiria*, leaving enough of the witch's legend for another film because the goddesses of pain are three. Levana is the mother of tears. Levana is the third sister, the evil mother who walks the world as a living shadow and rules a vast kingdom from behind the triple veil of crepe that covers her face. She is the mother of madness, the counselor of suicide, the slash of the tiger, the breath of the dragon. The tomb is sacred to her; she is the life of darkness. She will not rest until she has tortured hearts beyond the brink of madness.

While looking forward to playing Levana, Ann awakens at night and is attacked by the apparition of Levana, who proclaims that Ann will never show the face of Levana on the screen. Ann will die first, Levana promises. Suddenly Ann awakens in her bed. While she asks herself if it was all a dream, Mark chalks her experience up to stress.

Again Levana's voice awakens Ann, who goes downstairs to find a young girl holding a glowing sphere. Suddenly Ann is attacked by Levana. Again Ann awakens in her bed. Was it only a dream? She goes downstairs only to be shocked by explosions inside her refrigerator.

When Mark reveals his fears about Ann's sanity to Dan, the latter postulates that Ann is being affected by working in the production of Poe's "The Black Cat." When Mark asks what Poe's story has to do with witches, Dan explains that in Poe's story the narrator's wife has made frequent allusion to the ancient popular notion which regarded all black cats as witches in disguise. For the moment Mark is satisfied.

As Mark and Dan try to convince Levin to produce *Levana*, Ann has hallucinations regarding William, the cousin of Ann's housekeeper Sarah, and a phantom refrigerator repairman. As a result of these experiences, Ann fears for the life of her baby son.

When Levin agrees to produce the film, Mark and Dan pay a visit to a professor for further background on Levana. The professor, astonished that Mark and Dan know so little of the thirteenth-century witch's history, pulls out a book called *Suspiria de Profundis* by Thomas De Quincey, published in 1845. This book, she claims, is the earliest source related to Levana. The professor then warns them that making a film about Levana might conjure her. Mark an Dan leave the professor when she refuses to loan them the book. When they are gone, the professor reads from the book:

> But one day the third mother will return to the world of men to wreck her vengeance on the sons of the sons of those who had burned her at the stake. If she takes the body of a young woman born under the sixth moon, there will be no way to stop her. But if she is first reincarnated in the male form, she will have to sacrifice a newborn child in order to regain the power that will make it possible for her to carry out her complete revenge.

The professor, suspecting that some nefarious plot is afoot, is stalked by her black cat and killed by Levana before she can reveal her suspicions to Mark and Dan. The black cat then skulks about as Dan works on the screenplay at his country house. Soon he is attacked by an unknown assailant and rendered a bloody mess.

Meanwhile, Levana awakens Ann and tells her to go downstairs. When Ann obeys, she sees the little girl with the glowing sphere speaking to her from a television set. The girl identifies herself as a fairy named Sybil and insists that both she and Levana have always inhabited Ann's body. Intestines then burst through the television screen onto Ann's floor, along with a knife that Levana orders Ann to pick up and use on her baby. Ann obeys and goes to the baby's bedroom. Although Mark arrives just in time to prevent her from killing their child, the two end up stabbing each other to death. Suddenly Ann awakens in bed with Mark beside her. Was it all just another nightmare? Fearful for the baby, Ann runs into the baby's room only to find him gone. On the wall, she finds the words "You are not Levana." After Mark has left, the mortally injured Dan crashes his car through the wall of Ann's house. After telling her that someone else, not Levana, is behind the strange occurrences, he dies.

Meanwhile, Mark is at Nora's house. The two are having an affair, and Mark says that after Ann is confined to a mental institution, he wants Nora to play the part of Levana. As Mark and Nora make love, Ann drives to Levin's house with a pistol and accuses him of stealing her son. Levin, however, is a corpse animated by Levana. He tells her that Levana took the baby to protect him from Ann. He suggests that she kill herself, after which Mark will marry Nora. Unpersuaded, she shoots Levin instead. Sarah then shows up and tells Ann that Nora has the baby. After shooting Sarah, Ann drives to Nora's house and is given her baby. Nora informs Ann that Levana is controlling everything and that she should go home, where Levana is waiting. Nora and Mark follow Ann but are both killed by Levana for being too weak to carry out fully Levana's plan.

Upon arriving home with her baby, Ann cowers as Levana causes fiery disturbances in and around her house. Then Sarah arrives and proclaims herself a mutant, the next step in human evolution. She has taken the place of God, and whatever she thinks happens. She has been the cause of Ann's hallucinations. A power struggle ensues between Ann and Sarah, which Ann wins. Suddenly all who have died (in the film) return to life. Ann then goes to the television set to say good-bye to Sybil. Sybil says good-bye to Ann and Levana. Ann is sure now that all will be well. She has her husband and her son, she knows what love is, and she knows that *Levana* will be a hit movie. Then she hears the voice of Levana saying, "I will be back in the body of your child," and the eyes of Ann's baby glow just as do Levana's.

Production and marketing: Although the screen says "Edgar Allan Poe's *The Black Cat*," this film has precious little to do with Edgar Allan Poe or his title story. In fact, there are only four rather superfluous references to Poe in the film: (1) the opening credits, (2) the production of a film called *The Black Cat*, (3) black cats creeping about, and (4) a reference to Poe's story in which the narrator's wife reflects on the legend that black cats are the embodiment of witches.

Director and screenwriter Luigi Cozzi is probably best known for his *Contamination—alien arriva sulla terra* (1980), which rips off both America's *Alien* (1979) and Great Britain's *Quatermass II* (1958). Although Poe's is an oblique inspiration for *Il gatto nero*, the real (and acknowledged) inspirations are Italian horror-film directors Mario Bava and Dario Argento. The idea of a witch returning from the grave to take revenge against the descendents of those who killed her is taken directly from Mario Bava's classic *La maschera del demonio* (1960, aka *Black Sunday*). In Bava's film, the witch threatens to merge with another young woman (both are played by Barbara Steele), a theme also present in Cozzi's screenplay. Cozzi's witch is obviously intended to be another incarnation of Helena Marcos, the witch queen of Dario Argento's stylish shocker *Suspiria* (1977). Argento filmed a follow-up to *Suspiria* titled *Inferno* (1980), which he considered the second of his "Mother of Tears" trilogy. The third film was never made, and Cozzi, who began with the idea of completing the trilogy, ends by filming an homage to Argento instead. Not only do Cozzi's characters mention Argento by name, but parts of the eerie Goblin's *Suspiria* soundtrack are also included. Cozzi's Levana somewhat resembles Argento's Marcos, and in a scene of obvious homage, Cozzi superimposed churning maggots over what should be Levana's eyes and mouth. Maggots, of course, play a key role in one of *Suspiria's* more memorable scenes.

Cozzi also draws from De Quincey's and Baudelaire's separate works titled *Suspiria De*

Profundis (which literally means "sighs from the depths"). The quotations in the film attributed to De Quincey do not exist in his *Suspiria De Profundis*, however. De Quincey's work was intended as a sequel to *Confessions of an English Opium Eater*, a book of "dream paintings." The central theme of the work is the necessity of pain and sorrow for the growth of the human soul. In a section called "Levana and Our Ladies of Sorrow," De Quincey writes:

> Oftentimes at Oxford I saw Levana in my dreams. I knew her by her Roman symbols. Who is Levana? ... Levana was the Roman goddess that performed for the new-born infant the earliest office of ennobling kindness,—typical, by its mode, of that grandeur which belongs to man everywhere, and of that benignity in powers invisible which even in Pagan worlds sometimes descends to sustain it. At the very moment of birth, just as the infant tasted for the first time the atmosphere of our troubled planet, it was laid on the ground.... But immediately, lest so grand a creature should grovel there for more than one instant, either the paternal hand, as proxy for the goddess Levana, or some near kinsman, as proxy for the father, raised it upright, bade it look erect as the king of all this world, and presented its forehead to the stars, saying, perhaps in his heart, "Behold what is greater than yourselves!" This symbolic act represented the function of Levana. And that mysterious lady, who never revealed her face (except to me in dreams), but always acted by delegation, had her name from the Latin verb (as still it is in the Italian verb) *levare*, to raise aloft.... And hence it has arisen that some people have understood by Levana the tutelary power that controls the education of the nursery.... She therefore watches over human education.

Cozzi's Levana is interested in an infant, but for nefarious reasons. Also, Cozzi's Levana often acts by delegation, again for nefarious reasons. In fact, Cozzi's Levana more strongly resembles De Quincey's third lady of sorrow:

> Her kingdom is not large, or else no flesh should live: but within that kingdom all power is hers.... Through the treble veil of crape which she wears the fierce light of a blazing misery, that rests not for matins or for vespers, for noon of day or noon of night, for ebbing or for flowing tide, may be read from the very ground. She is the defier of God. She also is the mother of lunacies, and the suggestress of suicides.

In essence, Cozzi turns De Quincey's Levana into a cross between Argento's Helena Marcos and De Quincey's third sister, whom De Quincey identifies as "*Mater Tenebarum—Our Lady of Darkness.*" Although Cozzi's sphere-cradling Sybil is a good fairy, she somewhat physically resembles the little-girl-as-Satan in Fellini's "Toby Dammit" episode of *Histoires extraordinaires* (1967). Cozzi's skulking black cat seems lifted from Fulci's *Il gatto nero* (1981), and the television that emits entrails was probably inspired by similar scenes in David Cronenberg's *Videodrome* (1983).

The cast members most familiar to American audiences are Caroline Munro (1951–) and Brett Halsey (1933–). British actress Munro had appeared in a variety of horror films, including *The Abominable Dr. Phibes* (1971, with Vincent Price), *Captain Kronos: Vampire Hunter* (1972), *Dracula A.D. 1972* (1972, with Peter Cushing and Christopher Lee), *The Golden Voyage of Sinbad* (1973), *The Devil Within Her* (1973), *At the Earth's Core* (1976, with Peter Cushing), *Maniac* (1980), and *Slaughter High* (1986). American leading-man Halsey was best known for *The Glass Web* (1953), *Cry Baby Killer* (1958, directed by Roger Corman), *The Best of Everything* (1959), *Return to Peyton Place* (1961), and *Twice-Told Tales* (1963, with Vincent Price).

Critique: As explained above, *Il gatto nero* owes much more to Mario Bava, Dario Argento, and Thomas De Quincey than it does to Edgar Allan Poe. For whatever reason, the film received little if any distribution in the United States.

The Overlook Film Encyclopedia: Horror states: "Like Fulci's *Un gatto nel cervello* (1991), this would-be self-reflective movie combines gory exploitation with meaningless in-jokes about the Italian schlock industry." *Video Hound's Golden Movie Retriever 1996* awards the film only 1 1/2 bones.

The major problem with *Il gatto nero* is the screenplay. After three viewings, I still cannot adequately make sense of the confusing plot twists. Is Sarah from outer space? What is her connection with Levana? In what ways have Levana and Sybil always inhabited Ann's body? What is the significance of the black cat (except to justify the title)? What is Ann's true nature? At the end of the film, what is the significance of Levana's threat to possess the child? In other words, what is really going on here? So many confusing dreams within dreams make it difficult for the audience to follow the plot threads, and the lack of adequate explanation at the end leaves a taste of irritating dissatisfaction.

Although they cannot outweigh the film's negatives, the positives include an evocative main musical theme and eye-catching special effects, some of which are copied from Argento's *Suspiria*. Although Caroline Munro overacts, perhaps her gorgeous presence makes up for the defect; otherwise the cast is adequate. Also adequate, though uninspired, is the cinematography.

If Cozzi's reliance on dreams within dreams was meant to evoke the mood of Poe, it fails miserably. The contemporary Italian setting, rock music, and colorful special effects place *Il gatto nero* far from the universe of Poe. Although watchable and visually ambitious, the film ultimately fails.

Due occhi diabolici (1990); aka *Two Evil Eyes, Duo occhi mallochio*

ADC Gruppo Bema, Italy and U.S.A.
The film comprises two separate stories by two separate directors.

Credits: Executive producers—Claudio and Dario Argento; film editor—Pasquale Buba; music—Pino Donnaggio, complimented by Natale Massara. "The Facts in the Case of Mr. Valdemar": director—George A. Romero; screenplay—George A. Romero; director of photography—Peter Reniers. "The Black Cat": director—Dario Argento; screenplay—Dario Argento and Franco Ferrini; director of photography—Beppe Maccari.

Cast: "The Facts in the Case of Mr. Valdemar": Adrienne Barbeau (Jessica Valdemar), Ramy Zada (Robert), Bingo O'Malley (Ernest Valdemar), E. G. Marshall (Mr. Pike). "The Black Cat": Harvey Keitel (Usher), Madeline Potter (Annabel), John Amos (chief of police), Sally Kirkland (Eleanora), Kim Hunter (Mrs. Pym), E. G. Marshall (Mr. Pym), Holter Ford Graham (violin student).

Story: Opening narration: "It's the depravity that's in all of us. Perversity is one of the prime impulses of the heart. Who has never done something wrong just because it was forbidden, to be evil for the love of being evil?" "The Facts in the Case of Mr. Valdemar": Attractive Jessica Valdemar presents lawyer Stephen Pike with papers signed by her elderly and dying husband, Ernest Valdemar, liquidating his financial assets and giving them to Jessica. To answer Pike's suspicions, she phones home and has her husband reassure the lawyer that he intends to do what the papers allow. Pike remains suspicious but tells Jessica that the lion's share of the money will be held up for two or three weeks and that she had better keep her husband alive until then or she will have trouble collecting. Jessica boldly admits to Pike that as a former airline hostess she married the old man for his money. He got to show her off, she says, and now she is collecting what she earned.

Robert, Jessica's lover and Valdemar's

physician, has been placing the dying man in a hypnotic state, during which times the doctor methodically makes his patient sign away his assets to Jessica. To pull off the scheme, Robert and Jessica are keeping Valdemar at home in great pain. When Valdemar dies under hypnosis, the two schemers decide not to report the death until their financial fraud yields fruit. As Valdemar's doctor, Robert plans to sign the death certificate and bury Valdemar in a closed coffin. He convinces Jessica to keep Valdemar in a basement freezer for preservation purposes.

Shortly thereafter, the chain-smoking, hard-drinking Jessica imagines she hears groans coming from the basement freezer. Robert brushes off her concerns but agrees to stay the night. Later, while Robert lies in a self-hypnotized state, Jessica again thinks she hears groans coming from basement. In the morning, they open the freezer and hear a telepathic message from the frozen "corpse." "I have been sleeping," Valdemar moans, "but now I am dead." Having expired under hypnosis, the old man is obviously in a horrible state of limbo, neither living nor dead. In answer to Robert's questions, Valdemar states that he is in no pain. He can see a very bright light far away in the distance, but unable to reach the light, he remains in cold darkness. "Help me, Jessica!" he cries. There are others watching him, he says. And they want something.

Robert believes he has proven that consciousness exists after death. The next morning Jessica wakes up to a radio broadcast of the economic news, while downstairs, Valdemar pleads with the doctor to wake him from the hypnotic state and release him from limbo. "Wake me," he pleads, "and let me go." He then tells Robert that the "others" want to use him to "pass through."

Unable to stand the stress any longer, Jessica approaches the freezer and fires bullets into Valdemar's forehead and cheek, obviously making it necessary that they change their original plan. Jessica blurts out the suggestion that they bury the body in the woods

out back, sign off on the death certificate, and tell everyone that her husband was shipped to another state to be buried near relatives. Although Robert fears the new plan will not work, after dark he goes to the woods to dig a grave.

Meanwhile, as a thunderstorm rolls in, the freezer door opens and the horribly bullet-scarred Valdemar stalks Jessica to the second story of their home. "They're coming for you, Jessica," he groans. "They're coming for you. They don't want me to go into the ground." Jessica, nearly wild with fear, fires the pistol at Valdemar without effect. As Robert runs into the house, the old man gains his revenge by turning the gun to Jessica's temple and pulling the trigger. After crashing over the banister, Jessica lies dead at Robert's feet. Robert then awakens Valdemar from the hypnotic trance, at which point the old man says that the "others" are with Robert now, and drops dead. Hardly giving Jessica a second look, Robert takes the money out of the safe and leaves the house.

As police later examine the bloody scene, amid remarks about the depravity of the rich, they hypothesize that Jessica shot Valdemar, stored him in the freezer where blood was found, dragged the body upstairs, and shot herself. They must dispense with that theory, however, when it becomes apparent that Valdemar's corpse is in a hideous state of advanced decay.

Later, while Robert is sleeping under self-hypnosis in a hotel room, a band of shadowy figures—obviously the "others"—enter through the open window. Accompanied by gusts of wind that blow the stolen money about the room, they thrust Robert's pyramid-shaped self-hypnosis device into his chest.

Weeks later the hotel manager calls in the police to investigate a hideous groaning inside the hotel room. The same two officers who investigated the Valdemar murders show up to discover Robert still on his bed. "There's no one to wake me," the decaying corpse cries. The terrified detective fires repeatedly at Robert's advancing corpse, splattering blood on the bills that litter the room.

Story: "The Black Cat": As police investigate the scene where a young woman has been cut in half by a giant pendulum, a photographer reactivates the murder machine and begins snapping pictures. The photographer is Rod Usher, a professional photographer specializing in grizzly metropolitan murders.

That evening, as Usher develops the photographs, a black cat comes seemingly from nowhere and interrupts his work. Shortly afterward, Annabel, his lover, informs him that the cat, which has a white mark on its breast, is a stray she has adopted. In bed that night, as Usher perceives the cat malevolently staring at him, he finds his dislike of the animal growing. "In the Middle Ages," Annabel says, "Inquisitors burned women and black cats because they thought they were witches. Finally there weren't many black cats left. Cats remember, so they don't trust." When Usher is later awakened by the cat, he throws something at it and receives a growl in return.

Annabel, an accomplished violinist, teaches the instrument to several young students, one being an adolescent boy named Christian. All the while, Usher continues to resent the presence of the watchful cat. When he asks Annabel the cat's name, she tells him it is a secret. "Don't hurt her," she warns, as though sensing Usher's discomfort.

As time passes and Usher's work is not going well, he becomes increasingly irritable. One evening in the dark room, he twists the cat into contorted positions while snapping photos of it with a foot-activated camera. He ends up torturing the animal to death in order to take pictures for his upcoming book, *Metropolitan Horrors*.

Usher drinks, and as he drinks, he becomes impatient with Annabel's concern for her vanished cat. "I know you killed her," she says. He denies the charge and hits her. She flees upstairs, and he follows.

Later he has a nightmare during which he sees Annabel at a witch's sabbat. A hanged black cat is placed into Annabel's arms. She identifies Usher as the killer and shows him a white mark which looks like a gallows on the cat's breast. The celebrants then hoist Usher up by ropes and drop him vertically onto a wooden spear, which pierces his groin, travels through his body, and emerges from his mouth. Usher is understandably disturbed by the dream.

Some time later the photographer finds himself at another gruesome crime scene. This time a man has been apprehended at a cemetery after digging up his cousin and pulling out all 32 of her teeth. Again present is the police chief who headed the pendulum murder investigation. "How could a man do something like that?" the chief questions. "I'll never figure it out."

Meanwhile, Annabel, still mourning the loss of her cat, kisses young Christian, at which point the door opens, presumably marking Usher's appearance. Later she sees Rod's newly published book and discovers the pictures of her cat. She immediately decides to leave him and makes arrangements with a friend to go to New York. "I'm so afraid," she says.

At a tavern, Usher sees a black cat that stares at him. Oddly, it sports a white gallows mark on its breast. Eleanora, the bar maid, says he can have the cat, which is a stray. Usher arrives home just as Annabel is about to leave with her suitcases. She hides until she hears a cat crying and struggling. Rushing into the darkroom, she finds Usher strangling the black cat with a cord and knocks him unconscious with a metal pipe. He quickly regains his senses, however, and attacks the cat with a meat cleaver. When Annabel intervenes, he chops her to death, and the cat escapes.

At that point, Usher's landlord, Mr. Pym, knocks on the door and inquires about the noise. Usher explains it away as a domestic dispute and says that the blood on the floor and stairs is from his cut foot. When Pym leaves, Usher seals away Annabel's body behind a wall and bookshelves and tells the Pyms that he is taking Annabel on a brief vacation so they can patch things up. When he returns, he tells the Pyms that Annabel took a train home but has not yet arrived. He tells Christian that she has gone on an orchestra tour and will not return for some time. But when the boy finds her violin still in the house, he suspects foul play and alerts the Pyms.

About this time, Usher is startled to hear a scratching sound behind the wall concealing Annabel. When he investigates, he sees the black cat freeing itself through a hole it has scratched in the wall. Usher had apparently walled it up within the tomb. When the cat springs free and attacks Usher, he kills it with a saw, places its bleeding corpse in a trash bag, and tosses it into a dumpster.

The next day, however, acting upon the suspicions of the violin student and the Pyms, the police are at Usher's door. As usual, the chief is in charge of the investigation. When Usher seems to have answered all of the chief's questions satisfactorily and the police are leaving the premises, Usher calls out, "What did you expect to find behind these solidly put together walls?" At that point, the chief returns to have Usher autograph a copy of *Metropolitan Horrors*. It is then that the officers hear a scratching sound upstairs. The chief's assistant investigates, discovers the freshly plastered wall, and begins battering it down. Although a terrible stench from behind the wall almost overcomes the officer, he persists until the interior of the enclosure becomes visible. There inside, Annabel's rotting corpse is being eaten by kittens obviously left by the previously imprisoned black cat, which had been pregnant. Although handcuffed to the chief, Usher takes advantage of the shocking moment to surprise and kill both of his captors.

At that point, as shouts and knocks sound at the door downstairs, Usher, still handcuffed to the chief, ends up hanging himself from a tree while unsuccessfully trying to escape through an upstairs window.

Production and marketing: "The Facts in the Case of Mr. Valdemar": George A. Romero was already one of America's premiere horror-film directors when in 1990 he chose to film Poe's "The Masque of the Red Death" as part of *Due occhi diabolici*, but upon learning of Roger Corman's plan to produce a remake of his own 1964 classic, Romero chose Poe's "The Facts in the Case of M. Valdemar" instead.

Born in 1939, Romero left his Bronx, New York, home to enroll in the art and drama departments of the Carnegie-Mellon Institute. Five years later he founded a film production company and began making commercials for such clients as Alcoa, Calgon, and U.S. Steel. In 1968 he directed his first feature film, the shocking and infamous *Night of the Living Dead*, which went on to become one of the great cult classics of all time. Over the years, some critics and Romero himself have claimed the existence of a plethora of social statements in the film, but while such an interpretation is possible, the film largely works as a basic, gut-wrenching horror movie. Clearly, Romero took chances in the film by casting a black man in the lead among an otherwise white cast, by killing off all the principals, including the leading man, and by vividly depicting zombies hungrily devouring human flesh and entrails. Indeed, *Night of the Living Dead* surprises and shocks the viewer at every turn by defying most expected horror-film conventions.

After directing two low-budget pictures, one of which has horror elements, Romero returned fully to his roots with *The Crazies* (1973), a highly suspenseful film in which a biological plague is loosed upon a small Pennsylvania town. When the army arrives to restore order, the townspeople oppose the soldiers in a display of social disintegration. In his next horror film, *Martin* (1977), Romero explores and expands the contours of the vampire myth while extending a *Night of the Living Dead* theme of the diminishing individual in modern, sterile society. That theme and other social concerns reappear in both of his "Living Dead" sequels, *Dawn of the Dead* (1979) and *Day of the Dead* (1985). Although in the eighties his films became more commercial, they retained the inimitable Romero style that established his reputation.

In 1982, Romero directed *Creepshow*, a four-part film based on short stories by modern horror master Stephen King. Eight years later, in *Due occhi malocchio*, he undertook the challenge of bringing to the screen a story by the horror master for all seasons, Edgar Allan Poe. Romero had used sexy Adrienne Barbeau in *Creepshow*, and he brought her back for *Valdemar*. Following the lead of Richard Matheson's screenplay for the "Valdemar" segment of *Tales of Terror* (1962), Romero employed the revenge theme, which is not part of Poe's story. Unlike Matheson, however, Romero gambled by setting the story in contemporary times, a strategy that rarely works. The contemporary setting, however, allows Romero to explore some of the contemporary, yet in some ways timeless, themes that infused his earlier films with social relevance.

Production and marketing: "The Black Cat": If George A. Romero was the preeminent American horror film director in the seventies and eighties, then Dario Argento held the same title in Italy. His first four genre films, *L'uccello dalle piume di cristallo* (1970, aka *The Bird with the Crystal Plummage*), *Il gatto a nove code* (1971, aka *Cat O' Nine Tails*), *Quattro mosche di velluto grigio* (1971, aka *Four Flies on Grey Velvet*), *Profondo rosso* (1976, aka *Deep Red*), and *Suspiria* (1976) established Argento as a groundbreaking director. It was on *Dawn of the Dead* that Dario Argento first collaborated with George Romero. Argento had seen and greatly admired Romero's *Night of the Living Dead*. When the two agreed to meet in New York, they talked for hours and decided to make a "living dead" film together. Before co-writing the *Dawn* screenplay with Romero, Argento traveled around the Caribbean islands to study zombie legends and myths. He also worked with the rock group Goblin in preparing the musical soundtrack.

Particularly interesting is Argento's tendency to identify himself (and the audience) with the killer of beautiful women by filming the murders from the killer's perspective, a technique adopted by many lesser directors (and some quite good ones) in the eighties. Of course, this technique garnered its share of criticism, to which Argento replied:

> I like women, especially beautiful ones. If they have a good face and figure, I would much prefer to watch them being murdered than an ugly girl or a man. I certainly don't have to justify myself to anyone about this. I don't care what anybody thinks or reads into it. I have often had journalists walk out of interviews when I say what I feel about this subject.[224]

Of course, it was Poe who wrote in "The Philosophy of Composition" that "the death ... of a beautiful woman is, unquestionably, the most poetical topic in the world." While it is doubtful that Poe would have considered the slashing of beautiful women to death with butcher knives a poetical topic, there is nevertheless something in what Argento says, and there exists an artistic link between Poe and Argento on this topic,[225] which the director continues to explore. As was the case with Romero, however, the quality of Argento's work suffered in the eighties as he too seemed to have taken his style and subject matter as far as he could.

Then came *Due occhi mallochio*, the second Romero-Argento collaboration. Argento at first envisioned the film as featuring the work of four directors—George Romero, John Carpenter, Wes Craven, and himself. When persistent scheduling conflicts intervened to delay filming, Argento proceeded with only George Romero and made a film consisting of two segments.

Argento already had a great respect for Poe:

> Edgar Allan Poe is the origin of all horror. I re-read all his works while I was on holiday—the short stories, the poetry, the essays.

I understand his pain; I think it's important to make a picture that is different from the memory people have of the Corman Poe pictures, of all the other adaptations of his work. I think today we can make a picture that more accurately represents the spirit of Poe's work than was possible before, even though we changed many things in the specifics of the stories—both Romero and I. I think it's true to the spirit of Poe to set his stories in the present, because when Poe wrote he wrote about the present; he didn't set his stories on some safe, distant past. I feel Poe would have understood the world today very well.[226]

Unfortunately, the film did not get widespread distribution in the United States and showed up on premium cable television stations in 1993.

Critique: "The Facts in the Case of Mr. Valdemar": Without a doubt, the primary reason Romero chose *Valdemar* as his subject was that it provided him with the chance to return to the themes of his "living dead" films in the context of bringing a classic Poe tale to life in a contemporary setting.

In *Dawn of the Dead,* Romero made his strongest statement about the loss of human individuality in an America of mindless consumerism. Indeed, the walking dead are drawn to a shopping mall like moths to a flame because it vaguely reminds them of something that had been important to them in their lives. Of course, the not-so-subtle implication is that America's materialistic consumer culture is rendering people about as dead above the shoulders and as cold within the heart as the zombies are.

To make his point, Romero fills *Valdemar* with constant references to the greed and misplaced values of the principals. It seems that Valdemar himself knowingly and willingly "bought" his young wife in order to show her off and feed his own ego. Being a "lowly" airline hostess, she sold herself into marriage in order to reap rewards after Valdemar's death. Since the foundation of the marriage is based on material greed, as Valdemar is dying, he charges his "bitch" of

a wife with negligence, while she avoids the sight of the dying old man, whom she actually loathes. Jessica's lover Robert, suspecting that Mr. Pike is like everyone else, guesses that the lawyer won't blow the whistle on them as long as he gets his fees. On the morning she shoots her tormented husband as he suffers in limbo, Jessica wakes up to the radio financial news. When Jessica lies dead at Robert's feet, his only concern is to leave the house with the money, demonstrating that his main concern all along was green paper rather than a woman's well-being and love. One police officer, playing amateur psychologist, blames the carnage at the Valdemar residence upon the depravity of the rich.

At the end of the segment, the "others" thrust a pyramid into Robert's chest, splattering blood on the money littering the hotel room. On the back of a bloody dollar bill is a pyramid, an occult symbol of death and immortality. In the film, the pyramid symbolically links the greed for money with the limbo state of the living dead, harkening back to Romero's earlier themes as exemplified in *Dawn of the Dead.*

Although Romero derives none of this from Poe, he is quite successful in marrying his own directorial and authorial concerns with Poe's original conception of a man suspended between life and death for purposes of scientific investigation.

While Romero's direction and screenplay are most responsible for the segment's success, actress Adrienne Barbeau deserves praise for her splendid death-watch performance. While her work for husband John Carpenter in *The Fog* (1979) shows she can be soft and sexy and resilient, Romero cast her as a real bitch in both *Creepshow* and *Valdemar.* Having come a long way since her youthful appearance in *Wild Women of Wongo* (1958), Barbeau proves herself both versatile and talented.

Critique: "The Black Cat": Probably no single film product captures Poe's treatment of neurosis and psychosis as well as Argento's *The Black Cat.* In Poe's tale, the narrator is a man unaware of his own dark motivations, a man who refuses to acknowledge his own repressed hostility. As Argento's Usher photographs gruesome murder scenes, he vainly seeks explanations for the carnage, never realizing that the dark answers hide within himself. In the film segment, Poe's anonymous narrator becomes Rod Usher, chillingly brought to life by Harvey Keitel. Usher is a deeply troubled man. He is involved with a gentle, artistic woman, evidence of tenderness within him. He fulfills his artistic inclinations, however, by photographing the horribly mutilated victims of violence, a passive act masking his own repressed aggressive tendencies.

In the film, Argento also addresses Poe's theme of perversity. In "The Tell-Tale Heart," Poe first deals with the theme of people doing what they should not do just because they know they should not do it. He returns to the theme in "The Black Cat" and again in "The Imp of the Perverse." In the film, Usher displays perversity on two occasions: first, when he asks a concerned priest if he would like to see the dead rat he claims is in a blood-dripping garbage bag and again when he asks the police as they are leaving what they expected to find behind the solidly built walls of his house.

Unlike Fellini's *Never Bet the Devil Your Head,* Argento's *The Black Cat* is both contemporary and broadly true to Poe's original plot. Of course, Argento sometimes alters Poe just at those times when the viewer is lulled into expecting a faithful adaptation, such as at the end after Annabel's' body has been discovered.

Also present in *The Black Cat* are several examples of black humor that Poe would have appreciated, such as Usher's explanation that his wife should not be disturbed because she is upstairs sleeping—this after he has slaughtered her with a meat cleaver.

Argento also includes in the film many other elements drawn from the Poe canon. For example, the pendulum murder derives from Poe's "The Pit and the Pendulum," and the cemetery sequence derives from his "Berenice." The name Rod Usher derives from "The Fall of the House of Usher," the Pyms from "The Narrative of A. Gordon Pym," Annabel from the poem "Annabel Lee," and Eleanora from Poe's tale of the same name.

The Overlook Film Encyclopedia: Horror prefers Argento's adaptation to Romero's, largely because of Harvey Keitel: "Keitel's half-comic, half-horrific performance is as much in the spirit of Poe as Vincent Price's Corman protagonists, and, along with Potter's fragile presence, provides a focus for Argento's camera tricks, elaborate effects and narrative confusion."

Current opinion on the film is exemplified by Leonard Maltin's 1 1/2 star review in which he calls it "A pointless pair of tales with the second slightly more successful than the first." *Video Hound's Golden Movie Retriever 1996* gives the film only two bones. In my view, however, *Two Evil Eyes* is a well-crafted monument to Poe's memory by two of the best modern filmmakers in the horror genre. Both segments satisfy after repeated viewings, a sign of the film's potential staying power in a future when one can only hope that this masterpiece will receive the critical attention it so richly deserves.

Masque of the Red Death (1990)
Breton, U.S.A.

Credits: Directed by Alan Birkinshaw; produced by Avi Lerner and Harry Alan Towers; associate producer—John H. Stodel; cinematography by Jossi Wein; screenplay by Michael J. Murray, based on the story by Edgar Allan Poe; music by Coby Recht;

Video box art for *The Masque of the Red Death* **(1990).**

edited by Jason Krasucki; production design by Leith Ridley.

Running time: 94 minutes.

Cast: Frank Stallone (Duke), Brenda Vaccaro (Elaina), Herbert Lom (Ludwig), Michelle McBride (Rebecca), Christine Lunde (Colette), Christobel d'Ortez (Dr. Karen), Simon Poland (Max), Fozia Davidson (Kitra), Kindsay Reardon (Dallon), Godfrey Charles (Hans), Andy Barrett (Jimmy).

Story: Rebecca, a lovely photographer on an assignment to photograph aging actress Elaina Hart, drives to the Bavarian castle of the wealthy and eccentric Ludwig, who is giving a costume party based on Poe's "The Masque of the Red Death." Rebecca intends to crash the party dressed as Cupid in order to get her photographs. On the way she daydreams that she is taking photographs in a churchyard and following a trail of blood into a chapel. Inside, she finds her own heart on a slab, beating and spurting blood. Startled by her daydream, she glances at the book by Poe beside her on the seat and concludes that she has been reading too many Poe horror tales.

Rebecca successfully crashes the party and wanders among the masked revelers. As the celebration progresses, a waiter is murdered by a diminutive, deep-voiced figure dressed as the Red Death. On one side of the great hall, a giant pendulum left over from a previous party based on "The Pit and the Pendulum" keeps the time. When Ludwig appears and addresses his guests, he dedicates the night to "love and deception." "Of course," he says, "for some of you, they may be one and the same."

In time, Rebecca wanders near a table peopled by the loud-mouthed Elaina, Rebecca's former lover Max, and several other sycophants. Although Rebecca is unaware of it, the Red Death makes an attempt on her life. Shortly afterward, Max sees Rebecca snapping pictures with her camera disguised as a Cupid's bow and confronts her. He does, however, arrange for her to sit with him, Elaina, and others at Ludwig's table during dinner. Unknown to the revelers, a Dr. Karen is treating Ludwig for a terminal illness.

At dinner, Ludwig addresses those at his table as his friends. The women have obviously been his lovers, and they are all clearly jealous of each other. Besides Elaina, whom Ludwig helped into the acting business, there is struggling ingénue Colette and fashion model Kitra, both of whom Ludwig put on the road to success. Ludwig has helped his male friends too. At the table is Duke, a young actor whom Ludwig helped make a star. After Elaina leaves in a huff, she is strangled upstairs by the Red Death and left to be discovered on a stairway. Ludwig argues unpersuasively that she fell down the stairs and was not strangled.

The evening's special surprise is an Easter egg hunt featuring Fabergé eggs. During the hunt, the Red Death traps Rebecca in a torture device from which she kicks her way free. The Red Death then attacks Rebecca with a knife, but Rebecca escapes by warding off her attacker with a torch.

The clock strikes midnight, and the Red Death murders Kitra by sewing her to a giant textile loom. After this third murder, many of the guests leave the castle. Ludwig, intent that the party continue, locks the remaining guests in the castle and proclaims that the spiked gate will not reopen until 7 A.M. The Red Death locks Rebecca and Max in a room and tries to kill them with poison gas. Leaving Rebecca and Max for dead, the Red Death attacks Dr. Karen with a razor and ties her under the descending giant pendulum in the hall. Rebecca and Max escape from the room of poison gas, and Rebecca tries to free Dr. Karen from the pendulum. Rebecca is unsuccessful, however, and the pendulum decapitates Dr. Karen.

Afterward, an exhausted and depressed Ludwig admits to the remaining guests that he is dying from a disease he inherited from his father and that he gave the party in order to trick death—to outlive time itself by being with all his friends. Before her death,

Dr. Karen was working against the clock for a cure. Max accuses Ludwig of killing his friends in order to take all of them with him.

Duke finds Colette attempting suicide and persuades her to reconsider. He turns his head from her for a moment, but when he looks back, the Red Death has taken Colette's place. A sword fight ensues, and Duke becomes the Red Death's next victim.

The Red Death then attacks Max. Max pulls off the mask, gasps at the identity of the killer, but gasps for a final time when the Red Death's knife savagely penetrates his body. To finish the deed, the Red Death plunges a hatchet into Max's back for good measure.

The clock strikes 6 A.M., and Rebecca discovers the bodies of Max and Hans, a servant. She also finds the mask that Max pulled from the face of the Red Death and discovers mascara inside. Meanwhile, Colette confesses to Ludwig that she killed all of their friends so she could have Ludwig for herself. Rebecca intervenes and Colette accidentally shoots Ludwig, leading to a final struggle between Rebecca and Colette. As they fight, the clock strikes seven and the spiked castle gate opens. When Colette tries to close the gate so that she will have time to kill Rebecca, the gate impales Colette, bringing to an end the crimes of the Red Death.

Production and marketing: Michael J. Murray's screenplay loosely incorporates several Poe themes. First there is the main theme of Poe's "The Masque of the Red Death"—that of an individual's inability to escape death though wealth. Although set in contemporary times, Ludwig's Bavarian castle, with its rock bands and modern conveniences, still serves, in the mind of the wealthy eccentric, to lock death out and his friends in. In this case, death *is* one of his friends, again proving that nothing material can ultimately ward off death. Second, there is the giant pendulum of death, an echo of Poe's "The Pit and the Pendulum." Since Dr. Karen works against time to save Ludwig's life, the passage of time is of major impor-

tance to Ludwig, as it is to anyone living with death at his elbow. The pendulum in Poe's story symbolized the same concern. Third, the opening dream sequence is a reference to Poe's dream theme (illusion or reality?) as well as a harkening back to his "The Tell-Tale Heart." Fourth, a black cat makes two appearances in the film. In the first instance, Michelle McBride pets it and moves on. In the second instance, it startles her with its sudden appearance. The black cat, though reminding us of Poe's "The Black Cat," serves no other purpose here than to do just that.

Producer Harry Alan Towers returns to Poe yet again (see *Buried Alive* and *House of Usher,* both 1989) and tabs the director of his none-too-successful *House of Usher* to again mount the helm.

In a 1989 interview, Towers spoke of his approach to filming Poe:

> I'd always talked about redoing the Poes but they couldn't be done in Gothic style. They had to be done in a contemporary style, with a Gothic feel to them. So first of all, I came up with a concoction, *Buried Alive,* which has elements of "The Black Cat" and "The Tell-Tale Heart." Once that was launched, we did *The Fall of the House of Usher* and went on and did *The Masque of the Red Death.* We are planning one more, which will be *The Raven.* They're all contemporary, but they're always in a confined, Gothic kind of setting.[227]

Frank Stallone, Sylvester's brother, receives top billing as Duke, a relatively minor character. Receiving second billing is veteran actress Brenda Vaccaro (1939–), who appeared in *Midnight Cowboy* (1969) and was nominated for an Academy Award for her work in *Once Is Not Enough* (1976). She also earned a horror film credit for her starring role in *The House by the Lake* (1977).

Herbert Lom (see *Murders in the Rue Morgue* [1971]) plays Ludwig. The role was originally intended for Jack Palance, but when the legendary tough guy had to drop out at the last minute, Lom was the instant replacement. Newcomer Michelle McBride essays the costarring role of Rebecca.

Because Towers usually produces on a low budget, some sets in *Masque of the Red Death* were left over from his previous Poe films. Screenwriter Michael J. Murray explains:

> When *Buried Alive* was being finished, the sets were kept, and then they were recycled for *Usher*. At the end of *Usher* there's a fire in the house and sets that weren't burned down were recycled for *Masque of the Red Death*.... We did build a ballroom for *Masque of the Red Death*, which was our one concession to the story. But if you see all the films, you'll notice that the cellar for *Buried Alive* becomes the crypt in *Usher* where the Usher family members are buried. Then in *Masque of the Red Death*, it becomes a wine cellar.[228]

The film received limited release in the United States and quickly made its way to video. The video box warns that "Seductive terror—where you can't bear to look, but can't bear not to—is the hallmark of suspense master Edgar Allan Poe. And never has his work received a more chilling and thrilling film adaptation than *Masque of the Red Death*, a terrifying trip to the dark side of madness."

Critique: *The Overlook Film Encyclopedia: Horror* found *Masque of the Red Death* wanting, describing it as "made in the traditional Towers runaway fashion." Similarly, *Video Hound's Golden Movie Retriever 1996* awards the film only 1 1/2 bones, calling it an "Unrecognizable Poe mutation.... One scene features a pendulum, and that's it for literary faithfulness."

The *Video Hound* shortchanges the film just a bit as there are other elements of literary faithfulness in the film. Still the overall judgment of the *Encyclopedia* and *Video Hound* is correct. Nothing is more jarring at the beginning of a "Poe film" than an automobile motoring across the countryside. Because so few updatings of Poe are successful, the audience is immediately put on guard. In this case, though, there are some redeeming qualities. First, the themes from Poe's "The Masque of the Red Death" are apparent enough to merit the credit. Sec-

ond, the film is visually appealing because of more than adequate cinematography and editing. Third, the cast, with few exceptions, is strong. Lom, cast to type as the brooding Ludwig, delivers accordingly. Vaccaro is suitably disgusting as an aging, flamboyant actress on the downside of her career. Particularly impressive is Michelle McBride, without whose strong presence the film would not have worked at all. Where is she today? Fourth, the rock and roll sequences are carried off well, particularly the first song, which returns again during the closing credits. Also positive in this context is the work of Neil McKay and the Razzle Jazzle Dance Company.

On the negative side, though there are enough Poe themes to merit the credit, this film is the least Poe-esque of all the versions of "The Masque of the Red Death." Perhaps it is the over-the-top rock and roll updating by Towers; perhaps it is simply the modern concerns that thrive behind the castle walls at the expense of perennial themes. Either way, the effect is less than successful. In regard to the cast, though Frank Stallone receives top billing, his presence is such that no one could believe him to be a successful actor. He clearly does not project any of the qualities of such a character in the film. Instead, his Duke is relatively minor, largely, I assume, because Frank Stallone is a less than outstanding actor. In the same vein, Christine Lunde outrageously overacts as Colette (the Red Death). Her French persona is just too affectedly French. Perhaps she gives the kind of performance Towers and Birkinshaw wanted. Such a person would clearly not be a likely suspect in a murder scenario. Still, I hope no actress would contrive such a performance on her own.

Another negative is the large number of holes in the plot. For example, why does no one call Rebecca's hand? She has crashed the party. Yet she ends up at Ludwig's table without a question on his part. Also, the Red Death is hardly believable. The small figure out-wrestles and finally strangles the bigger, stronger Elaina. The Red Death also kills several men of greater build and strength. And how could Colette don the garments of the Red Death while sitting next to Duke without his noticing? And given her voice, how could she possibly manufacture the very deep voice of the Red Death? These are only a few of the holes. One could go on a hunt for holes in this film with much greater excitement than that generated by the Fabergé Easter egg hunt.

On the whole, the film (largely thanks to McBride and Lom) is mildly enjoyable as a time passer. It does not merit repeated viewings, however, and it will not survive the passage of time.

The Pit and the Pendulum (1991)
Full Moon Entertainment, U.S.A.

Credits: Directed by Stuart Gordon; produced by Albert Band; executive producer—Charles Band; screenplay by Dennis Paoli, adapted from "The Pit and the Pendulum" by Edgar Allan Poe; edited by Andy Horvitch; cinematography by Adolfo Bartoli; art direction by Giovanni Natalucci; music by Richard Band; special effects makeup by Greg Cannom.

Running time: 96 minutes.

Cast: Lance Henriksen (Torquemada), Rona De Ricci (Maria), Jonathan Fuller (Antonio), Francis Bay (Esmerelda), Stephen Lee (Gomez), Mark Margolis (Mendoza), Oliver Reed (The Cardinal).

Story: Toledo, Spain, 1492. Torquemada, Grand Inquisitor of the Spanish Inquisition, opens a tomb, pronounces the corpse guilty of heresy, and sentences it to receive twenty lashes. After Mendoza has administered the "punishment," Torquemada confiscates the property of the corpse's family and has the bones ground into dust. He then places the dust in an hourglass as a reminder of the shortness of life.

Maria loves the church but disapproves of the Spanish Inquisition. When she and her husband Antonio are in the marketplace selling their bread, they are swept up by the crowd to the scene of the public executions, where they are repulsed by the cruelty but forced to stay. When Antonio accidentally causes the powerful Don Carlos to fall from his horse, Maria pleads with Torquemada to forgive them and let them go. Believing Antonio dead from the accident, the Grand Inquisitor orders Maria arrested as a witch. Later he makes her take off her clothes so that his henchmen can look for the devil's mark. All the while, the Inquisitor is becoming increasingly attracted to the young woman. Later Maria is imprisoned with elderly, white-haired Esmerelda, an admitted white witch who uses charms and herbs to cure illness.

Realizing that he is falling in love with Maria, Torquemada asks Mendoza, who considers the Inquisitor his "savior," to scourge him and purify him of his lust for the baker's wife. Meanwhile, Antonio, who was only stunned by his encounter with Don Carlos's horse, discovers that his wife is imprisoned and bribes the Inquisitor's workman, Gomez, to smuggle him into the prison. Gomez agrees for a fee, but as Antonio is freeing Maria from her cell, Gomez tips off the troops, and they capture the young man.

Later, as Maria is being tortured on the rack, her spirit leaves her body. In a vision, Esmerelda offers to teach her elements of the hidden wisdom. Maria is willing, but when she looks down at her body on the rack, her spirit reenters the flesh, and she screams in agony. Torquemada soon arrives and frees Maria, offering to hear her confession himself. When she tries to convince the Inquisitor that she is not a witch, he escorts her to watch Antonio being tortured.

Antonio escapes and fights against his captors, finally taking Torquemada hostage. When Torquemada promises mercy if Antonio will let him go, Maria also pleads for him reminding her husband that the Inquisitor is a man of God. Antonio frees his captive but is locked in a cell for his trouble. "You promised mercy!" Maria cries, to which Torquemada replies in all seriousness, "In this place, death is mercy."

When a Cardinal arrives from Rome with a papal order designed to curb Torquemada's cruelties, the Inquisitor generously offers his visitor goblets of Amontillado, burns the papal order, and has the Cardinal sealed behind a brick wall, presumably to insure that he is never found. As the wall is erected, the Cardinal at first jests, then promises to forget all about the papal order, if only Torquemada will free him. Unmoved by his victim's pleas, the Inquisitor allows the workers to continue. Just before the last brick is put into place, the Cardinal cries, "For the love of God," to which Torquemada simply replies, "Yes, for the love of God."

Later, when Torquemada promises that he will let Antonio go free if Maria will confess herself a witch, live with him, and love him forever, she plays along. At that point, the Inquisitor confesses his love for Maria and tries to rape her, but fails because of impotence. To keep her from telling what he has said and done, which would discredit the Inquisition, Torquemada cuts out Maria's tongue and returns her to Esmerelda's cell. There, Esmerelda puts Maria into a death-like trance, promising to teach her the wisdom while her spirit is out of her body. While she is in the trance, however, the guards mistake her for dead and prepare her for burial. Torquemada appears, demanding to know who has cut out Maria's tongue, causing her death. When no one comes forward, Torquemada says that Maria was innocent of the witchcraft charge and that she must be entombed within the castle itself, almost as though she were a saint. Antonio observes the proceedings from his cell, pre-

sumes that his wife is indeed dead, and loses the will to live.

Esmerelda is blamed for Maria's death and is taken out to be burned at the stake. Before she is tied to the stake, however, she swallows a great quantity of gunpowder and curses Torquemada, the executioner, and all those present who approve of the Inquisition. She also predicts that Torquemada will be killed by one of his own torture instruments. As Esmerelda burns, the Inquisitor replies to the curse, saying "If I lie, may my tongue be …," at which point blood gushes from his mouth and Esmerelda explodes as a result of the ingested gunpowder.

At the sound of the explosion, Maria awakens in the tomb and struggles, but cannot budge the lid. After she has passed out, Torquemada kneels at her tomb, admitting aloud his part in her death and asking forgiveness. Unknown to the Inquisitor, however, Mendoza hears the confession and departs in a very troubled state. Shortly afterward, Maria reawakens and screams.

As Maria struggles within the tomb, Antonio, despondent because he thinks her dead, finds himself tied to the floor of the torture chamber as a giant, razor-sharp pendulum descends in the direction of his chest. It is then that he hears Maria telepathically call his name and frantically looks about for a means of escape. As Torquemada watches, hungry rats race across the floor and begin chewing Antonio's hands and feet. When the pendulum is so close that it cuts one of the rats on his chest in half, Antonio squeezes the blood and entrails out of the rat's remains onto the rope that binds his hand. The other rats immediately begin gnawing at the rope to get at the entrails and blood. Soon Antonio is free. Unfortunately, at the moment he frees himself, a pit opens under him and he hangs suspended by a rope over a circle of spikes.

Meanwhile, Mendoza, convinced that all those executed as witches and heretics were innocent, attacks Torquemada. The Inquisitor, however, manages to stab his attacker to death. When troops enter the torture chamber, Antonio fights them off, makes his way to Maria's tomb, and opens the lid. At that moment, the troops rush in, led by Torquemada, who orders them to kill Antonio. They fall to their knees, however, when Maria rises from the tomb and telepathically communicates to the gathering that Torquemada is the murderer. As the Inquisitor flees, he remembers Esmerelda's curse, which said in part that he would die by one of his own instruments of torture. As he runs, he knocks over the hourglass of human dust. Before Torquemada's eyes, the dust slowly becomes the rotted corpse it once was and moves toward him. Torquemada runs to the torture chamber, pursued by Antonio, Maria, and the troops. Finally, he loses his balance and falls into the pit, where he is horribly impaled on spikes.

Antonio is amazed that Maria can communicate telepathically, obviously the result of Esmerelda's teaching her while she was in the trance. With the Grand Inquisitor dead, Maria and Antonio free the others from their cells and leave the castle together.

Production and marketing: Director Stuart Gordon (1947–), whose *Re-Animator* (1985) and *From Beyond* (1986) were outlandish and gory black comedies based on stories by H. P. Lovecraft, set out in *The Pit and the Pendulum* to do for Poe what he had done for (or to) Lovecraft. Early on, Gordon announced that the stars of his new $5 million Poe project would be Peter O'Toole as Torquemada, Sherilyn Fenn as Maria, and Billy Dee Williams as Abdul the Infidel. When those plans disintegrated, Gordon acquired Lance Henriksen to play Torquemada. Henriksen's genre films included *Damien: Omen II* (1978), *Piranha 2: The Spawning* (1983), *The Terminator* (1984), *Jagged Edge* (1985), *Aliens* (1986), *Near Dark* (1987), *Pumpkinhead* (1988), and *The Horror Show* (1989). Gordon signed Rona De Ricci to play Maria, and the part of Abdul the Infidel was written out of the film.

The idea to do *The Pit and the Pendulum* came to Stuart during a London film festival showing of *Re-Animator*. While there, Gordon and *Re-Animator's* producer, Brian Yuzna, took a horror tour of Madame Tussaud's wax museum, where they saw wax renderings of various torture devices and prisoners' cells. Gordon tuned to Yuzna and said, "This is far more horrifying than anything we've ever done."[229]

The picture was shot half in London and half in Italy at a castle outside of Rome. Other scenes were shot at Rome's De Paolis studios, site of Sergio Leone's *Once Upon a Time in the West* (1968) and Dario Argento's *Opera* (1987).

In a preproduction interview, Gordon reflected upon the Corman film of 1961:

> Since Corman made his film in the early 60's, he could only scratch the surface of the story. We're going to deal with it much more directly.... Roger's film was set just after the Spanish Inquisition. We're going to deal with it directly and throw our audience right into the middle of it. We're going back to the Poe story, in which he describes a mechanical room that is really a torture device in itself. The walls heat up and close in as the pendulum comes down from above, a seemingly bottomless pit is centered in the room and the walls have demonic faces painted on them.... The great thing about the Corman film was that it introduced so many people to the work of Poe. I think it would be wonderful it I could do the same thing for today's audiences.[230]

Critique: Although the film revels in gore and violence seemingly for its own sake, a tongue-in-cheek attitude permeates. While Ricci and Fuller give believable lead performances, and while Oliver Reed is both amusing and pitiable as the ill-fated Cardinal, the focus of the film is Lance Henriksen's Torquemada. In tune with the film's overall mood, Henriksen broadly plays the Grand Inquisitor as a sexually repressed, psychotic religious zealot. When he mauls poor Maria, he is about as sexually appealing as Klaus Kinski's *Nosferatu the Vampyre* (1979). Henriksen sometimes successfully overplays and at other times successfully underplays. In either mode, he is effectively repulsive.

Screenwriter Dennis Paoli gleefully

infuses the film with black humor. For example: Mendoza says as he tortures Maria on the rack: "One good turn deserves another." An Inquisition official says to Esmerelda as she is about to be burned at the stake: "I'm sorry, Mistress, that you weren't able to properly confess. There wasn't enough time to torture you." Esmerelda replies, "Thanks anyway."

Although there is plenty of blood, torture, and murder, the most chilling moment of the film comes as Torquemada seals the Cardinal behind a wall of bricks. Paoli gives the Cardinal Fortunato's line from Poe's "the Cask of Amontillado"—"For the love of God." In this case the meaning is the same as in Poe's tale. However, when Torquemada replies as Montressor does, "Yes, for the love of God," the implications are larger than they are in "The Cask of Amontillado," for Torquemada truly believes that he must kill the Cardinal literally for the love of God, as he has tortured and killed so many others.

As far from Poe as this film is, it nevertheless includes more of Poe's original plot than do other feature film versions. Overall, this version works to the extent that it does because it wisely fails to take itself *too* seriously.

Haunting Fear (1991)
American Independent Productions, U.S.A.

Credits: Directed by Fred Olen Ray; produced by Diana Jaffe; cinematography by Gary Graver; edited by Chris Roth; music by Chuck Cirino; screenplay by Sherman Scott (Fred Olen Ray), based on "The Premature Burial" by Edgar Allan Poe; associate producer—Grant Waldman; coproducer—Jeffrey B. Mallian.

Cast: Jan-Michael Vincent (James Trent), Karen Black (Dr. Julia Harcourt), Brinke Stevens (Victoria Monroe), Jay Richardson (Terry Monroe), Delia Sheppard (Lisa), Robert Clarke (Dr. Carleton), Robert Quarry (Mr. Visconti), Michael Berryman (mortician).

Story: "The boundaries which divide life from death are shadowy and vague. Who shall say where the one ends and the other begins."

—Edgar Allan Poe

Victoria Monroe is having recurring nightmares and hallucinations about premature burial. Her husband, Terry, insists that she visit Dr. Carleton, the family physician, whom she blames for her father's death. Terry is having an affair with his secretary, Lisa, but he resists leaving Victoria because of the house and money she inherited from her father.

When Victoria reluctantly visits Dr. Carleton, she relates her persistent dream of being buried alive. Dr. Carleton gives her a prescription for pills designed to produce dreamless sleep. That night Victoria takes a pill and falls asleep, but the medicine fails to banish the dreams. This time Victoria dreams that Terry finds her in a cataleptic state and calls Dr. Carleton. As her brain cries out for them to realize that she still lives, Dr. Carleton has her "body" shipped to the morgue. There, an odd-looking, salacious mortician begins the processes of embalming and autopsy. She wakes up from the dream screaming.

For weeks Victoria has noticed a handsome young man sitting in a car across from her house. One day the young man comes to the door, identifies himself as Lieutenant James Trent, and says he is investigating reports of screaming. Victoria tells him that she has been screaming as a result of nightmares and that nothing is wrong. Trent, who seems enamored with Victoria, takes a look around the house and promises to stop by again just to see how she is doing. Victoria assures him that she will be fine.

Meanwhile, Terry is frantically wondering how he is going to pay off a large gambling debt to Mr. Visconti, a gangster. Trent, who is not a police lieutenant, has been hired by Visconti to watch the Monroe house and make sure Terry does not run out on the debt. Lisa suggests that Terry somehow kill Victoria and use the bonds left to her by her father to pay off the debt. Terry suspects that Victoria has inherited a bad heart and agrees to kill her.

Dr. Carleton phones Dr. Harcourt, a famed clinical hypnotist, and enlists her aid in Victoria's case. Dr. Harcourt accompanies Dr. Carleton to the Monroe house and hypnotizes Victoria, regressing her to a previous life. Victoria relives her wedding night when she was raped by her brother-in-law and buried alive by her husband. Now that Victoria knows the source of her dreams, Dr. Carleton hopes they will stop.

As Victoria sleeps that night, Terry and Lisa place her in a homemade coffin in the basement. When she awakes to find herself lying in a coffin, Terry and Lisa, who are waiting nearby, taunt her and attempt to frighten her to death. When Victoria loses consciousness, Terry and Lisa cover the coffin with a layer of dirt and go upstairs to have sex in Victoria's bed. As Terry and Lisa engage in rough sex, Victoria regains consciousness, goes mad, and claws her way out of the coffin. She then goes on a murderous rampage, killing both Lisa and Terry with a butcher knife. Trent, who is watching the house, sees Victoria kill Lisa on the lawn, follows her back into the house, and calls the police. With his gun ready to fire, Trent searches for the bloody, insane Victoria. Near the staircase, she attacks him and stabs him in the shoulder. He fires bullets into her until she falls down the stairs. When Trent goes down the stairs, Victoria, who is miraculously not dead, attacks him again. As the police arrive, Trent stands in the kitchen doorway. Victoria sits cross-legged on the kitchen floor, tapping the blade on the linoleum.

Trent turns his head for a brief moment, then looks back, only to find that Victoria has somehow disappeared. Only the knife remains. Where could she have gone?

Production and marketing: Director Fred Olen Ray (1954–) came to *Haunting Fear* after a long string of outrageous exploitation films including such titles as *Hollywood Chainsaw Hookers.* Around 1989, Ray began working on a screenplay based on Poe's "The Premature Burial." After completing about twenty-five pages of script, he decided that there were enough new Poe films in circulation at the time and instead decided to direct Robert Quarry in a film called *Empire of the Rats,* based on H. G. Wells's short story "Empire of the Ants" and on his novel *Food of the Gods.* When that screenplay proved too bad to fix, Ray canceled the project and broke the bad news to Quarry during a breakfast. Eager to go to work, Quarry asked Ray if he had another screenplay available. Ray thought for a moment and remembered the aborted Poe script on his computer at home. Returning to his computer, Ray had the screenplay ready in three days.

In the case of *Haunting Fear,* H.G. Wells's loss was Edgar Allan Poe's gain. The film's working title was "Edgar Allan Poe's *House of Babes.*" Ray later changed the title to *Haunting Fear,* inspired by the old EC comic book, *Haunt of Fear.*

Ray likes to use established actors in his films, and for *Haunting Fear* he paired Karen Black (1942–) and Robert Quarry (1923–) with top-billed Jan-Michael Vincent (1944–). The handsome Vincent was a popular leading man in the seventies, starring or costarring in such box office successes as *The Undefeated* (1968, with John Wayne), *The Mechanic* (1972, with Charles Bronson), *Buster and Billie* (1974), *Bite the Bullet* (1974), and *White Line Fever* (1975). Although he worked throughout the eighties, his career seems stalled in the nineties as a result of alcohol and drug-related arrests.

Karen Black appeared in *Easy Rider* (1969) but rose to fame as an Academy

Award nominee for her supporting role in the highly acclaimed *Five Easy Pieces* (1970). She went on to star in such fine films as *Cisco Pike* (1971), *The Great Gatsby* (1974), *Trilogy of Terror* (1975, made for TV), *The Day of the Locusts* (1975), *Nashville* (1975, directed by Robert Altman), *Family Plot* (1976, directed by Alfred Hitchcock), and *Burnt Offerings* (1976, with Oliver Reed). Amidst these hits, however, were a number of bombs, and throughout the eighties Karen found herself in considerably weaker projects, such as *It's Alive III: Island of the Alive* (1987), *Eternal Evil* (1987), and *Out of the Dark* (1989). In 1986, however, she starred with her son in Tobe Hooper's underrated remake of *Invaders from Mars*. In the nineties, she continues to appear in low-budget films, usually giving a good performance.

Robert Quarry boasted an impressive résumé dating back to the early years of television. He is best known today, however, for his starring roles in *Count Yorga, Vampire* (1969) and *The Return of Count Yorga* (1971). Other Quarry horror vehicles included *The Deathmaster* (1972), *Dr. Phibes Rises Again* (1972, with Vincent Price), and *Madhouse* (1974, with Vincent Price and Peter Cushing).

Although the established stars receive top billing, the actress with the central role and the most screen time is young Brinke Stevens, a Ray regular who had appeared in a variety of his earlier low-budget shockers.

The haunting fear of the title is, of course, premature burial. Although this film is about as far removed from the spirit of Poe as a film can be, screenwriter Ray tried to imbue the process with an atmosphere suggestive of Poe as Victoria explains the nature of her dreams to Dr. Carleton:

> Me, trapped inside a dream with no escape—buried alive. I've been buried alive, and I wake up in the coffin. It's black inside, but I can still see, and I can hear my heart beating in my ears like a drum. I scream, but no one can hear me because I'm so far underground. And it's cold—deathly cold and quiet. I scream, and then I claw at the coffin lid until my fingernails are broken and torn, raw and bloody from the frantic scratching

and digging at the hardwood of the casket. Nothing happens. No one can help me. I scream and scream. Then I wake up.

Another touch inspired by Poe is the burial of Stevens's Victoria. In Poe's "The Premature Burial," the narrator imagines himself buried alive when he actually is not. In the film, Victoria believes she is buried in the earth when in reality she is above ground in a makeshift coffin. Victoria's escape from her coffin and subsequent rampage were inspired by Poe's "The Fall of the House of Usher" and by Roger Corman's 1960 film of the same name.

The film, which had a production cost of $115,000, made $175,000 in the first year of its release.

Always a fan of Poe's writings, Fred Olen Ray visited the Poe house in Baltimore with Brinke Stevens when they attended a Fanex convention a few years ago. "The house is in a bad neighborhood," he said, "and we made the mistake of going on foot near dark. When we got there, the house was closed, so we walked around back for a moment and I took a loose brick from the house as a souvenir. It occurred to me that if I returned to Baltimore every year, maybe I could move the Poe house back with me to California—brick by brick."[231]

Critique: When asked if he considers *Haunting Fear* a success, Ray answered that he does—at least as much as a modernized version can be. His only regret is the inclusion of the past life regression conducted by Karen Black. "It was put in to explain Victoria's problem," Ray said. "It introduced a supernatural element into the story, and then we didn't go anywhere with it."[232]

I would agree that the film is about as successful as a modernized Poe film can be. Although the contemporary setting and gratuitous sex take it far from the Poe universe, the film has its moments. Particularly remarkable is a dream sequence in which a necrophilic mortician (Michael Berryman) begins to conduct an autopsy on Victoria while she is still alive. Later, Victoria's escape from her coffin is unnerving and believable.

The rampage of the mad Victoria is also effective. Although Trent shoots her repeatedly with his pistol, she recovers and resumes her attack. I believe these scenes were at least partly inspired by Michael Myers's similar resurrections in *Halloween*, but Ray denies the connection, explaining that because madness has its own strength, a normal human being can be shot repeatedly and still keep moving. Although Ray denies that Victoria becomes a supernatural being like Michael Myers, the film's conclusion suggests otherwise. After filling her full of lead, Trent traces Victoria to the kitchen, where she sits on the floor tapping a knife repeatedly on the linoleum. Of course, this scene was inspired by an almost identical one at the conclusion of *Trilogy of Terror* (1975) in which Karen Black sits on the floor with a knife after having been possessed by the spirit of a devil doll. Trent looks away for a second and then looks back. Victoria is gone. Only the knife remains. If she were not a supernatural being, where did she go? Perhaps we will find out in *Haunting Fear II*, a property currently owned by Brinke Stevens herself which so far remains unproduced.

Tale of a Vampire (1992); aka *A Tale of a Vampire*
State Screen, Great Britain

Credits: Executive producer—Noriko Shishikura; produced by Simon Johnson; co-produced by Linda Kay; Directed by Shimako Sato; screenplay by Shimako Sato and Jane Corbett; story by Shimako Sato; cinematography by Zubin Mistry; music by Julian Joseph; edited by Chris Wright; production design by Alice Normington. Cast: Suzanna Hamilton (Ann and Virginia), Julian Sands (Alex), Kenneth Cranham (Edgar), Marian Diamond (Denise), Michael Kenton (magazine man), Catherine Blake (Virginia at age 5), Mark Kempner (morgue official).

Story:

It was many and many a year ago,
    In a kingdom by the sea,
That a maiden there lived whom you may
    know
        By the name of Annabel Lee;
And this maiden she lived with no other
    thought
        Than to love and be loved by me.

A car explodes into flames as a bearded man in a slouch hat looks on. A young woman (Ann) goes to the morgue, where she is assured that the man in the car died instantly and did not suffer.

A young man (Alex) awakens from sleep, and a black cat enters the room. Alex lifts and caresses the cat. Then he suddenly bites into the cat's neck and holds the dying animal above his face as gouts of blood splatter into his mouth and onto his face.

News reports speak of a third unidentified body in the River Thames. At a library in a minimally populated section of London, Head Librarian Denise helps Alex find rare books. The bearded man in the slouch hat enters the library, apparently interested in Alex. Ann soon enters the library and presents Denise with a letter she says she received inviting her to apply for a vacant library position. Denise cannot remember writing the letter but admits that a vacancy does exist. All the while, Alex watches from his table.

After Denise hires Ann to work in the library, Ann goes to the cemetery and kneels before the grave of her deceased beloved. The bearded man in the slouch hat watches discreetly from a distance.

Later, Ann goes to a restaurant where she is joined by Alex. Ann recognizes him from the library, and they discuss literature together. Ann reads Alex's palm, informing him, among other things, that he may lose something precious to him, and if that happens, he will never be able to find it again. Alex sits quietly for a moment and then softly asks Ann how many men she has seduced in this way. Offended, she leaves.

Alex follows a five-year-old girl into an alley, kills her, and drinks her blood. Two men come upon Alex in the act. One is a homeless person to whom Alex has earlier given cigarettes. The homeless man runs, but the other intruder fires a shot at Alex.

It is raining. Unhurt by being fired upon earlier, Alex appears in Ann's room as she sleeps. As he watches her, he remembers having killed a woman in a forest clearing and being interrupted by the appearance of a little lost girl identifying herself as Virginia. Alex leaves the corpse and carries little Virginia out of the woods. Little Virginia looks like Ann as a child.

Next evening Alex approaches Ann in the library and hands her a beautiful brooch as a gift. Without explanation, he walks away, leaving Ann amazed.

The library closes. It is raining. Alex offers to walk Ann home under his umbrella. At her door, he again departs mysteriously. Ann is interested in Alex, romantically attracted in a strange way to this shy, quiet young man.

Fog crawls through the city streets, and Alex comes upon the homeless man to whom he once gave cigarettes but who saw him in the alley with the dead little girl. It isn't long till the frightened man becomes another victim of the vampire.

Alex remembers the teen-aged Virginia marrying Edgar and vowing that she and Alex will be together forever. As Alex remembers, he lies on his bed, caressing Virginia's wedding gown of years past.

The man in the slouch hat approaches Ann in the cemetery during her next visit to her boyfriend's grave, and introduces himself as Edgar. She recognizes him as the man from the library but is uneasy in his presence. Later, Edgar discovers Virginia's wedding gown on Alex's bed. Edgar is apparently the same person whom Virginia married years ago, and he is monitoring Alex and Ann with unusual interest.

During a thunderstorm, Alex knocks on Ann's door. There is a power outage, and the two sit in her living room and talk by candlelight. Ann admits that she is still pining for her deceased beloved and asks Alex if he ever loved anyone. He replies quietly and sadly that he indeed had someone "a long time ago." Ann notes that his choice of words makes him sound very old, much older than he can possibly be. "There are some things that cannot be destroyed," Alex says. "Love?" Ann asks. "Pain," he answers. Ann assures Alex that pain passes, but he remains quietly absorbed and apparently unconvinced.

When Ann accidently cuts her finger, Alex lifts her hand and begins drinking her blood, fantasizing that he expresses love for her, goes for her neck, and drains her of life. Recovering from his unholy reverie, he notes the shocked expression on Ann's face and quickly leaves her.

Alex remembers the distant past when he gave young Virginia a choice: to die a mortal death or live on as an immortal beast. Because of her love for Alex, she chooses vampirism.

Next day, Edgar approaches Ann in the library and begins speaking to her of Alex, saying that in his opinion, Alex needs the friendship of a strong, young woman such as Ann because there is something vulnerable about him. Edgar then persuades a reluctant Ann to have dinner with him.

At dinner, Edgar explains that he is a writer and a student of mysticism and the occult, especially of vampirism. He goes on to explain that he once had an unfortunate accident and lost the girl he loved. In flashback, Virginia escapes through a forest with Alex. She tries to explain to him that though villagers are pursuing her, she did not kill the person they are trying to avenge. Alex and Virginia separate, and as Virginia hides behind some bushes, a black cat approaches. "It is time, Virginia," a male voice intones. Virginia screams.

Alex visits Ann at her home and hugs her. "Virginia, I've missed you so much!" he says wearily. Then he explains that his Virginia is alive, but there is nothing he can do to ease her pain. No one can take away someone else's pain," Ann counsels, "but we can comfort one another a little." They kiss; he begins to bite her but hurries away before causing any harm.

Next day, Edgar invites Ann for a drink, explaining that he wants to tell her Alex's secret. Though Ann still believes that her private life is none of Edgar's business, she consents. At their meeting, Edgar tells Ann that Alex is a vampire who inhabits "the valley of unrest" between life and death. Vampires devour the living in a vain attempt to assuage their hunger, the emptiness and horror of everlasting life. They will devour you, too, he tells her. That is what a vampire calls love.

Edgar then shows Ann the diary of Virginia Clemm from 1846. "You cannot escape from the truth," he warns. Because of Alex's strange behavior, Ann has been considering the possibility that he might be a vampire. Still, both her reason and her emotions rebel against the idea.

In an effort to discover the truth, Ann, spike in hand, explores Alex's lair where she finds him apparently asleep. As she raises the spike over his heart Alex suddenly but calmly says, "Go ahead." Shocked, Ann steps back and Alex rises. Again, Alex asks Ann to destroy him though he doubts that he can ever really die. At that moment Ann realizes what Alex meant when he said that some things can never be destroyed. Unwilling to destroy Alex, she pleads with him to make her a vampire too, but he refuses, explaining that he "made this mistake before."

In the library, Edgar insists on looking at a magazine hoarded by a mentally unsta-

ble old man. When Denise asks Edgar to please return the magazine to the old man, Edgar reminds her that they are in a public library and that he needs the magazine only for a moment. True to his word, Edgar pages quickly through the magazine and returns it to the old man. When the library closes, Denise finds the bloodied old man, dead in his library chair.

Later, when Alex returns to his lair, he finds Ann unconscious on his bed, neatly decorated with red ribbons as though she were a gift. "I have longed to see your face like this, Alex," Edgar says, and drives a sword into the vampire. Edgar explains that Virginia is locked in a coffin at the bottom of the North Sea. Doomed to eternal torment for betraying Edgar, she cannot escape, and she cannot die. Alex recovers and knocks Edgar through a window into the water below. Alex then lies upon Ann and orders her to drink.

> For the moon never beams without bring-
> ing me dreams
> Of the beautiful Annabel Lee;
> And the stars never rise but I see the bright
> eyes
> Of the beautiful Annabel Lee;
> And so, all the night-tide, I lie down by the
> side
> Of my darling—my darling—my life and
> my bride,
> In her sepulchre there by the sea -
> In her tomb by the side of the sea.

As the last stanza of Poe's "Annabel Lee" ends the film, fog creeps across the night sky, clouding the face of the half moon.

Production and marketing: Though uncredited as such, *A Tale of a Vampire* is obviously inspired by Poe's poem "Annabel Lee." The poem's first stanza opens the film, and the poem's final stanza ends it. Screenwriters Sato and Corbett conceive of Poe's Virginia as a vampire. The real Virginia's death was indeed marked by blood as her tubercular, dying body coughed up crimson. That and the idea of Poe as a vampire seeking revenge through the ages lays the foundation for a unique production. In terms of Poe, the film also has Cranham's Poe apply the vampire's state to the title of Poe's poem "The Valley of Unrest," and at two points of the film, black cats appear, suggesting Poe's short story "The Black Cat."

British actor Julian Sands (1957–) had appeared in a wide variety of films before being cast as Alex the vampire, the most acclaimed being *The Killing Fields* (1984) and *A Room with a View* (1985). No stranger to dark cinema, however, he had also contributed to *The Doctor and the Devils* (1985, directed by Freddie Francis), *Gothic* (1986, as Percy Shelley, directed by Ken Russell), *Warlock* (1988, in the title role), *Arachnophobia* (1990), *The Turn of the Screw* (1992) and *Warlock: The Armageddon* (1993).

British veteran of stage and television Kenneth Cranham (1944–) had appeared in a small number well-received films, including *Oliver!* (1968) and *Prospero's Books* (1991). He also had turned in a chilling performance as the villainous asylum head in *Hellbound: Hellraiser II* (1988).

A Tale of a Vampire received limited release in the United States. Poster art featured the darkly staring countenance of Julian Sands above the words "Never ending life. Undying passion."

Critique: *A Tale of a Vampire* is a slow, moody depiction of vampirism's physical horror, sexual passion, and emotional loneliness. The blonde, soft-featured Sands speaks in soft tones of lost love and pain in some scenes and masks his face with gouts of blood flowing from both animals and humans in other scenes. Sands's Alex is some-what a cross between his romantically vulnerable Percy Shelley in *Gothic* and his vicious devil worshipper in *Warlock.*

Kenneth Cranham is both suave and downright creepy as Edgar Allan Poe. The film drops a number of hints that Poe himself is a vampire. If Poe is not a vampire, how is he able to pursue Alex for over a century, and if neither Virginia nor Alex killed that villager in the flashback, who did? Also, who dispatched the old man in the library? Edgar is obviously the prime suspect.

Suzanna Hamilton gives a sympathetic performance as the lonely Ann and as the naive Virginia, and Marian Diamond turns in a solid performance as Denise the librarian. Zubin Mistry's cinematography is evocative as the camera moves along blue-tinted, fog-bound streets in the present and glories in yellow autumn light on red and gold leaves in flashbacks. Julian Joseph's haunting musical score is also a strength, effectively enhancing the overall mood.

The loneliness and sexuality of the vampire has been cinematically addressed before, most notably in *Dracula's Daughter* (1936), *Dracula* (1973), and *Bram Stoker's Dracula* (1992), but the effective tying of those themes to the "undying" love of Edgar Allan Poe for Virginia is both quirky and creative—a unique combination of the ugliness and beauty permeating vampire mythology with the "life and afterlife" of literary icon Poe. As both director and co-screenwriter, Shimako Sato deserves praise for his sure-handed guidance and imaginative vision.

Afterword

No doubt many filmmakers and screenwriters who never made a film based on Poe's writings nevertheless responded to his influence, an influence that made its way into a large number of films. One major director who never made a film based on a work by Poe openly acknowledged the author's influence. The director was "the master of suspense," Alfred Hitchcock, who said:

At sixteen I discovered the work of Edgar Allan Poe. I happened to read first his biography, and [the] sadness of his life made a great impression on me. I felt an enormous pity for him, because in spite of his talent he had never been happy.

When I came home from the office where I worked I went straight to my room, took the cheap edition of his *Tales of the Grotesque and Arabesque*, and began to read. I still remember my feelings when I finished "The Murders in the Rue Morgue." I was afraid, but this fear made me discover something I've never forgotten since: fear, you see, is an emotion people like to feel when they know they're safe....

Very likely it's because I was so taken with the Poe stories that I later made suspense films. I don't want to seem immodest, but I can't help comparing what I've tried to put in my films with what Edgar Allan Poe put in his novels [*sic*]: a completely unbelievable story told to the readers with such a spellbinding logic that you get the impression that the same thing could happen to you tomorrow....

I never broke this rule. If "The Gold Bug" fascinated me then, it still does now, because I've always loved adventure, travel and the impression of somehow always being away from home.... I believe Poe has a special place in the world of literature. He's at the same time certainly a romantic and a herald of modern literature.[233]

Among the many films influenced by Poe that do not acknowledge the debt are *The Necklace of the Dead* (1910), *La Folie Du Docteur Tube* (1915, aka *The Madness of Dr. Tube*), *Verldens Undergang* (1916, aka *The End of the World*), *La Fin du Monde* (1930, aka *The End of the World*), *The Old Dark House* (1932), *Isle of the Dead* (1945), *Dementia 13* (1963), *The Comedy of Terrors* (1963), and *Spider Baby* (1968). Some films have tipped their hats in obvious ways to the gentleman from Virginia. Among them are *The Phantom of the Opera* (1925), in which Lon Chaney descends a staircase dressed as Poe's Red Death; *The Drums of Fu Manchu* (1940), in which villain Henry Brandon utilizes a murderous giant pendulum as a torture device; *Das Ungeheuer von London City* (1964, aka *The Monster of London City*), in which a killer resembling Jack the Ripper spreads terror near Whitechapel's Edgar Allan Poe Theatre; *Dr. Goldfoot and the Bikini Machine* (1965), which sends up Corman's *The Fall of the House of Usher* and *The Pit and the Pendulum* (even using Price and pendulum footage from the latter); *Cinque Tombe per un Medium* (aka *Terror Creatures from the Grave*), the United States advertising for which reads, "in the macabre tradition of Edgar Allan Poe."

Top: **Poe's influence is acknowledged in advertising for** *Cinque Tombe per un Medium* **(aka** *Terror Creatures from the Grave*).
Bottom: **Although the villain of** *Drums of Fu Manchu* **is Sax Rohmer's criminal mastermind, the torture device is Poe's pendulum.**

Television, of course, has tapped into the Poe vein. Following is a list of notable productions:

1. "Heartbeat" (1953)—a version of "The Tell-Tale Heart" directed by William Cameron Menzies for General TV Enterprises.

2. "The Premature Burial" (1961)—an adaptation of Poe's short story written by William G. Gordon and directed by Douglas Heyes for the *Thriller* television series. Boris Karloff, Sidney Blackmer, Patricia Medina, and Scott Marlowe starred.

3. "The Edgar Allan Poe Special" (1970)—adaptations of Poe's "The Cask of Amontillado," "The Tell-Tale Heart," "The Sphinx," and "The Pit and the Pendulum" narrated and interpreted by Vincent Price.

4. *The Fall of the House of Usher* (1979/1982)—a made-for-television movie directed by James L. Conway for Sunn Classic. Charlene Tilton, Martin Landau, and Ray Walston starred.

5. *The Murders in the Rue Morgue* (1986)—a made-for-television movie directed by Jeannot Szwarc and written by David Epstein. Bruno de Keyzer was cinematographer. George C. Scott, Rebecca de Mornay, Ian McShane, Neil Dickson, and Val Kilmer starred.

Notes

1. Vincent Buranelli, *Edgar Allan Poe* (Boston: Twayne Publishers, 1977), pp. 20–21.
2. *Ibid.*, p. 136.
3. Denis Gifford, "Pictures of Poe: A Survey of the Silent Film Era 1909–29," in Peter Haining (ed.), *The Edgar Allan Poe Scrapbook* (New York: Schocken Books, 1978), p. 129.
4. *Ibid.*, p. 130.
5. *Ibid.*
6. *Ibid.*
7. *Ibid.*
8. Claude Pichos, *Baudelaire* (London: Hamish Hamilton, 1989), p. 183.
9. Gifford, "Pictures," p. 131.
10. *Ibid.*
11. Siegried Kracauer, *From Caligari to Hitler* (Princeton, NJ: Princeton University Press, 1947), p. 29.
12. Carlos Clarens, *An Illustrated History of the Horror Film* (New York: Capricorn Books, 1967), pp. 10–11.
13. Gifford, "Pictures," p. 131.
14. Rose London, *Cinema of Mystery* (New York: Bounty Books, 1975), pp. 74–75.
15. Ken Hanke, "Robert Florey's *Murders in the Rue Morgue:* Almost a Classic," *Phantasma* 1, no. 3 (1981), pp. 33–34.
16. *Ibid.*, p. 35.
17. John C. Cawelti, *Adventure, Mystery, and Romance* (Chicago: University of Chicago Press, 1976), pp. 94–95.
18. *New York Times*, February 11, 1932.
19. *Ibid.*
20. Richard Bojarski, *The Films of Bela Lugosi* (Secaucus, NJ: Citadel, 1980), pp. 68–69.
21. Arthur Lenning, *The Count: The Life and Films of Bela "Dracula" Lugosi* (New York: G. P. Putnam's Sons, 1974), p. 125.
22. Hanke, "Robert Florey's *Murders*," p. 34.
23. *Ibid.*, p. 47.
24. Michael Brunas, John Brunas, and Tom Weaver, *Universal Horrors* (Jefferson, NC: McFarland, 1990), p. 34.
25. William K. Everson, *Classics of the Horror Film* (Secaucus, NJ: Citadel, 1974), p. 122.
26. London, *Cinema of Mystery*, pp. 37–38.
27. Gregory William Mank, *Karloff and Lugosi* (Jefferson, NC: McFarland, 1990), p. 82.
28. *New York Times*, May 19, 1934.
29. Richard Bojarski and Kenneth Beals, *The Films of Boris Karloff* (Secaucus, NJ: Citadel, 1974), p. 97.
30. Ivan Butler, *Horror in the Cinema* (New York: Paperback Library, 1971), pp. 169–170.
31. Chris Steinbrunner and Burt Goldblatt, *Cinema of the Fantastic* (New York: Galahad Books, 1972), p. 87.
32. Everson, *Classics*, p. 123.

33. Brunas, Brunas, and Weaver, *Universal*, p. 78.
34. Mank, *Karloff*, p. 82.
35. Brett Wood, "Maniac," in Gary J. Svehla and Susan Svehla (eds.), *Guilty Pleasures of the Horror Film* (Baltimore, MD: Midnight Marquee Press, 1996), p. 19.
36. *Ibid.*, p. 11.
37. *Ibid.*, pp. 20–21.
38. *New York Times,* June 15, 1934.
39. *Ibid.*
40. *Ibid.*
41. *New York Times,* July 5, 1935.
42. *Los Angeles Herald–Examiner,* July 10, 1935.
43. Bojarski and Beals, *Films*, p. 111.
44. Clarens, *Illustrated,* p. 75.
45. Mank, *Karloff,* p. 119.
46. Brunas, Brunas, and Weaver, *Universal,* p. 135.
47. *New York Times,* January 13, 1936.
48. *Ibid.*
49. *Ibid.*
50. London, *Cinema of Mystery,* p. 18.
51. Bojarski and Beals, *Lugosi,* p. 167.
52. Brunas, Brunas, and Weaver, *Universal,* p. 258.
53. Michael Weldon, *The Psychotronic Encyclopedia of Film* (New York: Ballantine, 1983), p. 60.
54. *New York Times,* May 5, 1942.
55. Brunas, Brunas, and Weaver, *Universal,* p. 296.
56. *New York Times,* September 21, 1942.
57. London, *Cinema of Mystery,* p. 75.
58. *New York Times,* November 28, 1951.
59. *Ibid.*
60. *New York Times,* March 20, 1954.
61. Denis Gifford, *A Pictorial History of Horror Movies* (London: Hamlyn, 1973), p. 174.
62. London, *Cinema of Mystery,* p. 89.
63. *Ibid.*, p. 58.
64. *New York Times* (The Tell-Tale Heart), May 16, 1963.
65. *Ibid.*
66. Donald C. Willis, *Horror and Science Fiction Films* (Metuchen, NJ: Scarecrow, 1972), p. 470.
67. London, *Cinema of Mystery,* p. 61.
68. Philip di Franco, *The Movie World of Roger Corman* (New York: Chelsea House, 1979), p. 97.
69. Ed Naha, *The Films of Roger Corman* (New York: Arco Publishing, 1982), p. 28.
70. *Ibid.*, pp. 30–31.
71. *Ibid.*, pp. 29–30.
72. *Ibid.*, p. 32.
73. *Ibid.*, p. 31.
74. *Ibid.*, pp. 148–149.
75. *Ibid.*, p. 149.
76. *Ibid.*
77. *New York Times,* September 15, 1960.
78. *Ibid.*
79. Clarens, *Illustrated,* p. 148.
80. Butler, *Horror,* p. 134.
81. *Ibid.*
82. London, *Cinema of Mystery,* pp. 78, 82.
83. Butler, *Horror,* p. 191.
84. *Ibid.*
85. Naha, *Films,* p. 32.
86. di Franco, *Movie,* p. 32.
87. Naha, *Films,* pp. 32–33.
88. Calvin Beck, *Scream Queens* (New York: Collier, 1978), p. 299.
89. *Ibid.*, pp. 300, 302.

90. *New York Times,* August 24, 1961.
91. Naha, *Films,* p. 155.
92. *Ibid.,* p. 155.
93. London, *Cinema of Mystery,* p. 65.
94. Weldon, *Psychotronic,* p. 550.
95. Jay R. Nash and Stanley R. Ross, *The Motion Picture Guide* (Chicago: Cinebooks, 1986), p. 3298.
96. Naha, *Films,* p. 159.
97. *New York Tribune,* May 24, 1962.
98. *Ibid.*
99. Butler, *Horror,* p. 135.
100. Ed Naha, *Horrors! From Screen to Scream* (New York: Avon, 1975), p. 233.
101. Weldon, *Psychotronic,* p. 360.
102. Naha, *Films,* pp. 160–161.
103. *Ibid.,* p. 161.
104. Steve Biodrowski and David Del Valle, "Vincent Price: Horror's Crown Prince," *Cinefantastique* 19, nos. 1, 2 (1989), p 55.
105. Naha, *Films,* p. 35.
106. di Franco, *Movie,* p. 33.
107. *Ibid.,* p. 33.
108. *New York Times,* July 5, 1962.
109. Naha, *Films,* p. 162.
110. Butler, *Horror,* p. 135.
111. Willis, *Horror,* p. 467.
112. Naha, *Horrors!,* p. 269.
113. di Franco, *Movie,* p. 108.
114. *Ibid.* pp. 33–34.
115. Biodrowski and Del Valle, "Vincent Price," p. 59.
116. Lawrence French, "Price on Poe," *Cinefantastique* 19, nos. 1, 2, p. 64.
117. Biodrowski and Del Valle, "Vincent Price," p. 61.
118. Naha, *Films,* p. 168.
119. *Ibid.*
120. *New York Times,* January 26, 1963.
121. Clarens, *Illustrated,* p. 149.
122. Willis, *Horror,* p. 397.
123. London, *Cinema of Mystery,* p. 47.
124. Naha, *Films,* p. 168.
125. Weldon, *Psychotronic,* p. 578.
126. Nash and Ross, *Motion,* p. 2546.
127. Naha, *Films,* p. 38.
128. Biodrowski and Del Valle, "Vincent Price," p. 59.
129. Everett F. Bleiler, *The Guide to Supernatural Fiction* (Kent, Ohio: Kent State University Press, 1983) p. 319.
130. Naha, *Films,* p. 174.
131. *Ibid.*
132. Butler, *Horror,* pp. 135–136.
133. Nash and Ross, *Motion,* p. 1170.
134. Naha, *Films,* pp. 179–180.
135. French, "Price on Poe," p. 66.
136. Naha, *Films,* p. 180.
137. *New York Times,* September 17, 1964.
138. Naha, *Films,* p. 180.
139. Butler, *Horror,* p. 137.
140. Clarens, *Illustrated,* p. 149.
141. Willis, *Horror,* p. 312.
142. Naha, *Horrors!,* 199.
143. Weldon, *Psychotronic,* p. 465.
144. Butler, *Horror,* pp. 138–139.

145. Beck, *Scream,* p. 306.

146. *Ibid.*

147. Weldon, *Psychotronic,* p. 107.

148. di Franco, *Movie,* pp. 34–35.

149. *Ibid.,* p. 34.

150. French, "Price on Poe," p. 66.

151. Naha, *Films,* pp. 39–40.

152. French, "Price on Poe," pp. 66, 119.

153. Naha, *Films,* p. 182.

154. *New York Times,* May 6, 1965.

155. James Robert Parish and Steven Whitney, *Vincent Price Unmasked* (New York: Drake Publishers, 1974), p. 225.

156. Butler, *Horror,* p. 140.

157. *Ibid.,* pp. 142–143.

158. Clarens, *Illustrated,* p. 151.

159. London, *Cinema of Mystery,* p. 24.

160. Nash and Ross, *Motion,* p. 3482.

161. Biodrowski and Del Valle, "Vincent Price," p. 68.

162. *Ibid.*

163. *New York Times,* June 3, 1965.

164. Weldon, *Psychotronic,* p. 761.

165. Nash and Ross, *Motion,* p. 437.

166. Robert W. Pohle, Jr., and Douglas C. Hart, *The Films of Christopher Lee* (Metuchen, NJ: Scarecrow, 1983), p. 116.

167. Christopher Lee, *Tall, Dark and Gruesome* (London: Granada Publishing, 1977), p. 225.

168. *Ibid.,* p. 257.

169. Pohle and Hart. *Films,* p. 115.

170. *Ibid.*

171. Weldon, *Psychotronic,* p. 70.

172. *Ibid.,* p. 652.

173. London, *Cinema of Mystery,* pp. 101–102.

174. *New York Times,* July 20, 1968.

175. Deborah Del Vecchio and Tom Johnson, *Peter Cushing* (Jefferson, NC: McFarland, 1992), p. 219.

176. Biodrowski and Del Valle, "Vincent Price," p. 69.

177. *Ibid.,* pp. 69–70.

178. *London Times,* May 12, 1968.

179. *Hollywood Citizen News,* May 15, 1968.

180. *New York Times,* August 15, 1968.

181. *Times Saturday Review,* May 11, 1968.

182. *Films and Filming,* July 1968.

183. David Pirie, *A Heritage of Horror: The English Gothic Cinema 1946–1972* (New York: Equinox, 1973), pp. 151– 152.

184. *Ibid.,* p. 152.

185. *Ibid.*

186. Don G. Smith, "A Defense of *Witchfinder General,*" *Gore Creatures* 25 (January 1975), pp. 14–17.

187. Butler, *Horror,* p. 213.

188. Naha, *Horrors!,* p. 47.

189. Peter Hutchings, *Hammer and Beyond: The British Horror Film* (Manchester: Manchester University Press, 1993), p. 145.

190. *Ibid.*

191. Biodrowski and Del Valle, "Vincent Price," p. 72.

192. Pohle and Hart, *Films,* p. 133.

193. Lee, *Tall,* p. 260.

194. Biodrowski and Del Valle, "Vincent Price," p. 73.

195. *New York Times,* July 24, 1969.

196. Naha, *Horrors!,* p. 223.

197. Weldon, *Psychotronic*, p. 526.
198. *Cine Weekly*, November 15, 1969.
199. Pirie, *Heritage*, p. 157.
200. Biodrowski and Del Valle, "Vincent Price," p. 74.
201. *Ibid.*
202. *Ibid.*, p. 75.
203. *Ibid.*, pp. 76–77.
204. *Ibid.*, p. 77.
205. Weldon, *Psychotronic*, p. 144.
206. Guy Woolsey, "An AIP Director Screams Again," *Fangoria* no. 53, (1986), pp. 26–27.
207. *Ibid.*, p. 27.
208. *Ibid.*
209. *Ibid.*
210. *New York Times*, February 3, 1972.
211. *Ibid.*
212. *Ibid.*
213. London, *Cinema of Mystery*, p. 89.
214. Naha, *Horrors!*, p. 215.
215. Weldon, *Psychotronic*, p. 493.
216. Daniel Hoffmann, *Poe Poe Poe Poe Poe Poe Poe* (Garden City, NY: Doubleday, 1972), p. 228.
217. Telephone interview with author, November 6, 1996.
218. *Ibid.*
219. John Wooley, "Towers' Tales of Terror," *Fangoria* No. 89 (1989), pp. 28–29.
220. *Ibid.*, p. 28.
221. *Ibid.*, pp. 27–28.
222. John Wooley, *"Masque of the Red Death:* The Next Dance," *Fangoria* No. 89 (1989), p. 29.
223. *Ibid.*, p. 22.
224. Kim Newman, *Nightmare Movies* (New York: Harmony Books, 1988), p. 105.
225. For a further exploration of this topic, see Don G. Smith's "Women: From Female Scientists to Chainsaw Leftovers," in Gary Svehla and Susan Svehla (eds.) *Bitches, Bimbos, and Virgins* (Baltimore: Midnight Marquee Press, 1996).
226. Maitland McDonaugh, *Broken Mirrors/Broken Minds: The Dark Dreams of Dario Argento* (New York: Citadel, 1991), pp. 248–249.
227. Wooley, "Towers' Tales," *Fangoria* No. 89 (1989): p. 27.
228. *Ibid.*, p. 28.
229. Charles Balun, "The Pit and the Pendulum," *Fangoria* No. 84 (1989), p. 10.
230. *Ibid.*
231. Fred Olen Ray, telephone interview with author, November 1, 1996.
232. *Ibid.*
233. Spoto, Donald. *The Dark Side of Genius* (New York: Ballantine, 1983), pp. 40–42.

Appendix A
Poe-Inspired Films in Chronological Order

This appendix contains a chronological listing of every Poe-inspired film addressed in this book. Not all films listed here receive a full entry in the main part of the book. Films in that category are indicated by an asterisk. Use the index to refer to films not accorded full entries.

1. *Sherlock Holmes in the Great Murder Mystery* (1908), U.S.A.
2. *Edgar Allan Poe* (1909), U.S.A.
3. *The Gold Bug* (1909), France*
4. *The Pit and the Pendulum* (1910), Italy*
5. *Hop Frog the Jester* (1910), Italy*
6. *The Raven* (1912), U.S.A.
7. *Une Vengeance d' Edgar Poe* (1912), France*
8. *The Pit and the Pendulum* (1912), U.S.A.
9. *The Bells* (1912), U.S.A.
10. *Le Système du Docteur Goudron et du Professeur Plume* (1913), France
11. *Der Student von Prag* (1913), Germany
12. *The Pit and the Pendulum* (1913), U.S.A.
13. *The Avenging Conscience* (1914), U.S.A.
14. *The Raven* (1915), U.S.A.
15. *Isle of Oblivion* (1917), Russia*
16. *Unheimliche Geschichten* (1919), Germany
17. *Die Pest in Florenz* (1919), Germany

18. *A Spectre Haunts Europe* (1923), Russia*
19. *Der Student von Prag* (1926), Germany and Austria
20. *La Chute de la Maison Usher* (1928), France
21. *The Chess Player* (1926), France*
22. *The Tell Tale Heart* (1928), U.S.A.*
23. *The Fall of the House of Usher* (1928), U.S.A.
24. *Unheimliche Geschichten* (1932), Germany
25. *The Murders in the Rue Morgue* (1932), U.S.A.
26. *The Black Cat* (1934), U.S.A.
27. *Maniac* (1934), U.S.A.
28. *The Tell-Tale Heart* (1934), Great Britain
29. *The Raven* (1935), U.S.A.
30. *The Crime of Dr. Crespi* (1935), U.S.A.
31. *Der Student von Prag* (1936), Germany*
32. *The Chess Player* (1938), France*
33. *The Black Cat* (1941), U.S.A.
34. *The Tell-Tale Heart* (1941), U.S.A.

35. *The Mystery of Marie Roget* (1942), U.S.A.

36. *The Loves of Edgar Allan Poe* (1942), U.S.A.

37. *The Fall of the House of Usher* (1949), Great Britain

38. *The Man with a Cloak* (1951), U.S.A.

39. *The Assignation* (1952), U.S.A.*

40. *The Tell-Tale Heart* (1953), U.S.A.

41. *Phantom of the Rue Morgue* (1954), U.S.A.

42. *The Cask of Amontillado* (1955), U.S.A.

43. *Manfish* (1956), U.S.A.

44. *El grito de la muerte* (1958), Mexico

45. *The Tell-Tale Heart* (1960), Great Britain

46. *The Fall of the House of Usher* (1960), U.S.A.

47. *The Pit* (1960), Great Britain

48. *Obras maestras del terror* (1961), Argentina

49. *The Pit and the Pendulum* (1961), U.S.A.

50. *The Premature Burial* (1962), U.S.A.

51. *Tales of Terror* (1962), U.S.A.

52. *Horror* (1963), Spain and Italy

53. *The Raven* (1963), U.S.A.

54. *The Haunted Palace* (1963), U.S.A.

55. *The Pit and the Pendulum* (1963), France*

56. *The Masque of the Red Death* (1964), U.S.A. and Great Britain

57. *La danza macabra* (1964), Italy and France

58. *El demonio en la sangre* (1964), Argentina

59. *Tomb of Ligeia* (1965), U.S.A. and Great Britain

60. *The City Under the Sea* (1965), U.S.A. and Great Britain

61. *The Black Cat* (1966), U.S.A.

62. *Die Schlangengrube und das Pendel* (1967), West Germany

63. *Histoires extraordinaires* (1967), Italy and France

64. *Torture Garden* (1967), Great Britain

65. *Witchfinder General* (1968), Great Britain

66. *The Oblong Box* (1968), Great Britain

67. *The Oval Portrait* (1969), Mexico and U.S.A.

68. *Cry of the Banshee* (1970), Great Britain

69. *Nella stretta morsa del ragno* (1970), West Germany and France

70. *Murders in the Rue Morgue* (1971), U.S.A. and Great Britain

71. *The Sabbat of the Black Cat* (1971), Australia

72. *La mansion de locura* (1972), Mexico

73. *Il tuo vizio è una stanza chiusa e solo io ne ho la Chiave* (1973), Italy

74. *The Tell-Tale Heart* (1973), U.S.A.

75. *The Spectre of Edgar Allan Poe* (1974), U.S.A.

76. *Il gatto nero* (1981), Italy

77. *Zanik domu Usherii* (1981), Czechoslovakia*

78. *Kyvadlo jáma a naděje* (1983) Czechoslovakia*

79. *The Haunting of Morella* (1989), U.S.A.

80. *Buried Alive* (1989), South Africa

81. *The House of Usher* (1989), Great Britain and U.S.A.

82. *Masque of the Red Death* (1989), U.S.A.

83. *Il gatto nero* (1990), Italy

84. *Due occhi diabolici* (1990), Italy and U.S.A.

85. *Masque of the Red Death* (1990), U.S.A.

86. *The Pit and the Pendulum* (1991), U.S.A.

87. *Haunting Fear* (1991), U.S.A.

88. *Tale of a Vampire* (1992), Great Britain.

Appendix B
Poe Films by Country of Origin

Films coproduced by two countries will appear under the headings of both countries, along with a note identifying the coproducing country.

Argentina
Obras maestras del terror (1961)
El demonio en la sangre (1964)

Australia
The Sabbat of the Black Cat (1971)

Austria
Der Student von Prag (1926), with Germany

Czechoslavakia
Zanik domu Usherii (1981)
Kyvadlo jáma a naděje (1983)

France
The Gold Bug (1909)
Une Vengeance d' Edgar Poe (1912)
Le Système du Docteur Goudron et du Professeur Plume (1913)
La Chute de la Maison Usher (1928)
The Chess Player (1926)
The Pit and the Pendulum (1963)
The Chess Player (1938)
La danza macabra (1964), with Italy
Histoires extraordinaires (1967), with Italy
Nella stretta morsa del ragno (1970), with West Germany

Germany
Der Student von Prag (1913)
Unheimliche Geschichten (1919)
Die Pest in Florenz (1919)
Der Student von Prag (1926), with Austria
Unheimliche Geschichten (1932)
Der Student von Prag (1936)

Great Britain
The Tell-Tale Heart (1934)
The Fall of the House of Usher (1949)
The Tell-Tale Heart (1960)
The Pit (1960)
The Masque of the Red Death (1964), with U.S.A.
The Tomb of Ligeia (1965), with U.S.A.
The City Under the Sea (1965), with U.S.A.
Torture Garden (1967)
Witchfinder General (1968)
The Oblong Box (1968)
Cry of the Banshee (1970)
Murders in the Rue Morgue (1970), with U.S.A.
The House of Usher (1989), with U.S.A.
Tale of a Vampire (1992)

Italy

The Pit and the Pendulum (1910)
Hop Frog the Jester (1909)
Horror (1963), with Spain
La danza macabre (1964), with France
Histoires extraordinaires (1967), with
   France
Nella stretta morsa del ragno (1970), with
   West Germany and France
*Il tuo vizio è una stanza chiusa e solo io ne ho
   la chiave* (1973)
Il gatto nero (1981)
Il gatto nero (1990)
Due occhi diabolici (1990), with U.S.A.

Mexico

El grito de la muerte (1958)
The Oval Portrait (1969), with U.S.A.
La mansion de locura (1972)

Russia

Isle of Oblivion (1917)
A Spectre Haunts Europe (1923)

South Africa

Buried Alive (1989)

Spain

Horror (1963), with Italy

U.S.A.

*Sherlock Holmes in the Great Murder
   Mystery* (1908)
Edgar Allan Poe (1909)
The Raven (1912)
The Pit and the Pendulum (1912)
The Bells (1912)
The Avenging Conscience (1914)
The Raven (1915)
The Fall of the House of Usher (1928)
The Tell-Tale Heart (1928)
The Murders in the Rue Morgue (1932)
The Black Cat (1934)
Maniac (1934)

The Raven (1935)
The Tell-Tale Heart (1928)
The Crime of Dr. Crespi (1935)
The Black Cat (1941)
The Tell-Tale Heart (1941)
The Mystery of Marie Roget (1942)
The Loves of Edgar Allan Poe (1942)
The Man with a Cloak (1951)
The Assignation (1952)
The Tell-Tale Heart (1953)
Phantom of the Rue Morgue (1954)
The Cask of Amontillado (1955)
Manfish (1956)
The Fall of the House of Usher (1960)
The Pit and the Pendulum (1961)
The Premature Burial (1962)
Tales of Terror (1962)
The Raven (1963)
The Haunted Palace (1963)
The Masque of the Red Death (1964), with
   Great Britain
The Tomb of Ligeia (1965), with Great
   Britain
The City Under the Sea (1965), with Great
   Britain
The Oval Portrait (1969), with Mexico
Murders in the Rue Morgue (1970), with
   Great Britain
The Tell-Tale Heart (1973)
The Spectre of Edgar Allan Poe (1974)
The Haunting of Morella (1989)
The House of Usher (1989), with Great
   Britain
Masque of the Red Death (1989)
Due occhi diabolici (1990), with Italy
Masque of the Red Death (1990)
The Pit and the Pendulum (1991)
Haunting Fear (1991)

West Germany

Die Schlangengrube und das Pendel (1967)
Nella stretta morsa del ragno (1970), with
   France and Italy

Appendix C
Poe Titles and Films Adapted from Them

"Annabel Lee"
  A Tale of a Vampire (1992)
"The Assignation"
  The Assignation (1952) Some sources
  credit this as a Poe adaptation, but I
  doubt that it is.
"The Bells"
  The Bells (1912)
"Berenice"
  Horror (1963)
"The Black Cat"
  The Raven (1912)
  Unheimliche Geschichten (1919)
  Unheimliche Geschichten (1932)
  The Black Cat (1934)
  Maniac (1934)
  The Black Cat (1941)
  Tales of Terror (1962)
  The Black Cat (1966)
  The Sabbat of the Black Cat (1971)
  Il tuo vizio e una stanza chiusa é solo io ne
    la chaiave (1973)
  Il gatto nero (1981)
  Il gatto nero (1990)
  Due occi diabolici (1990)
"The Cask of Amontillado"
  Obras maestras del terror (1961)
  Tales of Terror (1962)
"The City in the Sea"
  The City Under the Sea (1965)

"The Conqueror Worm"
  Witchfinder General (1968)
"A Descent into the Maelstrom"
  The Raven (1912)
"The Facts in the Case of M. Valdemar"
  Obras maestras del terror (1961)
  Tales of Terror (1962)
  Due occi diabolici (1990)
"The Fall of the House of Usher"
  La Chute De La Maison Usher (1928)
  The Fall of the House of Usher (1928)
  The Fall of the House of Usher (1949)
  The Fall of the House of Usher (1960)
  Horror (1963)
  Zanik domu Usherii (1981)
  House of Usher (1989)
"The Gold Bug"
  The Gold Bug (1909)
  The Raven (1912)
  Manfish (1956)
"The Haunted Palace"
  The Haunted Palace (1963)
"Hop Frog"
  The Masque of the Red Death (1964,
    uncredited)
  Hop Frog the Jester (1910)
"Ligeia"
  The Tomb of Ligeia (1965)
"Maelzel's Chess Player"
  The Chess Player (1926)
  The Chess Player (1938)

"The Masque of the Red Death"
   Die Pest in Florenz (1919)
   The Masque of the Red Death (1964)
   Masque of the Red Death (1989)
   Masque of the Red Death (1990)
"Metzengerstein"
   Histoires extraordinaires (1967)
"Morella"
   Tales of Terror (1962)
   The Haunting of Morella (1989)
"The Murders in the Rue Morgue"
   Sherlock Holmes and the Great Murder
     Mystery (1908)
   The Murders in the Rue Morgue (1932)
   Maniac (1934) uncredited
   The Phantom of the Rue Morgue (1954)
   The Murders in the Rue Morgue (1971)
"The Mystery of Marie Roget"
   The Mystery of Marie Roget (1942)
"Never Bet the Devil Your Head" or "Toby
  Dammit"
   Histoires extraordinaires (1967)
"The Oblong Box"
   The Oblong Box (1968)
"The Oval Portrait"
   The Oval Portrait (1969)
"The Pit and the Pendulum"
   The Pit and the Pendulum (1910)
   The Raven (1912)
   The Pit and the Pendulum (1912)
   The Pit (1960)
   The Pit and the Pendulum (1961)
   The Pit and the Pendulum (1963)
   Die Schlangengrube und das Pendel (1967)
   Kyvadlo, jáma a naděje (1983)
   The Pit and the Pendulum (1991)

"The Premature Burial"
   The Raven (1912)
   The Crime of Dr. Crespi (1935)
   El grito de la muerte (1958)
   The Premature Burial (1962)
   Horror (1963)
   Buried Alive (1989)
   Haunting Fear (1991)
"The Raven"
   Edgar Allan Poe (1909)
   The Raven (1912)
   The Raven (1915)
   The Raven (1935)
   The Raven (1963)
"The System of Dr. Tarr and Professor
  Fether"
   Le Système du Docteur Goudron et du Pro-
     fesseur Plume (1913)
   Unheimliche Geschichten (1932)
   La mansion de locura (1972)
"The Tell-Tale Heart"
   The Avenging Conscience (1914)
   The Tell-Tale Heart (1928)
   The Tell-Tale Heart (1934)
   The Tell Tale Heart (1941)
   The Tell-Tale Heart (1953)
   Manfish (1956)
   The Tell-Tale Heart (1960)
   Obras maestras del terror (1961)
   El demonio en la sangre (1964)
   The Tell-Tale Heart (1973)
"William Wilson"
   Der Student von Prag (1913)
   Der Student von Prag (1926)
   Der Student von Prag (1936)
   Histoires extraordinaires (1967)

Annotated Selected Bibliography

Books by Poe

Beaver, Harold (ed.). *The Science Fiction of Edgar Allan Poe.* New York: Penguin, 1976.
Contains Poe's "The Unparalleled Adventure of One Hans Pfaall" and *Eureka,* which are not collected in the Mabbott standard edition of Poe's poems, tales, and sketches.

Levine, Stuart, and Susan Levine. *The Short Fiction of Edgar Allan Poe: An Annotated Edition.* Urbana: University of Illinois Press, 1990 (originally published 1976).
Contains a bibliography and index.

Mabbott, Thomas Olive, with the assistance of Eleanor D. Kewer and Maureen C. Mabbott (eds.).
Collected Works of Edgar Allan Poe. Volume I: Poems. Cambridge, Mass.: Harvard University Press, 1969. *Volume III: Tales and Sketches 1843–1849.* Cambridge, Mass.: Harvard University Press, 1978.
The standard edition of Poe's collected poems, tales, and sketches.

Ostrom, John Ward (ed.). *The Letters of Edgar Allan Poe* (2 vols.). New York: Gordian Press, 1966.
Collects Poe's letters. Useful in checking details in films depicting Poe's life.

Peithman, Stephen (ed.). *The Annotated Tales of Edgar Allan Poe.* Garden City, N.Y: Doubleday, 1981.
Introductions to the annotated tales often refer to films based on those tales. Contains a bibliography.

Poe, Edgar Allan. *Complete Stories of Edgar Allan Poe.* Garden City, N.Y.: Doubleday, 1966.
Contains *The Narrative of A. Gordon Pym of Nantucket,* which is not collected in Mabbott's standard edition of Poe's poems, stories, and sketches.

_____. *Marginalia.* Charlottesville: University Press of Virginia, 1981.
Seventeen installments of Poe's commentaries that appeared in *Democratic Review, Godey's Lady's Book, Graham's Magazine,* and *The Southern Literary Messenger.* Not collected in the Mabbott standard edition of Poe's poems, tales, and sketches.

Prescott, F. C. *Selections from the Critical Writings of Edgar Allan Poe.* New York: Gordian Press, 1981.
Collects the best of Poe's critical writings.

Books About Poe or His Works

Bloom, Harold (ed.). *Edgar Allan Poe.* New York: Chelsea House, 1985.
Part of the Modern Critical Views series, this book edited by one of America's leading literary scholars includes eight essays by such important Poe critics as Paul Valery, D. H. Lawrence, Allen Tate, Richard Wilbur, and Daniel Hoffman. Includes an introduction by the editor (who is not a "fan" of Poe), a chronology, a bibliography, and an index.

_____ (ed.). *The Tales of Poe*. New York: Chelsea House, 1987.
   Part of the Modern Critical Interpretations series, this book edited by one of America's leading literary scholars offers seven modern critical essays on Poe's tales. Contains the same introduction
   that Bloom wrote for *Edgar Allan Poe*. Also includes a chronology, a bibliography, and an index.

Buranelli, Vincent. *Edgar Allan Poe*, (2nd ed.). Boston: Twayne Publishers, 1977.
   One of Poe's most ardent critical supporters argues that Poe might be "America's greatest writer—
   and the American writer of greatest significance in world literature."

Haining, Peter (ed.). *The Edgar Allan Poe Scrapbook*. New York: Schocken Books, 1978.
   Wonderful for browsing, this illustrated catch-all volume contains Dennis Gifford's "Pictures of
   Poe," an examination of Poe-based silent films from 1909 to 1929, Ron Haydock's "Poe, Corman,
   and Price: A Tale of Terrors," an assessment of the AIP Corman/Poe series, and a look at *The
   Spectre of Edgar Allan Poe*. No index. No bibliography.

Hoffman, Daniel. *Poe Poe Poe Poe Poe Poe Poe*. Garden City, N.Y.: Doubleday, 1972.
   Hoffman offers insightful and sometimes eccentric interpretations of Poe's works. His take on "The
   Tell-Tale Heart" probably accounts for themes stressed in the 1973 film version. Contains an
   index. No bibliography.

Regan, Robert. *Poe: A Collection of Critical Essays*. Englewood Cliffs, N.J.: Prentice-Hall, 1967.
   Contains twelve essays on Poe's works by such scholars/authors as Aldous Huxley, Allen Tate, Patrick
   F. Quinn, and Richard Wilbur. Includes a chronology of important dates in Poe's life and a bib-
   liography. No index.

Rosenheim, Shawn and Stephen Rachman. *The American Face of Edgar Allan Poe*. Baltimore: Johns
   Hopkins University Press, 1995.
   Collects thirteen critical essays on Poe's writings by academics such as Joan Dayan, Jonathan Elmer,
   and the editors.

Silverman, Kenneth. *Edgar A. Poe: Mournful and Never-ending Rememberance*. New York: HarperCollins,
   1991.
   Of the *many* Poe biographies available, this is my favorite. Others I have read and enjoyed to vari-
   ous degrees include *The Life of Edgar Allan Poe* (1903) by James A. Harrison, *Israfel: The Life and
   Times of Edgar Allan Poe* (1934), *Edgar Allan Poe: A Critical Biography* (1941) by Arthur Hobson
   Quinn, *The Histrionic Mr. Poe* (1949) by N. Bryllion Fagin, *The Extraordinary Mr. Poe* (1978) by
   Wolf Mankowitz, *The Tell-Tale Heart: The Life and Works of Edgar Allan Poe* (1978) by Julian
   Symons, and *Edgar Allan Poe* (1992) by Jeffrey Meyers.

_____. *New Essays on Poe's Major Tales*. Cambridge, England: Cambridge University Press, 1993.
   Silverman collects five excellent critical essays on Poe's most important tales. Contains an introduction by the editor and a bibliography. No index.

Thomas, Dwight, and David J. Jackson. *The Poe Log: A Documentary Life of Edgar Allan Poe 1809–1849*.
   Boston: G. K. Hall, 1987.
   A day by day account of Poe's life. An indispensable research tool. Helpful for checking the verac-
   ity of films based on Poe's life. Illustrated. Includes a list of sources and index.

Walsh, John. *Poe the Detective*. New Brunswick, N.J.: Rutgers University Press, 1968.
   An excellent study of the murder of Mary Rogers and the writing of Poe's "The Mystery of Marie
   Roget." Good background reading for anyone interested in the 1942 film adaptation.

Books About the Horror Genre and Poe Cinema

Andrews, Nigel. *Horror Films*. New York: Gallery Books, 1985.
   The illustrations, many of which are in color, are the main attraction of this coffee table book. The
   text is for novices only. Still, it contains a small section on the "Corman Canon" of Poe films. No
   bibliography. No index.

Annan, David. *Ape*. New York: Bounty Books, 1975.
   In the process of covering films featuring apes, this thin volume casts cursory attention on the screen's
   various adaptations of Poe's "The Murders in the Rue Morgue." Illustrated, with four color pages.
   No bibliography. No index.

_____. *Movie Fantastic: Beyond the Dream Machine*. New York: Bounty Books, 1974.
    A short examination of how archetypes of human thought and feeling are expressed in horror and
    science fiction films. The text deals with several Poe-inspired pictures. Slightly better than the
    average Bounty film book. Illustrated, with four color pages. Contains a title index but no bibli-
    ography.

Baraket, Mark. *Scream Gems*. New York: Drake, 1977.
    Riddled with errors, this horror film history includes a very brief and relatively worthless chapter
    on Poe's contribution to the dark cinema. Illustrated. No bibliography. No index.

Brunas, Michael, John Brunas, and Tom Weaver. *Universal Horrors: The Studio's Classic Films, 1931–1946.*
    Jefferson, N.C.: McFarland, 1990.
    Contains insightful, comprehensive treatments of Universal's *Murders in the Rue Morgue* (1932), *The
    Black Cat* (1934), *The Raven* (1935), *The Black Cat* (1941), and *Mystery of Marie Roget* (1942).
    Contains an index, but no bibliography.

Butler, Ivan. *Horror in the Cinema*. New York: Paperback Library, 1971.
    Though over twenty-five years have passed since the publication of this book, it remains one of the
    best introductions to the horror film. An entire chapter is devoted to "Roger Corman and Edgar
    Allan Poe," and other Poe-inspired films are addressed as well. Contains a bibliography and index
    of principal references.

Clarens, Carlos. *An Illustrated History of the Horror Film*. New York: Capricorn Books, 1967.
    For the casual reader, this and Ivan Butler's *Horror in the Cinema* remain the best introductions to
    the horror film. Contains brief historical accounts and critical appraisals of many Poe-inspired
    films. Contains an index and appendix with film credits. No bibliography.

Douglas, Drake. *Horror!* Toronto: Collier, 1966.
    Contains a lengthy chapter on the creators of horror, one of whom is Poe. Quickly dismisses
    Universal's Poe films and gives favorable attention to the Corman/Poe series.

Everson, William K. *Classics of the Horror Film*. Secaucus, N.J.: Citadel, 1974.
    Noted film historian Everson devotes one chapter to the Poe cinema and argues that most Poe adap-
    tations owe little to the author. Illustrated. No index. No bibliography.

Gifford, Denis. *An Illustrated History of Horror Movies*. New York: Hamlyn, 1973.
    This horror film history briefly mentions the Karloff/Lugosi Poe films at Universal and the later
    Corman/Poe series. The usual. Illustrated, some pictures in color. Contains a list of British films
    that received the "H" Certificate, book and magazine bibliographies, and an index.

_____. *Movie Monsters*. London: Studio Vista, 1969.
    In chapters devoted to "the ape" and "the cat," Gifford devotes limited space to several Poe-inspired
    films. Illustrated. Contains a filmography. No index.

Haining, Peter (ed.). *The Ghouls*. New York: Stein and Day, 1971.
    This book collects eighteen short stories that served as the bases for notable horror films and pro-
    vides a brief introduction to each story. Included are Poe's "The System of Doctor Tarr and
    Professor Fether," which inspired several films, and "The Oblong Box," which inspired the 1968
    film of the same name. The commentary accompanying "The System of Dr. Tarr and Professor
    Fether" is mildly interesting, but the commentary accompanying "The Oblong Box" was written
    before the film's release. Includes an introduction by Vincent Price and an afterword by Christopher
    Lee.

Hardy, Phil (ed.). *The Overlook Film Encyclopedia: Horror*. Woodstock, New York: Overlook Press,
    1995.
    The best horror film encyclopedia to date. Insightful, scholarly appraisals of horror films, world-
    wide. Excellent and sometimes controversial assessments of many Poe-inspired films. Illustrated.
    Includes an index.

Hutchings, Peter. *Hammer and Beyond*. Manchester, Great Britain: University of Manchester, 1993.
    Though this book is dedicated to a study of Hammer horror films, it includes a chapter on Michael
    Reeves, director of *Witchfinder General*, aka *The Conqueror Worm*. The book mixes enlightening
    insights with academic psychobabble. Contains notes and an index, but no bibliography.

Hutchinson, Tom. *Horror and Fantasy in the Movies*. New York: Crescent Books, 1974.
    This history of the horror film for the novice or casual reader touches briefly on some Poe-inspired
    pictures. Features a foreword by Vincent Price. Illustrated. Contains an index but no bibliography.

Kaminsky, Stuart M. *American Film Genres*. New York: Dell, 1977.
  In a chapter titled "Psychological Considerations: Horror and Science Fiction," Kaminsky devotes a paragraph to Corman's *The Masque of the Red Death* (1964) and mentions *The Conqueror Worm* (1968). A very informative book that examines how various American film genres reflect American society. Illustrated. Includes bibliographies and an index.

Kracauer, Siegfried. *From Caligari to Hitler*. Princeton: Princeton University Press, 1947.
  This is a classic study, the thesis of which is that German films of the twenties predicted the Nazi totalitarianism of the thirties. Presents a detailed analysis of *Der Student von Prag* (1913) and briefly comments on the two later versions. Illustrated. Contains a lengthy bibliography and index.

London, Rose. *Cinema of Mystery*. New York: Bounty Books, 1975.
  This thin volume covers Poe's films thematically. Lavishly illustrated. Four pages of poster reproductions are in color. As with most Bounty film books, the films themselves receive all-too-brief treatment. No index. No bibliography.

_____. *Zombie: The Living Dead*. New York: Bounty Books, 1976.
  This thin volume covers films featuring zombies and the living dead and in the process briefly touches on several films inspired by Poe. Not much of interest here for those desiring information on the Poe cinema. Illustrated, with four pages of color poster reproductions. No bibliography. No index.

McGee, Mark Thomas. *Faster and Furiouser: The Revised and Fattened Fable of American International Pictures*. Jefferson, N.C.: McFarland, 1996.
  A delightful read, this is the best history of American International Pictures, home of the Corman/Poe series. Illustrated. Contains a bibliography and index.

Naha, Ed. *Horrors from Screen to Scream*. New York: Avon Books, 1975.
  This illustrated horror film encyclopedia briefly covers some films inspired by Poe.

Newman, Kim. *Nightmare Movies*. New York: Harmony Books, 1988.
  The best, most comprehensive study of the contemporary horror film to date. Gives a quick glance at a handful of contemporary Poe-inspired films. Illustrated. Contains an index of alternate titles, a bibliography, and a general index.

Pirie, David. *A Heritage of Horror: The English Gothic Cinema 1946–1972*. New York: Avon, 1973.
  This classic book devoted to the British horror film includes a groundbreaking chapter on director Michael Reeves and his *Witchfinder General* (1968), as well as provocative insights into Gordon Hessler's Poe-inspired films. While some of Pirie's judgments can be questioned, they must all be taken seriously. Illustrated. Contains several valuable appendices, and a filmography and index.

Pollin, Burtin R. *Images of Poe's Works: A Comprehensive Catalogue of Illustrations*. New York: Greenwood, 1989.
  This exhaustive compendium includes entries from thirty-five countries. Entries are organized by country and listed chronologically. Contains four useful indices.

Prawer, S. S. *Caligari's Children: The Film as Tale of Terror*. New York: Oxford University Press, 1980.
  Prawer tries "to elucidate the rhetoric and iconography of terror in the cinema, its cultural context, and the links between German films of the silent era and subsequent horror films produced by other countries. Includes interesting insights into *Der Student von Prag* (1926) and briefly examines a number of other Poe-inspired films. A thoughtful book. illustrated. Contains a bibliography and indices.

Smith, Ronald L. *Poe in the Media: Screen, Songs, and Spoken Word Recordings*. New York: Garland, 1990.
  Smith describes the films and sound recordings in essays for each story and poem.

Steinbrunner, Chris and Burt Goldblatt. *Cinema of the Fantastic*. New York: Galahad Books, 1972.
  This book contains chapters on fifteen classic horror/science fiction films, one of which is *The Black Cat* (1934). Unfortunately, most of each chapter consists of a lengthy story synopsis. Illustrated. No bibliography. No index.

Svehla, Gary J., and Susan Svehla (eds.). *Bitches, Bimbos, and Virgins: Women in the Horror Film*. Baltimore: Midnight Marquee Press, 1996.
  This book contains ten chapters devoted to examining women in the horror film. In "The Women of International Pictures," Steven Thornton examines the female element in the Corman/Poe series. Illustrated. Contains an index but no bibliography.

Weldon, Michael. *The Psychotronic Encyclopedia of Film.* New York: Ballantine Books, 1983.
   An entertaining illustrated guide to cult films. Weldon remarks briefly on a number of Poe-inspired
   pictures.

Wright, Bruce Lanier. *Nightwalkers: Gothic Horror Movies: The Modern Era.* Dallas: Taylor Publishing
   Company, 1995.
   A delightful book that offers interesting and controversial critiques of modern gothic horror films,
   including the Corman/Poe series, except for *The Raven* (1963). Engaging on all levels. Illustrated,
   with nine pages of color poster reproductions. Includes a bibliography and index.

Books About Actors

Beck, Calvin. *Heroes of the Horrors.* New York: Collier, 1975.
   Beck offers chapters on five of the greatest horror film actors of all time. Chapters on Boris Karloff,
   Bela Lugosi, Peter Lorre, and Vincent Price provide some useful information concerning their
   Poe films. Illustrated. Includes filmographies. No bibliography. No index.

_____. *Scream Queens.* New York: Macmillan, 1987.
   Beck offers chapters on twenty-nine horror film heroines. The chapters on Barbara Steele and Hazel
   Court provide useful information regarding their Poe films. Illustrated. Includes a bibliography
   and index.

Bojarski, Richard. *The Films of Bela Lugosi.* Secaucus, N.J.: Citadel, 1980.
   All of Lugosi's films get the Bojarski treatment—credits, reviews, and production notes. Some interesting tidbits appear regarding Lugosi's *The Murders in the Rue Morgue* (1932), *The Black Cat*
   (1934), *The Raven* (1935), and *The Black Cat* (1941). Illustrated. Contains a foreword by Carol
   Borland and a filmography. No bibliography. No index.

_____ and Kenneth Beals. *The Films of Boris Karloff.* Secaucus, N.J.: Citadel, 1974.
   All of Karloff's films get the Bojarski treatment—credits, reviews, and production notes. Gives some
   attention to *The Black Cat* (1934), *The Raven* (1935), and *The Raven* (1963). Illustrated. Includes
   a filmography of Karloff's television work. No bibliography. No index.

Cushing, Peter. *'Past Forgetting.'* London: Weidenfeld and Nicholas, 1988.
   In this sequel to *Peter Cushing: An Autobiography* (1986), the author provides memoirs of his Hammer
   years and includes a brief, inconsequential reference to *Torture Garden* (1967), in which he costars with Jack Palance in Robert Bloch's "The Man Who Collected Poe." Illustrated. Contains
   theater, television, and film credits, and an index.

Del Vecchio, Deborah, and Tom Johnson. *Peter Cushing: The Gentle Man of Horror and His 91 Films.*
   Jefferson, N.C.: McFarland, 1992.
   This comprehensive study of Peter Cushing's career includes a look at *Torture Garden* (1967), in which
   the actor co-stars with Jack Palance in Robert Bloch's "The Man Who Collected Poe." Illustrated.
   Includes a bibliography and index.

Lee, Christopher. *Tall, Dark and Gruesome.* London: Granada Publishing, 1977.
   In Lee's autobiography, the actor reminisces about his work in *Die Schlangengrube und das Pendel*
   (1967) and *The Oblong Box* (1968). Illustrated. Contains an index.

Lennig, Arthur. *The Count: The Life and Films of Bela "Dracula" Lugosi.* New York: G. P. Putnam's Sons,
   1974.
   This first and most heart-felt Lugosi biography includes a detailed, insightful critical response to
   The Raven (1935). Also addresses Lugosi's other Poe pictures. Illustrated. Contains a filmography and index.

Mank, Gregory William. *Karloff and Lugosi: The Story of a Haunting Collaboration, with a Complete
   Filmography of Their Films Together.* Jefferson, N.C.: McFarland, 1990.
   This is a lively, well-researched, comprehensive study of the Karloff/Lugosi collaboration. Illustrated.
   Covers *The Black Cat* (1934) and *The Raven* (1935). Contains a detailed filmography and an index.
   No bibliography.

Nollen, Scott Allen. *Boris Karloff: A Critical Account of His Screen, Stage, Radio, Television and Recording
   Work.* Jefferson, N.C.: McFarland, 1991.
   This is the best critical account of Karloff's career to date. Looks at *The Black Cat* (1934), *The Raven*

(1935), and *The Raven* (1963). Includes an exhaustive list of Karloff's creative output, a bibliography, and an index.

Parish, James Robert, and Steven Whitney. *Vincent Price Unmasked*. New York: Drake, 1974.
   Though this book has recently been bested by Williams's *The Complete Films of Vincent Price* (1995), it still contains much biographical material missing from Williams. Includes information and reviews on Price's Poe films. Illustrated. Contains lists of Price's work on stage, in film, on television, etc. No index.

Pohle Robert W., Jr., and Douglas C. Hart. *The Films of Christopher Lee*. Metuchen, N.J.: Scarecrow, 1983.
   Includes brief discussions, reviews, and personal comments by Lee on his *Die Schlangengrube und das Pendel* (1967) and *The Oblong Box* (1968). Illustrated. Contains a bibliography and indices.

Smith, Don G. *Lon Chaney, Jr.: Horror Film Star, 1906–1973*. Jefferson, N.C.: McFarland, 1996.
   Includes a discussion of *Manfish* (1956), based on Poe's "The Gold Bug" and "The Tell-Tale Heart." Illustrated. Includes movie and television filmographies, a bibliography, and an index.

Svehla, Gary J., and Susan Svehla (eds.). *Bela Lugosi*. Baltimore: Midnight Marquee Press, 1995.
   Contains 24 chapters focusing on one or more Lugosi films, among which are *Murders in the Rue Morgue* (1932) by Gregory William Mank, *The Black Cat* (1934) by Don G. Smith, and *The Raven* (1935) by Gary J. Svehla. Illustrated. Contains a filmography, a bibliography, and index.

_____. *Boris Karloff*. Baltimore: Midnight Marquee Press, 1996.
   This book contains twenty-four chapters, each focusing on one or more films of Boris Karloff, among which is one Dennis Fischer on *The Black Cat* (1934). Illustrated. Contains a filmography, bibliography, and index.

_____. *Guilty Pleasures of the Horror Film*. Baltimore: Midnight Marquee Press, 1996.
   In this book, twelve noted horror film critics defend horror films which they enjoy but which were panned by the world at large. The highlight of the book is Bret Wood's chapter on *Maniac* (1934), a film based on several Poe short stories. Illustrated. Contains a bibliography but no index.

Underwood, Peter. *Karloff*. New York: Drake, 1972.
   This early Karloff biography has been bested by Scott Nollen's *Boris Karloff* (1991). Of little use to anyone interested in the Poe cinema. Illustrated. Includes a bibliography and index.

Williams, Lucy Chase. *The Complete Films of Vincent Price*. New York: Citadel, 1995.
   This is the most comprehensive book on Price and his work to date. Well-researched and profusely illustrated (with plenty of color), the book begins with a biography and follows with a discussion of every Vincent Price film, including, of course, all those based on Poe's works. Includes a reference list (bibliography). No index.

Books About Directors

di Franco, J. Philip (ed.). *The Movie World of Roger Corman*. New York: Chelsea House, 1979.
   Corman speaks for himself throughout most of this book. Contains useful information on the philosophy underlying his Poe series, as well as production anecdotes. Illustrated. No real filmography. No index.

Gibson, Arthur. *The Silence of God*. New York: Harper and Row, 1969.
   The author provides a creative response to seven of Ingmar Bergman's most provocative films, including *The Seventh Seal*, which influenced Corman's *The Masque of the Red Death* (1964). Penetrating analysis. Illustrated. No bibliography. No index.

McCarthy, Todd and Charles Flynn. *Kings of the Bs*. New York: Dutton, 1975.
   Includes chapters on and interviews with director Roger Corman, director Edgar G. Ulmer, and producer Sam Arkoff, all of whom made notable Poe films.

McDonagh, Maitland. *Broken Mirrors/Broken Minds: The Dark Dreams of Dario Argento*. New York: Citadel, 1991.
   This study of Italian director Argento includes a critique of Argento and Romero's *Due Occhi Diabolica* (1990), as well as an interview with Argento in which the director discusses Poe at some length. Illustrated. Contains a bibliography and index.

Naha, Ed. *The Films of Roger Corman*. New York: Arco Publishing, 1982.
  Presents a general overview of Corman's career, followed by a film-by-film treatment with plot summaries and reviews. Covers the Corman/Poe series. Illustrated. Contains an index but no bibliography.

Spoto, Donald. *The Dark Side of Genius: The Life of Alfred Hitchcock*. New York: Ballantine, 1983.
  In a lengthy quotation, Hitchcock discusses the influence of Edgar Allan Poe on his life and work and on Western culture. Illustrated. Includes a bibliography and index.

Articles

Biodrowski, Steve and David Del Valle. "Vincent Price: Horror's Crown Prince." *Cinefantastique* 19, nos. 1, 2 (1989).
  This is the most comprehensive article on Price ever to appear. Contains valuable interviews with Price and others involved in the actor's Poe-inspired films. Illustrated, many pictures in color.

Corman, Roger. "Vincent Price as I Remember Him." *Scarlet Street* No. 13 (1994).
  Corman eulogizes Price in this reminiscence of their Poe film days.

French, Larry. "Vincent Price: The Corman Years, Part I." *Fangoria* 6 (1980).
  Part one of an interview with Vincent Price on the subject of his Corman/Poe films.

_____. "Vincent Price: The Corman Years, Part II." *Fangoria* 7 (1980).
  Part two of an interview with Vincent Price on the subject of his Corman/Poe films.

Weaver, Tom, and Michael Brunas. "Richard Matheson and the House of Poe." *Fangoria* 89 (1989).
  Part one of an extensive interview with the screenwriter of many of the Corman/Poe films.

_____. "Quote Matheson, 'Nevermore!'" *Fangoria* 90 (1990).
  Part two of an extensive interview with the screenwriter of many of the Corman/Poe films.

Novelizations of Screenplays and Tie-ins

Bassett, Ronald. *Witchfinder General*. London: Pan, second ed. 1968.
  Bassett's novel of the brutal historical exploits of Matthew Hopkins, Witchfinder General, served as the foundation for Michael Reeves's *Witchfinder General* aka *The Conqueror Worm*. This edition, illustrated on front and back with scenes from the film, was published to coincide with the release of Reeves's film.

Danne, Max Hallan. *The Premature Burial*. New York, Lancer, 1962.
  Based on the *Premature Burial* screenplay by Charles Beaumont and Ray Russell. "He suffered the worst horror the human mind can imagine—living death!"

Green, Carl R., and William R. Sanford. *The Black Cat*. Mankato, Minn.: Crestwood House, 1987.
  Based on the 1941 *Black Cat* screenplay by Robert Lees and Fred Rinaldo. "In this comedy-mystery, Abigail Doone, the housekeeper, is suspected of killing strange old Mrs. Winslow, but she herself is murdered. Eduardo, the keeper of her pet cats, looks suspicious, but so do the rest of Mrs. Winslow's relatives. The cats lead to the murderer." This illustrated novelization is aimed at young audiences. Includes a prologue explaining the treatment of Poe's story at Universal Studios.

Lee, Elsie. *The Masque of the Red Death*. New York: Lancer, 1964.
  Based on the *Masque of the Red Death* screenplay by R. Wright Campbell. "The Master of Horror Edgar Allan Poe's sinister story of good vs. evil."

Poe, Edgar Allan. *The Murders in the Rue Morgue and Other Tales of Horror*. New York: Grosset and Dunlap, 1932.
  Published to coincide with the release of Universal's *Murders in the Rue Morgue*, this collection of sixteen Poe short stories features nine photos from the film.

Sheridan, Lee. *The Pit and the Pendulum*. New York: Lancer, 1961.
  Based on the *Pit and the Pendulum* screenplay by Richard Matheson. "She was enslaved by evil in a terror haunted castle."

Sudak, Eunice. *Poe's Tales of Terror*. New York: Lancer, 1962.
    Based on the *Poe's Tales of Terror* screenplay by Richard Matheson. "Three Chillers by the all-time master of Horror."
_____. *The Raven*. New York: Lancer, 1963.
    Based on the *Raven* screenplay by Richard Matheson. "Edgar Allan Poe's nightmare classic."

Comic Book Tie-ins

Masque of the Red Death. Dell Movie Classic, 12-490-410, 1964.
Poe's Tales of Terror. Dell Movie Classic, 12-793-301,1962.
Poe's The Raven. Dell Movie Classic, 12-680-309, 1963.
Tomb of Ligeia. Dell Movie Classic, 12-830-506, 1965.

Miscellaneous

Bergman, Ingmar. *Four Screenplays of Ingmar Bergman*. New York: Simon and Schuster, 1960.
    This collection of four Bergman screenplays includes *The Seventh Seal*, a film that influenced Corman's *The Masque of the Red Death* (1964). Illustrated. Includes an introduction by Bergman and a Bergman filmography.

Index